Margarine

AN ECONOMIC, SOCIAL
AND SCIENTIFIC HISTORY
1869–1969

Margarine

AN ECONOMIC, SOCIAL AND SCIENTIFIC HISTORY 1869–1969

EDITED BY

J.H. van STUYVENBERG

Professor of Economic History
in the University of Amsterdam

LIVERPOOL UNIVERSITY PRESS
1969

Published by

LIVERPOOL UNIVERSITY PRESS

123 Grove Street, Liverpool 7

Copyright © 1969 by
Liverpool University Press

85323 130 3

First published 1969

PRINTED AND BOUND IN GREAT BRITAIN BY
HAZELL WATSON AND VINEY LTD
AYLESBURY, BUCKS

Foreword

By Dr. A. BOERMA

Director-General
Food and Agriculture Organization
of the United Nations

O VER the past hundred years, the margarine industry has made a very great contribution to world food supplies, the expansion of trade, and the improvement of living standards in many countries. Starting from very modest beginnings in Western Europe it has developed into one of the most important and—as the authors of this book show—one of the most sophisticated food processing industries in the world. Production is now running at over five million tons a year and there is clearly room for further expansion, not least in the growing urban areas of Africa, Asia, and Latin America, where large numbers of people are today faced with food shortages of the kind which originally led to the growth of the margarine industry in Europe.

It is also worth recalling here the fact that the development of any one sector of food and agriculture can stimulate growth in others. The expansion of margarine production has had important repercussions on agricultural industry as a whole and on economic development in general. Let me take one example of this. Remembering that it was largely the shortage of butter which first led to the development of margarine, it is very interesting to note that the increase in oil-seed production and processing that has come with the expansion of margarine output has also contributed, as time has gone on, to the development of the livestock industry. This happened once it was recognized that the residual oil-seed cake was a valuable source of high protein feed.

Even more important, the need for vegetable oils for use in the production of margarine from the turn of the century onwards, has helped to stimulate a quite phenomenal expansion in the production and export of tropical oils and oil-seeds. These now represent a substantial proportion of world trade in all agricultural products. They

provide a considerable source of foreign exchange for many developing countries, so that it is not too much to say that the trade and
development prospects of these countries are closely linked with the
future of margarine.

It is with these thoughts in mind that I have been glad to write
these few words by way of a foreword to this volume which is
published to mark the centenary of the invention of margarine.

Contents

CONTENTS

xii   CONTENTS

Illustrations

PLATES

TABLES

The Contributors

J. H. VAN STUYVENBERG studied economics at the Netherlands School of Economics in Rotterdam, and graduated in 1947 with a thesis entitled: 'Enkele economische aspecten van de kersenteelt in Nederland' ('Some Economic Aspects of Cherry-Growing in Holland'). During and after the Second World War he was employed by the price control authorities for agricultural produce.

His book, *Het Central Bureau, een coöperatief krachtveld in de Nederlandse landbouw* (*The Central Agency: a Co-operative Force in Dutch Agriculture*), brought him recognition as an agricultural economist. In 1949 he was appointed head of the Horticultural Department of the Agricultural Economics Institute; from 1951 to 1960, he also held the post of special lecturer on the co-operative movement at the University of Amsterdam.

With his appointment to the post of full professor of economic and social history in the Netherlands School of Economics in Rotterdam in 1954, he abandoned his agricultural specialization. Since 1962 he has been part-time professor of social and economic history in the Royal Military Academy in Breda; before that, he was for several years a part-time professor in the Free University of Brussels. From 1967 onwards, he has held the post of professor in economic history in the University of Amsterdam.

Other works he has published include *De Bloemisterij in Nederland* (*Floriculture in Holland*) (editor), 1961; *De Nederlandische Economische Hoogeschool, 1913–1963* (*The Netherlands School of Economics, 1913–1963*). He has also written brochures and essays including: 'Consequenties van de vorming van centrale organisaties op coöperatief gebied' ('The Consequences of forming Central Organizations in the Co-operative Sphere'), 1951; 'De industriële revolutie in discussie' ('The Industrial Revolution: A Discussion'), 1961; 'Geschiedenis als cultuurcomponent' ('History in its Social Context'), 1964; (Economische groei in Nederland in de negentiende eeuw: een terreinverkenning' ('Economic Growth in Holland in the Nineteenth Century: A Survey'), 1967.

WALTHER G.HOFFMANN was born in 1903 in Hartmannsdorf, Silesia. He received his grammar school education in Laubers and Görlitz, and then studied economics at the University of Tübingen and the Institute for World Economics in Kiel. In 1929 he obtained his doctorate in economics at Tübingen, and until 1946 he worked at the Institute for World Economics. In 1943 he became part-time professor at Kiel and in 1946 professor at the University of Münster, a post that he still holds. He was the director of the Institute for Economic and Social Sciences in Münster until 1965 and from 1953 to 1955 he held the Robert Schumann chair in Brugge. In 1964 he was given an honorary doctorate by the Economic Sciences Faculty of the Free University of Berlin.

Professor Hoffman has held, and holds, many posts; member of the scientific advisory board of the Ministry of Economic Affairs, chairman of the Society of Economic and Social Sciences, member of various commissions of the High Authority of the European Coal and Steel Community, and honorary member of the Real Academia de Ciencas Economicas y Financieras and the Economic History Association.

He has published many works on European integration and the problems brought by industrialization, including *Stadien und Typen der Industrialisierung* (1931—revised edition published in 1958 as *The Growth of Industrial Economies*), *Wachstum und Wachstumsformen der englischen Industriewirtschaft von 1700 bis zur Gegenwart* (1940—revised edition published in 1958 as *British Industry 1700–1950*), *Das deutsche Volkseinkommen 1851–1957* (1959), *Die branchenmässige Lohnstruktur der Industrie* (1961), and *Das Wachstum der deutschen Wirtschaft seit der Mitte des 19. Jahrhunderts* (1965).

KENNETH EDWARD HUNT was born in 1916 at Evesham, England. He was educated at Prince Henry's Grammar School, Evesham, and Emmanuel College, Cambridge. He took his degree in Natural Sciences in 1937, and then studied for the Diploma in Agricultural Science. In 1939 he joined the staff of the Animal Nutrition Research Institute of the University of Cambridge. During his postgraduate studies, and in subsequent work on poultry and the wartime feeding of livestock, he developed an interest in the economic aspects of livestock feeding and in national planning of food supplies generally. After working on these topics for the Ministry of Food and various international organizations, he was appointed lecturer in the Agricultural Economics Research Institute of the University of Oxford. He has since worked mainly in the field of commodity market information, including the statistical techniques of collection of basic information in developing areas, which he studied in Africa and the West Indies, and the dissemination of economic information to farmers. He has studied and advised on poultry marketing in Europe for the O.E.C.D. In 1964 he became part-time director of the Institute of Agrarian Affairs of the University of Oxford, while continuing to lecture in agricultural economics. He has prepared and edited publications for the International Association of Agricultural Economists, and his other publications include the six-volume *The State of British Agriculture*.

ROBERT FERON was born in Caen, Normandy, on 20 February 1910 and completed the first part of his studies there. After he had obtained his chemical engineer's diploma at the University of Caen, he prepared his thesis for his doctorate in Paris, in the laboratory of Professor H. Colin. He presented his thesis in 1936 and received the degree of Doctor of the University of Paris.

In 1934 he joined the Société Astra, the French affiliate of the Unilever group, and has spent all his career with this company. He became head of laboratory, head of the Margarine Department, assistant director, and then director of the factory at Asnières; he was appointed a technical director of the company early in 1961. His present post is that of scientific director. This involves mainly the promotion of research and development in co-operation with Unilever specialists.

ALASTAIR CAMPBELL FRAZER, C.B.E., was born in London on 26 July 1909. He was educated at Lancing College and the University of London, graduating in medicine in 1932, and was a lecturer in Physiology, Biochemistry, and Pharmacology at St. Mary's Hospital Medical School from 1929 to 1942. He was the first holder of the Chair of Pharmacology (later Medical Biochemistry and Pharmacology) in the University of Birmingham, from 1943 to 1967. At present he is Director-General of the British Nutrition Foundation Ltd. in London, Honorary Consultant in Metabolic Diseases to the British Army, Consultant to the Atomic Energy Authority, President of the British Food Industrial Biological Research Association, and Scientific Adviser to the Minister of Agriculture, Fisheries, and Food. He is a member of the Medical Advisory Committee of the Ministry of Overseas Development, and the president of the Food Section of the International Union of Pure and Applied Chemistry, and chairman of Commission I of the International Union of Nutritional Sciences. He is a member of the Joint F.A.O.–W.H.O. Expert Committee on Food Additives, and he has served on a number of other W.H.O. expert committees. He was awarded the Buckston Browne Prize of the Harveian Society of London in 1944. He is an Honorary Member of the Royal Flemish Academy of Sciences, the Société Philomathique de Paris, and the Société Gastro-entérologie de Belge.

JAN BOLDINGH was born on 3 January 1915 at Buitenzorg in the former Dutch East Indies. He studied organic chemistry at the State University Utrecht from 1933 to 1939 and took his doctor's degree in June 1942 under the supervision of Professor Dr. F. Kögl with a thesis called 'Synthetic Studies of the Chromophoric System of Lumi-auxon'. He worked as a scientist at the Physical Laboratory of N.V. Philips' Gloeilampenfabrieken at Eindhoven from July 1942 to April 1944, then joined Unilever N.V. as a research scientist, first at Rotterdam and then at Zwijndrecht. In April 1952 he was appointed Research Manager of the Unilever Research Laboratory which was transferred to its present site at Vlaardingen in 1955. In 1964 he was appointed ordinary member of the Royal Netherlands Academy of Sciences, and in 1966 followed his appointment as Professor extraordinary at the State University Utrecht to teach Chemistry and Biochemistry of Lipids.

He received an honorary doctor's degree from the Agricultural University at Wageningen on 9 March 1968, and on 28 May 1968 was presented with the Chevreul Medal by the Groupement Technique des Corps Gras de la Société de Chimie Industrielle, Paris. On 8 October 1968 he was awarded the Normann Medal by the Deutsche Gesellschaft für Fett-wissenschaft at Münster, Western Germany. He is at present a member of the Committee for Biochemistry and Biophysics appointed by the Royal Netherlands Academy of Sciences; International Conference on the Bio-chemical Problems of Lipids (national representative for the Netherlands and Secretary of the Steering Committee); Board of the Institute for Organic Chemistry T.N.O.; Advisory Council of the Netherlands Heart Foundation; Board of the Foundation for the Study of Technological Forecasting (Royal Netherlands Institute of Engineers).

Professor Boldingh is Past-President of the International Society for Fat Research, and has published a number of articles which cover, amongst other subjects, reversed phase partition chromatography for fatty acid analysis; accurate vitamin A analysis in fatty products; isolation of phospholipids by dialysis through nonpolar membranes; isolation and identification of trace constituents, particularly flavour components such as various lactone classes in butter; isolation of crystalline aflatoxin; chemical action of linoleic acid hydroperoxided isomerase. He has also published a number of articles of a review nature on biochemistry and nutrition, and has given plenary lectures on specific occasions.

RAYBURN D. TOUSLEY is professor of marketing in the College of Economics and Business at Washington State University, Pullman, Washington, U.S.A., where he joined the faculty in 1940. After a period of government service between 1942 and 1945 he returned to Washington State University where he served as Chairman of the Department of Business Administration between 1950 and 1964. In 1964–5 he was the Fulbright Lecturer at the Nederlandsche Economische Hoogeschool in Rotterdam.

Professor Tousley holds two degrees from the University of Missouri; the B.S. in Business Administration and the A.M. in Economics. He obtained his Ph.D. at Northwestern University in 1943. He is a member of the American Marketing Association and the American Economic Association. His interests in marketing include particularly marketing management and the development and history of marketing thought.

Professor Tousley is co-author with Eugene Clark and Fred E. Clark of *Principles of Marketing* (1962). He has also contributed to numerous other books and monographs, including *Trends in Distribution, Services and Transportation* (1966), *The Spokane Wholesale Market* (1951), and *Marketing in the West* (1946). He has published articles and papers on marketing topics in the *Journal of Marketing*, the *Harvard Business Review*, and other professional journals.

Acknowledgements

The contributors have made their individual acknowledgements to persons assisting them, or to special source materials, in the appropriate place in the text. I should like to express my personal satisfaction that Dr. A. Boerma, Director-General of the Food and Agricultural Organisation of the United Nations, kindly undertook to write the Foreword.

Permission to use illustrative material has been given by the Royal Tropical Institute; the Unilever Museum, Amsterdam; the Margarine-Institut, Hamburg; Kurt Bunckenburg, Frankfurt am Main; Feldhaus-Archiv, Wilhelmshaven; Historishes Bildarchiv-Handke, Bad Berneck; Uwe Lacina, Hamburg; Technisch Film Centrum, Velp, (Gld.); Fotobureau John Klaver, Rotterdam; KLM Aerocarto N.V., Amsterdam; URL Photodienst, Vlaardingen; and VOZ, Zwijndrecht. The drawings which constitute Plates 21 to 26 and 28, were drawn by R. Das, Aerdenhout, Netherlands.

Permission to use other material was given by Unilever N.V.; the Institut National de la Propriété Industrielle, Paris; and by the Controller, H.M. Stationery Office.

Many friendships grew out of the preparation of the English edition for which Miss E. Huggard translated Chapters 1, 3, and 5, and the preparation of the manuscript owes much to the generous help of Mr. A. Braakman, and Mr. F. J. M. Tummers of Unilever N.V., and Mr. A. H. Clerkx who drew the text figures. On the other side of the North Sea the contributors and myself have received equally generous assistance from Mr. Sidney Blackhurst, Special Projects Editor, Unilever Limited.

The Members of Liverpool University Press, through their Chairman, Professor F. W. Walbank, expressed their interest in this project from its inception. An international symposium of this kind involves special publishing problems. We are indebted to Miss K. Christie, Mr. T. R. Hall, and Mr. D. Deacon for technical and sub-editorial assistance, and to Mr. B. Hunter who, with Miss K. Christie, prepared the index. To Mr. J. G. O'Kane, Secretary of the Press, Mr. H. L. Brook its Production Manager, and Mr. Bernard Crossland, designer, who saw the book through the press, I should like to say a special word of thanks for the care they brought to this task.

Introduction

By J.H. VAN STUYVENBERG

WITHIN the process of industrialization, which began in England towards the end of the eighteenth century and which, in the long run, brought a great increase in prosperity, three phases can be recognized. At first, the process was mainly characterized by the growth of the cotton and iron industries, and by the construction of railways. A hundred years later, around 1870, the emphasis was more on new industries: the chemical, electrical, and steel industries made a contribution towards increasing the general standard of living. In the present era other new industries have come to the fore, particularly those which manufacture durable consumer goods, such as cars and television sets; and undreamt-of prospects are now looming on the horizon.

The rise of the margarine industry belongs to the second phase of the industrialization process. This industry made a great contribution to the growth of prosperity by meeting an existing demand for fats, and by providing people with what has now become an indispensable foodstuff. It was invented in 1869 after a period of intense scientific research by a French chemist, Mège Mouriès, a brief biography of whom follows this introduction.

The industry's enormous expansion—of which the following pages bear ample evidence—has been helped by growth factors similar to those which influenced other sectors of industry: the creative urge of the people at the top, the expansion of the market, the investment in increasingly more modern production machinery, in scientific research and development of the product, and in human capital, particularly in the training and selection of senior staff.

It will be noted that one factor is missing from this summary: government encouragement. In this respect—right from the time the industry had achieved a certain stage of growth—a complete contrast with other industries was evident, in that the latter could at least rely on the government creating a climate conducive to their expansion, and even giving them powerful support in the form of numerous helpful measures.

Yet the margarine industry was hampered in its development in almost every country by government measures, of varying degrees of severity. This meant that a negative growth factor was created. I know of no other industry which had to swim so much against a tide of adverse government policy and which nevertheless succeeded in becoming one of the great modern industries. Seen in this light, the development of the industry has been unique.

When I was asked if I would act as editor for a symposium on margarine, to appear in 1969, the hundredth anniversary of the discovery of margarine, I accepted the invitation with pleasure. During the ensuing discussions, certain points were agreed upon.

The chapters were to correspond to the various stages in the production process, from the raw materials to the finished product offered to the consumer. The growth factors were to be included within this framework; especially the development of technology, of scientific research, and product development, as well as market expansion and government intervention. The provision of labour and capital—never any real problem—was to be left out. The subjects to be dealt with were therefore chosen deliberately; there was no attempt at a comprehensive treatment of the subject. We agreed in principle not to discuss the influential role played by executive staff in the expansion of the industry: Charles Wilson gave an excellent treatment of this in his *History of Unilever*, even though he did not cover the entire margarine industry. It will be apparent, therefore, that the book is historical in nature. Experts in the relevant fields of science were invited to write the various chapters. In view of the international nature of the industry, we were very pleased to have the co-operation of writers of various nationalities.

With a book of this kind there is always the danger that certain subjects may be omitted, whilst others will be treated more than once. There are some subjects—the hardening of vegetable oils for example—which have various aspects and which are consequently dealt with in more than one chapter, looked at each time from a different angle.

I leave it to the reader to decide whether this book meets with the aims we had in mind. Editing this work has, of course, brought me into contact with a great number of people, and I retain very pleasant memories of our meetings. I would like to thank all those who helped in any way towards the production of this study. I am particularly grateful to the contributors for their willingness to write the relevant chapters, for the dedication they showed in their work, and for their readiness to listen to suggestions on my part. My thanks go to the representatives of the many organizations whose co-operation and encouragement sustained the contributors and myself in our work, and made this book possible.

Hippolyte Mège Mouriès

THE French Second Empire was a period marked by great economic activity and substantial industrial development. Napoleon III himself exercised much influence on public affairs, and the atmosphere was one of busy economic life contrasted with the false splendour of society. Hippolyte Mège Mouriès undertook numerous research projects during this period, mainly in the field of food.

Until quite recently little was known of him except that he produced margarine in 1869. There was even confusion about his name. He was born on 24 October 1817 in Draguignan, an old town in the south of France, where his father was a schoolmaster. His name was registered as Hypolite Mège, but in later life he usually spelt his Christian name Hippolyte. In 1850 he discovered that there were other inventors surnamed Mège, so he added his mother's name to his own. He is therefore usually known as Hippolyte Mège Mouriès, except in official documents.

He began his career as a chemist's assistant in Draguignan when he was 16. After a period of practical training in Aix-en-Provence he went to Paris, and after a competitive examination on 1 April 1838 he became a resident pharmacist's assistant at the Hôtel Dieu hospital. He held this position until about 1846, but never sat the pharmacists' examination.

When he began his research work it soon became obvious that he had a good head for business, and he took good care of his financial affairs and his patents in several countries. However, it seems that what he earned from his more lucrative inventions was frittered away on others.

His first invention was a very practical one. One of the remedies commonly prescribed at that time for syphilis, copahin, could not readily be taken orally by some patients. Mège treated the drug with nitric acid, which eliminated the unwanted effects. He was awarded a prize for this work.

He took out his second patent for effervescent tablets, and then turned his attention to paper-making. After that came patents for sugar-making (1845) and the use of egg-yolk in the tanning of leather. By this time he was no longer an assistant pharmacist but a consultant chemist.

In 1852 Mège began to carry out research on food. He deduced, from analyses, that more active species of animals have more calcium phosphate in their blood. He therefore made up a calcium phosphate-protein preparation and marketed it as health chocolate and semolina. He sent a treatise on the subject to the Académie des Sciences, which encouraged his work with a contribution of 500 francs. One of the members of the committee who decided on this grant was the world-famous fat chemist Chevreul, who was later to have considerable influence on Mège's career.

In the years 1854–60, Mège carried out research into the preparation of bread; this work made him famous at the time, but it is now forgotten. He devised a method of making 14 per cent more white bread from wheat than had previously proved possible. Mège lectured on his process in Berlin, Brussels, and Paris, and was awarded two gold medals for it. On Chevreul's recommendation, Napoleon III awarded him the Legion of Honour. Mège's new bread-making process was comparatively cumbersome and so did not recommend itself to the bakers; thanks to the government subsidies then in force they had no interest in increasing their output anyway. The army bakeries apparently used it for some time, but the introduction of modern milling methods rendered it obsolete.

Meanwhile, Mège was making headway financially. He moved to a better house, on the Boulevard de Strasbourg. He married in 1861, but his wife died four years later. In 1860–2 he became interested in impracticable machines, apparently *perpetua mobilia* of some kind. We now know only their names.

After 1862 he concentrated on fats. He obtained some patents on the cold saponification of milk (at 40–5 °C.) in fat emulsions, a process about which Chevreul was very enthusiastic, but which proved disappointing in practice.

The margarine patent (F.P. 86480) was lodged on 15 July 1869 and granted on 2 October. The English provisional specification was lodged on 17 June.

We know very little of how Mège made this discovery. At the time he was either in the service of the French government or had been commissioned to carry out research that might improve food and he was assigned the task of preparing a product that could take the place of butter, but would be cheaper and have better keeping properties. Napoleon III was personally interested in the project, and Mège was able to carry out his experiments at the Ferme Impériale de la Faisanderie in Vincennes, which was the personal property of the Emperor.

Fasting cows produce milk from which it is impossible to make butter. Mège concluded that butter fat must therefore be derived from beef suet. By pressing beef suet at 30–40 °C. he obtained a fat that melted at 20–5 °C.; this, in the terminology of the day, was oleo-margarine. In 1813 Chevreul had isolated impure palmitic acid and called it margarine. Later this name was given to impure tripalmitin, and impure oleopalmitin was called oleomargarine. Mège's product was a household fat which could replace various other fats, even butter, for cooking purposes. In 1872 it was put on sale in Paris as margarine but was sold abroad as 'margarine butter'.

By churning this product Mège made what he called *beurre économique* (economical butter). He had to change this name to 'Margarine Mouriès', as names reminiscent of butter were illegal. In his patent he dealt relatively briefly with the preparation of this butter substitute. He assigned his rights to the Société Anonyme d'Alimenta-tion, and they took out a *certificat d'addition* to Mège's original patent in 1874.

Mège seems not to have done any more work on margarine. In 1871 he sold his knowledge to the Dutch firm of Jurgens for 60,000 francs. (There was no patent law in the Netherlands at that time.) He sold his British, American, and Prussian patents to various buyers in 1873 and 1874.

In 1875 he took out a patent dealing with the preparation of canned meat; a subject of considerable interest in view of the great expansion of the meat industry in South America. His last patent, which dates from a few months before his death in 1880, deals with the nutritional advantages of raw sea-salt as a food additive.

Mège was a man of great energy who worked his own way up in his profession. His theoretical knowledge was always slight, although he liked to formulate hypotheses, but he was an accurate observer. He deserves to be remembered for having found a new food for mankind.

1. This portrait of Mège Mouriès drawn by his son René in 1887 shows the inventor in his sixtieth year.

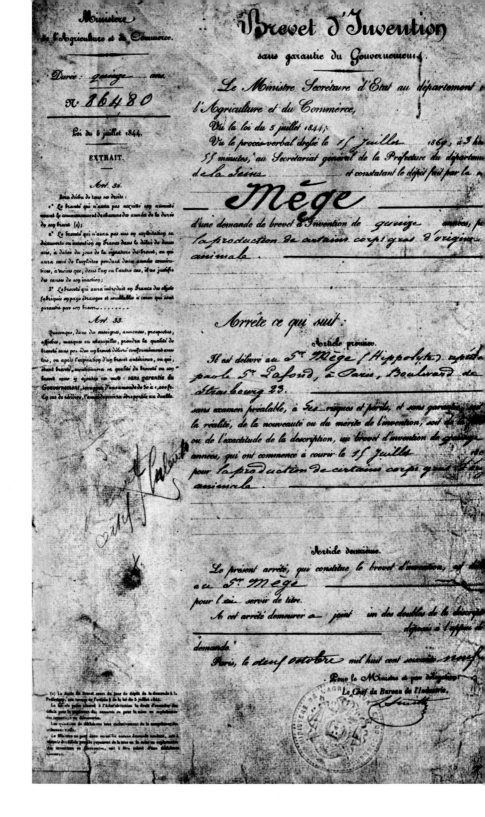

2. On 15 July 1869 the French Ministry of Agriculture and Trade granted Mège Mouriès a patent for fifteen years for the processing and production of certain fats of animal origin.

A.D. 1869, 17th July. N° 2157.

Producing Fatty Bodies.

LETTERS PATENT to Hippolyte Mège, of Paris, Boulevart de Strasbourg, No. 70, Chemist Manufacturer, for the Invention of " THE
PREPARATION AND PRODUCTION OF CERTAIN NEW ANIMAL FATTY BODIES."

Sealed the 1st January 1870, and dated the 17th July 1869.

PROVISIONAL SPECIFICATION left by the said Hippolyte Mège at
the Office of the Commissioners of Patents, with his Petition, on
the 17th July 1869.

I, HIPPOLYTE MÈGE, of Paris, Boulevart de Strasbourg, No. 70,
5 Chemist Manufacturer, do hereby declare the nature of the said Invention for " THE PREPARATION AND PRODUCTION OF CERTAIN NEW ANIMAL FATTY
BODIES," to be as follows :—

The object of my Invention is to make neutral products new by their
nature and superior in quality.

10 The Invention is based on the deductions of modern science, which
prove, first, that odoriferous coloring matters volatile and becoming
rancid (acres et rancissantes) do not preexist in the natural fats called

3. On 17 July 1869 this patent was also registered in England.

Der Geist des Erfinders

und sein Urteil nach 60 Jahren.

Sie lösten mein Problem am besten. In Ihrer Marke liegt die höchste Vervollkommnung meiner Erfindung

Rama-Qualität-Blauband-Qualität vereinigt zur Höchst-Qualität:

MARGARINE

MÈGE MOURIÈS,
*ein bekannter Chemiker, erfand 1869
die Margarine; das darauf erteilte
Patent ging 1871 in den Besitz der
Firmen Jurgens-Van den Bergh
über, welche zuerst die Margarine
fabrikmäßig herstellten.*

Rama im Blauband

doppelt so gut

½ ℔ 50 Pfg.

mit Garantie-Zeichen für frische Qualität

4. This German advertisement published in 1929 is one of the few which feature the inventor of margarine.

CHAPTER ONE

100 Years of the Margarine Industry

W.G.HOFFMANN

THE REASONS FOR THE EMERGENCE OF THE INDUSTRY IN THE NINETEENTH CENTURY

IN the second half of the nineteenth century various social and economic factors combined to create the margarine industry. These were population increase (1), urban development, industrialization, the general rise in purchasing power, and the need for sufficient and above all better nutrition. This development had its starting point in Europe.

There is truth in the dictum that in economic terms the Middle Ages did not end until the nineteenth century. In fact the industrial era, from the political, economic, social, and technical aspects, provided entirely fresh conditions, built on new foundations, for the everyday life of mankind. The decided improvement in living conditions in Europe is clearly shown by the figures given here. During the past 100 years Europe's population has more than doubled; in the same period agricultural production has increased fivefold, industrial production about twentyfold, and world trade about fiftyfold. Expectation of life, which in earlier centuries has been a mere 18 years and even in the first half of the nineteenth century had only reached 37, has in the course of the past 100 years doubled to over 70 years. Population research experts have shown that the great increase in population began as early as 1750. This extreme population pressure explains why famine continued without a break until late in the nineteenth century.

Burgdörfer (2) showed that the population of Europe increased from 140 million people in about 1750 to 187 million in 1800 and 266 million in 1850. Between 1850 and 1900 the population increase was especially great, and the number rose from 266 million to 401 million.

The figures refer to Western and Eastern Europe including the European portion of Russia. The same area today has a population of far more than 600 million.

Statistics on population in England (3), the first country to be industrialized, show an increase for the period from 1871 to 1911 of more than 50 per cent in England and Wales from 22·7 million to 36 million people. In Germany (4), the population rose from 35·3 million people in 1850 to about 50 million in 1900.

In that period the pressure of population was so heavy in some areas that many millions of Europeans emigrated to countries in other continents which offered more ample space; especially to that land of promise, the United States of America, whose population of 59 million in 1850 rose to 144 million in 1900. Today it has over 200 million inhabitants (5).

Hand-in-hand with this rise in population came the Industrial Revolution, which began about 1760 in Great Britain and in the course of the nineteenth century spread to Belgium and Northern France; finally, in the second half of the nineteenth century, especially after the foundation of the German empire, it swept into Germany in 1871. Meanwhile, the massive emigration from Europe to North America was the precursor of industrialization in the New World; and then advances in engineering and scientific techniques brought about a vast expansion in industrial as well as agricultural production. In this particular sphere it was the agricultural chemistry developed by Justus von Liebig about 1840 that made possible a gradual manifold increase of the yield per acre. Thanks to mineral fertilizers, agricultural production could be stepped up faster than the rate of population growth. This made it possible to utilize an increasing proportion of agricultural production in the form of animal feeding-stuffs, and thus to keep more livestock and produce meat, milk, eggs, and dairy products in greater quantity. In preceding centuries the ill-nourished beast had served the unprolific farmland as a scraggy donor of stable manure: now the productive farmland and the meadows and pastureland too in their improved condition could enter the service of stock-rearing as sources of animal fodder. The increase and improvement in the yield of stable manure obtained by this means was at the same time a prerequisite for the corresponding increased use of mineral fertilizers. For the yield of stable manure, as we know, helps to enrich the soil; a point already emphasized by Albrecht von Thaer in 1809.

Naturally enough, decades had to pass before industrialization could be reflected in a general increase of prosperity throughout all sections of the population. The industrial employers could not pass on the profits either immediately or in sufficient amounts to the employees, as industrial investments had to be financed and costs of depreciation met. Experience shows that development and growth of this kind imply a very slow process of penetration, and consequently a very long time had to pass before the increasing population could afford more and better food. This is the explanation of the severe social stresses in the second half of the nineteenth century. Employers had a strong interest in the existence of healthy and able-bodied employees; for this, the essential condition was a fundamental improvement in the food situation; and accounts of that situation at the time bring home the urgent need for such a development.

Thus Brugmans (6) writes: 'The diet of the Dutch workers is very poor; since 1800 their staple food has been the potato, which they cook with vinegar and mustard. Even the children have to be content to live on potatoes, often in consequence suffering from scrofula. Only on special days potatoes are served with some oil or fat. Bread very seldom appears on the table, and if there is any it will be made of rye, potatoes, or barley. Wheaten bread, on account of the high tax on wheaten flour, is out of the question. Meat is a luxury which only some few better-off workers can afford. In the first half of the nineteenth century even meat consumption per head diminishes, and it does not revive until after the abolition of excise duty on mutton and pork.'

Similar observations were made in Great Britain. One chronicler (7), for example, wrote that it was almost a mark of prosperity if the housewife in a working-man's home was able to serve bread, oatmeal, ham, a little butter, treacle, tea, and coffee. Higher bread consumption at this time was a sign of increase in prosperity.

On the diet of the French worker Kuczynski (8) writes: 'Soup, soup, and again soup—a piece of dry bread for "second breakfast" for a miner, meat for a miner six times in the year, but every day in a family with a high standard of living.'

A summary of these observations, which owing to lack of statistical data on the period are very incomplete, will show that the diet of the European worker in the nineteenth century was unbalanced and quite inadequate from the physiological aspect: it was particularly lacking in protein and fat content. Carbohydrates were sufficiently available

on the whole, although this varied greatly. Even among the carbohydrates, only bread, porridge, and potatoes were commonly available; sugar at that time was still in short supply and very expensive.

The following figures show how serious the food problem was. In
the hundred years or so from 1850 to the present day, bread consumption per head per year in Western Europe has fallen from 300 to
less than 100 kg. Sugar consumption has risen from about 5 kg to
almost 30 kg. Meat consumption has improved from 10 kg to 50–70
kg, egg consumption from about 50 per head yearly to over 200, consumption of potatoes from about 50 to 100 kg. The amount of milk
consumption, in liquid milk and in dairy products, has risen during
this space of time from about 100 litres per head per year to over
300. Consumption of pure fat including butter has doubled from 10
to 20 kg per head per year; but at the same time, the supply of invisible fats for the population has improved, because meat and eggs
contain a fair amount of fat. The improvement in the supply of fats
was particularly important, because industrial work demanded a diet
with minimum ballast and maximum energy value, something best
obtained through higher fat consumption; 1 kg of fat supplies considerably more calories than 1 kg of carbohydrates or protein. The
calorie content of fat is about 9,000 per kg; of sugar about 4,000, rice
about 3,000, bread and moderately fat meat about 2,000; a kilogramme of eggs contains 1,300, a kilogramme of fish 1,000, a kilogramme of potatoes or liquid milk 600, and a kilogramme of fruit or
vegetables only 200–600. Furthermore, among the fats butter is the
one containing the important vitamins A and D, which are soluble in
fat and are necessary for the body's maintenance. Around 1850, however, the fat supply was not only inadequate in amount, but also un-
satisfactory in its composition. In Germany in 1850, for example, the
fat consumption was about 12·5 kg a head, made up of 40 per cent
butter, 32 per cent suet, 16 per cent lard and bacon, and 12 per cent
vegetable oil. The butcher's meat fats—suet, lard, and bacon—made
up 48 per cent of the pure fat consumption. The drawbacks of these
fats are their low vitamin content and indigestible nature. Besides,
suet is no use as a spread. Consequently the popular demand in
general was not just for more fat, but quite specifically for more butter; because it can be spread, is universally available, and relatively
more wholesome. These facts account for the severe shortage and
high cost of butter after 1850; between 1850 and 1870 butter prices
in Europe rose by almost 100 per cent (9).

Long-term price quotations in the retail trade for 1 kg of butter are available for Hamburg for the years since 1792. 1 kg of butter in 1792 cost the consumer 1·02 marks, in 1800 1·94 marks, in 1850 1·32 marks, and in 1869 2·44 marks. A Prussian miner about the year 1870 received a wage of 2·59 marks for one shift; this meant that he needed almost the whole wage for one shift to buy himself 1 kg of butter. In other urban consumer centres of Europe, particularly in Paris, the dearth of butter between 1850 and 1870 was in some cases even much greater. Since industry, still in its infancy, found it impossible to provide the improved purchasing power for butter through correspondingly higher wages, there was now a question of creating a substitute fat. This would have to possess all the properties of butter—wholesomeness, taste, ease of spreading, and universal availability—without costing so much. This important function in the policy of social economics fell to the lot of margarine, the price of which for the consumer, when it was introduced, was only 1·20 marks, half the price of butter (10).

THE BEGINNINGS OF THE INDUSTRY AND ITS REGIONAL DEVELOPMENT AFTER 1870

The manufacturing process for margarine was developed in France; there was good reason for this. In 1852, France under Napoleon III had recovered its imperial status and was a country where forces of change were simmering in the political, economic, social, and scientific spheres. French achievements in the chemistry of nutrition were world-renowned in the nineteenth century. Political tensions were increasing in relations with Prussia, which was now rapidly advancing under Bismarck. As the dearth of butter in France was worse than ever after 1850, the government was particularly anxious about an adequate supply of fats for the army and the working population, especially in the event of a war against Prussia. For that reason, it took advantage of the Paris World Exhibition in 1866 to invite offers for a research undertaking on the development of a reasonably priced nutritive fat. The French food research chemist Mège Mouriès applied for the assignment, and was successful (see pp. 5–7). His method, basically very simple, made it possible—thanks to the addition of liquid milk—to produce, on the basis of beef tallow as the raw material, a nutrient fat which could be spread and which was universally available and comparatively easy to digest. As beef tallow is a cheap by-product of meat production and skimmed milk is also cheap, the price-rating of the nutrient fat obtained from these two constituents was only half that of butter.

Soon after this, in 1870, the expected war between France and Prussia broke out, but in 1871 it was over and France defeated. Napolcon III had to abdicate and leave the country. All this meant that, politically speaking, Mège Mouriès's hands were tied, so that he could not himself exploit his patent as he had intended. In the post-war chaos in France the margarine patent might easily have come to grief had it not been bought up abroad. Particular interest in this new fat was shown in Holland, which at that time was a centre for the most important butter wholesalers of Europe; in fact Holland in about 1870 was still the major butter-exporting country of the world, especially to the English market. England, at that time already rela-tively well forward with industrialization, imported the bulk of its butter requirement from abroad. As shortage and high prices were making butter exports to England exceptionally difficult, it was understandable that the Dutch butter wholesalers should become interested in the new fat, margarine.

So it was in the spring of 1871 that the news of the French margarine patent penetrated to the butter wholesale firm of Jurgens in Oss, Holland. This was a family business, which for 100 years had been engaged in the butter trade and butter export, and now it immediately realized the importance of the margarine patent in the task of im-proving the fat supply for the population of Europe.

Through the agency of I. & E. Cordeweener, a firm doing business near Oss, Jan Jurgens made contact with Mège Mouriès in Paris and bought the margarine patent from him. After a few improvements of the factory process the Jurgens family then very quickly took up the production of margarine. In the marketing of margarine the firm of Jurgens found that the good international business relations they had built up for some decades stood them in good stead. The firm of Van den Bergh, also with headquarters at Oss, and having been, like Jurgens, wholesalers and exporters of butter for many years, took up margarine production also. Other Dutch firms followed suit, so that the margarine industry in Holland developed rapidly. A. Meyer (11) reports that by 1884 a number of Dutch margarine factories were already in existence.

In some other European countries also margarine factories were built in the early 1870s. In Germany (12) the first of these came into being under the name Frankfurter Margarine-Gesellschaft in about 1872. In 1873 the Austrian Sargs began the building of a factory in Leising near Vienna (13). In Norway the first one was opened in Oslo in 1876 under the trade name of August Pellerin & Fils (14) and in Sweden the first was built in 1884; in the same year a factory was established in Denmark (15). England's first factory came very late; it was founded by the Dane, Otto Mønsted (16) in 1889.

In the United States of America the production of margarine began between 1874 and 1876 in Manhattan (17); this earliest North American factory was known by the name Oleo Margarine-Facturing Company. In Russia (18) the industry was comparatively late in developing, and there were only a few primitive little factories before the Russian revolution of 1917. Factories on a larger scale did not exist in Russia till after 1930.

This survey shows that the margarine industry, cradled in Holland, very soon attained significance in other countries too. Naturally its increasing importance in these countries quickly led to the enactment of margarine laws by the various governments concerned (see Chapter Seven). The purpose of these was to ensure that this new industry was integrated in the general design of the objectives of national economic policy, with a view in particular to the protection of agricultural interests in the matter of butter prices. Thus in Germany for example, the year 1887 saw the enactment of the first margarine law, which was amended in 1897. As the margarine legislation of the individual countries is discussed elsewhere in this book, suffice it to say that—as the statistics show—the price of margarine has not in fact had the effect of depressing the price of butter. Cheap margarine has simply prevented a further rise in butter prices.

Moreover it was really not possible, up to the turn of the century, for margarine to compete with butter, because margarine consumption up to that time, though it had been steadily increasing, remained relatively small compared to butter consumption. At first, the market for margarine was mainly to be found with the poorer classes, who could hardly, or not at all, afford butter; they had to rely almost entirely on tallow and lard. So after 1870 margarine did not compete with butter at first, but with beef tallow and lard. A more rapid expansion of the margarine industry up to the turn of the century had to face certain limitations, in that the raw material of margarine, beef tallow, became increasingly scarce because agriculture was obliged to change from fat mast to meat mast, in view of the popular demand for more and more and better meat. Towards the end of the century it became increasingly difficult for the melting plants to supply the factories with sufficient amounts of refined tallow.

A turning-point in the provision of raw materials for the margarine industry came with the invention in 1902 of the oil-hardening process. Even in this matter, it was once more the French food chemists who had pioneered the scientific work at the crucial early stage. The Frenchmen Sabatier and Senderens as early as 1897 had discovered that the fluid consistency of vegetable oils is due to their having a lower hydrogen content than solid fats such as butter, tallow, and lard. Of course, they did not evolve any method of converting fluid oils into fats of solid consistency by the addition of hydrogen: it was only in 1902 that the German research scientist Wilhelm Normann succeeded in this, and took out a patent for the process on the 14 August of that year in Berlin (19). Hence in the twentieth century it became possible to include tropical and subtropical regions of the earth as sources of basic stocks of raw material for the industry in Europe and North America. This extension of the raw material supply was a decisive factor in accelerating a global expansion of the industry.

THE WORLD-WIDE EXPANSION SINCE THE END
OF THE NINETEENTH CENTURY

Once the margarine industry, originating in Holland after 1870, had acquired importance in the other industrialized countries of Europe, from about 1880 onwards it gradually extended throughout the world. Wherever the population was increasing, or urbanization, industrialization, rise in prosperity, and improvement in nutritional conditions were evident, the margarine industry grew in importance. Following the advance of industrialization, factories were first built in the U.S.A. in about 1880. After 1900, the first steps were taken in Russia and the other countries of the world. The growth of the margarine industry and its world-wide expansion in the period from 1875 to 1965 are illustrated in Tables 1.1 and 1.2.

From Tables 1.1 and 1.2 it is clear that the growth of margarine production between 1875 and 1913 was at first slow. It was only after the First World War that it rapidly gained impetus; after the Second World War it achieved boom conditions. In 1895 world margarine production had reached merely 300,000 tons, an amount that was only about 10 per cent of world butter production at that time. In 1913 world margarine production amounted to 550,000 tons. In 1925, after the First World War, it was already 1 million tons, in 1950 over 2 million tons, and today it is over 5 million tons. With this order of magnitude, margarine production has now almost caught up with the world production of butter.

Years	Western Europe	U.S.A.	U.S.S.R.	Other countries	Total
1875	100	—	—	—	100
1895	250	50	—	—	300
1900	300	60	20	20	400
1913	400	75	35	40	550
1925	750	100	50	100	1,000
1932	1,050	150	75	125	1,400
1938	991	175	93	141	1,400
1950	1,313	425	193	169	2,100
1951	1,510	472	226	292	2,500
1952	1,603	583	277	337	2,800
1953	1,675	586	338	301	2,900
1954	1,751	619	392	338	3,100
1955	1,821	605	399	375	3,200
1956	1,894	622	437	747	3,700
1957	1,867	592	449	892	3,800
1958	1,813	713	395	879	3,800
1959	1,873	731	452	944	4,000
1960	1,910	769	431	990	4,100
1961	1,816	782	474	1,128	4,200
1962	1,808	783	516	1,193	4,300
1963	1,829	814	566	1,191	4,400
1964	1,886	842	606	1,266	4,600
1965	1,876	864	670	1,390	4,800

TABLE I.I. The margarine production of the world (in thousands of tons). Data taken from the Commonwealth Economic Committee publications on *Dairy Produce* from 1953 onwards, and the *F.A.O. Coconut Situation* (no. 3 onwards).

Tracing this evolution of production in the individual states is not entirely possible, because long-term statistics of production are available only for a few countries, for instance Denmark, Germany, Great Britain, Holland, Norway, Sweden, the U.S.S.R., and the U.S.A.; and even for these countries the statistical sequences are incomplete. Especially for the initial period only sporadic annual data are available for various periods. For the war periods the production statistics are full of gaps.

Although the number of countries at our disposal for this inquiry is very small, those countries are representative of the over-all picture, being themselves the most important economic units in national production of margarine. As regards the total amount of production the

Years	Western Europe	U.S.A.	U.S.S.R.	Other countries	World production (1,000 tons)
1875	100	—	—	—	100
1895	83·3	16·7	—	—	300
1900	75·0	15·0	5·0	5·0	400
1913	72·7	13·6	6·4	7·3	550
1925	75·0	10·0	5·0	10·0	1,000
1932	75·0	10·7	5·4	8·9	1,400
1938	70·8	12·5	6·6	10·1	1,400
1950	62·5	20·2	9·2	8·1	2,100
1951	60·4	18·9	9·0	11·7	2,500
1952	57·3	20·8	9·9	12·0	2,800
1953	57·8	20·2	11·7	10·3	2,900
1954	56·5	20·0	12·6	10·9	3,100
1955	56·9	18·9	12·5	11·7	3,200
1956	51·2	16·8	11·8	20·2	3,700
1957	49·1	15·6	11·8	23·5	3,800
1958	47·7	18·8	10·4	23·1	3,800
1959	46·8	18·3	11·3	23·6	4,000
1960	46·6	18·8	10·5	24·1	4,100
1961	43·2	18·6	11·3	26·9	4,200
1962	42·1	18·2	12·0	27·7	4,300
1963	41·6	18·5	12·9	27·0	4,400
1964	41·0	18·3	13·2	27·5	4,600
1965	39·0	18·0	14·0	29·0	4,800

TABLE I.2. The share of Western Europe, the U.S.A., the U.S.S.R., and other countries in the world production of margarine, 1875–1965 (percentage). Data from Commonwealth Economic Committee: *Dairy Produce*, 1953 onwards, and *F.A.O. Coconut Situation* (no. 3 onwards).

U.S.A. is today at the head of the list, followed by the U.S.S.R., West Germany, Great Britain, and the Netherlands.

In the course of the world-wide expansion of the industry, as Table I.2 shows, the share of Western Europe in world production, immediately after 1870 amounting to 100 per cent, showed a steady decline. In 1900 it was only 75 per cent, in 1950 62·5 per cent, and in 1965 a mere 39 per cent. The share of the U.S.A. between 1895 and 1965 fluctuated between 15 and 20 per cent. The share of the U.S.S.R. rose gradually from 5 per cent in 1900 to 14 per cent in 1965.

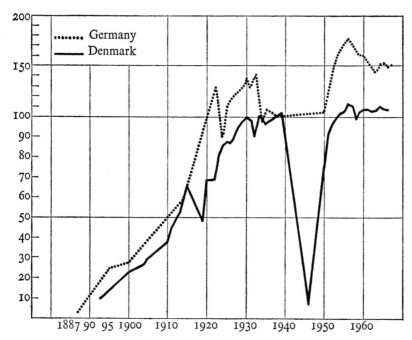

FIG. 1.1. Margarine production in Denmark and Germany (Federal Republic), 1887–1964.

The development of margarine production is especially remarkable in the other countries of the world, particularly even in the Asiatic countries and in South America. The share of these groups of countries rose from 5 per cent in 1900 to 29 per cent in 1965. And a further rise can be expected there in the future, since industrialization is still only in the early stages in these areas of the world.

Figs. 1.1–1.4 show the development of margarine production in eight countries. For the sake of easy comparison between the progressions they are all indicated on the basis of 1938 = 100. The absolute figures are given in Table 1.3. However incomplete the statistics, in all these countries a vigorous upward development of margarine production can be detected. In Denmark, for instance, the production index of margarine rose from 9·5 per cent in 1893 to

109·8 per cent in 1964. In Germany the index in 1887 amounted to 4·1 per cent as against 173·7 per cent in 1964. It has to be borne in mind here that the German figures up to 1913 cover the area of the empire, up to 1938 the former imperial territories, and from 1950 on

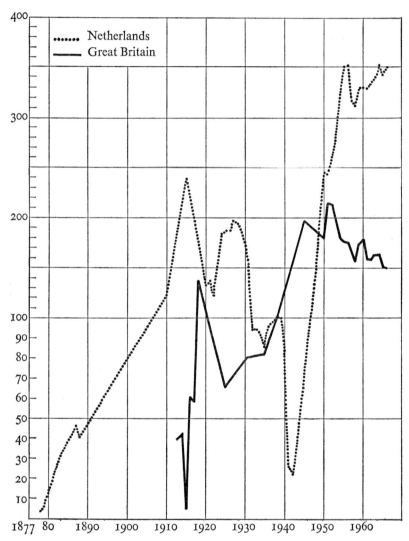

FIG. 1.2. Margarine production in the Netherlands and Great Britain, 1887–1964.

only the area of the Federal Republic of Germany including West Berlin. In Great Britain, margarine production increased from 39·8 per cent of the 1912 level to 163 per cent in 1964, and in the same period in the Netherlands from 122 per cent to 353 per cent. For Sweden the index in 1964 more than quadrupled that of 1913, and the volume of production in Norway increased to a similar extent. In the U.S.S.R. production between 1938 and 1964 actually showed a

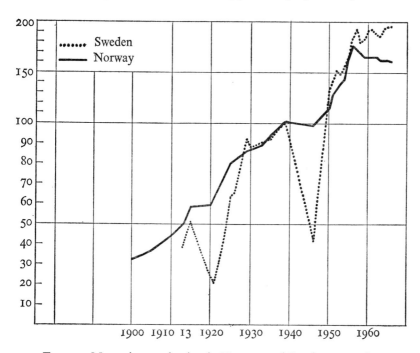

FIG. I.3. Margarine production in Norway and Sweden, 1913–64.

sixfold increase. For the U.S.A. in 1965 an index figure of 494 points in 1965 contrasted with the 11·7 points of 1885.

Despite the evidence of a steady upward trend in margarine production in all countries during this long interval of about a hundred years, the fact must be faced that in the various countries there had been considerable differences in the levels of growth. Owing to the difficulties experienced under wartime conditions in procuring raw materials, there were breaks in production, above all in the European countries, during the two world wars. In the U.S.A. and the U.S.S.R., on the other hand, such interruptions in the upward trend are not recognizable, though indeed it appears that production in the U.S.A. both in 1902 and in 1931, after a margarine tax was introduced in these years, suffered a temporary decline. In Germany, after 1933, government policy and quota restrictions on margarine production

	Denmark 1	Germany 2	Great Britain 3	Netherlands 4	Norway 5	Sweden 6	U.S.S.R. 7	U.S.A. 8
1874				0·1				
1875				0·2				
1876				0·2				
1877				2·5				
1878				2·9				
1879				4·4				
1880				9·6				
1881				13·4				
1882				18·8				
1883				22·8				
1884				25·1				
1885				27·9				20
1886				29·9				
1887		15		33·3				
1888				29·7				
1893	7·7							
1894								32
1895		90						
1900		100						
1901								
1902								57
1903					19·4			
1904	21·1							
1909								53
1910								67
1911	35·4							48
1912								64
1913	42·3	210	84	88	27·4	23·6		69
1914			90					64
1915			11					64
1916			129					85
1917			125					130
1918			286					159
1919	39·6							167
1920	55·5				32·7			167
1921	55·5			99		12·7		98
1922	55·9	480		88		17·7		84
1923	65·2	360		108		23·0		103
1924	69·4	340		131		29·5		105
1925	70·2	410	140	132	44·3	38·5		106
1926	69·6	450		134		40·0		110
1927	71·8	455		141				126
1928	76·5	480		140	46·6			144
1929	78·9	508		133	47·2	56·6		161
1930	80·6	516		128				148
1931	79·3	480		111				104
1932	73·3	525		68				92

	Denmark 1	Germany 2	Great Britain 3	Nether- lands 5	Norway 6	Sweden 6	U.S.S.R. 7	U.S.A. 8
1933	80·9	370		68	48			111
1934				66				120
1935				62				173
1936				69				178
1937				70				180
1938	81·0	376	211	72	55	61	93	175
1939				72				137
1940				61			119	145
1941				20				167
1942				16				193
1943				27				279
1944							126	267
1945								279
1946				68				260
1947				79				338
1948				107				412
1949				144				391
1950	61·0	387	380	176	63	79	193	425
1951	73·0	469	453	175	71	86	226	472
1952	77·0	530	452	188	74	93	277	583
1953	80·0	594	413	202	76	91	338	586
1954	84·0	614	385	231	79	96	392	619
1955	85·0	641	372	252	92	101	399	605
1956	91·0	663	370	253	98	112	437	621
1957	90·0	648	357	232	96	117	449	664
1958	80·0	624	334	226	94	110	395	714
1959	86·0	615	364	239	92	112	452	731
1960	88·0	609	374	239	92	116	431	769
1961	88·0	576	336	237	92	117	474	782
1962	86·0	557	336	241	92	115	516	783
1963	87·0	549	343	245	90	113	566	814
1964	89·0	569	345	254	90	118	606	842
1965	88·0	570	319	248	90	119	670	864
1966	87·0	558	316	252	89	120		
1967		564						

TABLE I.3. Margarine production of eight countries (absolute figures), 1874–1967 (in thousands of tons). Data from technical groups of the margarine industry.

led to interruption of the trend. In the Netherlands also production of margarine in the 1930s was checked by state action. In Denmark on the other hand the consumption *per capita* was very high at an early stage. But on the whole it may be said that margarine production in individual countries after 1920 was double that of 1913. After 1950 it doubled yet again.

It is clear that in so long a period as 100 years, influences arising from war and crisis conditions, and in this context interventions by the government, had varying effects on the expansion of the margarine industry in the individual countries. Yet the trend makes it plain that

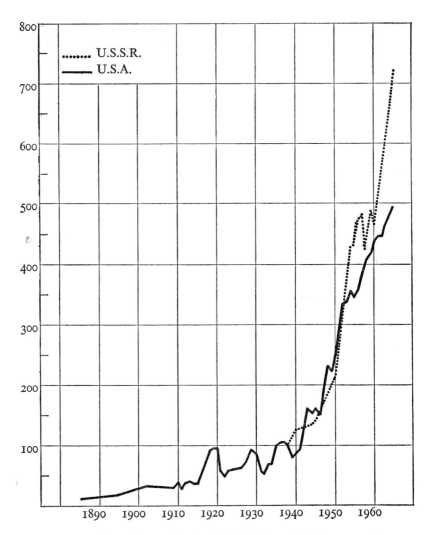

FIG. 1.4. Margarine production in U.S.S.R. and U.S.A., 1939–65.

the margarine industry in all the producing countries, despite interruptions by wars, crises, and government intervention, has steadily maintained dynamic growth.

The history of the margarine industry of the world is a representative passage in world economic history over the last 100 years. The transition then effected from the uni-concentric world economy, which at first was represented by Europe alone, to the multi-concentric world economy with new kernels of industry in the U.S.A., in Canada, in the U.S.S.R., and in Japan, together with the formation of further industrial centres in South America, in Africa, and in Asia, provides the background for the world-wide expansion of the industry. This evolution has been described most impressively by Andreas Predöhl (20). Naturally, the trend of growth in the margarine industry of the world for 100 years—leaving technical, physiological, and political factors out of account—has been continually influenced by economic factors dependent on market conditions and structural patterns; particularly in fact by movement in incomes among the population on the one hand, and by price trends in margarine and butter on the other. These influences require closer consideration and explanation in detail.

ECONOMIC STRUCTURE AND ECONOMIC CHANGES IN RELATION TO DEVELOPMENT

In the course of this expansion throughout 100 years and the extension of its boundaries, the margarine industry has been constantly faced with economic changes resulting from market conditions and structural patterns; these changes are reflected in prices and incomes. The initial position in the free market economy after 1870 was very favourable for the industry, and that tendency has always been maintained. Around 1870, as we have said, incomes were very low and butter prices very high, while the price of margarine was only half that of butter. One explanation of the difference in price is that butter is produced with losses due to its circuitous refinement process through the animal stomach, whereas oil-bearing fruits are a direct product of the soil, a fact which accounts for the double yield per hectare in vegetable oils and even multiple yields in palm oils as compared with the production of milk fat. A corollary of these facts is that European vegetable oil is cheaper than European butter.

The influence of prices and incomes on sales of butter and margarine was discussed repeatedly in the literature of past decades; but it is only within the last twenty years that a statistically accurate

M.—4

measurement of this influence has proved possible, with the use of improved mathematical methods. Here the terms price elasticity and income elasticity respectively are used in speaking of the quantitative demand for butter or margarine (21). Elasticity of demand is a factor calculated from the effect of relating the percentage change of price or of income to the percentage change of demand. For example, if the price of margarine drops by 10 per cent and the demand for margarine because of that increases by 5 per cent, this corresponds to a price elasticity of 0·5. If income rises by 10 per cent and margarine consumption increases by 5 per cent, this corresponds to a positive income elasticity of 0·5. Of course negative elasticities are calculated also; as for example when, in spite of a decline in price or in spite of rising income, the demand falls off. At this point a distinction must be drawn between two types of elasticity reaction, one static and vertical according to classes of income at a definite moment, and one dynamic and horizontal pertaining to all the income classes in the period. Both considerations are important, for the margarine industry in its 100-year development found its sales in the first instance mainly in families of the low-income groups and those with higher income and many children. Consequently, margarine did carry out its intended task, that of improving the fat supply for families in the low-income groups who could not afford to buy fat in sufficient amounts. On that account economic theory has classed margarine among the so-called inferior goods, the consumption of which is higher in low-income households than in those which are better off. This negative income elasticity already noted, of the quantitative demand for margarine in the static income vertical of the income groups, still remains today. In the dynamic and horizontal time-phases of all the income groups, the consumption both of margarine and of butter shows a positive income elasticity during these 100 years, although neither margarine nor butter consumption *per capita* rose in the individual countries in the same proportion as real income. The purchasing power of an hour's wages has shown a multiple increase in the course of 100 years, both for margarine and butter. This centennial development both in margarine and in butter consumption was interrupted in the individual countries for shorter or longer periods under the influence of varying conditions in politics, economic activity, and the structural basis. In West Germany, for example, from 1957 to 1963 and in 1965–6 margarine was an inferior commodity, with decreasing consumption in spite of continued growth in real income.

After 1870 the butter supply also improved. In many households it turned out that butter was used in the first instance more for spreading on bread, and margarine more for cooking, roasting or frying, and baking. Individual countries and regions varied to an extraordinary extent in this development, according to the nature of their social or economic structure and their habits—for example, in having more or fewer hot meals. The prices of both butter and margarine were subject to sharp fluctuations in the earlier decades after 1870, and this also affected short-term decisions to purchase. It may be said that up to and into the present century, with the growth of prosperity in all the so-called margarine countries, the consumption both of butter and of margarine has increased, because the population is demanding more and more of these fats which are easily digested because of their moisture content, whereas consumption of tallow is declining. In the course of this development—apart from cases of temporary government regulation of the prices of butter and margarine—in free market conditions both butter and margarine rose in price, though the price rises tended to be smaller for margarine than for butter, and there have been fewer and fewer extreme fluctuations in price. This has led to a structural change in the butter–margarine price ratio in favour of margarine. In many countries margarine consumption has climbed higher than butter consumption; this applies to the Netherlands, Denmark, Sweden, Norway, Germany, and the U.S.A. Nowadays margarine is bought by members of all income groups, a situation definitely aided by the continuous improvement in the quality of margarine, particularly by the use of vegetable oils. It may be said that today the consumer's decision to buy margarine in many margarine countries has become less dependent on price, while the consumer classification for butter has remained to some extent price-dependent. Marais (22) and Ellinger (23) among others have referred to this. Rajko (24) and Mork (25) also explain the reduced influence of price on margarine consumption, and draw attention to the decline in the influence of income on margarine consumption. With the increase of prosperity in highly developed industrialized countries, where margarine accounts for 30–60 per cent of the total consumption of nutrient fats, the consumption of margarine is influenced by quite different factors such as habits of diet, health awareness, durability, packaging, advertisement, and so on.

In the two decades since 1950 the consumption of margarine *per capita* in Western Europe has increased rather more than that of butter. In the U.S.A., Canada, and Australia butter consumption *per capita* declined in the same period, while there was a rise in individual consumption of margarine. These phenomena have been discussed by Ellinger (26) and Schüttauf (27). Schüttauf's explanation is that the prosperity of the individual increases faster in the age of automation than it did before, and this factor has accelerated an expansion in the range of consumer goods. When a motor-car stands in front of a house that is one's own, it is no longer a status symbol to buy butter. With the purchase of a car and a home of his own the consumer also accepts responsibility for expenses of maintenance and obsolescence, which induce him to economize in other respects. Thus a level of income is reached at which the consumer has become more price-conscious even about butter.

As awareness of health factors grows keener the consumer also becomes more quality-conscious. The prosperity that is increasingly widespread in the highly developed industrialized countries is giving rise to a community which is free of consumer classification and in which everyone can afford anything. It reflects an age of total consumption in a classless society (28).

The present-day writers cited do, however, point out that the consumption of nutrient fats in the industrialized countries, with high fat consumption *per capita*, has reached, or will soon reach, saturation point. According to Engel's law, expenditure on food does not increase in the same ratio as income, but in fact becomes relatively lower. Thus as prosperity rises the income elasticity of the quantitative demand for foodstuffs generally loses its strength, finally declining to almost zero. Consumers have grown richer and richer, more and more numerous and difficult-to-please, comfort-loving, and health-conscious to an ever greater extent, increasingly aware of quality, but also more prone to question prices.

In the U.S.A. where the level of individual prosperity is highest, this income elasticity still only amounts to between 0·1 and 0·2. In Western Europe, where individual prosperity is at only half the level existing in the U.S.A., it is as yet only 0·3–0·4. With increasing prosperity it turns out also that among the three food categories the consumption of carbohydrates (bread and potatoes) actually decreases, consumption of animal protein (meat, eggs) increases while there is little or no change, or even a falling off, in the consumption of food fats. This trend of so-called visible fat consumption is further explained, as already indicated, by the fact that with constantly increasing consumption of meat and eggs, which both contain fat, consumption of invisible fat increases, with a resulting influence on visible fat consumption. In the U.S.A. for example, where consumption of invisible fat in meat and eggs is particularly high, visible fat consumption has gone down from 25 kg thirty years ago to 20 kg today. In the other industrialized countries of the world similar phenomena may be observed or anticipated.

Among the individual types of visible fat in the U.S.A. butter consumption is falling and margarine consumption is rising. In Western Europe the income elasticity in butter and margarine fluctuates between slightly positive and slightly negative, with variations in the individual countries. In the newly industrialized areas of the world, where fat consumption per head is still moderately high, fat consumption, especially consumption of margarine and vegetable oils, but also butter consumption, continues to increase. Of course, the changes occurring in structure of consumption in general, and of food consumption including that of fats in particular, in the other continents are taking place with greater speed as prosperity increases than in the past 100 years in Western Europe and North America. The margarine industry of the world will be prepared for this. For it is clear that the industry will find conditions for expansion where the process of industrialization is under way, and where there is constant movement by lower-income groups of the population from rural areas into new industrial centres in which opportunities for a better income can be expected.

It has been shown that these changes have occurred and are occurring at many levels, extending beyond the economic and social spheres to those of technology and nutritional physiology. Continual adjustment of the margarine industry was and is possible only with the adoption of appropriate locations and forms of enterprise.

LOCATIONS AND FORMS OF ENTERPRISE

For the choice of industrial location three factors are crucial: supply of workers, supply of raw materials, and markets (29). The problem of obtaining the labour force played no part in the choice of location for the margarine industry, since the industry is low in labour requirements and in return, owing to the use of machinery, its prime requirement, it makes heavy demands on capital. On the other hand, the interest of the margarine industry has always been concentrated on raw materials and sales. In the matter of obtaining raw materials it was home agriculture, supplying tallow and milk, that was in the van until the turn of the century. The tallow-melting plants established as auxiliary industries for margarine were similarly located. After 1900 emphasis was increasingly shifted towards oil-seeds and oil-bearing fruits imported from tropical and the subtropical countries, and thus navigable waterways became increasingly important for the industry. Towns on navigable waterways, growing with the expansion of the export trade, gained ever greater significance as markets for margarine. These facts largely account for the transfer by the butter wholesalers Jurgens and Van den Bergh (30) of the headquarters of their firms from Oss to Rotterdam; the move also facilitated the seaborne exports of margarine to England. At the same time, the Dutch margarine industry was interested in exports up the Meuse and the Rhine to Belgium and Germany, especially to the Ruhr, an area of heavy consumption. From 1879 on, however, after the introduction of Bismarck's protective tariffs, that was no longer possible to the extent that the Dutch would have wished. In 1888 Jurgens built a large factory on German soil, in Goch on the Lower Rhine, and in the same year Van den Bergh built a factory in the neighbouring town of Cleves.

In this choice of location lay the most favourable opportunities both for the raw material supply and for market openings, and it assured in addition a supply of milk from the country around. The industry has maintained its alignment in regard to raw materials and markets up to the present day. Thus, for example, the German industry has about 25 per cent of its productive capacity concentrated in Hamburg, about 25 per cent on the Lower Rhine, and about 25 per cent on the Upper Rhine (Mannheim). The rest is allotted to Bavaria, Holstein, Berlin, and the margins of the Ruhr area.

Once vegetable oils had increasingly come into use as raw materials for the margarine industry, from the turn of the century onward, there had to be concentrations of the oil-press industry and of refining and hardening plant. The oil-press industry, for similar reasons of dependence on raw materials and market availability, located itself near the margarine industry. Like the margarine industry, the oil-press industry is low in its labour requirement and makes heavy demands on capital. So the German oil-press industry is located 50 per cent on the Elbe (Hamburg) and 50 per cent on the Lower and Upper Rhine.

5. Good rail and water connections are essential to a margarine factory. An artist's impression of the Van Den Bergh factory, Rotterdam, 1918.

6. The Van Den Bergh factory, Rotterdam, 1926.

The geographical concentration (31) of the margarine industry on the one hand, and the vertical integration of this industry with the oil-press industry on the other, have during the past 100 years constantly confronted the controlling bodies of both industries with difficult commercial problems. Geographical concentration and the great advances in technique required from the outset factory plant of the most appropriate size, and a broad basis of capital for raising funds. Accordingly the joint-stock company as a form of enterprise very soon attained significance in both industries. In both industries, too, the passage of time has seen the progress of a technical revolution leading up to the present age of automation. The productivity of labour in both industries, owing to their high capital intensity, is very high and far above the average for industry as a whole. Naturally the value added is also low in both, being much under the average for industry in general, as is proved by a glance at the cost structure of the two industries. The dominant factor here is the cost of raw materials, which in the margarine industry is about 60–70 per cent and in the oil-press industry still higher. The share absorbed by labour costs is below the industrial average of about 20 per cent.

The over-all productivity of both industries is very high. For, in spite of a difficult cost structure adjusted to world conditions on account of raw material costs, the industries have always been able— thanks to rational methods of purchase and processing of raw materials—to offer their end products at advantageous prices. Moreover the production process yields, in addition to crude oil, margarine, salad oil, and cooking fat, a number of derivatives; particularly those used for process finishing in the soap, paint and varnish, pharmaceutical, and textile industries, to name only the most important. Nor should we omit agriculture. From oil-seeds and oil-bearing fruits only an average of 33 per cent is extracted in quantity in the form of oil, but 66 per cent in the form of oil-cakes, which have become the most important feeding concentrates in agriculture. Without these concentrates the milk yield of cows and the meat output from cattle, pigs, and poultry in the world would be considerably lower. The importance of oil-cake as a feeding-stuff for cattle has initiated another entirely new branch of world industry: the production of animal feeding compounds.

Increasing demands have been made on enterprising achievements and a sense of responsibility towards the national economy by the

factors just mentioned, with their many levels—location, cost structure, advance in technique, the world-wide risk in raw materials,
financing, industrial integration, and the relationship between raw
materials and many other industries. Yet in the course of 100 years
there has at no time in this industrial complex been any lasting use
of the horizontal cartel to contain the risk attached to enterprise,
with the purpose of reducing the price risk; it has aimed rather at
horizontal and vertical concentration with common action in the
cause of rationalization and cutting costs. One special problem was
to keep a hold on the rising fixed costs. This process of concentration
has been reflected in enterprise on an international basis in the
Unilever concern (32), which has grown up by degrees since the
beginning of this century, and from 1927 on has functioned as a
commercial unit under the law. Side by side with the Unilever concern
further horizontal and even vertical concentrations and groupings have
been formed throughout the world. In this industrial complex, free
competition prevails in good trading co-operation within the national
and supra-national associations. At no time have monopolies made
their way within it. So that process of concentration recognized for
all sectors of the economy in the world, to which the margarine
industry is no exception, has also been achieved in the cause of
economic effort and hence of general well-being.

The Unilever concern has a share of about 50 per cent in margarine in Western Europe, equivalent to an oligopoly. In spite of this
strong market position there is stiff competition in the margarine
industry of Western Europe, which exerts a favourable influence on
the prices and quality of margarine in the interest of the consumer.
The Unilever concern, notwithstanding the strength of its market
position, is not free to dictate margarine prices. On the contrary, it
has to pursue an extremely cautious price policy in order to maintain
its share of the market.

THE INDUSTRY IN THE LIGHT OF
POLITICAL INTUITION AND SCIENTIFIC RESEARCH

From Napoleon III to the highly developed margarine industry, with
its precursory and consequential industries, there runs like a golden
thread the idea of an economy fulfilling its social obligation to
benefit society. Here the law applies, developed about the year 1826
by Johann Heinrich von Thünen, of the retroflective force of pros-

perity for all. Similar conceptions of the economy were in the mind of Count Saint-Simon (33) in France early in the nineteenth century.

It is well known that Napoleon was greatly attracted by the economic theory of Saint-Simonism. This was a movement which attempted to synthesize the trends of thought that characterized the Age of Enlightenment and the Romantic Era and to abolish the antithesis between capital (34) and labour. These ideas are put into practice today in the modern industrialized society, so to speak, as concerted action. From this idea of *action concerté* is derived the *planification* of France.

Napoleon III was ambitious and gifted, and in addition kindly and sympathetic towards his fellow men. He feared that owing to the great poverty and grave social tensions of his time he could not achieve the fulfilment of his political ideas in Europe. He had every excuse for being anxious about nutrition, since it is the basis of human creative power. People in his time had to spend 60-70 per cent of their income on food, yet had little hope of good or sufficient nourishment at reasonable cost. Conditions were worst at that time— as has been shown—in the supply of food fats. Today, after 100 years, people in industrialized countries need only spend from 35 to 52 per cent of their income on food, and despite this reduced proportion can have plenty, of good quality, at reasonable cost. Napoleon III had good reason to find support for his ideas in the science which was especially advanced in France at the time: for the work of the food chemists Chevreul (1786-1889) and Pasteur (1822-95) in research on fats and on milk is still world-renowned today. In economic science there were many researchers before and after Saint-Simon, who placed man and his well-being foremost and thus strove to reconcile liberalism and socialism. The margarine industry for its part during 100 years has invested vast amounts of money in technical, physiological, and economic research on fats, and has thus succeeded in creating in margarine a food for all mankind. Margarine is therefore a creation of political intuition and scientific research.

NOTES AND REFERENCES

1.There is a comprehensive survey of the population problem in MACKENROTH, G. *Bevölkerungslehre Theorie, Soziologie und Statistik der Bevölkerung* (*Study of population, theory, sociology, and statistics of population*) (Berlin, Göttingen, Heidelberg, 1953).

2. BURGDÖRFER, F. *Bevölkerungsdynamik und Bevölkerungsbilanz* (*Population dynamics and balance*) (Munich, 1951), p. 19.

3. MITCHELL, B. R. *Abstract of British historical statistics* (Cambridge, 1962), p. 6.

4. HOFFMANN, W. G., with GRUMBACH, F., and HESSE, H. *Das Wachstum der deutschen Wirtschaft seit Mitte des 19. Jahrhunderts* (*The growth of the German economy since the middle of the 19th century*) (Berlin, Heidelberg, New York, 1965).

5. BURGDÖRFER, op. cit., p. 19.

6. BRUGMANS, I. S. *De arbeidende Klasse in Nederland in de 19e Eeuw* (*The working class in Holland in the 19th century*) (The Hague, 1929), p. 151.

7. The data are taken from WILSON, C. *The History of Unilever. A study in economic growth and social change* (London, 1954), vol. 2, p. 24.

8. KUCZYNSKI, J. *Die Geschichte der Lage der Arbeiter in Frankreich von 1789 bis in die Gegenwart* (*A history of the conditions of workers in France from 1789 to the present*) (Berlin, 1955), part 2, p. 13.

9. *Die Grosshandelspreise in Deutschland von 1792 bis 1934* (*Wholesale prices in Germany from 1792 to 1934*). Institut für Konjunkturforschung Special Issue No. 37 (Berlin, 1935), pp. 58–9.

10. Data taken from SCHÜTTAUF, W. *Die Margarine in Deutschland und in der Welt* (*Margarine in Germany and the world*) (Hamburg, 1966), p. 3; and MULHALL, M. *History of prices since the year 1850* (London, 1855), p. 93.

11. LINDEMANN, W. 'Die deutsche Margarine-Industrie und die öffentliche Margarinepolitik bis 1935' ('The German margarine industry and public margarine policy up to 1935') (dissertation, unpublished, 1936).

12. HAGER, H. *Die Entwicklung der deutschen Margarineindustrie unter besonderer Berücksichtigung ihrer Arbeitsverhältnisse* (*The development of the German margarine industry with regard to its working conditions*) (Geissen, 1928), p. 7.

13. VON GOHREN, TH. 'Kunstbutter-fabrikation' ('Synthetic butter production'). *Frühlings landwirtschaftliche Zeitung*, 1 (1877), 38.

14. LINDEMANN, op. cit.

15. HEFTER, G. *Technologie der Fette und Oele: Handbuch der Gewinnung und Verarbeitung der Fette, Oele und Wachsarten des Pflanzen- und Tierreichs* (*Technology of fats and oils; a handbook of extraction and processing of vegetable and animal oils and waxes*) (Berlin, 1910), vol. 2, p. 50.

16. DRUMMOND, J. C., and WILBRAHAM, A. *The Englishman's food: a history of five centuries of English food* (London, 1957), p. 306.

17. RIEPMA, S. F. 'Margarine in the United States, 1873–1967' (unpublished).

18. SLASTCHEV-GREGOROVITCH, N. N. 'The development trends of the margarine industry in the U.S.S.R.' (unpublished).

19. SCHÜTTAUF, op. cit., pp. 5–6.

20. PREDÖHL, A. *Das Ende der Weltwirtschaftskrise; eine Einführung in die Probleme der Weltwirtschaft* (*The end of the world economic crisis; an introduction to the problem of world economics*), Rowohlts Deutsche Enzyklopädie (Hamburg, 1962), p. 80.

21. STONE, R. 'The measurement of consumer's expenditure behaviour in the United Kingdom 1920–38', *Studies in the national income and expenditure of the U.K.* (Cambridge, 1954), vol. 1, p. 98.
   GOLLNICK, H. *Ausgaben und Verbrauch in Abhängigkeit von Einkommen und Haushaltsstruktur 1927–8 und 1950–1* (*Expenditure and consumption depending on income and budgetary patterns 1927–8 and 1950–1*), Arbeit aus dem Institut für Landwirtschaftliche Marktforschung, Braunschweig-Völkenrode (Hanover, 1959), p. 30.
   MARAIS, G. *Butter and margarine; a comparative study of supply and demand in the Republic of South Africa* (Pretoria, 1966), p. 4.
   HESSE, M. 'Die Elastizitäten der mengenmässigen Nachfrage nach Milch und Milcherzeugnissen in der Bundesrepublik Deutschland' ('The elasticities in the quantitative demand for milk and milk products in the German Federal Republic'), *Agrarwirtschaft*, Sonderheft 24 (Hanover, 1967).
   KRELLE, W. 'Elastizität von Angebot und Nachfrage' ('Elasticity of supply and demand'), *Handwörterbuch der Sozialwissenschaften* (Göttingen, 1961), vol. 3, p. 176.

22. MARAIS, op. cit., p. 34.

23. ELLINGER, K. R. 'Some factors affecting butter and margarine production', *F.A.O. monthly bulletin of agriculture economics and statistics*, **12**, 7–8 (1963), 4.

24. RAJKO, A. S. 'The demand and price structure for dairy products', *U.S. Department of Agriculture technical bulletin no. 1168* (1957).

25. MORK, R. 'Interrelationships and variations of prices and sales levels for butter and margarine', Report made for the annual conference of the International Dairy Federation (Munich, 1966).

26. ELLINGER, loc. cit.

27. SCHÜTTAUF, W. 'Bestimmungsgründe des Absatzes von Nahrungsfetten unter besonderer Berücksichtigung des Einkommens' ('Determining factors in the sale of nutrient fats, with special reference to incomes'), *Ernährungswirtschaft*, **11** (1963), 970.

28. —— 'Fat consumption in Western Europe', *Soyabean digest*, Export Issue, **25**, 8 (1965), 26.

29. WEBER, A. et al. 'Über dem Standort der Industriën' ('On the location of industries'), *Zur Frage der Industrialisierung der Welt* (Tübingen, 1929).
   PREDÖHL, op. cit.

30. The naming here of only Jurgens and Van den Bergh among the controllers of the margarine industry seems justified, as they were the pioneers. Those engaged in the industry who are not mentioned by name here have also done great service over the past 100 years in the development of the world margarine industry and its commitment to public welfare.

31. LIEFERMANN, R. *Kartelle und Truste und die Weiterbildung der volkswirtschaftlichen Organisation* (*Cartels and trusts and the evolutionary progress of the national economic system*) (Stuttgart, 1920).

ARNDT, H. (ed.) *Die Konzentration in der Wirtschaft* (*Concentration in economic activity*) Schriften des Vereins für Sozialpolitik (Berlin and Munich, 1960).

POSTAN, M. M. *An economic history of Western Europe 1954–64* (London, 1967). This book gives an account of the influence of modern forms of enterprise on growth and increase of productivity in the industry of Western Europe after the Second World War.

32. WILSON, op. cit.

33. SAINT-SIMON, C. H. de R. *Nouveau christianisme* (Paris, 1825).

BOON, H. N. *Rêve et réalité dans l'œuvre économique et sociale de Napoleon III* (*Dream and reality in the economic and social achievement of Napoleon III*) (The Hague, 1936).

GIDE, C., and RIST, C. *Geschichte der Volkswirtschaftlichen Lehrmeinungen* (*A history of economic theory*) (Jena, 1923). This book gives a detailed account of Saint-Simonism.

34. SOMBART, W. *Der moderne Kapitalismus* (*Modern capitalism*) (Munich and Leipzig, 1924–7).

SCHUMPETER, J. A. *Theorie der wirtschaftlichen Entwicklung* (*Theory of economic development*) (Leipzig, 1912).

CHAPTER TWO

Raw Materials

K. E. HUNT

Introduction

IN setting out an orderly account of the raw materials on which the margarine industry has been based, logical considerations do not seem to be very helpful. There can be very few groups of commodities which are so intimately linked in their practical applications while having their roots in such a wide diversity of situations. If any central theme can be found on which such an account might be ordered, it probably lies in human action and endeavour. The story of the supply of raw materials required over the past 100 years by this rapidly expanding industry is a story of human enterprise in technology, in business, and in agricultural production, and of man's attempts to mould his world nearer to his liking through the machinery of government.

The history of raw materials for margarine production is largely an account of the interaction of these several lines of activity, and their influence on the manipulation of a wide range of biological products which are capable of contributing to this now essential section of the food industry. Oil-bearing plants and land and marine animals have all contributed to the raw material supply at one time or another; even within these groups there has been great diversity. The plants have been grown on a large or small scale in tropical and temperate countries. The animal sources have included farm livestock, marine mammals, and fish.

A further strand in the network is introduced by the use of by-products from oil-seed extraction—in the form of oil-seed cakes and meat and fish-meals—as part of the feeding-stuff supply for the farm livestock industry.

From this whole complex, world-wide, and century-long pattern this chapter seeks first to give a factual description and then to describe some influences. These influences have often been powerful, sometimes subtle, but they have been mainly responsible for the evolution of the sources of raw material on which the world's margarine industries depend today. After the brief sketch of the main issues the chapter is divided into three parts—the facts, the influences, and the outcome. The aim of the first part is to give a brief sketch of the main features of the seeds, nuts, and other raw materials, and their production. Then the main features of the marketing processes through which they pass from the producer to the user are indicated, with an outline of the general economic features of the trade in these products and of the businesses which have been engaged from time to time in their production, distribution, or use.

The second section is concerned with forces such as technological developments and government policy which have shaped the evolution of the supply of raw materials over the last 100 years. It is not possible to keep descriptive facts and influences wholly separate, since often the circumstances of production and marketing were the consequences of the forces, and vice versa.

Finally, the evolving pattern of the supplies of raw materials since 1869 constitutes the 'outcome'. A particular fat or oil may be especially favoured by users because of its technical qualities for the manufacture of a particular product. However, if economic or other considerations make it desirable, it is now usually possible to substitute at least a proportion by one or more other fats or oils, without changing the final product to any commercially important extent. Although certain food products are highly specific in their requirements of raw materials, these possibilities of marginal substitution mean that there are a dozen or more raw materials which contribute to what is, broadly speaking, a single unified supply. One result of this is that the effects on the price of an individual raw material of fluctuations in its supply are cushioned by the stabilizing effect of the supplies of possible substitutes. This has not always been so; indeed part of the history of the raw materials for margarine is the story of the emergence of this degree of free interchangeability. In all these materials the oil is the energy storage product, having generally about twice as much energy value per unit weight of dry material as any of the other tissues in the plants or animals concerned. In plants the oily material is mostly in the seed, although it may be in the seed coat. In animals it may be in various sites.

Looking back over the last 150 years, one could say that there have been, at one time or another, six or seven main uses for oil-bearing nuts and seeds, and for fats and oils generally. They have been used for burning to give light and heat; for lubrication; for food, directly in their original form or as frying oils, margarine, compound cooking fat, lard, butter, and so on; for soap; for paint and varnish; and for linoleum manufacture. During the nineteenth century mineral oils (and later electricity) took over most of the functions which had previously been performed by vegetable and animal fats and oils in lighting and in lubrication. Paint, varnish, and linoleum are still affected by the fats and oils situation, although in recent years synthetic substitutes have become actively competitive. The two big outlets that have had the greatest effect on raw material supply are the use for edible purposes—in Western Europe principally as margarine and compound cooking fats—and for soap.

Both uses have been described, in periods of optimism, as 'depression-proof'; and certainly once a population reaches a reasonable living standard, it will continue to use soap even under conditions of some stringency. Under such conditions it may even turn to a still greater extent towards margarine and away from butter. In the main, the history of raw materials for the margarine industry runs from the 1870s—when soap could more or less have its choice of oils and fats while margarine was still severely restricted to certain animal fats by technological considerations—through to a period when manufacturers of the general run of margarines have had at their disposal techniques which opened practically all supplies of oils and fats to their use (1).

There was, therefore, a period during which the competition of soap with margarine was increasingly keen, and during which their combined demands stimulated enormous increases in the supply of the raw materials in which they were jointly interested. In the course of this development, not only were very extensive commercial enterprises created in the supplying countries, with a complex commercial network leading, generally speaking, from the southern and tropical areas to North America and Western Europe, but also a whole new industry for the crushing, refining, and hardening of oils was set up. As we can see from other chapters, the demand for margarine was strong, and once new techniques applicable to the refining and hardening of oils were discovered one might perhaps have expected an even more rapid change in the picture than actually occurred. The explanation is probably that these commercial and industrial organizations for assembling and processing raw materials needed time to

develop, their capital had to be raised, and their special skills learnt—
on the distant transport route as much as on the factory floor.
Further, though the principles for the new technical advances might
have been worked out, their application to individual oil-bearing
products often presented very considerable challenges which took
some time to meet. In other words, innovation, as always, lagged behind invention.

National governments have intervened at many points. Perhaps
margarine and oil-seeds, by their nature, are specially liable to attract
government intervention. Margarine has competed directly with butter, and as dairying has been among the means through which farmers
have tried to sell their skill and labour for reasonable incomes,
farmers everywhere have brought pressure to bear on governments
to prevent farm incomes from becoming too low and too variable.

Again, a number of countries have depended very heavily for their
foreign earnings on exports of oil-seeds. In a period of colonial rule
it was natural that the oil-seed situation would be affected by any
policy measures designed to link more closely the central government
and its colonial territories. When such territories became independent, it was natural for these same products to be taxed directly
or indirectly to provide revenue for current needs or to help in the
economic development of the new sovereign country.

Even such a relatively straightforward matter as the way a specific
crop is grown and marketed may be less clear-cut than it seems. The
method may have changed completely since the product first became
important in the margarine business, and at any one time the practice may differ greatly from country to country. Again, one country
may use a selection of oil-bearing materials for margarine production
which is quite different from that used by another; hence a particular
raw material may be highly important in one place and negligible in
another. However, it seems sufficient for the present purpose to include a commodity in the discussion if it is, or has been, a major
constituent of margarine somewhere in the world.

THE ORGANIZATION OF THE INDUSTRY

Production and procurement

We are mainly concerned with those features of the various oils and
oil-bearing commodities that affect their behaviour in trade. Of course
their chemical constitution has some influence on the extent to which

one can substitute for another, but the notes which follow are mainly concerned with such matters as the general characteristics of the products from the point of view of perishability and portability, location of production, the agricultural systems under which they are produced, and the kinds of people who have been concerned with the main management decisions relating to production and trade. Each commodity in each country of origin shows its special production and marketing features, but only a very general survey can be made here. In particular, the discussion of marketing and distribution is confined to examples illustrating the practices which have prevailed for moving peasant crops from up-country districts to the central buying points in the country of origin, and to an outline of the international trade in oil-seeds.

The principal raw materials fall into three broad groups; the vegetable oil-bearing materials, animal fats from farm-reared animals, and marine fats. A list of vegetable oil-bearing materials might be arranged with some logic either in order of magnitude of the world production of oils, or of the magnitude of world exports (2) (see Fig. 2.1).

Soya beans would now come at the top of both lists. After that, on a list based on world production, would come sunflower, groundnuts, cottonseed, coconut, rape-seed, palm, olive, and linseed oils. The list based on exports would have a different pattern; after soya bean oil would come coconut and groundnut oils. The bulk of the cottonseed is not exported from the countries of production (U.S.A., Egypt, Sudan, etc.), nor is the substantial Indian crop of rape-seed, Burmese sesame, or Russian sunflower. These crops would, therefore, come further down the trade than the production list. In round terms, vegetable oils and fats account for about one and a half times as much production as animal and marine fats and oils. Although agricultural and botanical details are not discussed here, it might be noted that the yields per unit area of the crops in current production vary enormously from one part of the world to another, and from one crop to another. Not unreasonably, bearing in mind that they are an energy product and that all energy comes from the sun, the tropical plants come out highest and yields of oil per acre in tropical palm plantations may be many times the yield of reasonably well-farmed, temperate, oil-seed crops.

Coconuts (*Cocos nucifera*). The coconut palm has been in cultivation since prehistoric times. Its origin is conjectural, but it now grows

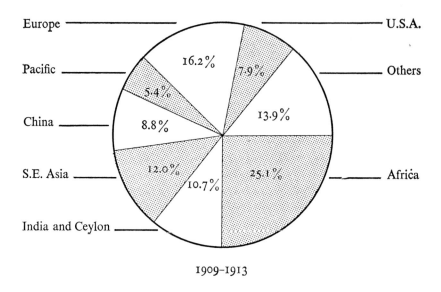

1909–1913

1959–1963

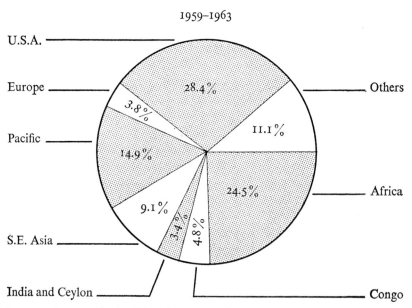

FIG. 2.1. Geographical origin of exports of major vegetable oils 1909–13 and 1959–63. (Expressed as percentages of total exports of oil and oil-equivalent of seeds, palm products, copra, soya beans, groundnuts, and cottonseed.)

along the shores of most tropical countries within 20° of the Equator; it is particularly important for food and as a source of income in, for example, the Philippines, Indonesia, Ceylon, and Malaysia. The trees bear from about 5 years old, under favourable conditions, up to perhaps 60 years old or more, by which time they may be anything from 50 to 80 ft in height. The nuts ripen in a period of 9–12 months but are ready for harvesting at all seasons of the year. This is important because it makes it possible for labour, whether hired or family, to be kept fairly evenly occupied all the year round. The management of the coconut palm has been the subject of a good deal of experimental work, and is still controversial.

The fruit consists of an outer fibrous casing, within which there is a hard shell which itself contains the white meat of the coconut. In preparing the product for market the outer husk is torn off and the shell split in two in some areas; in others, the shell is split without dehusking. The halves are then dried in the sun, if this is practicable. When it loosens from the shell, the separated meat, which provides the copra of commerce, is dried further. Usually some form of artificial drying is essential, sometimes in ovens heated by burning the shells.

Coconuts are grown on holdings of very different sizes in different parts of the world; family smallholdings and substantial estates compete side by side. Generally speaking, the very great increase in the coconut area which has taken place since about 1890 has been concentrated in a very limited number of places. Consequently, over 90 per cent of the world's supply of copra has come from Indonesia, the Philippines, Malaysia, and Ceylon. Traditional coconut-growing has been located in coastal areas, and industrialized development of coconut production also seems to have been more successful when it has been tried in the traditional coconut areas. The advantages of coastal areas may, however, have been partly a matter of ease of access to export points. Moreover, these areas have also tended to be ones where alternative profitable export crops such as coffee, tea, cocoa, or rubber could not readily be grown. As with rubber-growing, the family-type holdings had some resilience in the depression periods which the European-owned estates lacked. The coconut has traditionally been thought of as providing home, clothes, and food, and smallholding producers could cut overheads under slump conditions, such as those of the early 1930s; a facility denied to plantation operators. At the end of the Second World War it was reckoned that about 85 per cent of copra was produced on smallholdings.

Coconut oil has been exported to Europe since about 1820, largely for soap production to begin with, and a good deal of attention was paid to it in the middle of the nineteenth century. The characteristics of the oil pressed from copra makes it suitable both for soap-making and margarine manufacture.

Oil palm (*Elaeis guineensis*). This palm originated in West Africa, and this area has supplied a large part of the international trade in palm oil products. The oil palm begins to bear somewhat earlier than the coconut palm, usually in its third to fifth year, and continues bearing for twenty-five years or more (3). Most of the West African trees are grown between 15° N. and 15° S. of the Equator, but they are most abundant in the coastal belt 100–50 miles deep from Sierra Leone to the Cameroons (4). The natural palms are scattered in the forest country, competing with other vegetation. If they get no assistance they tend to grow tall and thin, and their useful life is cut short as they are too tall for easy harvesting. Where they receive at least a minimum of management attention the vegetation is cut down from around the young palm when it is discovered in the bush, and it is given the chance to grow somewhat more stoutly and become a tree of better economic characteristics. Oil palms have also been planted under plantation systems in parts of West Africa and South-east Asia.

The fruit is carried in bunches at the head of the palm; it varies considerably in weight with variety and the age and nutrition of the tree. The range might be put as from about 10 to 50 lb. Each individual fruit in the bunch consists of a fleshy exterior containing a hard shell with a kernel within. The palm yields two quite distinct kinds of oil. The fleshy pericarp yields an oil which is liquid at the ordinary temperature of the producing country, and distinctly reddish in colour. This is traditionally extracted by the West African peoples for food use, but where this is done by primitive means or by a much more efficient process in factories equipped for the purpose, it must be done near the growing area because the palm fruit, like the olive, will not survive transport. The kernel carried within the hard shell also contains an oil, but one with a higher melting point. There is no local use of the kernel oil, and the organization for kernel collection and use has been linked almost entirely to the demand in Europe and North America.

Because of the nature of the equipment required, the crushing of the shelled kernels is normally done in large factories under close control. Several methods are in use, however, for the production of oil from the pericarp. The factories attached to the concessions in the former Belgian Congo and to the plantations in Malaysia and Indonesia all take great care to control the quality of the oil produced. Substantial quantities of pericarp oil have, however, been produced for many years by local methods in West Africa, and ultimately shipped for overseas use. These have varied considerably in their free fatty acid content, a high fatty acid level being undesirable for use in the food industry.

Cottonseed (Gossypium). When the cotton is grown for fibre the seed is separated from the fibre at the ginning stage, and may be pressed to produce an oil. Cottonseed oil has been in use for a long time, in several countries, for edible purposes and for the production of soap. The fact that cottonseed is produced along with another important, but quite different, commercial material, the fibre, makes it somewhat unusual amongst the vegetable oil-bearing products. The big producing areas for cotton are the U.S.A., India, U.S.S.R., Brazil, China, Egypt, and the Sudan. All sizes and types of producer contribute to the world total. As man-made fibres are now in competition with natural fibres it is to be expected that the supply of cottonseed available for crushing will depend in large measure on the competitive success of the cotton fibre. Though the use of cottonseed oil for food has been known for a long period in the United States, the bulk of each year's crop was not in fact crushed until towards the end of the nineteenth century.

In other producing countries, the seed has often been fed to livestock in its whole state. Though cottonseed oil was to some extent brought into food use fairly early, its refinement presented many problems in the early days of its application to margarine production.

Peanut or groundnut (Arachis hypogaea). This annual legume originated in South America and is believed to have been carried to Africa by Portuguese slave-traders. It spread there, and worked its way back to the U.S.A. by similar routes. It seems to have been taken across the Pacific in the sixteenth century and subsequently passed on to the Far East. It is rather precise in its climatic and soil requirements, but has happened to find what it needs in highly dispersed areas of the world. As a legume, and therefore capable of fixing atmospheric nitrogen, it is useful in contributing to the nutrient status of the soil.

Although it is grown on a substantial scale in North America and in some other producing areas, a high proportion of the world supply has always been produced on family-run holdings. The scope for the crop on such holdings is limited, as it is for other crops with especially heavy labour requirements at certain seasons, by the family's effective work capacity. It was one of the first vegetable oil sources to respond to the demands of the margarine industry in Europe. France was then supplying oil crushed from groundnuts exported from Senegal. The trade expanded vastly in the following half-century, but West Africa, India, and China came to provide over three-quarters of world exports of nuts.

Soya bean (*Glycine max*). This plant has been cultivated in China since ancient times. It has a comparatively low oil content (of the order of 18 per cent) and it has been used until the last few decades mainly for food in a more or less complete form. It spread from China to neighbouring countries, but did not enter into international trade until the early years of the twentieth century. Japan imported soya bean cake for fertilizer about that time, and the first shipments of whole beans to Europe are reported to have occurred about 1908. From this time onwards there were large exports of soya beans from the Far East to the crushing industries in Europe. The development of the very substantial Manchurian export trade was probably due in part to the Russo–Japanese war of 1904–5 which led to a heavy demand for food to supply Japanese troops in Manchuria.

When the troops were withdrawn, a surplus developed which was the start of the export trade to Europe. Subsequently, through the following decades, until it reached its peak in the 1920s and early 1930s, the production was developed by immigrant workers into Manchuria. The crop was tried in the U.S.A., and was found to do well and to fit the machinery and other equipment which had already been developed for 'row' crops in the American farming system. With the difficulty in importing requirements of oil-seeds during the Second World War, the American agricultural authorities encouraged the development of soya beans, and production continued to expand after the war. The consequences in terms of the place of the U.S.A. in the world trade in oils and fats is illustrated in Fig. 2.1.

Sunflower (*Helianthus annuus*). Although native to North America, this plant has never been a commercial crop there. The only areas where it has occupied any notable place are Argentina and Russia and Eastern Europe, all largely as a result of official encouragement. Argentina followed a development policy for sunflower from about the middle of the 1930s, with substantial results by the end of the 1940s. The major Russian developments have been more recent. Research on the crop resulted in major improvements in seed yield and in oil content; together these contributed largely to the expansion in output which by the 1960s has generated a substantial export trade to countries in Eastern Europe, which themselves produce substantial quantities, and elsewhere. As a valuable source of highly unsaturated fatty acids sunflower oil is of special interest (see p. 146).

Other vegetable oil-bearing plant materials. Out of the long list of other vegetable oils which have from time to time been used in margarine the following might be noted as having had some significance: Rape oil (from *Brassica napus*)—China and India have been the largest producers but it is the oil-seed crop best suited to Europe; corn oil (from *Zea mays*), perhaps more commonly thought of as a source of carbohydrate, but yielding an oil used in speciality margarines and as a source of unsaturated acids; sesame oil (from the seed of *Sesamum indicum*), grown in many countries, especially China, but the bulk of the crop is used in the producing country; shea butter (from the fruits of an African tree *Butyrospermum parkii*), growing in inland tropical Africa from the Equator to about 15° N.; babassu oil (from the Babassu palm *Orbignya martiana*), found largely in Brazil; olive oil (from the *Oleaceae*), much used, of course, for food purposes in Europe. Of all of these minor vegetable oils, only olive is no more in use as a raw material for margarine.

Animal fats. In the course of their growth and fattening, animals lay down in various parts of their bodies deposits of fat of a texture which depends largely on the species. Some deposits are laid down inside the abdominal cavity, others on the tissues associated with the abdominal organs, on the outside of the muscular layers under the skin, and between the muscle bundles. The proportion of fat in a beast at any particular stage depends in part on the age and degree of feeding, and in part on the animal's inherent characteristics. Part of the fat is removed from the carcase and set aside in the ordinary process of dressing the animal, but the details of practice have varied. In the days before meat could be readily transported, relatively imperishable products could be obtained by rendering fats from the whole carcase; fat products of this kind formed part of the exports from Australia and from Argentina in the years before the start of seaborne refrigerated transport. In recent years, with the increasingly sedentary nature of city life, consumers have shown an increasing dislike for fatty meat; the custom has developed of trimming from the carcase a good deal of fat which would formerly have been eaten with the meat. The characteristics of the extracted product depend partly on the kind of animal and the portion of the body from which it is obtained and partly on its subsequent treatment, including the temperature and conditions under which the fat is separated from the remaining tissue. Broadly speaking, body fat from cattle and sheep when rendered provides oleo stock (or *premier jus*). It was this material which in Europe formed the basis for margarine in its earliest form. Lard is rendered fat from the pig. It may originate in the internal fat or, particularly where pigs are deliberately fed up to heavy weights, from the fatty tissues cut off the back of the carcase. A variety of forms have been marketed, differing in their manner of preparation. 'Neutral lard' is extracted at low temperatures from back fat; 'prime steam lard' at a rather higher temperature from fatty tissues from almost any part of the body. It was neutral lard which, particularly in the U.S.A., entered into the manufacture of margarine at certain periods. Though once highly important, these animal fats are now of limited significance in margarine production. Their replacement to a substantial extent by vegetable oils is a key feature of the development of the industry.

Marine oils. This category includes whale oil and a wide range of fish oils; the latter group including the special category of liver oils used primarily as vitamin concentrates. Marine oils other than whale oils have been used in margarine in a number of countries, for instance Japan, Norway, and the United Kingdom, and the supply increased sharply in the 1960s. None the less, whale oil has so far contributed most to the marine materials supplied for margarine in the world as a whole, and it provides an important part of the history of raw materials (5).

Whales lay down a layer of fat between their muscular tissue and skin, presumably partly as a reserve, partly for cushioning against pressure and impact, and for heat insulation. They have been hunted

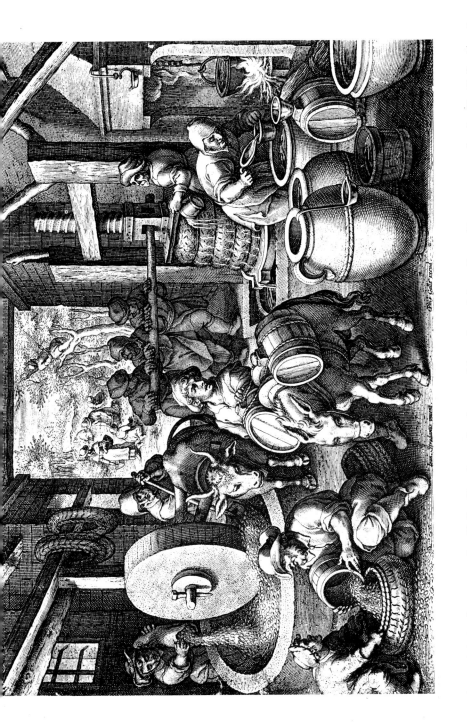

7. An eighteenth-century oil-mill. Small-scale production requiring a large labour force. From an engraving by Ph. Galle, based on a drawing by Ioan Stradanus.

8. Melting animal fats for margarine production at the Oleo Margarine-Facturing Company, Manhattan, New York, 1876.

Fig. 1.

9. Oil-mill, 1800. From an engraving by J. C. Pelletier.

10. High-pressure expellers in a modern oil-milling factory. Large-scale production requiring a minimum of employees.

for their oil and their meat in the Northern Hemisphere for centuries, but the modern whaling industry stemmed from the invention of the pistol harpoon in 1865. This provided a means of killing whales, but the demand for the oil was limited. Some was used for lubrication, some for lamps, and a little for soap. The material was greasy and smelly, and no developments were possible until efficient refining processes had evolved. The stock of whales in the Northern Hemisphere was fished out, and in the early years of the twentieth century attention turned to land-based whaling stations in the Southern Hemisphere. It proved difficult to find stations that were suitably placed with respect to the catching areas; moreover, little was known of the distribution of whales in the Antarctic fishing zones. This led to the development of the factory ship for the processing of the whale carcases and for the servicing of the catching ships. Some increase in production occurred after 1906, with improvements in refining techniques which allowed the whale oil to be used for a useful range of purposes. The First World War disrupted the organization, but in the middle 1920s there was a boom period for whale oil, which continued more or less through to the Second World War. Under postwar conditions, with the establishment of control of whaling to conserve the whale population, the industry began to decline.

A substantial international trade in fish body oils is a recent development, which began towards the end of the 1950s. The oils come from various species of oily fish—herring, menhaden, pilchards, anchovies, and others—which are caught and processed to yield a high-quality protein feed for farm animals as well as the oil. The main source areas for exports have been the Scandinavian countries, Peru, and southern Africa.

Structure and organization of production

The structure and organization of the production of these various raw materials has shown great variety. It has been one of the features of the oil-using industries in the main oil-seed importing countries that they have come to be dominated by a few large firms. One might have looked for something approaching this simplicity at the other end of the supply chain for raw materials, but the experience has been totally different. The outline of the features of production already given suggests that the animal fat supply system in the earlier days of the industry and the whaling organization in the 1930s were the main examples of business concentration in the supply sector. For the most part, the rest of the raw materials have been produced by a wide range of different types of producer, many of them of smallholders or peasants. Only in the case of palm oil in the former Belgian Congo, Indonesia, and Malaysia, and of coconuts in the Far East and Oceania, have plantation methods on a substantial scale contributed to the oil-seed supply.

From the point of view of the possible economic advantages of plantations, an important feature of a number of oil-bearing raw materials is that they can be prepared for export by relatively simple methods (6). This applies to groundnuts, palm kernels, to copra, and to a lesser extent to palm oil. Consequently, when the demand opened up and business contacts were made between producers at one end of the chain and users at the other, the producer could fairly readily learn the processes required to convert the natural product into an acceptable commodity for trade. European firms in colonial days tended to be concerned with the commercial side; often financing either the commodity stockholding, or the construction of the structures necessary for warehousing or such processing as demanded fair amounts of capital—for example, ginning. As has been noted, groundnuts and most of the other annual crops, seem not to have lent themselves to production on any larger scale than was usual for other field crops in the countries concerned. Coconut and oil palm, however, have been the subject of plantation-type production in many parts of the world. Estate production has been carried on in units of many sizes, from quite modest ones to units of many square miles. They have varied, too, in the extent of control; some in effect being little more than organized handling of fruit bought from natural stands of palm trees, others being plantation systems of a closely controlled kind. Probably the best known have been those with which Viscount Leverhulme was originally concerned and which became the property of Unilever or its associates in later years. Others of the big vegetable-oil users explored this possibility from time to time, and some took an active part in it.

Social considerations of some complexity have played a part in the West African oil-seed producing industry. Broadly speaking, in the greater part of the oil palm belt of West Africa, excluding the former Belgian Congo, the land was regarded as being held by the community with the individual having usufruct so long as he worked it. The right to work a piece of land did not necessarily give the right to harvest the product of the oil palms which were growing on it, but in any particular area there was usually a fairly clear local custom in this matter. Thus, the man who planted the tree or cleared the vegetation from around it might have the right to the product throughout its life. As is noted below in the discussion of plantations, this system of rights was protected by some colonial powers and alienation for industrial-type development was not permitted. However, developments in this direction were instituted from 1911 in the Belgian Congo. Under the British system, most local community heads were reluctant to see pure groves of oil palm being planted even by members of their own community, in case this gave the planter some continuing rights to the land. Consequently, there was little encouragement to pay special attention to the trees. A further social feature of some economic importance has been the fact that the disposal of kernels in a number of areas was the perquisite of the women. They cracked the kernels, and retained any money they obtained for their sale. Consequently they have, on occasion, resisted measures which tried to streamline the cracking of fruit for export.

The Unilever interest began in the late 1890s when Lord Leverhulme sought some degree of control by his firm of its sources of raw materials (7). He began initially with coconut production in the Solomon Islands. However, as plantation owners often have found since, labour was a problem there; the British authorities who controlled the Solomon Islands did not allow indentured labour to be brought in. This meant that the prospects for plantations were not promising. Subsequently, Lord Leverhulme explored prospects in British territories in West Africa, but government policy did not permit alienation of large areas of land, or even long leasing; and short leases offered no prospect of remunerative investment in tree crops.

Leverhulme did, however, find the opportunity to develop centralized production in the Belgian Congo, and in 1911 a convention was signed bringing into existence La Société Anonyme des Huileries du Congo Belge. The arrangement provided for the operation of processing-plant for pericarp oil and kernels bought from local producers harvesting from native palm over agreed areas (8). Under certain conditions areas could also be cleared for intensive plantation production. In the years which followed, plantations were also set up in Nigeria, the Cameroons, and the Gold Coast. Among the advantages claimed for plantations have been that they permitted better husbandry practices—use of better varieties, more careful observation of the trees, scientific fertilizer application, more systematic and cheaper harvesting methods—and soon that they provided a more regular supply of produce throughout the year, which justified the use of power-driven extraction processes; and offered scope for the productive use of waste products. These arguments have always held to a greater or lesser extent but, at least until recent years, plantations have not found it easy to compete with producers operating on a family scale (9). In a slump period such as the early 1930s, the advantage a family producer had in being able to cut back his expenses by growing food rather than spending his labour on harvesting his cash crop gave him a resilience not matched by the plantation producers. If, as we earnestly hope, such conditions do not return, then the advantage to the more industrialized producer of using better stock and employing better husbandry may well give effective competitive advantage. However, the attraction of establishing new plantations and continuing the control of existing ones is likely to turn very much on the economic and political policies of the independent governments concerned. Expatriate capital is unlikely to be invested if there is any risk of appropriation.

Marketing organization

How does this great variety of products find its way to the users who can employ them to the best advantage? The organization for marketing primary products varies greatly from place to place, and through time in the same locality. None the less, whatever the pattern, there must be someone to collect an export product from the producers, to bulk it, to provide transport to some export point, to provide such finance as may be required for purchase, stockholding, and equipment, to arrange shipment overseas, and the sale to users at the importing end.

Throughout this chain there are risks to be borne, labour and facilities to be organized, and the changes in ownership to be arranged. None of this is carried out without personal effort on someone's part, whether as a contractual duty for which he gets a wage, or as a speculative activity from which he expects to obtain reward.

In the oils and fats field, amongst the shortest and simplest of the marketing chains was probably that used in the early days of the margarine industry when the Dutch manufacturers bought by-products of the American meat-packing plant on the spot in Chicago. They then maintained ownership right through to the sale of their own manufactured products. The system changed when the meat packers began sending their products to commission agents in Holland; these agents organized the last ownership transfer in the light of their expert knowledge of the raw material supplies on offer and the potential buyers of the particular kind of material. Such expert knowledge—which is provided nowadays by international firms with branch offices in the main commercial cities—was, and is, essential if the range of potential buyers is to be matched, to everyone's satisfaction, with the range of materials of diverse specifications available for sale.

It is quite impossible to select wholly typical examples of the main marketing processes, but one or two examples will indicate important features. First, consider the marketing of palm kernels in Nigeria in, say, the 1930s. The first change of ownership took place in the producer's home village when he or she sold to a small-scale buyer. This buyer then carried the kernels on foot or by bicycle to some point where a middleman, in a rather larger way of business, was prepared to buy. He probably bought by volume rather than by weight. The original buyer then returned to prospect for trade in other villages.

The middleman's income from this business contained two elements. First, he performed a useful service by bulking the small quantities collected by the first-hand buyers into consignments suitable for sending on to the next stage in the chain, and could expect some remuneration in return. The second point arose from the fact that he bought and sold under rather different conditions. He generally sold dry kernels to a branch of an exporting firm, but he bought individual small parcels of moist kernels of a range of qualities. Between the two transactions his skill and position gave him scope to earn a profit.

A more complicated example of the marketing of a product linked into a traditional economy was that of West African palm oil, where the producer might set aside small quantities for sale over and above what he made for his own use. This supply for sale—perhaps no more than a gallon or so—was probably carried by head-load for several miles to the first sale point. There is was bulked to 4-gallon cans, which could be transported by any available transport to the local sales point. At this point some might be diverted for local use and the rest blended to give a homogeneous parcel for sale to the main branches of exporting houses. The dealer made his margin partly on the bulking service and partly by his skill in mixing oils so that they were just within the grade requirements. Probably the buyer had to provide cash for the operations of the smaller men who were buying in the country. From this buying point onwards there was transport to be arranged, packaging suitable for movement on lorries or river steamers to be provided, probably bulk handling facilities at the export point, and finally the produce had to be dispatched by ocean freight. For much of the history of the trade the ownership of the material in the case outlined would have stayed with the main exporting company up to the destination port where it was sold onwards to the user through intermediaries operating in all the main markets (10).

Other products in other countries went through different hands. The picture of West African marketing outlined in the previous paragraphs does not describe the present situation. Statutory marketing boards now purchase the product from the firms who would, broadly speaking, have been exporters in pre-war times, and perform the export services from that point onwards, sometimes using brokers, sometimes bypassing this stage and dealing directly with ultimate users.

Philippine production has passed through a pattern often not dissimilar to that outlined for West Africa. Malayan plantation producers of palm oil pooled their products and sold through intermediaries to users in Europe. In these ways the trade bridged the time lag between production and consumption of the raw materials and the distance between the places of production and consumption. It also adapted the quality and quantity of raw materials to consumption requirements, and acted as a financier.

Whale oil has always tended to have few links in its distribution chain. Norwegian producers in the interwar period had sometimes virtually sold their product to specified users before the factory ships left port for the catching season. Japanese whale oil has been marketed through three main producing companies to three firms of Japanese merchants operating on an international scale, who sold to users through intermediaries.

Marketing of fish oil has varied from country to country—some has been sold from a producer's association direct to users, some by government agencies, some by private enterprise (11).

Perhaps it is especially enlightening to view a marketing system by considering its reaction to changing conditions and the extent to which it has mobilized the skills necessary for the job in hand. Before railways penetrated to the northern part of Nigeria there was no groundnut industry to supply the requirements of European margarine manufacturers. When the transport line was opened, the initiative of the Hausa peasant in extending the production of the crop, and of innumerable operators—some miniature, some large-scale—in building up a system which moved produce 1,000 miles to the export point for the overseas market, was no mean feat of organization. The incentive to continue production and distribution was sharpened by the concurrent development of merchandizing arrangements which made consumer goods widely available. Thus the producer had something worth having to buy with what he earned by growing groundnuts.

The final link in the chain usually had the benefit of the services provided by the produce exchanges in the importing countries. Produce exchanges were set up by the corporate action of those engaged in the produce trading business in the big commercial centres, mainly to facilitate the efficient conduct of trade. Among their contributions were the provision of market buildings, the development of standardized contracts and codes of operation, facilities for arbitration in disputes, and provision for settling accounts between members. Such arrangements have made possible the development of 'futures' markets. These are considered by some to be the most highly developed form of market organization. They might be said to make their particular contribution to the marketing process by making possible increased specialization of function. Thus some operators have been enabled to apply their capital and judgement to risk bearing, others to providing storage facilities, others to securing raw materials to meet the precise specifications required by individual users, others to manufacturing based on the raw material, all earning their profit accordingly. Naturally, firms have chosen to operate in more than one of these specialized fields, but those who preferred otherwise could, for example, make their living by selling their skill as processers and could look to others to carry the risks, provide storage in an economical manner, and so on. The valuable feature of risk transfer is discussed later in connection with instability of prices.

This outline implies that those operating at the various stages in the marketing of oil-bearing raw materials have operated without restraint on competition in a largely free market. In general this has been so, but none the less it is well known that at least as early as the turn of the century firms got together to restrain competition on various occasions. However, this is not a subject which lends itself to definitive discussion, if only because the more nearly monopolistic the activities become at any point, the less likely it is that any clear account of operations will be available for reference. It is generally recognized that in the difficult 1906-7 period an uneasy, but more or less effective, pooling of purchases by the main users was operating, though not necessarily for long. Before the First World War the meetings of users of whale oil gradually evolved to a point where the conference was dividing supplies into agreed portions, and this continued and hardened into a whale oil 'pool' for distributing world supplies of whale oil amongst the leading buyers. A combination of West African oil-seed importers was believed to exist when Germany had withdrawn from the market after the outbreak of war (12). In the late 1920s Nigerian groundnut exports were subject to pooling and pool-breaking. Soya beans were successfully pooled from time to time, and Bauer indicates (13) that a market syndicate was operating for palm oil, palm kernels, and groundnuts. This appears to have ended in 1950, but it is believed that various arrangements were in operation in the procurement field for many years before the Second World War. These are, of course, instances of privately sponsored departure from free competition. The war and postwar period brought various examples of statutory monopoly such as the commodity marketing boards which are discussed below.

The general marketing arrangements described here have been highly successful in collecting raw materials from the ends of the earth, and transferring them into the hands of the industries which could use them. However, the prices at which they have changed hands have been far from stable (see Fig. 2.2). The destabilizing influences are too complex to be analysed here; some are concerned with the supply and demand for individual fats and oils, some with over-all supply and demand position for the whole group, some with cyclical variations in business activity. They have on occasion embarrassed producers of the raw materials and users of the oils and fats, though usually not simultaneously, and no doubt others concerned in the trade too.

Regarding the longer-term fluctuations and their influence on the sectors using oils and fats, the view has been expressed that the recovery phase of a business cycle is the best time for the soap industry (14). In the prosperity phase of a cycle, raw materials tend

11. Oil palm, *Elaeis guineensis*, has been used for centuries as a source of fat and oil by the inhabitants of tropical Africa. Extensive plantations were started in South-East Asia in the first decades of this century. Oil palm is one of the few palms which yield a commercial oil from both the pericarp and the seed kernel.

Above. Harvesting a full fruit bunch.

Right. A full fruit bunch growing in a leaf axil. Weight about 50 lbs or 22.5 kilos.

12. Cotton, *Gossypium sp.*, is grown in every tropical country under either irrigation or rain cultivation.

Below. A cotton boll showing the lint surrounding the seed.

13. Coconut, *Cocos nucifera*, is widely distributed in the coastal areas of the tropics and sub-tropics where rainfall is more than 60 inches or 1500 mm., and a humid climate is found.

Above. Fruit ready for de-husking on a farm in Ceylon.
Left. Stages in the growth of coconut shell and kernel.

14. Sunflower, *Helianthus annuus*, is grown extensively in Central Europe and the Soviet Union.

Above. Inflorescence.

Below. A field crop of sunflower in Central Europe.

15. Soya bean, *Glycine soja*, a plant of great antiquity, was extensively cultivated in China and Manchuria before written records were kept. It is grown throughout the tropics for its oil and high nutritional content.

16. Groundnut, *Arachis hypogaea*, is grown throughout the tropics and its importance in the world economy is increasing every year.

Right. A groundnut farm in West Africa.

Below. A storage pyramid before shipment.

17. Maize, *Zea mays*, is a principal cereal crop of tropical and semi-tropical areas.

Below. A maize ear showing 'corn on the cob'.

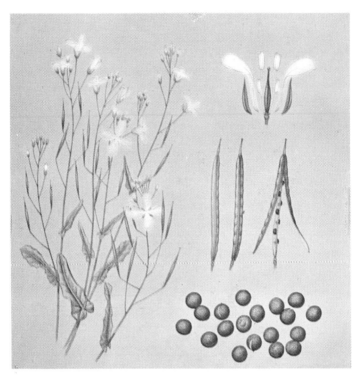

18. Rape
Brassica sp.

Left.
Inflorescence.

Top right.
Single flower.

Middle right.
Fruit.

Bottom right.
Seed.

Below. A field
of mature rape.

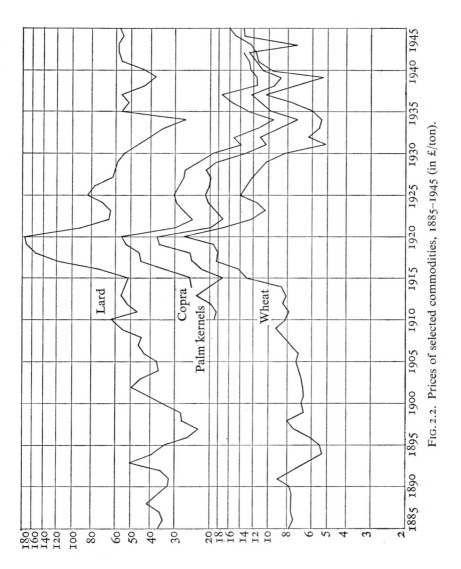

FIG. 2.2. Prices of selected commodities, 1885–1945 (in £/ton).

M.—6

to be dear and it is raw material prices that have unsettled the profit position of soap makers. No doubt the margarine producers were similarly placed. The skill with which businesses have dealt with adverse prices of raw materials has largely determined their success.

Turning to shorter-run fluctuations, crushers of oil-seeds and nuts and users of fats and oils, like others whose business is the transformation of materials, find that a substantial period may elapse between taking delivery of the raw material and the disposal of the product. If prices fluctuate, they stand to make speculative gains or losses on the stocks they hold. In practice, individual firms' operating policies may be determined by several considerations. However, some have preferred to transfer the risks of price fluctuations. The 'futures' markets, for example, for soya beans in Chicago and cottonseed in New York, through the hedging facilities they have offered, have made this possible. Various influences, among them wartime dislocation of markets, government intervention in price determination for farm products in various countries, and the tendency for large firms to carry their own risks, have tended to curtail the place of the 'futures' markets in recent years.

The instability of world prices of oil-seeds, which has from time to time embarrassed the final users, bears even more hardly on the producer, particularly if he is heavily dependent on one crop for his income. It is equally embarrassing for a country with a heavy dependence on a single export product (15). Helleiner noted that groundnuts, with rubber, cotton, and cocoa, were amongst the most highly unstable earners of export receipts (16). Such instability can arise in different ways. In rubber and cocoa price has been the destabilizer; for groundnuts it has tended to be the volume. Palm kernels and palm oil have been relatively stable for both volume and price. Where prices vary from year to year, there would be some attraction to the producer in an arrangement by which part of the first-hand sale value in a high-price year could be carried over to supplement the producer's return in a low-price year.

In principle, such a pooling over time might be provided by an individual firm or co-operative marketing society, but these operators might have a very difficult time in the high-priced periods in competition with others following different policies, unless their suppliers were exceptionally loyal. More usually a central marketing organization is seen in this role; for example, one to which all supplies of a particular product must be sold by producers or which has a monopoly of exports. It could then sell onwards for what it could get and pool the proceeds. From this pool it could pay producers a price somewhat below the equivalent of the wholesale price in a good year, and offset this by paying somewhat above the corresponding level in a bad year. It would also be in a position to announce its buying price for a period ahead. In principle, such an organization could also engage in other pooling operations; it could act as a discriminating monopoly seller, charging different buyers different prices if this were financially advantageous, and pool the proceeds of the several selling sectors.

Marketing organizations, often called boards, with functions such as these have been envisaged and set up in many countries since the depression of the 1930s. Some statutory basis has normally been necessary in order to secure the completeness of coverage desired, but the details of responsibility have varied. Some have been producer-operated within the statutory terms, but others have not had such representation of sectional interests. It has sometimes been difficult to assess the extent of government influence, but such an organization would need to be unusually favourably placed to be able to follow for long a line of action contrary to official policy. The operation of such boards has been outlined in various publications (17).

Oil and oil-seeds from Ghana, Sierra Leone, and Nigeria have been marketed through boards of this nature, which grew out of the purchasing arrangements instituted during the war as part of the Allied food control system, and others have operated elsewhere. In territories for which the United Kingdom had responsibility there were, as early as 1952, over sixty boards or similar organizations concerned with marketing over fifty agricultural products, including copra, coconut oil, cottonseed, groundnuts and their cake and oil, palm products, soya beans, and sunflower (18).

Their precise organization varied. Often when they were set up the existing arrangements for collecting and transporting the produce to the export point were left in operation, with few changes (19). In the case of the West African boards handling oil-seeds, provision was generally made for the agents to buy at not less than the scheduled prices and to sell onwards to the board at other prescribed prices. The difference between the two went towards paying the expenses and profits of the agents. Subsequently the produce was exported using channels similar to those used before the boards began operations.

The creation of a board did not, in itself, greatly change the way most of the basic marketing functions were performed, and in the early days of their operation the main change was in the processes by which prices were arrived at.

The basic concept of a stabilization programme along the lines described has an appealing logic and simplicity. Study shows that it needs close definition. For example, does stabilization relate to produce prices alone, or to producers' money incomes, or their real incomes? Stabilization of any one of these may destabilize the rest. In the process of pooling the proceeds, over what period should retention of funds in good years and disbursements in bad be made to balance? At what level should the stabilized price to producers be set, compared with the average price if the board were not operating (20)? Commentators on the operations of such boards have pointed to examples of destabilization of producer receipts, of prices to producers well below the equivalent of the free market prices. Accumulated surplus funds had not been returned to producers in these cases; indeed, they had often been diverted to other purposes (21).

INFLUENCES ON RAW MATERIAL PRODUCTION

Influences on the raw materials economy

The prosperity of consumers in developed countries, incomes of oil-seed producers, the business opportunities of traders in oil-seeds, techniques of exploiting marine resources, innovations in the manufacture of margarine; all these and other factors have played a part in the development of the raw material supply structure as it stands today. Moreover, each tended to influence the others. It is practically impossible to follow a single thread of argument through a discussion of any such developments without being subject to the strongest temptation to turn aside to other issues. However, the major factors directly affecting oil-seeds, over and above the consequence of the general upward trend in prosperity in the countries where the end products were marketed, can be regarded as falling under two broad headings. Firstly, there were all the technological advances concerned with the production of margarine and the provision of the raw material for this process, together with those which influenced the situation of competitive products. Secondly, there were the consequences of government action, direct or indirect. Since there are few matters that are not the indirect consequences of government action, a limit must be set on the scope of this heading. In fact, the relevant part of the subject is concerned either with tariff policy affecting the pattern of international trade in raw materials or with policy relating to margarine manufacture. The latter is dealt with in Chapter Seven, leaving us with the tariff issue. It has often seemed that a third category of indirect influences might usefully be considered, namely the business outlook and performance of those engaged in the production of products or supply of materials; certainly its importance was consistently evident. The consequences of a new technological advance or a new government policy measure were not rigorously determined by the nature of that advance or the terms of that measure. They might depend to a substantial degree on the extent to which those businessmen who were in a position to act on their judgement of prospects in their particular field fully understood the developments in sight, and their implications. Even if these men had the necessary shrewdness of appraisal, what they could achieve might in turn depend on the characteristics of the human material with which they had to work. These remarks have applied just as forcefully to the distribution chain at remote points in a developing country as to the board-room of a large manufacturing firm. The prospects of building up a marketing chain which would tap distant production potential might depend to a critical degree on having, at a suitable point in that chain, people who could see the chance of making a profit. When they are there, then there is a good prospect that produce will flow in trade. In principle, a whole chain of minor entrepreneurs stretching over 1,000 miles of bush paths, roads, and rivers could be replaced by one central organization with regional and local staff. In practice, however, such a system, widespread geographically, would demand skilled and careful supervision at all points. Top-quality supervisors at all levels have usually been amongst the scarcest of skilled men in developing countries.

Thus, any system which harnessed individual enterprise to secure the same ends had much to commend it.

Influence of technological advances

The complex of products on which the margarine industry has been built has already been described. For the present purpose, it is important to bear in mind the competitive balances that have been shifted by the influences with which we are concerned. When margarine came on the scene, among the current conflicts were those between vegetable oils and fats and electricity and gas for the provision of heating and lighting, and between vegetable oils and mineral oils for lubrication. Margarine has always competed with soap for raw materials, although the situation has changed. Later, the compound cooking fats came into the picture in North America, the United Kingdom, and a few other countries. During the First World War glycerine requirements, normally met from the soap-making process, became a direct and active influence in the choice between different oil-producing products. Since marginal adjustments were possible between oil-cakes and cereals in making up the feeding-stuffs requirements of farm livestock, there has been some significance, too, in the competition between oil-seeds and grains as it has borne on the preference for raw materials with a high yield of oil-cake.

It is tempting to dramatize two innovations in this field; the original invention of margarine and the discovery of the hydrogenation of oils. Clearly without them the situation would not be as it is today. However, their part was probably less clear-cut than one tends to think at first, both in the sense that they did not burst into life at one move, and also in the sense that their results could only be fully achieved through the assistance of many other changes in associated areas of the economy.

After the first discovery of the technique of margarine production, a notable and influential change was the development of refrigeration, which opened up a supply of suitable animal fats from the packing houses of North America to the producers of margarine, especially in Holland. Until then, European producers had been dependent on that proportion of the home supply of animal fats that was available over and above that required for direct human use. This source of animal fats gave to the European industry its opening for expansion through the 1880s and up to the end of the century. However, on both technical and price considerations, margarine producers had been exploring the possibility of incorporating vegetable oils into margarine during the period when the prices of animal fats had been increasing, i.e. up to the early years of the twentieth century. They had found the possibilities limited by the colour and flavour characteristics of the vegetable oils. Developments became possible here with the discovery about 1900 of refining processes that could greatly improve the odour and flavour of cottonseed oil. This development made it possible for margarine producers to use cottonseed oil in reasonable quantities whereas previously they had been precluded from doing so. Also it ensured a fuller use of supplies of seed for crushing, as there was a greater demand for oil (22).

Progress continued with the discovery of refinement techniques suited to more kinds of oil, techniques that made suitable for edible purposes grades of oil that would previously have been used for non-edible purposes, and the development of manufacturing skills that allowed a wider range of products to be used successfully in producing a margarine which was acceptable to the consumers. Developments in refining, for instance, allowed certain firms in the middle 1920s to use—to considerable business advantage—a greater proportion of palm oil than their competitors could. Their advantage gave them, in effect, access to cheaper raw materials. As the rest of the industry took up each new technique such raw materials became available to them all. As a consequence, the producers of raw materials at the other end of the distribution chain received an encouraging stimulus.

Hydrogenation, or hardening, was first introduced in about 1906. This process makes it possible to add hydrogen to unsaturated liquid oils and to produce, in a controlled manner, products of a desired degree of hardness at normal temperature. Mixes of ingredients can be chosen to give a type of margarine conforming to desired specifications. The discovery and patenting of the basic hydrogenation technique was not by any means the end of the story, even for those who had immediate access to it. The enormous potential value of the process for the whole industry was only beginning to be properly appreciated by about 1908 or 1909. In the years which followed, the application of the process to more and more raw materials was worked out, although the First World War intervened. Among the last major raw materials to be successfully dealt with was whale oil; the process was fully under control by about 1930.

The history of whale oil and the new technical developments showed very clearly the inter-relationship between processes. The original technique for catching whales in a reasonably organized manner was developed before the discovery of margarine. The techniques of operating from floating factories were being successfully mastered in the first few years of the twentieth century, but so long as the use of whale oil was confined to certain sectors of the oils and fats market the full potential of the source of supply could not be exploited. When the hardening process was at last successfully applied to whale oil the way was open, and production was heavy through the

1930s to the outbreak of war. However, the opportunities for the supply source to respond to the technical possibilities were limited by the nature of the harvesting process.

Whaling was really a seaborne version of the 'collecting and hunting' economy as practised by our nomadic forefathers. When they had over-hunted a locality they had to move on to somewhere not yet tapped; so did the whalers. They moved on from the Arctic to the Antarctic; when that failed there were no untapped hunting grounds and in recent years the supply has declined. Still more recently, the fish body oils have gained in importance. The weight to be given to the several tendencies in these later years must, so far, be a matter of opinion.

The decline of the whaling industry led, among other things, to a search for alternative enterprises, especially by Norway. New fishing techniques—for example, the use of nylon nets with associated changes in technique—greatly increased the catching potential. Fiscal changes made expansion more commercially attractive in Peru. Fish body oils are a joint product, one might almost say a by-product, of fishmeal production for animal feeding, and the world price for this product was attractive enough to encourage rapid expansion in the 1960s.

In the past few paragraphs the concern has been with the oil as it appeared on the market and the factors which influenced its use thereafter. A great many important, but not spectacular, developments operated also at the crushing stage. In the early days in a number of countries that are now important in the business, the crushing industries were organized to handle only soft seeds. With the change to hard seeds new processes, capable of dealing with the whole range of materials on the market, evolved.

Generally speaking, equipment for extracting oil from oil-seeds and nuts on an industrial scale can be classified into three categories. In many countries where vegetable oils are a part of the traditional diet small-scale extraction equipment is used, much of it using the screw-press principle. Originally the same principle was employed in extraction presses for industrial use, but this is by its nature a batch method. It gave way to the expeller process in which the raw material, after suitable pre-treatment, is, in effect, driven through a narrowing pipe with arrangements for the oil expressed in the process to flow away. This system has in its turn been largely displaced by a process in which the oil is removed from the prepared seed by extraction with a solvent, which is subsequently recovered. The solvent process has a higher yield of oil from the original material, but while it is favoured for most modern mills in developed countries, many installations in developing countries have used expeller types. They have been preferred for their lower capital costs and simpler operation; moreover, it has often been possible to secure a premium for oil-cake with the slightly higher oil content which they yield.

A special feature of the technology at the crushing stage has been the fact that oil-seed crushing firms have been geared to handle a wide range of raw materials so that they could use whatever was economically most attractive for the time being. Further, they were not dependent on the seasonally varying supplies of an individual seed, and so could maintain a reasonably level throughput. The fact that in a good many instances the capacity was only partially, perhaps 60 per cent, used, has itself often been a reflection of technical developments. New equipment tended to be installed without discarding the old and, since the latter—often of the expeller type—was largely written off in the accounts, it was maintained against sudden rushes and special demands. Governmental measures have played a considerable part in the location of the crushing industry as is outlined below.

In passing, one might note that the highly important by-product of oil-seed crushing, oil-cake for livestock feeding, has reached the importance it now holds in many temperate countries as a result of much careful investigation and development work on the part of academic and commercial research workers, a process which is still continuing (23).

It would be to miss much of the reality and importance of the more sophisticated technical developments to view them merely in terms of the chemistry and physics of the engineering which went into their exploitation. Equally significantly, they were one of the weapons with which firms using oil-seed fought each other for increasing shares in the market. The original discovery of margarine has been called a child of wartime necessity. It is perhaps open to argument whether the original discovery of refining and hydrogenation techniques was a child of commercial necessity. However, it is perfectly certain that the adoption of such techniques once they had been developed was a life or death matter for the businesses concerned if competition was open and keen. The fight to use the hydrogenation process very largely determined the shape of the oils and fats, margarine, and soap industries in Europe from the years just before the First World War up to the present day. In discussing this kind of in-fighting it must be kept in mind that it was not simply the right to use a particular technique that was important in giving a controlling influence; equally necessary was the acquisition of staff with experience in transferring the principles from the laboratory and pilot stages to industrial use. Even know-how in industrial application would not have been enough to develop the industry from a minor trade using slaughter-house waste to its present scale had there not been, not only in the periods of greatest competition but also in anticipation of such periods, a restless seeking for new possibilities in types and sources of oil.

Early in the period it was known that it could be useful to incorporate olive oil with animal fats in margarine production; but it was dear. Exploration of other possibilities, after sesame oil and a few others had been tried, showed that there were advantages in groundnuts. Subsequently, the French processing industry in Marseilles and other southern ports responded with developments which led to the emergence of the large Senegalese groundnut-exporting organization. It is fairly easy to recognize in the early history the individuals whose restless inquiring minds led to the transformation of the scene over the first half-century of the history of margarine (24). However, their successors who provide the leaven today will probably remain lost in the anonymity of large enterprises when present-day history comes to be written.

So far, this account is still firmly focused on the practical technological developments and the consequences immediately associated with them. One ought not to close a section devoted essentially to innovations without also stressing those innovations that were not directly connected with processes and machines but that nevertheless played a highly significant part in the raw materials business. The development of techniques of organization which permitted the operation of firms as big as those who have used oils and fats in North America and Europe represents a very substantial innovation. But this may still be focused too firmly on the industrial and the large scale. In many instances raw materials moved because, at each of half a dozen stages in the distribution process, problems which initially seemed insuperable were successfully solved. The use of kerosene tins and bicycles for the transport of palm oil where no road existed in West Africa was a technical development which must stand high as a contributor to the raw materials economy as it had evolved by the

1960s. Equally significant was the discovery of effective arrangements for supplying enough credit to impecunious but energetic and resourceful middlemen. With funds made available by this means it was possible for them to bring produce from distant producing areas to a point where it could be picked up by more formally organized assembly processes (25).

THE ROLE OF GOVERNMENT

Turning now from private enterprises to governments, which have influenced the raw material situation for oils and fats both with specific intention and as a result of general action affecting a broad sector of the economy. Furthermore, many governmental activities, begun without any particular reference to oil-bearing materials, have come to affect them. Two examples might illustrate this. First, many developed countries have followed a policy of protecting their agricultural industries and, since the Second World War, a number have succeeded in making livestock production reasonably profitable.

However, many farmers could look after more livestock than they could feed from the products of their own farmland; by buying feeding-stuffs from elsewhere they effectively increased the size of their farming businesses and their incomes. This economic climate, together with changes in the technology of livestock production, gave general encouragement to use concentrated feeding-stuffs and hence tended to underwrite the market for oil-cakes. Second, to take an example from quite a different setting, the bringing of the railways to northern Nigeria in effect created the possibility of a groundnut industry in the north. However, governments can also be influential without actually taking explicit action. As will be noted later, oilseed crushing plants have been set up in seed-producing countries without the aid of funds or direct assistance from the government, where it became known that the government favoured a move in this direction. This reduced the uncertainty in the minds of potential investors sufficiently to lead them to put money into a business which they judged on current prospects to hold promise of profit. It is rarely easy to trace the full extent of government influence, but it seems that general government approval was important in the setting up of crushing plants in, for example, New Guinea and the Sudan (26).

Before turning to the more specific and direct government activities, it should be noted that the general contribution of government in securing the maintenance of law and order has been itself a major matter in determining the possibilities of development, particularly in less-developed countries. In many countries raw materials to the value of hundreds of thousands of pounds a month are bought in innumerable small transactions in the earlier stages of their route from the farm to the crushing plant. The transport of cash in such quantities to dispersed buying points is difficult enough under any conditions—no more than about £10,000 worth of coin can be carried on a fully loaded 3-ton lorry—and it is only practicable if at least a minimum of law enforcement is provided by the central authorities. Governments have also contributed to the growth of trade in raw materials by providing inspection services and by setting up standard grades to facilitate commercial arrangements and to maintain buyers' trust in the products of the country concerned.

Since the import tariff policies have a long history of considerable complexity it might be appropriate, before turning to them, to make a brief reference to export duties. A number of developing countries, for example, Nigeria, have depended for over two-thirds of their export earnings on oil-seeds (27). Since, under their social and administrative conditions, direct taxation of all incomes was not feasible except for a small proportion of the population, it was natural to turn to export duties as a revenue-raising device. It was, of course, possible to use them in a discriminating manner; it was also possible to use them as a means of forcing investment in the exporting country, whatever might be the views of the producers and the exporting firms. Either producers or exporters had usually to provide the duty, since only exceptionally could it be passed on to the consumer, at any rate in the short run. It is perhaps sufficient to leave this as a general revenue tax and not explore its more devious operations.

If we now turn to import tariffs, it seems that they have usually been applied to the protection of one of three groups; the agrarian interests, industrial interests in the importing countries, or the agrarian interests in the colonies or associated countries. All three can be seen in the history of the tariffs affecting margarine and its raw materials. However, one might say that probably the most important were those measures, by no means confined to import tariffs, which were applied to margarine itself. These are the subject of Chapter Seven.

If we now look very broadly at the trade in raw materials for oil and fats over the whole period from about the 1890s to the present day, we can trace a short list of major policy tendencies through an immense variety of short-run detailed or minor policy steps. There was the policy of agrarian protection which has continued on and off in Germany right up to the present time. Much the same held in France and in a number of other agrarian countries in continental Europe; it can be discerned in the U.S.A. in her policy towards the import of oil-seeds and oils from the early part of the twentieth century. Towards the end of the inter-war years such activities took the form not only of protection of agrarian interests by import duties, exchange control measures, quota restrictions, etc., but also of an export subsidy war, for example for butter, which served to increase the prices to producers well above the equivalent of the final export sale price. The impact of national agricultural policies on international trade in agricultural products continues to be critically important in the 1960s.

Secondly, we can discern over long periods steady imperialization of the international trade in oil-seeds through preferences granted to their associates by colonial powers. Much the same pattern was followed for other agricultural products. This tendency became particularly evident in the post-depression period, and in connection with France, Britain, and the U.S.A. To take France as an example; in the 1930s fats and oils produced in France and abroad competed embarrassingly with French butter, and with olive oil from associated territories in North Africa. The situation was politically insupportable and some protective measures would have been necessary in any event; colonial interests urged that they be applied more forcefully against produce from outside the French Association. In 1933 the import duties on tallow, suet, whale fat, and lard oils were trebled, and various other restraints were added in the following months, even to the point of export bounty on lard in the early months of 1936. Tariffs and quotas were imposed on imported oils. The proceeds of certain duties on seeds in the mid 1930s were used to assist colonial oil-fruit growing. British measures showed a similar trend. Her Empire preference policies gave preference to producers of oil and oil-bearing materials within her Empire, as she did to producers of other Empire products. Such national measures naturally came into conflict with one another, with consequent arguments and misunderstandings. French measures against imports of Indian shelled groundnuts could be represented as reprisals for the British action in discriminating against groundnuts from French West Africa in

1932. The U.S.A. had been pursuing since the First World War, and even before, a policy of increasing protection by giving specially favourable terms to her own dependencies. An important result here was the building up of the copra trade of the Philippines.

Superimposed on these protective measures and imperialization tendencies was a general policy of encouraging the export from producing areas of raw materials before crushing, to the benefit of industry in the importing countries. This subject is discussed below, but, broadly speaking, it operated by metropolitan governments setting heavier duties against imports of oil than against the original material, probably by a margin about equal to the value added by the crushing process. In consequence, the whole international oil-seed economy entered the period after the Second World War with the majority of the crushing facilities located in the importing and using countries. In the years since the Second World War much international effort has gone into reducing the restraints on international trade of all kinds, with some success.

With agricultural products, it was increasingly realized that the complex of national policies which countries had set up to protect their own agricultural producers constituted the most significant barriers. These were much more influential in moulding the pattern of international trade than measures, such as tariffs, quotas, or exchange control measures, designed to influence it directly. The developing countries particularly felt that their efforts were hampered by the virtual reservation of large sections of the internal market in developing countries for those countries' own producers. The treatment of oils and oil-seeds in the E.E.C. continues to have special arrangements for the associated territories. However, since regulations provide for freedom of trade within the whole assembly, certain territories will no longer have the special advantage that they did when they enjoyed special preferences in the metropolitan countries. Thus, oil-seed exporting territories are likely to find this important when their crushing industries are competing freely with those in Holland and Germany.

Few government actions are quite devoid of impact in the economic sphere. However, one might perhaps distinguish such policies as those noted above, which arise directly from economic and political considerations and result in measures designed to have a fairly direct and immediate economic consequence, from others which may only have such effects at second hand. One might include here the consequences of government-sponsored research, which has led to enhanced crop yields and better quality in many countries—the sunflower crop in the U.S.S.R. is an example. Trade barriers imposed to prevent the spread of animal diseases is an example of a different nature, and international agreements restraining whaling might come in the same category. The whale oil boom, made possible by the successful solution of the problem of hardening whale oil, reached a point where there was grave danger of overkilling. Anglo-Norwegian agreements in the early 1930s were made ineffective by German and Japanese competition. Two international conferences were held. One in 1937 sought to provide for protection of breeding stock, and consequently some replenishment of populations. However, this did nothing to control the total kill or the level of oil production. The 1938 conference agreed that only a limit on the total kill by all whaling countries would prove effective, but with war imminent this was not a time when countries were prepared to forego the opportunity to stock up with oil (28). However, the groundwork that had been done then was fruitful in 1945. The solution arrived at, under which the whaling operators regularly reported the number of whales killed and ceased killing for the season when the total permitted number was reached, left competition between countries and between ships within countries to operate unimpaired.

LOCATION OF THE OIL-SEED CRUSHING INDUSTRY

The location of the oil-seed crushing industry can to a considerable extent be regarded as a consequence of government measures. In most areas where oil-seeds or nuts have been produced there were facilities for crushing. This was the origin of the crushing industries in European centres; local crushing is often to be found in developing countries even where there are no large-scale crushing plants in the big towns or the ports. The original European industry was set up to crush linseed and rape-seed in the north and west of Europe, and olive and sunflower in the south and east, but its scope was gradually expanded to take in imported raw materials—copra, groundnuts, cotton, and soya in particular—as the demand for fats as foodstuffs grew in the early years of this century. The forces which, at least up till the Second World War, caused a general concentration of crushing in the countries using oil-seeds were complex, and some were not easy to isolate.

In general terms, it can be noted that the value added by crushing is relatively small, probably not more than 10 per cent of the value of the raw material. While a particular operator might find it profitable to earn this margin, relatively minor adverse influences could transform his position. One important factor is the advantage of being able to spread the load through the year, or more evenly, by drawing a variety of seeds for crushing from several countries. The concentration of crushing in the metropolitan countries has often been explained by this advantage. However, many crushing industries in developed countries in the period after the Second World War operated well below capacity, which robs the argument of some of its force. Equally relevant might be the advantage open to a crusher in an importing country of buying his raw materials as his skill and the market allowed. In fact, crushing and using stages have been integrated to an extent that practically rules out simple generalizations.

Probably a more powerful reason than the mere advantage of a level throughput has been the opportunity—provided by having the crushing in close association with the using industry—of ensuring that the latter obtained the kinds of oil it needed with that precision of quality definition which has made possible the close technical control of modern margarine production. The history of the European margarine industry in its earlier days underlines the advantages the operators saw in having the oil-crushing plant, as well as the oil-using plant, under a central control. Probably the subsequent emergence of technical finesse has increased rather than diminished this advantage.

Quite apart from this subtle consideration and from governmental influences which we will discuss later, it may not be particularly easy for a developing country to reap the benefit of local crushing industry. Thus palm-kernel crushing mills were erected in Nigeria in 1910, but local suppliers made purchasing difficult, labour supply was uncertain, and shipping was costly. Again, conditions in the First World War led to a considerable increase in the crushing of copra in the Philippines, the oil being exported to the U.S.A. However, in the years that followed, the Philippine producers of oil found it increasingly difficult to survive, and probably not only in consequence of the tariff pattern. The demand for oil-cake has often played a part in the siting of crushing. This element has probably had more effect on the choice of oil-seed than on the actual location. Thus, in Germany in the inter-war period grains were heavily taxed and this might have been expected to favour palm-kernel cake as a grain substitute, but the effect was probably minor. There have been a number of exceptions to this tendency to crush in Europe and North America. One was China which, between the wars, was one of the major exporters of oil, the mills having been set up in her ports from early in the century. The Belgian Congo had a crushing industry largely based on the

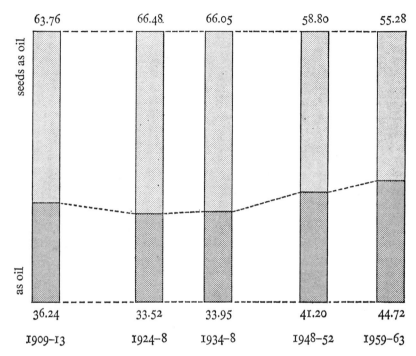

FIG. 2.3. Comparative importance of international trade in vegetable oils and oil-seeds as an indication of the location of oil-seed crushing. (Expressed as percentages of total oil equivalent of groundnut, soya, cottonseed, palm kernel, and copra, exported as seed or as oil.)

plantation system. Phillippine crushing built up again, probably assisted by a useful economy in freight and the avoidance of deterioration in transit when copra is converted into oil and cake before dispatch. In fact they need much of the oil locally. There is more to be gained by economy in transport costs from crushing copra at the production point than most other oil-bearing products (29).

These technical features were undoubtedly influential on occasions in determining the location of the crushing industries, but governmental action played its part, too, as the earlier discussions of tariffs

M.—7

underlined. One might sum up the situation in the words of Stopforth and O'Hagan, '. . . most important countries impose tariffs which protect to some degree the domestic crushing industry against competition from imports of oils, i.e. structure of import duties favours imports of oil-seeds including the oil-seeds from other developed countries. In general the level of the tariff appears to be somewhere around the value added by processing.' They went on to point out that exceptions to these protective duties were chosen on political rather than on other grounds. Broadly, however, these lines of action tended to reinforce technical factors and left the bulk of oil-seed processing in the user's area, at least until the 1950s. After that a number of industries built up, some with local assistance (e.g. the long-standing private-enterprise crushing industry in Ceylon benefited from export duties which were set to favour home crushing). A private industry for crushing groundnuts was set up in Senegal, which processed probably two-thirds of their groundnut crop. It appeared that taxes neither hindered nor helped that particular industry. Developing countries have naturally been anxious to improve the earnings and employment of their own industries and there has been increasing international recognition of the risk that developing countries would fall further behind the developed in prosperity and trade generally (30). The over-all trend in the location of crushing is illustrated in Fig. 2.3.

THE OUTCOME

The outcome of all these intermingling influences has been the pattern of production of oil-bearing materials in all its present breadth and complexity. All the technical, economic, and political features outlined in the preceding paragraphs served to mould the flow of raw materials of fats and oils, in a way which makes the pattern today utterly unrecognizable as the successor to that of even fifty years ago. When margarine was first made, the outlet for animal and vegetable fats and oils was in part for soap, in part for lubrication, and in part for lighting. Both in Europe and America the first margarine was derived from animal fats, and the U.S.A. had sufficient supplies of these to allow her to continue until the First World War without being under heavy pressures to find substitute products. It was in Europe that the influences of technology and demand were the most evident. European margarine production began in the hands of butter traders, and in the first few years they used animal fats of European origin.

Even in the 1870s, however, the supply of these, in addition to what was required for sale with the meat, was not enough to meet the demand readily. Users began exploring the possibility of using vegetable oils to combine with animal fats. The pressure on European supplies of animal fats was eased somewhat by the opening up of the North American supplies to the European margarine users, and for two decades there was a flow of by-products from the Chicago packing-houses to Western Europe.

However, oil prices were still high enough to encourage Dutch margarine manufacturers to go on investigating all possible cheaper substitutes. Palm, coconut, groundnut, cotton, soya, sunflower, and whale oils were all known, many of them for soap production; but generally speaking they could not be refined satisfactorily for food use, and they were too soft. Despite the advent of the margarine industry the middle 1880s was a good time for soap makers in Europe; but the history of that industry indicates that by about 1888 the force of the new competition was evident to most operators.

At this stage the bigger manufacturers were overcoming the technical problems of margarine production, but then and for nearly another twenty years, they were more confident when using animal fats than vegetable, and would turn to them when the price was right. Even so, each was using as much of the cheaper oils as his knowledge allowed and the requirements of the market made feasible. The incentive to solve the problems of using vegetable oil increased with the rise in prices of raw materials from the packing industry in 1901 and 1902.

About 1900, an effective process for refining cottonseed was discovered, and subsequently extended to coconut oil; within the next two or three years coconut oil became useful for food purposes. This was a critically important development coming at a time when it was generally recognized that the world demand for fats and oils had well overtaken the supply.

Emerging about this time was a feature of organization which was to be an increasingly important factor in the supply system. The margarine producers, probably because of the technical nature of the process they were operating, were more compactly organized than the soap industry and in consequence were better able to buy effectively. The year 1906 brought critical conditions for users of fats and oils, with prices rising very rapidly, and most operators realized that this was not a transitory effect.

The first few years of the twentieth century brought the second main technical feature of the oils and fats story—the development of the process of hardening. These years, and this technique, laid the foundations for much of the large-scale organization of the European and American margarine industry in the twentieth century. It could be said by about 1910 that there was practically no good oil or fat that could not be used for the manufacturing of food products, though some considerable time elapsed before most products could be handled with almost equal facility. In the few years from then until the outbreak of war a number of features began to come into prominence. Soya beans, for instance, suddenly appeared on the world market, and coconuts and coconut oil, palm and palm products, and groundnuts, increased greatly in international trade. Just before the First World War plantations were initiated in the Belgian Congo. Generally speaking, at about this time Germany was the largest crusher of many of the world's traded oil-seeds.

The speed of the change from a manufacturing regime virtually dependent on animal fats in the first few years of the century to one using a considerable proportion of vegetable fats by the outbreak of war was governed in part by the need to apply new techniques on a large scale, and in part by the need to build a crushing industry suitably linked both to oil users and to the animal feeding-stuffs industry.

The war gave increased incentive to use vegetable oils; it killed the German oil-crushing industry, broke up her contacts with supply areas in the developing countries, and largely focused the Allied interest in oil-seed crushing in the United Kingdom. In due course American interest encouraged both home production of oil-seeds and a very substantial local crushing of copra in the Philippines.

These years saw changes begin in the structure of the organizations which handled the seed-crushing industries in Europe, which have left their mark up to the present time. The United Kingdom which had tended before the war to choose oil-seeds for the cake they yielded began to favour high oil-yielding products from nearer sources, particularly palm products from West Africa.

The oil-seed industry had many troubles between the wars. A number of tropical countries had been encouraged to expand their production, and enjoyed the income that they earned. The increase in supply in this period was one of the main influences on the oils and fats industries. In many countries there was a rationalization of cultivation and resulting increases in productivity. New links between countries formed after the dislocation of the war, the recovery of farming in war-devastated areas, the impact of the output from recovered sectors on those which had expanded to fill the wartime gap in oil-seed supplies, and, finally, the governmental reactions to the slump and later the preparation in all its various forms for another war. Within the oils and fats-using sector, technical advance progressed step by step. One firm might be a little more successful with its technique of handling groundnuts, another with its use of palm oil. Whale oil, too, was being used, but some years were to elapse before the solution of the problem of incorporating it in margarine was achieved. Nevertheless Europe was using hydrogenated whale oil and fish oil for food to a considerably greater extent than the U.S.A.

The years from 1929 to 1933 were ones of reaction to the overproduction of oils and fats. One million more tons of oil-seed crops were produced in the middle 1930s than in the previous decade; and whale oil production had doubled in that period. Government protective action emerged in various forms.

Such features as the Imperial Preference under the Ottawa Agreements Act of 1932, instituted in the United Kingdom, gave rise to a chain reaction; France increasing her tariffs against oil-seed products from outside her own empire. The second half of the 1930s in Europe was very substantially affected by the operations of Germany.

If we pause at this point and look back, the most important feature of the change over the seventy years of the margarine industry was the ending of the dependence on animal fats, and the prospect of raw materials supplies embracing, without substantial technical restraint for the manufacture of most types of margarine, practically all the animal and vegetable oils and fats, with the exception of the drying oils like linseed. That the trade was not moving wholly as supply possibilities and demand interests might suggest was the result not of technical considerations or even matters of business organization, but largely of governmental intervention for one purpose or another.

Nonetheless, one should note that over this period the structure of the industry handling oil-seeds from the farm gate to the kitchen had profoundly changed. Both in North America and in Europe the tendency, probably inevitable in view of the technical demands of the industry, had been for large firms to emerge, and the significance of specific patents for the manufacturing processes had increased. Moreover, the margarine manufacturers, the soap manufacturers, the crushers, and the feeding-stuffs manufacturers were often in very close association with one another. Under such conditions it was usually very difficult to identify the scope of competition in the various areas of the complex of activities, and to form even a tentative view of the long-term consequences of the structure.

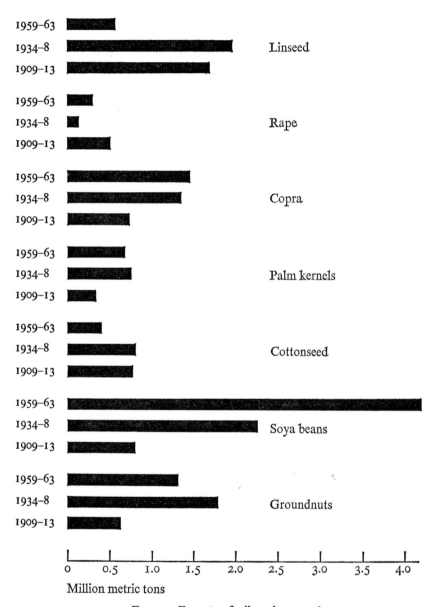

FIG. 2.4. Exports of oil-seeds 1909–63.

The Second World War might be said to have repeated many features of the First World War so far as the oils and fats industry was concerned. International arrangements were made to handle supplies but still the markets were distorted, old connections broken,

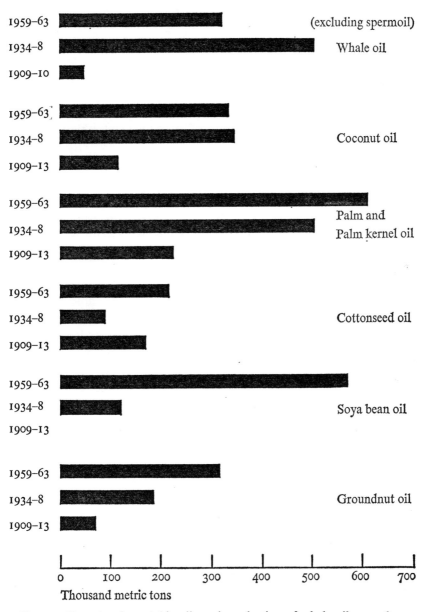

FIG. 2.5. Exports of vegetable oils and production of whale oil 1909–63.

and output reduced drastically in some countries and expanded in others. By 1947 it was reckoned that the world supply of fats and oils was 10 per cent below pre-war levels, but the demand, with increased population was substantially greater. Moreover, for a diversity of reasons, a number of the old sources were no longer available. These matters gradually righted themselves; partly through business initiative, and partly through national and international assistance.

Many wartime emergency efforts disappeared with the end of the war, but one that survived was the expanded United States soya bean industry. The American exports of soya beans increased to make her the largest exporter of oils and fats in recent years. Before the war she was exporting about 100,000 tons of oil-equivalent out of world exports of something over 4 million; by 1960 she was exporting some 2·4 million tons out of world exports of about 6 million. For the most part, this trade was conducted at world prices, but the assistance of PL 480 laws permitting concessional sale made the overseas marketing of soya somewhat easier. For her own margarine, soya supplied about 70 per cent by the late 1950s compared with no more than 15–20 per cent in the middle 1930s. The long-term over-all trends for the major products are summarized in Figs. 2.4 and 2.5 for the world as a whole up to the early 1960s.

The 1960s have seen still further developments, among them increased production of sunflower and fish oils and increased plantings of oil palm. They are too close to us to be seen in their proper place in the pattern. However, it is clear that improved varieties, new techniques of production, changes in governmental policies, and resources released from the production of quite different products, have played a part. Thus at the end of the century, as at the beginning, we see the complex network of interlinked individual commodity situations in which oils and fats are set, and the great diversity of influences that play their part in this history.

NOTES AND REFERENCES

1. ANDERSEN, A. J. C., and WILLIAMS, P. N. *Margarine* (Oxford, 1954). This book gives, among other things, examples of special-purpose margarines for which only a limited range of raw materials may be suitable.

2. EKEY, E. W. *Vegetable fats and oils* (New York, 1954). This gives a comprehensive account of the characteristics of vegetable fats and oils and the production and utilization of natural sources of raw material.

3. HARTLEY, C. W. S. *The oil palm* (London, 1967). This gives a comprehensive account of the cultivation and general management of the oil palm.

4. RAYMOND, W. D. 'The oil palm industry', *Tropical science*, **3**, 2 (1961), 69.

5. BRANDT, K. 'Whale oil: an economic analysis', *Fats and oils studies no.* **7** (Stanford, California, 1940).

6. PIM, A. *Colonial agricultural production* (Oxford, 1946), p. 134.
ROWE, J. W. F. *Primary commodities in international trade* (Cambridge, 1965), p. 223.

7. WILSON, C. *The history of Unilever. A study in economic growth and social change* (London, 1954), see especially vol. 1, p. 165.

8. DRACHOUSEFF, V. 'Agricultural change in the Belgian Congo: 1945–1960', *Food Research Institute studies*, **5**, 2 (Stanford, California, 1965).

9. See, for example, ROWE, op. cit.

10. For an account of the marketing of palm produce in West Africa see *United Africa Company statistical and economic review no.* **3** (1949).

11. WEDD, W. B. 'The marketing of oilseeds, oils, and fats', *Agricultural producers and their markets* (ed. WARLEY, T. K.) (Oxford, Basil Blackwell), p. 244.

12. WILSON, op. cit., vol. 2, p. 159.

13. BAUER, P. T. *West African trade* (Cambridge, 1954), p. 217.

14. EDWARDS, H. R. *Competition and monopoly in the British soap industry* (Oxford, 1962), p. 270.

15. STEWART, I. G., and ORD, H. W. (eds.). *African primary products and international trade* (Edinburgh, 1965). See, for example, HELLEINER, G. K. 'Peasant agriculture, development and export instability. The Nigerian case', p. 44.
UNITED NATIONS ORGANIZATION, DEPARTMENT OF ECONOMIC AFFAIRS, *Instability in export markets of under-developed countries* (New York, 1952), p. 94.

16. STEWART and ORD, op. cit., p. 54.

17. ABBOTT, J. C., and CREUPEANDT, H. 'Agricultural marketing boards and their establishment and operation', *F.A.O. marketing guide no.* **5** (Rome, 1966), p. 236.

18. *A review of colonial marketing organizations and related bodies* (United Kingdom Colonial Office, 1952).

19. See, for example, BAUER, op. cit.

20. BAUER, P. T., and PAISH, F. W. 'The reduction of fluctuations in the incomes of primary producers', *Economic journal*, **62** (1952), 750.

21. See ibid.
HELLEINER, G. K. *Peasant agriculture, government, and economic growth in Nigeria* (Homewood, Illinois, 1966).

22. For details of earlier refining processes see, for example, LEWKOWITSCH, J. *Chemical technology analysis of oils, fats and waxes*, 5th edition (London 1907). For a modern account see ANDERSEN, op. cit.

23. See LANDMANN, U. *Struktur und Dynamick des Ölkuchenmarkts* (*The structure and dynamics of cooking-oil markets*), Institut für Landwirtschaftliche Markt-lehre (Göttingen, 1961), p. 252.

24. See WILSON, op. cit.

25. See JONES, W. O. 'Economic man in Africa', *Food Research Institute studies,* **1**, 2 (Stanford, California, 1960). This is not specifically concerned with oil-seeds, but it underlines the fact that economic behaviour does not stop where the asphalt road ends.

26. See STOPFORTH, J., and O'HAGAN, J. P. 'Structure of the oil-seed crushing industry and factors affecting its location'. *F.A.O. monthly bulletin of agriculture economics and statistics,* **16**, 4–5 (1967).

27. See STEWART and ORD, op. cit.

28. BRANDT, K. 'The German Fat Plan and its economic setting', *Fats and oils studies no.* **6** (Stanford, California, 1938).

29. See, for example, STOPFORTH and O'HAGAN, op. cit.

30. Aspects of this problem are considered in *Trade in agricultural commodities in the United Nations Development Decade*, a special supplement to the *F.A.O. commodity review* (Rome, 1964).

CHAPTER THREE

Technology and Production

R. FERON

RAW MATERIALS AND THEIR TREATMENT

MARGARINE is an emulsion composed of two phases: a fatty phase, which is the more important, and an aqueous phase of milk or water or a mixture of both. Small quantities of other ingredients, which are of considerable importance if a product is to meet all the consumer's requirements, complete this brief description.

The fatty phase

The sole ingredient in the margarine which Mège Mouriès invented was fat from the fluid fraction of beef tallow, then known as oleo-margarine.

The raw material, beef tallow, was collected from slaughtered animals or supplied by butchers who removed some fat when preparing the meat for retail sales. The tallow was washed, minced, and rendered in one of two ways.

The oldest method and the one that supplies the best product is to render the fat on a water bath at a moderate temperature: 60 °C., for example. With this method the fat floats on the surface of the water, whilst the residual protein gathers in the bottom of the equipment. The fat is collected by decantation. This method was in use long before the invention of margarine. The high quality of the product gave it special significance at the very outset of the new industry, but the constantly rising demand very soon made it imperative to adopt processes that were more productive. Thus the dry bath with air flowing freely or under light pressure has almost completely superseded the water bath.

The second method is to put the washed and minced fat into vats or autoclaves with double jackets. Steam is blown in at normal pressure (in vats) or a little above atmospheric pressure (in autoclaves). The fat is drawn off, whilst the residue or greaves is collected on the screens of the autoclave; it is used in animal foods. The original process has been very much improved upon, first by a substantial reduction in the time during which the fat is exposed to a high temperature, and then, about 1925, by the introduction of a continuous procedure. The continuous and improved procedure is nowadays used for the preparation of very good-quality lards.

The beef tallow, or *premier jus* as it is called, is then crystallized slowly at about 30 °C. The crystallized product, which is a granular mass, is filtered and pressed, yielding about 60 per cent liquid with a melting point between 28 and 34 °C. This is oleomargarine. The solids, which have a melting point of 48–54 °C. and are known as oleostearine, remain on the filter cloths of the presses. They are used for some foods and, of course, in stearin production.

The rapid success of margarine and the increasing demand for it by consumers soon made oleomargarine hard to come by. In 1873–4 some manufacturers therefore contrived to increase their resources by using vegetable oils. These also had the advantage of producing a more plastic product with a lower melting point. In some cases even fractionation of the *premier jus* could be omitted, as vegetable oils gave a product with the desired physical properties.

In those days only certain liquid oils could be used in foods. Solid vegetable fats were generally not of a quality suitable for human consumption. Towards the end of the nineteenth century refining processes for solid vegetable oils enabled manufacturers to use these oils in margarine-making, and about 1907 margarines were coming on the market which contained larger or smaller amounts of coconut, palm kernel, or palm oil, obtained by the same refining processes as we know today.

The extraction of vegetable oils. Vegetable oils are obtained from oil-bearing seeds or fruits in two ways.

The first method is pressing. The seed is crushed, heated, moistened with a little steam, and then pressed. In the past, mechanical or hydraulic presses were used; the oil-bearing material was contained in bags or placed between metal plates. Pressure is applied, sometimes as much as 300 kg/cm^2, forcing out the oil which is then collected and filtered. The residue, or cake, still contains 10–12 per cent oil.

In a screw press the heated material is then pressed against the walls of a barrel by means of a screw, which also keeps the substance moving. There are slots in the walls through which the oil can escape.

Squeezing efficiency is far higher and the residue which emerges may only contain 4–5 per cent oil. Moreover, it is a continuous process.

Oil can also be extracted by the use of a solvent. The oil-bearing material is washed with a solvent which dissolves only the oil. The solution is filtered and the solvent evaporated. The result is oil with a meal which is almost free from oil—modern processes leave less than 1 per cent oil in the meal.

This process, suggested by Deiss in 1854, has been much improved upon since the beginning of the century. It has the advantage of a high yield and is continuous. The solvent used in the early years was carbon disulphide, which has been practically abandoned in favour of very volatile and perfectly harmless fractions of petrol. The most commonly used solvents are hexane or hydrocarbons with a boiling point of 60 °C., which are comparatively easy solvents to remove. The operation can be carried out batch-wise in pots, in which the meal is washed with solvent then steamed free of it. There is also a continuous-extraction process; this uses a counter-current in which the substance is drained with an increasingly pure solvent. The mixture of oil and solvent, called the *miscella*, is distilled in simple or multiple equipment and the last traces of solvent are stripped off with steam.

The most usual procedure is pressing followed by extraction. About two-thirds of the oil can be removed from the seed by the moderate and consequently inexpensive pressing process. The rest of the oil is extracted with solvent.

Refining crude oil. Crude oils are not fit for human consumption at this stage. They contain various impurities: vegetable residues, gummy or mucilaginous substances, colouring matter, and metabolic products of the oil-seed which taste unpleasant and cannot be used in foodstuffs.

A preliminary refining process purifies these oils and makes them fit for human consumption. Then they become the raw material of margarine production and are transformed into margarine in a second series of operations. Fig. 3.1 shows the different stages in the production of the finished product.

Reception of the crude oils. Although the harvesting of oil-bearing seeds is usually seasonal it is possible to spread the pressure and extraction processes throughout the year by stocking seeds in silos or warehouses. The need to make up stocks is thus reduced to the requirements of commerce and transport only. The crude oils consequently leave the oil-stores all the year round and are stocked in the crude state in tanks adjoining the refineries, as experience has shown that in this form deterioration is reduced to a minimum. It is important for the oils to be thoroughly dry and for their temperature to be carefully checked. For oils gathered only once, such as whale oil, the only solution is to build up large stocks at the end of the whaling

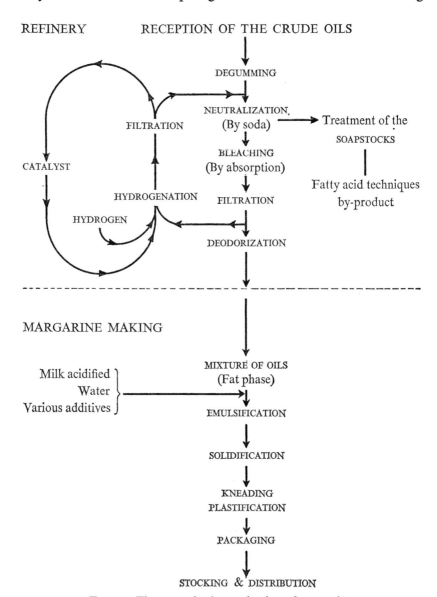

FIG. 3.1. The stages in the production of margarine.

season and draw from them as required. If certain precautions are taken (e.g. moisture and temperature control) crude oil keeps well.

Degumming. The crude oils contain, in suspension, vegetable fragments and components of the seed cells which are very small, even colloidal. Decantation, which is slow and efficacious, has always been used to clarify oils meant for human consumption. Industrial use of certain oils (for lighting and paints) necessitated more complete purification to obviate the formation of injurious precipitates. Rather ruthless methods such as the addition of a small quantity of sulphuric acid to the oil, which had been known for a long time (Gowen, 1790), although they accelerated the formation of mucilages, were ill-suited for the treatment of oils to be used for food. Gowen's process, perfected by Baron Thénard (1811) remained in use for lighting-oil, especially rape-seed oil, until the arrival of alkaline refining towards the end of the nineteenth century.

It was then noticed that the gums caused considerable losses, although promoting emulsification. Various processes and additions were suggested: Villon, for instance, in 1893, added a 1–2 per cent solution of ferrous sulphate (green vitriol) 'to eliminate the water and precipitate the protein substances'. Water alone, or with an admixture of sodium chloride or a weak organic acid, produces the same effect; this alternative was soon turned to account by the new industry of oil refining, as precipitation of the gums or mucilages when refining begins ensures better yields. Since 1921 soya lecithin (the mucilages of crude oil) has been prepared industrially by this method, which is thus part of current practice. The crude oil is heated to 60–80 °C., and 2–5 per cent of water or a weak solution (about 5 per cent) of an edible acid (phosphoric, citric) is added; the emulsion is then stirred for 20–30 minutes. The hydrated mucilages form a precipitate and are separated by decantation or, more rapidly, by centrifugation. The viscous mass is either put aside or treated for preparation of lecithin. The oil, unless it is neutralized at once, ought to be dried.

Neutralization or deacidification. The free fatty acids in the oil, which are metabolic products of the seed, are combined with an alkaline reagent, usually caustic soda, to form a soap. This soap, which is insoluble in oil but soluble in water, sinks to the bottom of the tank and is drained off. The oil is washed with hot water and then dried by evaporation of the water under reduced pressure. This process yields neutralized oil.

The neutralization method is more than a hundred years old, having been used in France, England, and Germany in the middle of last century (Evrard, 1855); and in the U.S.A. in 1842 Schmersahl had already suggested using soda for the treatment of cottonseed oil. However, it was from the 1880s onward that alkaline refining was developed, largely owing to the considerable demand for edible vegetable oils that were neutral in taste, for the manufacture of margarine; and by 1900 refining had its established principles which have scarcely varied since then. Oil, degummed if necessary, is heated to 80–90 °C. in a vat with coiled piping and a stirrer. Then enough caustic soda solution is sprinkled in to neutralize the free fatty acids of the oil (a slight excess of soda is usually used) while the stirrer is operating; after 20–30 minutes the stirrer is stopped and the soap, in a fairly concentrated solution, is decanted in the base of the apparatus, forming the soapstock. It is drawn off, and the oil is washed with hot water and stirred two or three times. Finally, the neutralized and considerably bleached oil is dried in a moderate heat under vacuum.

It is also possible to make the operation continuous, and industrial installations for this have been in use since 1928. The long decantation phase is replaced by a series of centrifugations, and special efficient mixing-machines ensure correct mixtures. This method results in a gain of time and space, and often, though not always, a better yield. Quite recently methods have come into vogue which are based on a new principle: instead of the lye being introduced into the oil, the oil is put into the lye, without any stirring. This is said to give better yields than the older methods.

Also, in order to improve the yield, efforts have long been made to remove the fatty acids only from the already purified oil, without carrying off the neutralized oil. In the last ten years or so this principle has been ratified by industry, a fact proved by the existence of a good many plants for refining by distillation.

Bleaching. The colouring substances of crude oils are either natural pigments or those formed as degradation products. They are inconvenient for use in foods, and have to be eliminated.

It has been known since about 1810 that certain products bleach solutions by selective absorption of pigments: at that time the problem of bleaching sweet juices by means of bone carbon (also called animal black) was solved. In 1855 Poll suggested the use of this same product for bleaching oils, and in 1889 Bornemann suggested using charcoal. The discovery at the beginning of the century of considerable deposits of absorbent clays (fuller's earth), already in use for fulling woollen materials in England and in Florida, made it possible to use these for improving the filtration of oils and even removing some of the colour. Up to 1910 no other method was known in industry; but that year saw the appearance of clays treated with a strong mineral acid to increase their retentive capacity for dyes, and the German activated clay (*terres activées*) industry came into being in 1924. Since then, the bleaching of oils has been carried out with small quantities (1–2 per cent, seldom any more) of active clays and sometimes of activated vegetable charcoal. The clay is added to the oil in a beater at 60–80 °C. under reduced pressure to lessen the risks of oxidation. The oil is then filtered; the absorbents containing pigments remain on the filter, while the uncoloured or very slightly coloured oil passes through.

Deodorization. The oils still have certain oil-soluble 'off-odours' or flavours which must be removed. This operation uses the principle of removing the volatile odours and flavours from the oil by steam-distillation. All other methods (washing in spirit, various additives to disguise the taste) were entirely unsuccessful, but this method made progress, though slowly. An English patent of 1841 covers the use of superheated steam for the deodorization of fats, an idea taken up again in France in 1854 (Cassgrand) and in 1855 (Bardies Moutié and Mme Decoudun). In 1873, Wurtz and Willin treated rape-seed oil with steam at 116–20 °C.; but it was in 1893 that a combination of superheated steam and a vacuum was first used in deodorization apparatus. British Patent Number 9205, granted to the Fabriques de Produits Chimiques de Thann et de Mulhouse in 1893, marks the birth of modern deodorization. The first continuous deodorizer was erected in 1895 by Rocca in Marseilles for the treatment of coconut oil, which was a problem of importance at that time, as can be seen from the multiplicity of patents for deodorization of this oil (Rocca, 1895, 1900, 1902; Klimoret, 1902). The same principle is still followed today: the superheated steam is blown in a certain proportion through the oil which has been heated to between 160 and 200 °C., and the pressure in the apparatus is kept at 2–8 mm Hg. The operation takes from 2 to 5 hours, according to the oil and the taste desired. To check the progress of the operation the oil is tasted; this is the only method known even today. When the taste is considered satisfactory the steam insufflation is stopped and the oil, still under vacuum, is cooled inside or outside the deodorization apparatus. After cooling,

M.—8

the neutralized oil, white and deodorized, is ready for consumption
or for the manufacture of margarine.

The modification of raw materials. Since 1907 margarines with a solid
vegetable-fat content have been coming on the market (mainly
coconut and palm kernel) which soon reached one-third of the total

Name	Iodine number	Saturated fatty acids %	Unsaturated fatty acids %	Polyunsaturated fatty acids %
Animal fats				
Beef tallow				
(*premier jus*)	42–8	48	52 especially oleic acid	
Oleomargarine				
(oleo oil)	44–5	*c*45	*c*55	
Pressed tallow				
(oleostearine)	18–28	*c*70	*c*30	
Mutton tallow	40–8	*c*50	*c*50	
Lard	52–68	40	60	
Animal oils				
Whale oil	105–20	25	75	
Fish oils				
Herring	135–40			
Sardine	170–90			
Menhaden	160–75	20	80	
Pilchard	180–90			
Vegetable oils				
Olive	85	10–12	83–90	7
Groundnut	85–40	17–20	80–3	20–40
Cottonseed	104–12	25 (palm)	75	45 (linol)
Soya	130–5	12–15	86–8	60
Sunflower	127–37	10–14	86–90	55 (linol)
Sesame	109–14	13–17	83–7	38–48
Maize	115–20	12–18	82–8	40
Vegetable fats				
Coconut	8–10	90–2	8–10	
Palm kernel	15–18	83	17	
Babassu	15	82	18	
Palm	53–60	48	52	
Shea	± 60	46	54	

TABLE 3.1. The main edible fats used as raw materials in the manufacture of
margarine together with their characteristic figures.

fat. Oleomargarine was still an important raw material in the industry, but events, notably the First World War, were soon to necessitate the use of vegetable oils in larger quantities. Since then the proportion of vegetable oils and fats has gone on increasing and they now play a predominant part in the supply for margarine production.

Table 3.1 gives the most important oils with their characteristic figures.

Hydrogenation. Another invention was again to widen the choice of raw materials for the margarine industry: this was hydrogenation.

It is known that the physical state of fats depends on their chemical composition, particularly the ratio of glycerides of solid saturated fatty acids to those of liquid unsaturated fatty acids. The chemical difference between saturated and unsaturated fatty acids is not great; oleic acid, which is liquid, and stearic acid, which has a melting-point of 72 °C., differ only in that the former has two hydrogen atoms fewer. The basic idea of adding hydrogen to the unsaturated fat—or hydrogenation—was studied by the French chemists Sabatier and Senderens at the turn of the century. But Normann, the German chemist, was the one to apply the technique to fats; he patented it in 1903, but hydrogenated fats did not actually appear on the market until around 1912.

Hydrogenation consists of adding very pure hydrogen to oil, with a finely divided nickel catalyst. Only the major installations are interested in preparing their own catalysts; excellent catalysts are supplied by industry, and there is a selection for special uses. On the other hand, every installation must prepare the necessary hydrogen. Three methods are in use for this:

(*a*) Electrolysis of water which has been made conductive with potassium hydroxide. 5 kWh must be reckoned for obtaining 1 m^3 of hydrogen. Equipment of different capacities is available.

(*b*) Reduction of steam by iron. The familiar reaction

$$Fe + H_2O \rightarrow FeO + H_2$$
$$3FeO + H_2O \rightarrow Fe_3O_4 + H_2$$

is followed by a phase of reduction of the iron oxide with a gas reducer, usually water-gas (or blue gas) a mixture of carbon monoxide and hydrogen.

$$Fe_3O_4 + 4CO \rightarrow 4CO_2 + 3Fe$$
$$Fe_3O_4 + 4H_2 \rightarrow 4H_2O + 3Fe$$

Thus the operation goes on in alternate cycles of production and reduction. The hydrogen obtained must be purified.

(c) By the action of steam on the hydrocarbons

$$C_3H_8 + 3H_2O \rightarrow 3CO + 7H_2$$
(propane)

Most of the carbon monoxide is converted into carbon dioxide which is eliminated by absorption. The last traces of CO are converted into methane. The hydrogen obtained is almost as pure as that supplied by electrolysis of water.

Hydrogenation is carried out in closed apparatus into which oil and the catalyst (0·2–1·0 per cent of nickel) are inserted in suspension. The remaining space is occupied by pure hydrogen. The presence of oxygen would incur a serious risk of explosion.

These appliances, 5–20 tons in capacity, had been equipped by Normann with a stirrer intended to keep the catalyst in suspension while the hydrogen, at a pressure of about 3 kg/cm², circulates in the oil and hydrogenates the double bonds. In some types of the apparatus the stirrer was omitted; in this case the hydrogen, entering at the base through a distributor, itself agitated the mixture. More recently the stirrer, in a much improved form, has been restored to favour among industrialists.

Two techniques are mainly in use; the first is circulation. In this method the hydrogen, under about 3 kg/cm² pressure, enters at the base of the apparatus; any portion that has not reacted escapes at the top, is purified, and returns at the base of the apparatus.

In the dead-end process, the apparatus is shut off. The hydrogen necessary for the reaction is let in under 5–6 kg/cm² pressure. Stirring makes the hydrogen settle on the oil and the pressure in the apparatus decreases, so that it is possible to follow the progress of the reaction.

In both cases the temperature of the operation is around 180 °C. The hydrogenated oil is filtered and usually refined a second time. The catalyst can be used several times.

Hydrogenation makes liquid oils more or less consistent, depending on how far the hardening is continued, i.e. according to the proportion of molecules of saturated fatty acid formed. This enables the chemist really to manufacture tailor-made raw materials. An important result of hydrogenation has been the use for edible purposes of marine oils (whale and fish) which, as they were highly unsaturated and consequently very unstable, were previously unusable. These marine oils now form a reasonable proportion of raw material supplies to the margarine industry.

Interesterification. There are other ways of modifying fats if their physical properties make them unsuitable for use in foodstuffs.

One is interesterification. This consists of modifying the position of the fatty acids in relation to the glycerol molecule. In natural oils the fatty acids are not randomly arranged on the three alcohol groups of glycerol. The number and position of the saturated and unsaturated

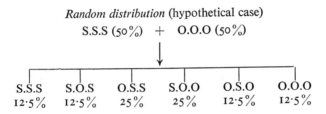

FIG. 3.2. Interesterification. When the mixture, with equal parts, of the two homogeneous triglycerides tristearin (S.S.S) and triolein (O.O.O), is interesterified, it supplies the above mixture of mixed glycerides in which the fatty acids are distributed at random.

fatty acids contained in the triglyceride molecule largely determine its melting point and plasticity. Glycerides containing one or two unsaturated fatty acids are generally liquid or melt at a low temperature, whereas the trisaturated glycerides are generally high-melting solids; tri-unsaturated glycerides are generally liquid. The melting point of margarine should be around 35 °C., and we can see that by rearrangement of the fatty acids on the glycerol molecule so as to obtain the maximum number of mixed glycerides (containing both saturated and unsaturated fatty acids), we can alter the fat favourably for margarine-making.

A diagram of the operation is given in Fig. 3.2. It is a very simple process. The oil is heated to a moderate temperature together with a catalyst, usually 0·1 per cent sodium alcoholate. Rearrangement is very fast. Washing the oil with water removes what is left of the catalyst, and refining can proceed in the usual way.

In industry, however, interesterification is comparatively recent practice. The first patents, granted to C. van Loon in 1920 and 1924, were followed by many others, especially those by Eckey in the U.S.A., describing either new uses or modifications of the process extending its field of application. Controlled interesterification operates at a temperature lower than the melting point of the higher-melting solid constituent. Thus this constituent is withdrawn from the reaction medium as it forms, and interesterification is controlled in the direction desired, either to form the maximum of constituents of high melting point or, on the contrary, to give the maximum yield of liquid products.

The method is extensively used in the U.S.A., Great Britain, Germany, and the Netherlands, either for the rearrangement of lard to produce shortening, or for vegetable oils and fats to produce fatty substances with specific rheological properties.

There are no statistics about the industrial importance of the process, but it would appear that the quantity of interesterified fats in the world may be estimated at between $\frac{1}{2}$ and $\frac{3}{4}$ million tons annually.

Fractionation. This process seems to have been applied in France from 1810 onwards for preparing edible fats by fractional separation of the high-melting constituent. This method was the one used by Mège Mouriès and his successors for the preparation of oleo-margarine. It has been modernized, and fractions can be obtained from certain fats such as palm oil and beef tallow with different melting points and rheological properties from those of the original product.

If the fat is cooled under controlled conditions, crystallization of high-melting glycerides is induced; coarse crystals are formed which are easy to separate off by continuous filtration. The solid crystals of fat are wetted with detergent to effect continuous separation by washing and centrifugation. Continuous operation is possible in both processes.

Fractionation makes it possible not only to obtain raw materials that are well suited to their uses, but also to increase the value of some raw materials by separating the fractions; these are more valuable than the products from which they are derived.

Some components of fats are so important that they are crystallized from a solvent. This gives a very clear separation and enables, for instance, fractions to be obtained from palm oil with all the properties of cocoa butter, which as we know is a valuable product.

Another important use of fractionation is the treatment of oils called winterization. Some oils contain a considerable quantity of glycerides which solidify at temperatures such as those experienced in temperate countries in winter. These glycerides are crystallized and

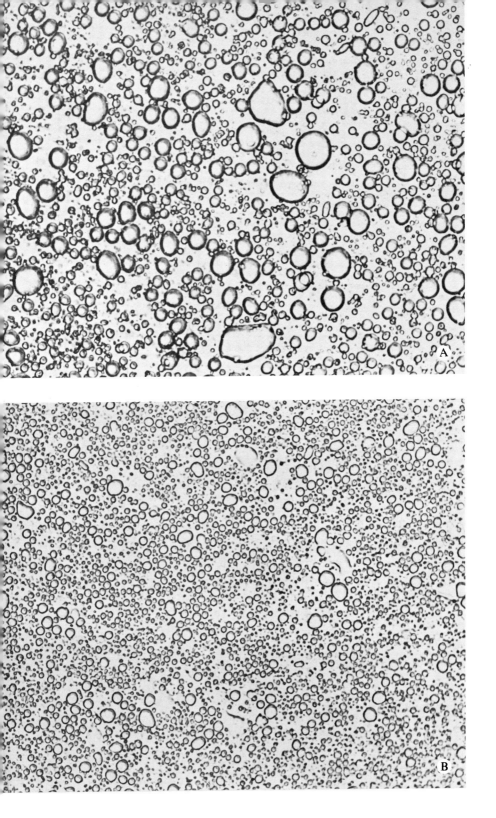

19. The aqueous phase is dispersed in the fat phase, coarsely in specimen A, more finely in specimen B.

20. Manually operated oil-press, of East-Nigerian origin, in the neighbourhood of Oron. Capacity: one ton of oil per week.

separated, and an oil is obtained which remains clear even at 0 °C. In this way the huge quantities of cottonseed oil in the United States could come on to the market for salad oil and cooking oil. The solid portion, cotton stearin, is used in margarine manufacture, either just as it is, or after interesterification.

In short, margarine manufacturers are not only able to use all the resources of edible fats for their products, but can also modify these fats in various ways so that the finished product is as perfect for its purpose as it can be.

The aqueous phase

This may be simply water. Even so, one must make sure that it is fit to drink, is tasteless, and contains no metals that would spoil the keeping properties of margarine. However, more often than not the aqueous phase is whole milk or skim milk, which must first be prepared.

After it has been received from the dairies it must be treated to destroy all micro-organisms that are pathogenic or liable to taint the milk later. This is the object of pasteurization, introduced in dairy practice by Soxhlet in accordance with Pasteur's universally known work on the action of heat on micro-organisms.

The pasteurized and cooled milk has only a slight flavour. To produce a flavour like that of fresh butter, the milk is exposed to the action of lactic bacteria, pure cultures of which have been in use since 1890. The labours of bacteriologists have made it possible to isolate the micro-organisms that help to produce this flavour. They are lactic bacteria of the type *Bacterium acidilactis* which convert lactose into lactic acid (which causes coagulation of the casein) and also produce other shorter acids, such as acetic acid, which help to produce the fresh taste of curdled milk. It was only after the discovery by Kluyver and Derx in 1928 of the really aromatic elements of butter—acetyl methyl carbinol and especially diacetyl—were the micro-organisms which form these compounds isolated. *Streptococcus cremoris* and *S. diacetylactis* will form these compounds from milk constituents and citric acid. The selected lactic ferments, now available commercially, are mixtures of pure cultures of acidifying bacteria and flavour-producing bacteria.

The pasteurized milk, cooled to 20 °C., is then seeded with 1–2 per cent of a leaven obtained by controlled culture on sterile milk of the commercially available ferments. After twelve hours or so the maturing process is complete and the milk is cooled to about 5 °C., pending its use in margarine in a proportion of 5–15 per cent.

Additives. Emulsifiers. The emulsification of the margarine is facilitated if small proportions (generally less than 0·5 per cent) of some emulsifying agents, which are also found in natural products, are added. They reduce the interfacial tension, a force that opposes proper dispersion of the water in the fat.

The first emulsifying agent used was certainly egg yolk. It is mentioned as being in use from before 1900, but it is expensive and not without risk to the keeping quality of the product; it was replaced by dried egg yolk, until in 1902 Fresenius suggested using egg lecithin. This in turn, still being costly, was superseded by soya lecithin, which from 1921 on gained importance as an industrial product.

Other emulsifiers, themselves derived from fatty substances, are in use also. A 1922 Schou patent covers the preparation of an emulsifier based on oxidized and polymerized soya oil, known as 'Palsgaard emulsion oil'; but certainly the most important advance was the introduction of the mono- and diglycerides. These are derived from triglycerides by glycerolysis, i.e. the action of glycerine. A mixture of partial glycerides is formed

$$
\begin{array}{llll}
CH_2 \cdot OOR & CH_2 \cdot OOR & CH_2 \cdot OH & CH_2 \cdot OOR \\
| & | & | & | \\
CH \cdot OOR & CH \cdot OOR & CH_2 \cdot OOR & CH_2 \cdot OH \qquad R = \text{fatty acid} \\
| & | & | & | \\
CH_2 \cdot OOR & CH_2 \cdot OH & CH_2 \cdot OH & CH_2 \cdot OH \\
\text{Tri-} & \text{1–2 tri-} & \text{2-mono-} & \text{1-mono-} \\
\text{glyceride} & \text{glyceride} & \text{glyceride} & \text{glyceride}
\end{array}
$$

and these, since they contain both lipophile (R) and hydrophile (—OH) groups, have an affinity with both oil and water and considerably reduce the interfacial tension. They are very generally used today and, although the American patent by Harris dates from 1933, it is practically certain that they were used in Europe before that date.

The list of emulsifying agents is constantly being added to.

Colouring materials. The colour of margarine is obtained either by using naturally coloured oils, such as palm oil (which contains substantial amounts of β-carotene) or by adding yellow and red colouring matters to the margarine. These are usually a mixture of carotenoids, or pure β-carotene which can now be synthesized. Rocou, or annatto, is a yellowy-orange dye extracted from roucou-tree seeds (*Bixa orellana*), containing the carotenoid bixine; it has long been used in the making of margarine and of butter.

Before the introduction of synthetic β-carotene, colouring agents synthesized from aniline were proposed and in fact used. Nowadays they are hardly used at all.

Using dyes in margarine involves very accurate manipulation if a uniform product is to be obtained. The particular colour of the oils must be determined, as must that of the colouring agent, suitably diluted. Not only the intensity (or concentration) of the colour but also its hue must be measured, the preferred hue for margarine being an orange-yellow with a pink tinge. Lovibond's colorimeter, which is well known and much used, gives a good approximation, yet has to call upon the eye of the experimenter. Light absorption measurements, with definition of the colours of the spectrum at certain wavelengths, are now used; this gives results which are more uniform and above all do not depend on the observer, as the measurement is by photo-electric cell.

Flavouring agents. Margarine, even when made with milk and with diacetyl added, tastes quite different from butter. It took till the 1950s to discover the nature of the constituents of butter flavour; only then could analytical methods reveal and identify the components, which, in minute quantities, are responsible for it. Exhaustive work was carried out for about ten years by the Unilever Research Laboratory team in Vlaardingen, Holland, terminating in the identification of an impressive number of components, of which the δ-lactones are the most important.

These components, which can be synthesized, make a decisive contribution—in very few parts per million—to the flavour of margarine, both when used in its natural state and in cookery.

Additives are also used to improve the keeping properties of margarine which, particularly if it contains milk, is subject to deterioration caused by bacteria. Salt is a bacteriostatic which has been known and used for many years. The quantity used depends on the consumer's taste, but rarely exceeds 3 per cent. For unsalted margarine, harmless preservatives such as benzoic acid or sorbic acid are used. Boric acid was used in the past for preserving butter and margarine, but it has been proved to endanger health and has now been abandoned completely.

The bacteria are not the only agents which affect margarine. The taste and odour of fats are subject to change caused by certain chemical agents, the chief of these being oxygen, the action of which may be promoted by traces of certain metals (iron, copper) acting as catalysts. Effects caused by oxidation of fatty acids are many and various. Hydroperoxides may be tasteless, but we know that aldehydes and ketones are discernible even when only traces are present. Some aldehydes produced by oxidation of isomeric fatty acids of linolenic acid, to which J. G. Keppler devoted special research, can be detected with a concentration of 1 or 2 parts in 10^9, as for example, the trans-6-nonenal. All the effort concentrated on the treatment of oils, especially during hydrogenation, is directed towards avoiding the formation of these isomers, which are veritable heralds of rancidity.

It is very difficult to eliminate the action of oxygen completely, but it can be slowed down by the use of substances known as anti-oxidants since the famous memoir submitted to the Paris Académie des Sciences by Moureu and Dufraisse in 1922. There are anti-oxidants in vegetable oils, the tocopherols (or vitamin E). If the fat does not contain this substance, or has too little of it, some can be added; it can also be replaced by harmless synthetic products with the same properties (BHA and BHT, gallates).

Formulation of the fatty phase

This is the preliminary stage and it is very important. Margarine originally had only one fatty constituent, oleomargarine, and therefore fixed physical properties; it is thus easy to understand what an interest would be taken in modifications of such properties as plasticity, resistance to heat, etc., and the potential economic importance of such changes. In the U.S.A. about 1880 cottonseed oil was introduced into margarine, a move that introduced the first compound fatty phase and made possible the development of an industry which, but for that, would have been at risk owing to shortage of its raw material.

In fact the physical properties and the uses of the product depend to a great extent on the composition of this fatty phase. The physical properties affected are melting point, consistency, plasticity (over a given temperature-range which is usually required to be as wide as possible), and stability in atmospheric oxygen. A final very important point is the price of the finished product.

The materials used are the refined, hydrogenated, fractionated, interesterified, edible oils available on the local market, as described above.

The first step is to determine the properties desired for the product. Is it to be a table margarine for family use? If so, it should have good plasticity at temperatures usually found in the home, and a fairly low melting point; and it must, of course, be possible to store and distribute the product without impairing its quality at the prevailing temperatures in the country of use. In other words, when the physical properties are determined, considerations of climate and season will play a part.

Plasticity is governed largely by the ratio between solid and liquid glycerides at the moment of testing. The percentage of solid glycerides can be determined in many ways: calorimetry, differential thermal analysis, dye dilution, refractometry, and even nuclear magnetic resonance. However, the method most frequently used is the dilatometric study of fats (1) which is based on the fact that the dilatation coefficient of liquids is higher than that of solids. The rise in temperature of a sample of fat is reflected by the melting of some of its components and an increase in volume greater than if the sample had remained solid, the rise in temperature being, of course, taken into account. This difference between the observed dilatation of the sample and the dilatation if it had remained solid has been called the dilatation coefficient and enables the percentage of solid fat at the moment of testing to be determined by calculation of a simple ratio. Instead of a dilatation coefficient a solid fat index (SFI) can be calculated, which gives the percentage of solid fat directly (see Fig. 3.3).

In general it is assumed that 15–30 per cent solids are required to achieve good plasticity at temperatures normally found in a temperate climate. These temperatures vary by 10 °C. or much more, and plasticity should preferably remain the same over this range—in other words the percentage of solid fats should not vary. This is impossible owing to the composition of the fats, and so a compromise must be made to ensure that the observed changes are as small as possible.

The melting point of a fat, as it is described in fat technology, is usually a few degrees lower than the temperature at which it is truly liquid. It is a good guide, but is not sufficient by itself to give information as to plasticity.

It must be recalled that neither melting point nor dilatation index is an additive characteristic. The different glycerides which make up fats have properties of intermiscibility and formation of mixed crystals that cannot possibly be predicted in the present state of our knowledge. One must apply trial and error methods: making a mixture, measuring its characteristics, correcting its composition in the desired direction, and repeating this procedure until the desired characteristics are obtained.

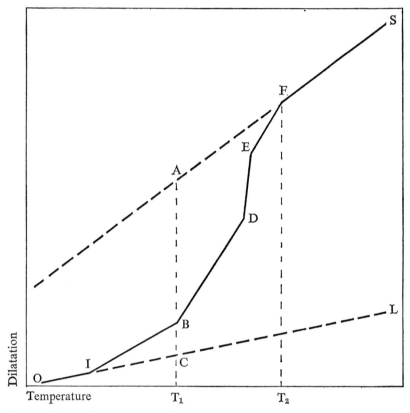

FIG. 3.3. When the temperature is raised the sample, which is solid at O, dilates to O–I. If it were a pure component, it would continue to dilate according to O–I–L, and once it had become liquid it would increase in volume (CA) and dilate according to the line AFS. A fat consisting of several glycerides liquefies in several stages IB–BD–DE–EF, as the solid:liquid ratio changes progressively.

In addition to the plastic properties of fats, we may also wish to fix the content of some specific component, such as essential fatty acids, at a particular level. In this case the choice of liquid components will, of course, take into account the fatty acid composition of the oils in question, which can be found in the tables.

Table 3.2, for example, gives a few margarine compositions taken from recent sources.

1. *Formulae for animal fats (table margarine)*

oleomargarine	60	oleomargarine	40
lard	30	*premier jus*	20
liquid oil	10	lard	15
		liquid oil	25

2. *Formulae for coconut and palm kernel oils*

coconut oil	50	palm oil	50
vegetable oil hydrogenated		palm oil hydrogenated	
(P.F. 42 °C.)	25	(P.F. 44 °C.)	20
liquid oil	25	liquid oil	30

3. *Formulae for hydrogenated oils*

groundnut hydrogenated		palm kernel hydrogenated	
(P.F. 32–4 °C.)	70	(P.F. 34 °C.)	70
coconut	10	coconut	15
liquid oil	20	liquid oil	15

4. *'Single oil' formulae*

cottonseed hydrogenated		sunflower hydrogenated	
(P.F. 28 °C.)	85	(P.F. 44 °C.)	20
cottonseed hydrogenated		sunflower hydrogenated	
(P.F. 42–4 °C.)	15	(P.F. 32 °C.)	60
		sunflower liquid	20

5. *Formulae for bakery margarines*

premier jus	25	groundnut hydrogenated	
palm oil hydrogenated		(P.F. 42 °C.)	30
(P.F. 46 °C.)	25	coconut oil	20
groundnut hydrogenated		palm kernel oil	20
(P.F. 34 °C.)	10	liquid oil	30
liquid oil	40	(For biscuits and raised pastry)	
(For puff pastry)			

6. *Standard margarine made in the United Kingdom during the 1939–45 war*

coconut oil }		whale oil hydrogenated	
palm kernel oil }	40	(P.F. 46–8 °C.)	20
palm oil	7	groundnut oil	20
groundnut oil hydrogenated			
(P.F. 34 °C.)	13		

7. *Recent formulae for products with special characteristics*

(a) *Margarine rich in essential fatty acids*

coconut oil	30	palm oil hydrogenated	
palm oil	10	(P.F. 42° C.)	10
palm kernel oil	15	liquid sunflower oil hydrogenated	35

(b) *Margarine very rich in polyunsaturated fatty acids*

liquid sunflower oil	88	palm oil hydrogenated	6
palm kernel oil hydrogenated	6		

(c) *Margarine using a mixture of interesterified oils*

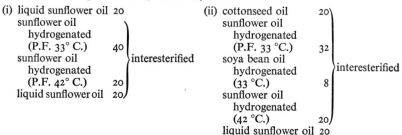

(i) liquid sunflower oil 20
  sunflower oil
    hydrogenated
    (P.F. 33° C.)   40
  sunflower oil   interesterified
    hydrogenated
    (P.F. 42° C.)   20
  liquid sunflower oil 20

(ii) cottonseed oil   20
   sunflower oil
     hydrogenated
     (P.F. 33 °C.)   32
   soya bean oil
     hydrogenated   interesterified
     (33 °C.)   8
   sunflower oil
     hydrogenated
     (42 °C.)   20
   liquid sunflower oil 20

TABLE 3.2. The composition of the fatty phase of margarine may be varied *ad infinitum* and allows for the properties required of the product as well as the raw materials available (formulae collected from the literature from the late nineteenth century up to 1967).

The number of possible combinations is unlimited, as we can see, so availability of supplies and nutritional and other requirements can be taken into account; this is one of the great advantages of margarine.

PRODUCTION PROCESSES

Mège Mouriès's original process was derived direct from butter technology—the only source of information in those days. The use of new raw materials, the necessity of checking, emulsifying and cooling, and later kneading conditions, have effectively brought about a special margarine technology which is very far from those early beginnings. However, a fundamental point has survived from the original process: the necessity for emulsification.

An emulsion is a fine dispersion of a component, called the internal or discontinuous phase, in another in which it is insoluble, which is called the external or continuous phase. In margarine the internal phase is water or milk, the external the fat.

The force which opposes dispersion of immiscible ingredients is interfacial tension. It has to be overcome; to begin with this was achieved by mechanical means such as vigorous agitation of the two components under conditions whereby they remain liquid. Even before 1900 the idea of using emulsifiers was introduced (see p. 96). They facilitate dispersion by reducing the interfacial tension; i.e. the mechanical energy necessary for a given dispersion will be less, or at constant mechanical energy dispersion will be better. The dispersion must be very fine. A good emulsion contains 95 per cent water droplets of a diameter of between 1 and 5 μm, 4 per cent between 5 and

10 μm, and 1 per cent between 10 and 20 μm. There are 10–20 million water droplets in 1 g of margarine.

Besides contributing to the plasticity of the product, a fine emulsion also makes it more resistant to bacterial attack. In a very small droplet a bacterium cannot multiply and soon dies. If the dispersion is coarser the bacterium can live and reproduce, thus causing the product to deteriorate.

Too fine a dispersion, however, can destroy the flavour of the margarine; the flavourings if they are to be perceived must be in aqueous solution, as only water can wet the taste buds. Too fine an emulsion may be absorbed without being broken and the flavour will then remain hidden.

It is probable, if not certain, that the emulsive state favours digestion and assimilation of fats. Emulsification is, in fact, known to be the step preceding digestion of fats.

For all these reasons emulsification must be considered an essential stage for the quality of the product.

The stages of production

These have remained basically the same as in the original process though they have been improved upon considerably.

First the emulsion. It is unstable at the temperature at which it is made, so it has to be stabilized (or fixed) in its finely dispersed state. This is done by cooling. The fat solidifies, trapping the fine droplets forming the aqueous phase. The fat is then solid, but not plastic.

Plasticizing requires kneading, a mechanical process which modifies the arrangement of the crystals, reduces their size, and makes it possible to obtain the plasticity desired. The plasticized product must then be prepared for sale; this is the packaging stage.

In modern processes these various stages, which used to be separate, can be carried out successively or simultaneously.

Batch processes

In the processes the four stages of production, emulsification, solidification or crystallization, kneading, and packaging, are carried out in succession.

This type of process, called the churn–drum, is derived from, and has succeeded, Mège Mouriès's original process. The latter, which has been improved by the construction of metal churns with a double jacket and temperature control, still suffered from the defects of the ice-water solidification method, in spite of the ingenuity of the technicians. The appearance of drums, or, in the terminology of the time, dry crystallization, was such an improvement that the process was adopted very quickly, and the year 1905 in fact saw the birth of the churn–drum process as we know it today.

Emulsification takes place in an enclosed vessel, called a churn, with a double jacket and temperature control. Its capacity may be as much as 2,000 l. It is equipped with two stirrers driven by a powerful motor. The two phases, which are weighed or measured out separately, are brought to the required temperature, then let slowly into the emulsion churn. The stirrers are started up while a temperature slightly higher than the melting point of the fat phase is maintained. When the entire batch has been put into the apparatus, stirring is continued for about 10 minutes, then it is slowed down to enable the emulsion to be removed to the cooling equipment.

The first systems for cooling the emulsion used ice-water, which was brought into contact with the emulsion and then dispersed the emulsion by means of various devices. This was wasteful of refrigeration and fat. The invention in 1905 of cooling-drums, on the surface of which a very thin layer (0·1–0·25 mm) of emulsion could be spread, brought about a considerable improvement (2).

A coolant (brine or liquid ammonia) circulates inside the drums and lowers the surface temperature to -12 to -18 °C. The emulsion sets immediately. It is then scraped off with a knife, which makes the cooling surface available again. The emulsion is distributed in different ways: with two parallel drums, distribution rollers, or troughs. The diagrams which follow give a clear idea of these processes, which were the only ones in use until recently, and are still widely used today (see Fig. 3.4).

The solidified emulsion is in the form of flakes or crystals which complete crystallization in wagons. The temperature rises to about the ambient temperature, but the product should be compacted and then kneaded to obtain its final consistency. The traditional butter kneaders were succeeded about 1880 by rollers with one pair of cylinders, and then between 1910 and 1920 with several pairs; finally continuous kneaders with orifice plates and knives, very similar to those used in soap-making, appeared about 1930. The process is perfected by trough-type kneaders which exercise considerable mechanical action in a very short time.

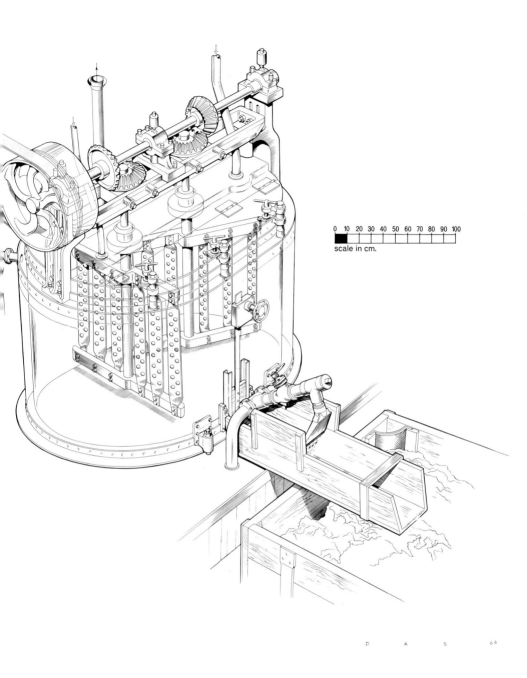

scale in cm.

0 10 20 30 40 50 60 70 80 90 100

D   A   S   66

21. Margarine churn, 1910.

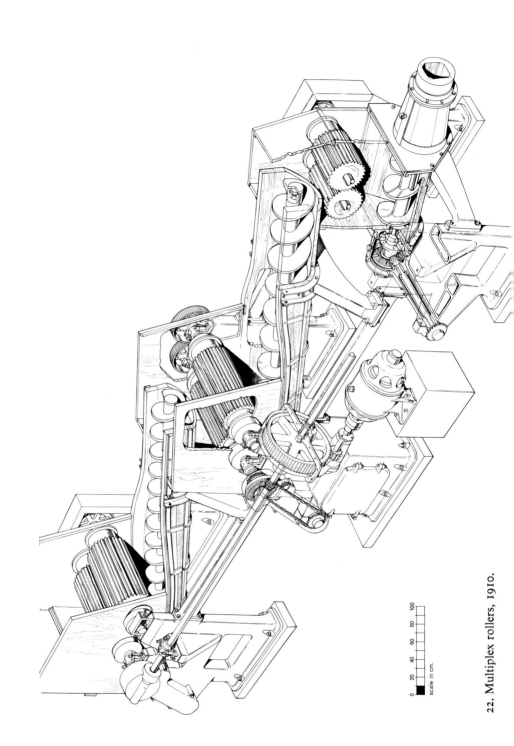

22. Multiplex rollers, 1910.

scale in cm.

0 20 40 60 80 100

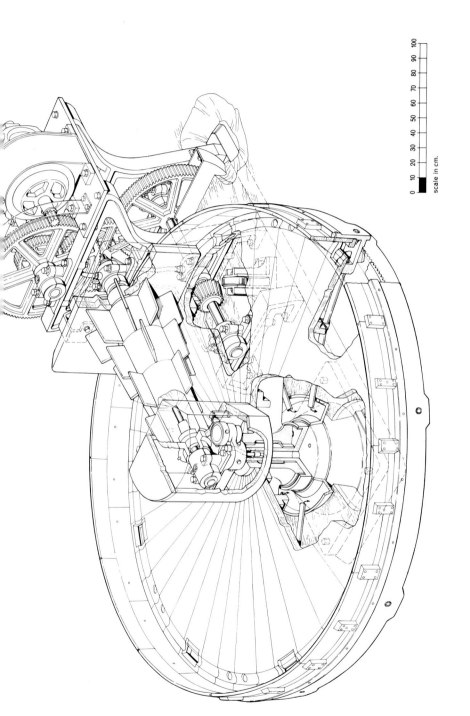

23. The first kneaders came to the margarine industry from the butter industry. They were called 'French Table'.

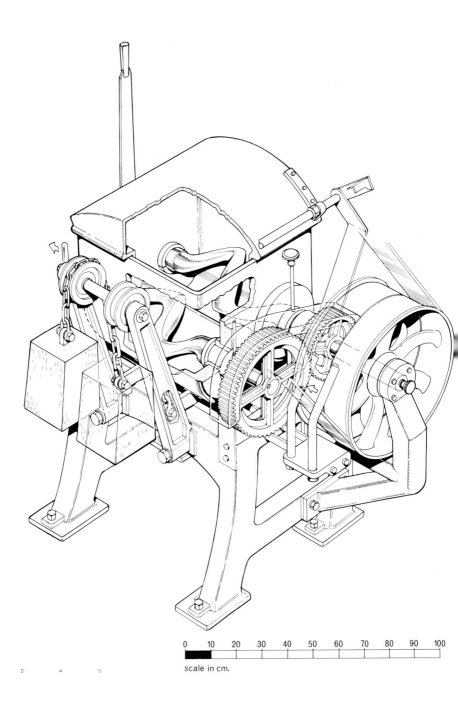

0   10   20   30   40   50   60   70   80   90   100

scale in cm.

24. Mixer of the 'pétrin' type, 1910.

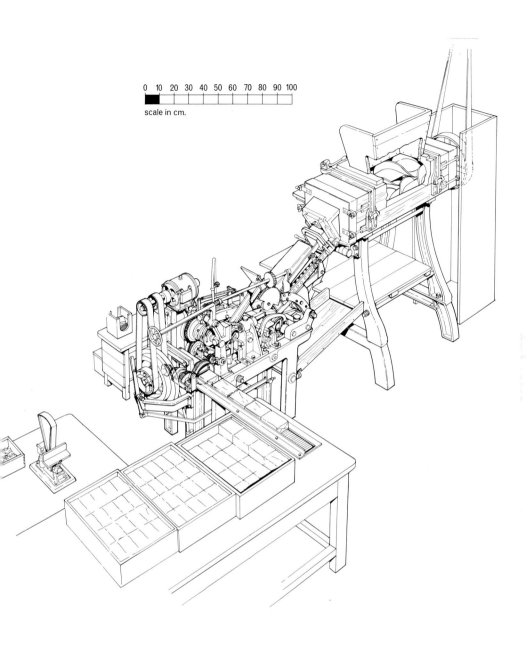

scale in cm.

25. One of the first packing machines, 1910.

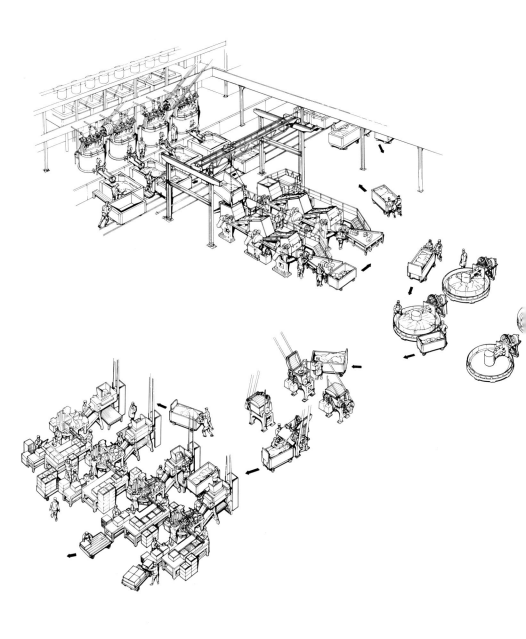

26. General arrangement of a production line, 1910.

27. Cooling drums in the Bromborough, Cheshire, margarine factory, 1932.

28. General arrangement of a production line, 1968.

After kneading the margarine is put back into wagons to await packaging.

Packaging machines are the same for all processes, and they are described at the end of the chapter.

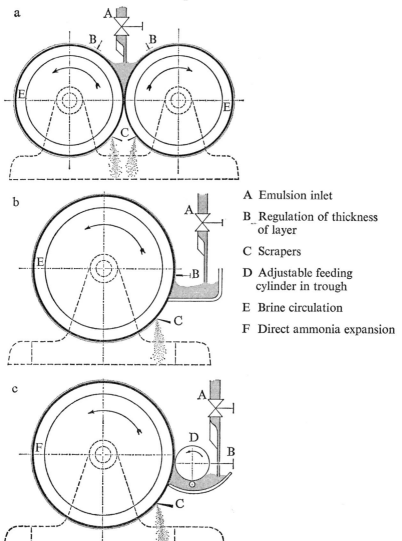

A Emulsion inlet

B Regulation of thickness
   of layer

C Scrapers

D Adjustable feeding
   cylinder in trough

E Brine circulation

F Direct ammonia expansion

FIG. 3.4. (*a*) The emulsion arrives between two drums; its thickness is regulated by rods B. (*b*) The emulsion arrives in a trough and rod B facilitates regulation of the thickness. (*c*) Application is effected by a cylinder which turns in a trough. The distance of cylinder D from the drum regulates the thickness of the emulsion on the drum.

Semi-continuous processes

With these processes, emulsification, cooling, and kneading are carried out continuously; only packaging is separate.

It is easy to imagine different procedures for feeding a cooling-drum continuously. There may be two or more churns working to a programme, or the pre-mixtures (fat plus aqueous phase) may be made in large tanks and conveyed to the drums with an emulsifier system

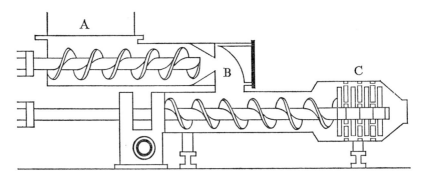

FIG. 3.5. Diagram of a Gerstenberg vacuum complector. The solidified margarine enters at A. It is conveyed by the two worm-screws to kneader C which is made up of orifice plates and knives. The two parallel screws form a sluice at B, enabling a partial vacuum to be obtained in the equipment.

consisting of a pump and a homogenizer under pressure. These continuous emulsifiers were studied in the first instance in the pursuit of a finer and more regular emulsion. The earliest one was Schröder's proposal in 1905, and various more or less improved versions were developed up to 1920, the year that saw the inauguration of continuous systems. The appearance of votators (see Fig. 3.8) about 1938 accounted for greatly reduced interest in continuous emulsification systems.

Lastly, a more modern method: the emulsifier can be fed by a proportioning pump which supplies the required quantities of fat and aqueous phase from separate tanks. This technique was already described, though for the votator, in 1938.

The emulsion thus obtained is applied to a drum similar to those described in the foregoing section, but turning faster and cooled to lower temperatures, around −20 to −25 °C. The fine layer of solidified emulsion is removed as a continuous film and passes straight to the kneading equipment via a buffer tank.

This equipment, involving a roller with a succession of knives and orifice plates, arranged so that they compel the substance to move forward, breaks up the substance a great deal. The kneader, the best-known one being called the complector (3), is fed by continuous

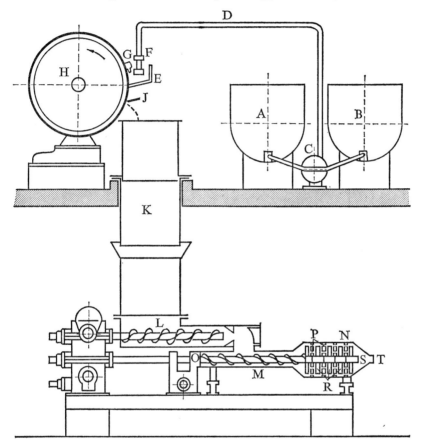

FIG. 3.6. Diagram of a Gerstenberg plant. The plant consists of two pre-mixing vats which supply the emulsifying pump C continuously. The emulsion which solidifies on drum H is removed by scraper knife J and is retained for a few minutes in hopper K before entering the continuous mixer (see Fig. 3.8).

screws which turn in the tubes and, thanks to an ingenious device (see Fig. 3.5), enable kneading to be carried out under a partial vacuum. When the margarine leaves the kneader it passes into wagons and is taken to the packing-room.

Fig. 3.6 gives a diagram of a complector plant; other manufacturers make similar ones. They have a capacity of up to 4·5 tons an hour, and are certainly very attractive if products are to be made in short runs.

Continuous processes

These follow quite a different principle. In the processes described above the emulsion was obtained first, then cooled on the outside of a

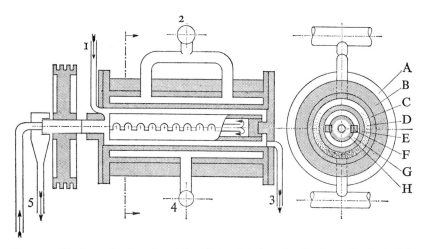

Fig. 3.7. The ingredients enter at I and circulate in tube G, the wall of which is scraped continuously by knives F. The mixture leaves, cooled, from 3. The liquid ammonia enters at 4, circulates in the insulated double jacket D, evaporates and is drawn off at 2 to return to the compressors. Rotor H can be heated by circulation of hot water 5.

drum; continuous methods require a plant which carries out emulsification, cooling, and kneading in one operation. The essential element is the votator cylinder or tubular cooler, introduced by the Girdler Corporation for ice-cream, and subsequently put to numerous other uses, in particular the manufacture of margarine in 1938. A cooling plant (see Fig. 3.7) consists of a pure nickel tube, surrounded by an annular space in which ammonia or any other cooling agent can be expanded. The annular space is itself surrounded by a heat insulator. Inside the nickel tube is a coaxial rotor, the diameter of which is about 20 mm less than that of the tube. This rotor is fitted with scraper blades which are fixed in a special way so that they are brought by centrifugal force to scrape the inner wall of the nickel tube. The speed of the rotor can vary from 400 to 700 rev/min.

The ingredients are brought by a proportioning pump into the end of the tube under a pressure of 15–25 kg/cm². As the substance passes through the cylinder it undergoes vigorous stirring, cooling, crystallization, and kneading in the last parts of the tube when the emulsion is cool and almost solid.

A continuous margarine plant generally consists of a proportioning pump to feed the chilling tubes, and two or three chilling tubes in series (these make up the A-unit). A post-crystallization tube, or B-unit, where the cooled emulsion completes its crystallization, is connected direct to the packaging machine.

The advantages in this method are immediately apparent: the product is kept moving in a closed apparatus, safe from any atmospheric contamination; it is untouched by hand, and the whole process, including packing, lasts 1–2 minutes; the hygienic conditions are practically ideal.

There are of course different ways of connecting the chilling tubes. Fig. 3.8 shows some examples of the possibilities of this process, which is coming more and more into use.

Packaging

The packaging operations prepare the products for distribution and sale. In the early days of the margarine industry the most prevalent packagings were large units; blocks, small barrels, and tubs, which the merchant sold as the customers required, as still occasionally happens with butter and lard. Packets of 250 or 500 g ready for retail sale were originally made up by the manufacturers as a service. It is also a way of making the manufacturer's name and trade-mark known, of ensuring that the customer receives a packet with a standard known weight, and of ensuring that it is handled under strictly hygienic conditions. In Mège Mouriès's day packaging in 250- and 500-g sizes was usual as it was for butter, but very expensive since it was done by hand. Retailing of 5- or 10-kg blocks was also current practice. Commercial requirements, and later the legal regulations, gradually enforced the extension of packaging in units for retail sale. Nowadays almost all margarine is sold in made-up packets, and this may soon become compulsory. Industrial users obtain margarine in larger units, blocks or containers, suited to their needs.

Packaging has progressed in two respects, as regards machines and materials for wrappers and packings.

A good packaging machine should supply packets of correct, uniform weight and suitable shape, at the highest possible rate under very strict conditions of hygiene, and should employ a minimum of

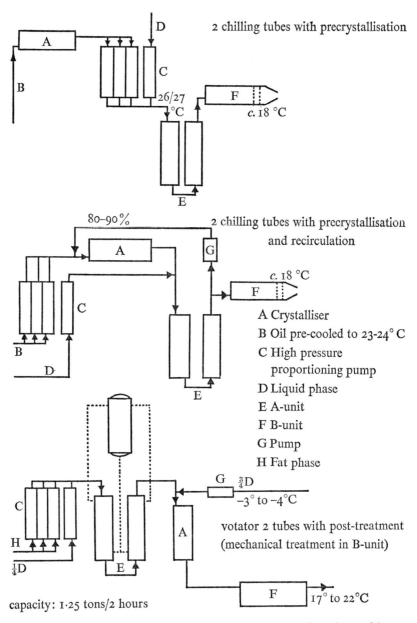

FIG. 3.8. Different votator arrangements. The elements of a plant with continuous production can be combined in different ways as required.

staff. The first packets of margarine were made by hand, probably moulded in wooden blocks, as is still done in some regions for farmhouse butter. They were also wrapped and placed in packing-cases by hand.

The first step towards the perfecting of packaging, dating probably from the 1920s, was to form, by means of a continuous moulding machine—consisting simply of a hopper with two screws which pushed the margarine into a mouthpiece or extruder—a bar of margarine which was cut into regular lengths and produced blocks to be wrapped by hand. The weight was more or less uniform; the labour ratio was high, as a firm producing 1,000 tons of margarine a week had up to 800 people working on packaging.

The second improvement occurred around 1925, when wrapping machines were introduced which, in conjunction with the relevant machines for moulding and cutting, could mould and wrap 60 packets a minute to within 10-15 g. Three or four operators were needed.

About 1930 machines were developed which formed the blocks separately. The margarine was introduced under pressure into a moulding chamber of constant, adjustable size and then ejected by a piston on to a piece of paper above the mould. Precision was greater (2-4 g), and the rate was increased to 70 blocks a minute. Between 1940 and 1950 these machines were improved further; speed and precision increased (80-90 blocks a minute to within 1 or 2 g per block). The emergence of the votator, necessitating fast packing machines connected direct to the B-unit, led to moulding and wrapping machines being developed after 1950 to produce 180 blocks per minute, accurate to within 1-2 g. The latest machines, in which the different steps are carried out in a continuous cycle and not successively, can mould and wrap 220 packets of margarine per minute to within 1 g of the desired weight.

The quality demands made upon wrapping-materials are: impermeability to outside agents, strict bacterial cleanliness, and sufficient mechanical resistance to enable them to be used in high-speed packing machines and stand up to all the hazards of transport.

Greaseproof paper or vegetable parchment, the traditional wrapping-material used in the butter and margarine industries, proved irreplaceable for quite some time. Its main feature is that it is impermeable to grease and water, but lets through light, oxygen, and water vapour. If margarine is to be kept satisfactorily it requires, as do other fats, a packaging material which forms an effective barrier against all outside influences including oxygen, light, water vapour, mechanical impurities such as dust, bacteria, and so on. Great efforts have therefore been made to find something more effective than greaseproof paper.

Much work has been carried out since the Second World War on combining greaseproof paper and thin aluminium foil with the aid of a glue or wax, and such combinations are much used nowadays. Added to the indisputable qualities of aluminium as a barrier, is the fact that it can be decorated in a very attractive fashion; but it does, of course, cost more than greaseproof paper. Plastic films cannot be used direct for margarine as they are scarcely compatible with the high speeds of the packaging machines. However, paper, whether greaseproof or not, combined with plastics, which form a good barrier against oxygen, such as polyvinyl chloride and polyvinylidene chloride, is now used for packaging materials which are already widely used and will probably undergo further development.

During the last few years very soft margarines, rich in unsaturated liquid oils, have made their appearance. These have necessitated the use of containers made either from PVC- or PVCD-covered cardboard or even metal—tin-plate or aluminium.

The wrapped margarine is packed in larger units for transport and distribution. The days of wooden cases seem to be over for good, except occasionally for remote destinations, and the cardboard box has conquered the market. Either compact or corrugated board is used, the latter having the advantages that it weighs and costs less but has the same resistance and better heat insulation. The outers are still largely filled by hand at the output end of the wrapping machines, but for the last twenty years or so machines which carry out this operation automatically, case-packers, have been in existence. If we take into account that machines can open the cases (which are supplied flat) and transfer them to the case-packers, and other machines can seal the filled cases, either with glue or gummed tape, it is clear that a modern production and packaging line really requires a minimum of manpower. To complete this picture, machines have recently made their appearance which arrange the cases on pallets in groups of 1 ton ready to be put on lorries or vans.

29. In 1890 margarine was packed by hand in a labour-intensive packaging department.

30. Modern automatic packing machine used in the Van Den Bergh and Jurgens factory, Rotterdam, 1969. This machine delivers 250 packs per minute and is supervised by one man.

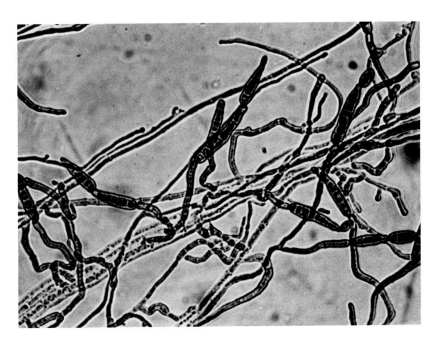

A. *Alternaria* x 400

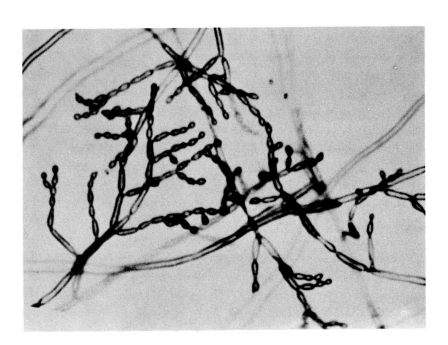

B. *Cladosporium herbarum* x 460

31. Examples of micro-organisms which may cause deterioration in margarine.

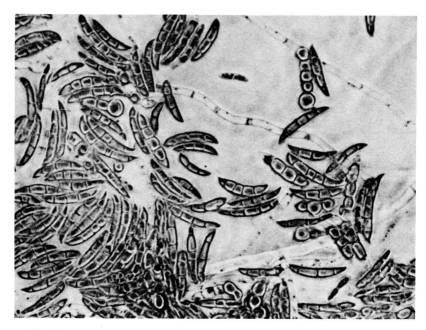

A. *Fusarium* x 400

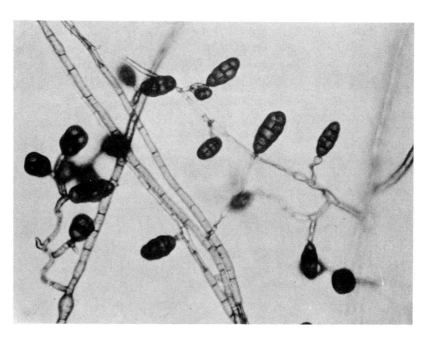

B. *Stemphylium* x 400

32. Other examples of micro-organisms which may cause deterioration in margarine.

PRODUCTIVITY

The margarine industry in Mège Mouriès's day had only one raw material and it was normal to associate the margarine factories with plants for making the raw material oleo.

This link between rendering-plant and margarine factory was customary until the end of the last century, and has in fact been maintained to a point when it might be detrimental to the product (4). In the public mind rendering-plants are associated with extracting the by-products of the meat industry; and from there it is only a short step to looking upon margarine itself as a by-product. This is by no means the case as the history and development of margarine bear witness.

Unlike oleo oil, vegetable fats are found practically all over the globe, and oil-mills are situated for preference near the ports where the oil-bearing seeds or fruits arrive. The oil-mill prepares the refined oils and can thus supply the margarine factories in the area. The crude oils or oil-bearing seeds needed in the making of margarine can also be obtained as such, then refined on the spot and used in margarine. In this way numerous breaks in the transport chain and ever-troublesome handling operations can be avoided. There are many examples of this vertical integration which leads from seed to margarine and which resembles, on quite another scale, the situation in the days of the rendering-plants (raw material and finished product being dealt with on the same premises).

This is only one aspect of the quest for productivity. Like all other industries, the margarine industry has been forced to keep costs down, the more so because margarine is traditionally a relatively cheap commodity.

Productivity can be raised in many ways, but there are two standard methods: the first is to increase the capacity of the plant and exploit the economies of scale, the second is to automate the plant.

Industrial plants rendering beef tallow were localized because the quality of the product could be maintained only by keeping down the time of transport by the slow means then available. The result was obviously to spread production over many small- or medium-sized factories. Equipment suited to the requirements of small-scale production, and a direct imitation of the equipment used for butter-making, favoured this dissemination.

The introduction of vegetable oils and the necessity of refining, then hydrogenating them, was the main reason for building larger units. In fact the pressing of the seed, the extraction of the vegetable oils, hydrogenation, and refining, are almost continuous processes which require little or no extra labour for large-scale production. Investment in buildings, equipment, etc., is not directly proportional to capacity, and even the power consumption per unit of output can be reduced by large-capacity plants.

Oil-mills processing less than 50,000 tons of seed a year are regarded as comparatively small; the number of units handling 200,000–500,000 tons is increasing constantly. Large supplies of refined oils in one locality make it attractive and profitable to install a large-capacity margarine factory there. In this way the large factories, particularly in the Netherlands, Germany, Britain, and France were born. They are near to, or include, a large oil refinery which supplies them with raw materials.

We have shown in the chapter on production how equipment has developed, combining hygienic methods with good quality and economical operation, permitting a higher output with a small staff.

Packaging and handling are still a considerable source of potential saving in many companies. A production chain comprising a continuous plant of the votator type, a high-speed wrapping machine, a case-opener, a case-packer, a case-sealer, and an automatic palletizer (which can serve several lines) can be supervised by two people, and has a capacity of around 2 tons an hour. If we compare these figures with those for the period 1920–30, when in a normal factory the allowance was 30–40 man-hours per ton, we shall have a clear idea of the productivity gains obtained by the margarine industry in the last three or four decades.

There are hardly any precise statistics concerning utilization of labour in the industry. Some figures given by a French company show that the number of man-hours per ton decreased from 40 to 10 between 1930 and 1950, and this decrease has continued since 1950.

The era of change is probably not yet past. The coming about of the European Economic Community may cause a regrouping of the European oil refineries and margarine factories into a small number of very large units. There has not been the same degree of automation everywhere, but this has now become feasible. The only problems are time and money.

HYGIENE AND KEEPING PROPERTIES

Margarine, being made up essentially of milk, water, and partially unsaturated fats, is a perishable food. It may undergo chemical or bacterial deterioration, the main chemical attack coming from oxygen in the air. Refineries also treat the crude oil with great care and use high temperatures only when they have to. They process the oil under vacuum to reduce the oxygen concentration. Some oils that are very susceptible to oxidation are handled under inert gas such as nitrogen or carbon dioxide.

During manufacture margarine is inevitably exposed to the air unless continuous processes are used, with the votator for instance. It is not usually exposed for long, and as the normal temperature in the factory is about 20 °C. the risk of oxidation is considerably reduced. A good air-tight wrapping well-applied to the product will preserve it quite long enough to reach the consumer in good condition.

The action of oxygen on fats is much accelerated by the ultraviolet rays in sunlight. Any direct or prolonged exposure to daylight is a mistake. For this reason the best wrappers also filter the light. Margarine should be stored in the dark or in closed cases. Antioxidants (see p. 159) make it possible to postpone the moment when the change in taste is apparent. Vegetable oils contain natural antioxidants, notably tocopherols, which afford a certain protection.

As mentioned above, some substances encourage oxidation of fats: for instance, metals such as iron and, in particular, copper, which are avoided as far as possible in the production equipment and especially in the water which goes into the margarine. Even sodium chloride, common salt, induces oxidation. Other heavy metals, such as lead and zinc, should also be banned for the same reason. It is, however, most unlikely that they would be present, even accidentally.

The changes undergone by the fats during oxidation are well known. They are particularly evident in deterioration of the taste, generally termed tallowiness or tallow-taste, the technical term being oxidative rancidity. At the final stage of oxidation, very strong-tasting products appear and even in very small concentrations make the fats uneatable.

Other forms of chemical attack on margarine are only accidental: for example, if it is kept near very strong-smelling products in a warehouse or shop it may acquire their taste or smell, for fats easily attract odours. In these cases too a good wrapping may provide effective protection.

Deterioration starting in the aqueous phase, especially if this is milk, is mainly of a bacterial nature. Some of the micro-organisms in our environment are pathogenic, i.e. harmful to human beings, others are useful in the conversion of organic matter, particularly some foods. Good examples of this are the lactic fermentation induced by different species of lactic streptococci, and the action of moulds and yeasts on cheese which induce the much-sought-after ripening. But micro-organisms that are useful for one process may be harmful elsewhere; cheese moulds cause rancidity of fats, especially margarine and butter.

The risks of contamination by bacteria are numerous, and all the greater for being generally invisible or unsuspected. The oils incorporated in margarine are usually sterile, because deodorization requires temperatures which few micro-organisms can survive. If a little water were to be introduced accidentally, micro-organisms would be present again. The aqueous phase is far more vulnerable, and milk, even when pasteurized, easily forms an excellent culture medium for micro-organisms. Water, especially from the mains, is undoubtedly fit to drink, but rarely sterile. It may not be dangerous to drink a few yeast cells, but they should not be contained in margarine. The other ingredients might all be contaminated to some extent by micro-organisms, and so they are generally pasteurized before use.

Besides the contamination arising from ingredients in the manufacture, some may also be carried by the staff or the equipment during production. As a rule the workers have no need to touch the product, but they may touch wrappers or machines and leave behind some micro-organisms, even if they are very strict in their personal hygiene. The packaging materials are rarely sterile and the equipment may be soiled accidentally.

There are, therefore, hazards. Margarine may be contaminated by pathogenic bacteria from water, milk, perhaps even the workers. It could then become a vehicle for disease, as other foods can. All precautions are taken to prevent this. The milk is pasteurized, the water, even drinking water, is re-sterilized, and in modern plants the product is not accessible before it is wrapped. Thorough cleaning of the installations makes it possible to keep microbes at bay and to ensure the complete absence of pathogenic micro-organisms. There is no record of an epidemic being spread by margarine, which makes it something of an exception among foods.

The margarine may be contaminated by bacteria which, though they are not harmful on their own, act on its ingredients and make it unpalatable. This is especially the case with bacteria, yeasts, and moulds which attack the fats, liberate the fatty acids and oxidize them to free fatty acids, aldehydes, and ketones which impart smells and flavours. A wealth of observations has been added to the bacteriology of margarine since Jacobsen's days (1910), making it possible for some of these unwanted micro-organisms to be studied, their origins to be determined, and research to be carried out for their elimination (see Pl. 31, 32).

Apart from water and milk, the main source of infection used to be the equipment, especially when it was made from wood. Extensive use of stainless steel from 1948 on was a great step forward, especially as the engineering experts in the construction of margarine equipment realized the necessity of absolute cleanliness and the limitations that this imposes on the form of the equipment, which must not contain any parts where water can settle and become a seat of contamination.

When describing the battle against micro-organisms we must not forget the bacteriostats and the antiseptics. Bacteriostats are substances which, without killing the micro-organisms, stop their growth and consequently suppress their organoleptic effects. The best-known bacteriostat is salt in a concentration of more than 10 per cent in the aqueous phase, i.e. 1·6 per cent in margarine; but it induces oxidation, and in some countries salted margarine is not liked. For taste reasons too, sugar, which is bacteriostatic in high concentrations, cannot be used either.

Antiseptics destroy good and bad micro-organisms alike; the human body needs assistance from some micro-organisms and strong antiseptics cannot be introduced into the gastric tract without inconvenience. For this reason only antiseptics with a moderate effect, which are often specific in their action, are used in foods; in the margarine industry benzoic and sorbic acids are most used.

Ideally, the action of micro-organisms can best be prevented by producing a sterile product, which the majority of manufacturers do in fact achieve these days. This is thanks to improvements in equipment and procedures and to long training in the principles of hygiene for the staff, who have to be convinced of its importance, not only to themselves but also to the products they make and which, tomorrow, will be foods for them and for others.

Though in many important respects Mège Mouriès's objective has been attained, there are others where more progress can always be made.

In appearance, colour, lustre, and plasticity, margarine is superior to butter; in taste and flavour the recent improvements show excellent results. We have seen that conservation poses no problems provided the raw materials are wisely chosen and sensibly treated, and that elementary precautions are taken in storage. As regards price, though differences exist between the markets of various countries, here too, broadly speaking, the objective has been attained.

In the matter of emulsion success has been only partial. Margarine is, in fact, chiefly an emulsion of water in oil, and consequently there is quite a perceptible difference in the plasticity of the products. On the rheological level the resemblance does not come up to expectations.

On the other hand the model has been surpassed in at least two points. The plasticity of the product can be adjusted at will, either by action on the constituents of the fat phase or by alteration of the production conditions. This accounts for the fact that margarines can be produced that have the same plasticity in different climates; some are fit for spreading directly they leave the refrigerator, and there is also a whole range of products designed for food manufacture or cake- and pastry-making, where the melting point and plasticity are adapted to all the technological pressures of the industries concerned. The nutritional qualities of margarine, too, can be modified with comparative ease, either by action on the constituents of the fat phase, or by the inclusion of useful additives. When the formula is worked out, the newest developments in the field of nutrition can be, and indeed are, taken into account, in many countries; for example, many household margarines today contain a significantly higher percentage of polyunsaturated fatty acids than the traditional products; it may indeed be very high in some cases if the advantage of this addition is recognized. The same thing might happen for every constituent of the fat phase if its advantage came to be recognized by the medical authorities. Nowadays margarine is a product which can be tailor-made; it is important to know the right measurements to make it suit all consumers. The calorific value, which is almost identical for all pure fats, including margarine and butter, might be modified, perhaps lowered. Alteration of the ratio between aqueous and fat phases would do this.

We may also mention that, of the additives, vitamin A and vitamin D have been made compulsory in many countries; margarine thus becomes an excellent vehicle for special fat-soluble nutrients which are beneficial for the health of the community.

Thus margarine functions as a traditional fat, which can be used in all the ways customary for emulsified fats, but is extremely adaptable as regards physical characteristics, chemical make-up, and even economic value (since some raw materials can be replaced by others on considerations of cost). Recent progress in the spheres of production and packaging ensures that the product can be kept for a long time, thus facilitating distribution.

Obviously more progress can always be made: we have already mentioned the nature of the emulsion and some rheological aspects of margarine. Production methods will undoubtedly develop further, leading to more constant quality and even better keeping properties.

But above all we believe that full use will have to be made of the adaptability of margarine, to ensure the best and most economical use possible of the world's raw material resources, and diversification in its range of production in accordance with new patterns of life and consumption and the important achievements in nutritional sciences.

All this unquestionably involves fundamental research, in fields as diverse as physiology and the keeping properties of fats, with particular application in the field of packaging.

NOTES AND REFERENCES

1. Although many writers used the thermal properties of fats to study their composition, notably Normann (1931) and Jensen (1931), the first publication on dilatometry as we now understand the term seems to be Hofgaard's study of 1938.

2. In 1892 Dr. Möllinger had invented a drum filled with ice. This was immersed in the emulsion and removed a film which, when set, was detached before the surface entered the emulsion again. This was the ancestor of the present-day drums.

3. The term 'complector' applies to the plant made by the Gerstenberg Company in Denmark.

4. The French authorities officially linked rendering-plants and margarine factories. During the period 1940–5 the two industries depended on one organization committee, but at that time vegetable oils and fats had already captured a very large share of the market.

The following books and articles, not explicitly referred to in the text, are recommended for further reading:

5. UBBELHODE,W. *Handbuch der Chemie und Technologie der Oele und Fette* (*Handbook of the chemistry and technology of oils and fats*) (Leipzig, 1929).

6. HEFTER,G., and SCHÖNFELD,H. *Chemie und Technologie der Fette und Fettprodukte* (*Chemistry and technology of fats and fat products*) (Vienna, 1937).

7. DEVINE,J., and WILLIAMS,P.N. *The chemistry and technology of edible oils and fats* (London, 1961).

8. BAILEY,A.E. *Industrial oil and fat products* (New York, 1964).

9. ANDRÉ,E. *Les Corps gras* (*Fats*) (Paris, 1964).

10. COCKS,L.V., and VAN REDE,C. *Laboratory handbook for oil and fats analysts* (London, 1966).

11. DEHOVE,R. *La Règlementation des produits alimentaires et non alimentaires* (*Regulations on nutritional and non-nutritional products*) (Paris, 1967).

12. FRITSCH,J. *Fabrication de la margarine et des graisses alimentaires* (*The manufacture of margarine and food fats*) (Paris, 1927).

13. PORCHEZ,G. *Le Raffinage des corps gras* (*The refining of fats*) (Paris, 1938).

14. SCHWITZER,M.K. *Margarine and other food fats* (London, 1956).

15. RUDISCHER,S. *Fachbuch der Margarine Industrie* (*Technical handbook for the margarine industry* (Leipzig, 1959).

16. Reports of the general meetings of the International Federation of Margarine Industries (Scheveningen, 1964) (Munich, 1965) (Geneva, 1966).

17. BOEKENOOGEN,H.A. *La Margarine et sa valeur en physiologie de la nutrition* (*Margarine and its value in nutritional physiology*) (1964).

18. ANDERSEN,A.J.C., and WILLIAMS,P.N. *Margarine* (London, 1965).

19. PORTER LEE,A., and KING,W.G. 'Edible oil—deodorizing equipment and methods', *Oil and soap*, **14** (1937), 263.

20. ROBINSON,A.A. 'Some recent developments in the manufacture of margarine', ibid. **15** (1938), 203.

21. BROWN,L.C. 'Margarine production', *Journal of the American Oil Chemists Society*, **33** (1956), 506.

22. VACHEROT,C. 'Technologie des margarines' ('Technology of margarines'), *L'Alimentation et la vie*, **45**, 4–6 (1967), 115.

23. GONZALEZ MARTINEZ,A. 'Moderna producción de sucedáneos de la manteca. La Margarina' ('Modern production of butter substitutes. Margarine'), *Ion.* **17**, 195 (1957), 562.

24. CRUMP, G. B. 'The technology of margarine', *Progress in the chemistry of fats and other lipids*, **5** (1958), 285.

25. ALLEN, R. R. 'Hydrogenation', *Journal of the American Oil Chemists Society*, **37** (1960), 521.

26. I.T.E.R.G. *Journees d'information sur les corps gras alimentaires* (*compte rendu*) (*Report on information conferences on food fats*), Institut des Corps Gras (Paris, 1962).

27. TOY-RIONT, M. 'La margarine sur le plan international' ('Margarine on the international scale'), *Revue française des corps gras*, **9**, 7 (1962), 395.

28. HEESCH, A. 'Neuzeitliche Margarine Herstellung' ('Modern margarine manufacture'), *Fats and soaps*, **65** (1963), 125 and 205.

29. TUYENBURG-MUYS, G. 'Détermination et numération de la microflore d'association d'emulsions alimentaires' ('Determination and counting of the associated microflora in food emulsions'). 'II. Etude microbiologique de la margarine' ('Microbiological study of margarine'), *Laboratory practice*, **15** (1966), 975.

30. BOLDINGH, J. *et al.* 'Constituants de la graisse de beurre présents à l'état de traces' ('Constituents of butter fat present in trace amounts').
'I. Isolement et identification de lactones aliphatiques saturées' ('Isolation and identification of saturated aliphatic lactones'), *Revue française des corps gras*, **13** (1966), 235.
'II. Activité optique des lactones aliphatiques saturées par la technique de dilution isotopique' ('Optical activity of saturated aliphatic lactones by the technique of isotope dilution'), ibid. **13** (1966), 327.
'III. Détermination quantitative des δ-lactones saturees par la technique de dilution isotopique' ('The quantitative determination of saturated δ-lactones by the technique of isotope dilution'), ibid. **13** (1966), 463.
'IV. Isolement et identification de lactones aliphatiques insaturées' ('Isolation and identification of unsaturated aliphatic lactones'), ibid. **13** (1966), 731.

CHAPTER FOUR

Nutritional and Dietetic Aspects

ALASTAIR FRAZER

HISTORICAL DEVELOPMENT OF THE NUTRITIONAL SCIENCES

THE discovery and development of margarine spans a century during which the science of nutrition was born and has undergone great changes. Over the same period there have been vast developments in the wider fields of science, technology, and medicine that have also been of interest to margarine manufacturers. As new knowledge relevant to margarine production became available, it was used to develop and improve the product for the benefit of the customer.

Nutrition is currently defined as the science of food and its effect on life and health. To appreciate the great use that has been made of advancing nutritional knowledge in the development of margarine, we must review the scope of the nutritional sciences as we know them today.

The chemistry and physics of raw materials and of food

The first consideration is the chemistry and physics of the raw materials from which food is made and of the final product. When margarine was first invented, knowledge of the chemistry and physics of fats was rudimentary. It is now known that in examining the chemical composition of a food material, it is necessary to consider detail at the molecular level, as small differences in molecular structure can significantly alter biological effects. Chemical considerations must include not only major ingredients, but also incidental components or contaminants, as well as any substances that may be added for technological or other reasons. Physical characteristics of the raw materials or the food made from them may be important: for example, solubility, melting point, plasticity, crystal or fibre structure, and texture. The physical properties may have a technological role in the manufacturing processes involved in making the food material or they may impart desirable properties to the end-product so that it is more acceptable to the consumer. To obtain the most suitable raw materials and foods detailed specifications are necessary for all substances used, as well as for the end-product. In this way it is possible to ensure that the raw materials possess the characteristics needed, that they are of suitable quality for food manufacture, and that any undesirable impurities are excluded or controlled. At the turn of the century remarkable developments in oil and fat technology, especially the introduction of hydrogenation, brought radical changes to margarine manufacture. It was now possible to use a much wider range of fats and oils, while still controlling the physical properties of the final product.

The basis for specifications for raw materials or foods

These specifications are largely determined as a part of quality control procedures and they may have to conform to legislative requirements. In general the specifications of raw materials and of foods tend to be based more on technological and legal than on nutritional requirements. This seems a rational approach in a community that consumes a varied and individually chosen mixed diet. However, it presupposes that individuals in the community are sufficiently well-informed about the principles of nutrition and about the foods they buy to provide a balanced and nutritionally sound diet for themselves and their dependants. Taking into account the complexity and variety of modern foods, the lack of adequate knowledge about many of the effects of food on the body, the emotional attitude that often develops about our daily food, and the difficulties of achieving a high level of understanding of scientific matters in the community as a whole, it seems likely that many people are unable to devise a nutritionally sound diet for themselves or others. The increasing knowledge of positive nutrition, which involves the consideration of the effects of food on the body and not just the results of nutritional inadequacy, now makes it possible and desirable to pay more attention to the nutritional properties of food in times of plenty as well as in periods of deprivation.

This change of attitude is reflected in the historical development of the use of raw materials for margarine manufacture. In the early days the main objective was to make margarine as like butter as possible. Particular attention was therefore given to appearance, texture, flavour, and fat content, and preference was often given to fats of animal rather than vegetable origin. However, with the possibility of using a wider range of fats, and especially those of vegetable origin, the fatty acid composition of margarine also changed. The full importance of this change was not immediately appreciated and for a number of years no special effort was made to retain the *cis cis* polyunsaturated fatty acids present in many vegetable oils in the finished margarine. Advancing scientific knowledge revealed, however, that these fatty acids do not have the same effect on metabolism as saturated fats. This has resulted in the development of margarines rich in these polyunsaturated fatty acids, an appropriate choice of raw materials and processing to give an acceptable product.

The development of food from raw materials

A food is developed from the appropriate raw materials by the application of various technological procedures. During this process it may be necessary to alter the natural nutritional properties of the raw material, for example, its vitamin content might be modified. It is also possible to add certain substances that may facilitate production of an acceptable food by modifying texture, consistency, flavour, or appearance, or may improve storage properties, or enhance nutritional value, or replace lost nutrients. Some of these technological procedures are illustrated in Fig. 4.1. The food material may also be packaged and treated in other ways before it is finally consumed. It is important that any modifications that these various procedures may make to the chemical and physical properties of the food should be fully known and their nutritional significance, if any, appreciated.

The technological processes used in margarine manufacture have undergone great changes since margarine was first invented. At each step, however, extensive studies on the nutritional effects of the modifications introduced have been undertaken. About the beginning of the twentieth century vitamins were discovered. It was soon appreciated that margarine is an excellent vehicle for the fat-soluble vitamins, and they were either included in the raw materials used or added to the final product. Nowadays synthetic vitamins A and D are available and it is a statutory requirement in most countries today that they should be added to margarine. Many other advances have also affected margarine manufacture. For example, the wide use of domestic refrigerators has resulted in the production of margarines that spread easily even when kept at a low temperature.

Digestion and absorption, metabolism, and utilization
Shortly before margarine was invented, Claude Bernard (1) had
demonstrated the importance of the preparation of fat for absorption
by the action of bile and pancreatic juice. Controversy persisted

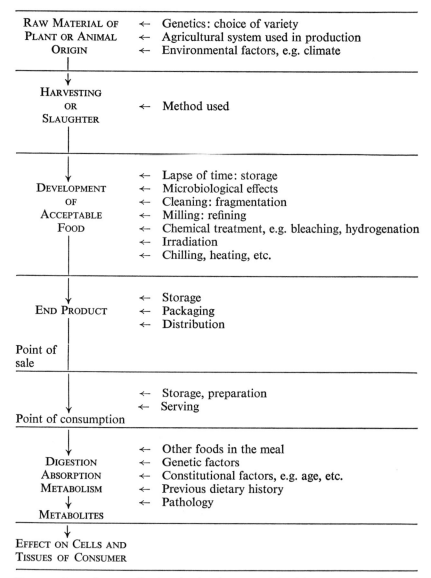

FIG. 4.1. Some factors affecting the development of food from raw materials and
its eventual effect on the tissues of the consumer.

about the absorption of fats throughout most of the following century (2). However, there is now fairly general agreement on the main mechanisms of fat absorption. This controversy has not been of great moment to margarine manufacturers, since the fats in margarine were shown to be efficiently absorbed from the intestine and to be comparable in this respect with other dietary fats.

The absorbed material has to be transported from the intestine to the various tissues and it becomes distributed and mixed with a great many similar molecules already present in the body. The body generally works like a competent housekeeper. Considerable stores of many important commodities are kept; these are continually being drawn upon and replenished as they are used up for various purposes, such as provision of energy, building or replacement of cells and tissues, or other bodily activities. Thus, for each molecular species there is a metabolic pool; the body draws on this pool for its needs and the pool is replenished by the absorbed nutrients. Thus, each metabolic pool is regularly turned over. While this concept of metabolic pools is helpful in the better understanding of many nutritional phenomena, it must be emphasized that there may be more than one metabolic pool for some molecular species and these pools may be turned over at different rates. Changes may also occur due to shortages or excessive amounts of other substances or to other factors. Such complications are, however, well known to the housewife.

Of greater importance to the margarine manufacturer was the discovery that the type of fatty acid in the diet has metabolic implications. Thus, there are certain fatty acids, such as *cis cis* linoleic acid, which are necessary dietary constituents for many animals and probably also for man. These essential fatty acids are needed for the formation of many other important substances in the body. Furthermore, many polyunsaturated fatty acids, not only linoleic and linolenic acids, but other acids, such as those in fish fats, have an effect on the level of blood lipids. The resting level of blood lipids may have some significance in relation to such important medical problems as deposition of fat in blood vessel walls, the rate of ageing, or even ischaemic heart disease. The possible relationship of unsaturated fats in the diet to these various medical problems is complex. Nevertheless, the nature of the fatty acids in the dietary fat must be given careful consideration. Margarine is undoubtedly an important potential source of unsaturated fatty acids. Margarine manufacturers have consequently carried out extensive studies in this field. This is the most important area of scientific development at the present time so far as margarine manufacturers are concerned.

Food safety

Until relatively recently it was generally thought that food was inevitably good for the consumer and that only gross impurities, such as adulterants or contaminants or deteriorated food materials, could do harm. The early margarine manufacturers took good care to ensure that the materials they used were of good quality and free from such hazards. However, more recently, and especially in the last twenty years, a much greater awareness of potential hazards to the consumer from foods themselves or from food additives has developed. This is a natural outcome of the much wider range of raw materials used, the greater complexity of technological processes applied, and the increased number of food additives available. It is now well recognized that many natural food materials may include components that can have undesirable effects; the technological preparation of such materials will include procedures to control such hazards. Substances not usually found in foods may be added for technological reasons, and the biological effects of such additives require careful study to ensure their safety-in-use. The food additives may induce changes in the food material that give rise to toxic substances, so that treated foods as well as the food additive itself should be examined. Methods have been devised for the effective evaluation of the safety-in-use of new food additives, and their use is nowadays largely controlled by permitted lists. Margarine manufacturers have been fully aware of these developments, and the various ingredients included in margarine and the processes employed for its manufacture have been subjected to extensive study along generally accepted lines.

THE COMPOSITION OF MARGARINE

The main components of margarine are shown in Table 4.1. (3). Of these the most important is fat, which usually forms about 80 per cent of the product; some 16 per cent is water and salt, and the remainder consists of other ingredients added for technological purposes. Some of the differences in composition required by law in different countries are summarized in Table 4.2.

Examination of Table 4.2 shows the effect of legislation on margarine composition in several countries. The permitted levels of fats and oils and water and salts are fairly uniform, in the region of 80 per cent and 16 per cent respectively. The amount of milk products or butter-fat permitted varies widely. In many countries addition of

I. FATS AND OILS	About 80 per cent
Beef tallow or products	Coconut oil; palm kernel oil
Mutton tallow or products	Palm oil, olive oil, arachis oil
Pig lard	Cottonseed oil
Whale oil: fish oils	Soya oil; sunflower seed oil

II. OTHER COMMON FOOD INGREDIENTS	About 16 per cent
Water and salts, mainly sodium chloride	
Milk and milk products	Usually restricted to 10 per cent if
Vitamins, mainly A, D, and E	permitted
Other food materials:	
lecithin, egg yolk, wheat flour,	Small quantities
soya flour	

III. ADDITIVES

Colours: various, especially carotene and annatto
Flavours: various, especially diacetyl
Emulsifiers and stabilizers: various, especially lower glyceride polymerized oils
Preservatives: boric acid, benzoic acid, sorbic acid, if permitted
Anti-oxidants: tocopherols, gallates, BHT, BHA, if permitted
Anti-spattering agents
Indicators: potato flour, sesame oil

TABLE 4.1. Ingredients of margarine.

butter-fat is prohibited; in those countries in which it is allowed, it is commonly limited to 10 per cent or less. Rather more surprising is the variation in the permitted quantities of vitamins A and D. In relatively few countries the addition of these vitamins to a certain level is a statutory obligation; in most of the others addition is permitted, but not enforced; a few prohibit it. Preservatives other than common salt are prohibited by a number of countries. Where a preservative is allowed, benzoic acid is the most popular; sorbic acid has been introduced by two countries. The use of anti-oxidants other than those already present in raw materials is generally prohibited; some countries allow the use of approved anti-oxidants. The most popular added colours are annatto and carotene; it is difficult to see why colours permitted for other foods should be prohibited on

Country	Fat or oil Min. per cent	Milk fat Max. per cent	Water Max. per cent	Vitamin additions	Preservatives other than common salt	Anti-oxidants other than those naturally present in oils used	Colouring agent	Flavouring agent	Indicators	Comment
Argentine	80	5	16	—	Prohibited	—	Prohibited	—	Sesame oil (10%); wheat or potato starch (0·1–0·3%)	
Australia	No statement	0·1	16	—	Prohibited. Tasmania — boric acid (0·3%)	—	Prohibited in some states	—	Potato starch (0·1%) in some states	State variations
Austria	80	Prohibited	18	Permitted	Benzoic acid (0·2%)	Not generally permitted	Permitted list	Permitted	Potato flour (0·2–0·3%)	
Belgium	82	10	No statement	Permitted	Sorbic acid	Permitted list	Permitted	Permitted	Sesame oil (2·5%); potato flour (0·2%)	
Brazil	82	10	16	A obligatory; D optional	Sodium benzoate (0·1%)	Permitted list	Vegetable colours permitted	Diacetyl permitted	Cottonseed or sesame oil (5%)	
Canada	80	0·02 (varies)	16	Newfoundland A and D obligatory. Permitted other provinces	Benzoicacid (0·1%)	Permitted list	Some prohibition (varies)	—	—	Province variations
Czechoslovakia	82	Prohibited	18	—	Benzoic acid (0·2%)	—	Permitted list	—	Potato starch (0·2–0·3%)	
Denmark	80	3	16	A and D obligatory	Prohibited	Permitted if lard or tallow used	Permitted	Permitted	Sesame oil (0·3%)	
Eire	No statement	10	16	No statement	Prohibited	—	Permitted	Permitted	None	
Finland	80	5	16	With permission	With permission	With permission	Permitted list	With permission	Potato flour (0·5%)	
France	No statement	10	16	Prohibited	Prohibited	Permitted list for industrial margarine	Prohibited (Natural coloured oil permitted)	Diacetyl permitted	Rice or potato starch (0·2%)	
West Germany	80	3	No statement	Permitted	Sorbic acid (0·12%)	Ascorbic acid and tocopherol permitted	Annatto and carotene permitted	Permitted list	Sesame oil (10%) or starch (0·2–0·3%)	
Great Britain	80	10	16	A and D obligatory	Prohibited	Permitted list	Permitted list	Permitted	None	New

Country									
Italy	84	Prohibited	No statement	Prohibited, except with special permission	Sorbic acid (0·05%)	Permitted list	Permitted in table margarine	Permitted list	Sesame oil (5%)
The Netherlands	80	1	16	A obligatory	Benzoic acid (0·2%); Sorbic acid (0·1%)	Prohibited	Annatto and carotene permitted	Permitted	None
Poland	80	4	—	—	Benzoic acid (0·2%)	—	Permitted list (includes phenylazo β naphthol)	—	Potato starch (0·2%)
Portugal	80	10	16	—	Prohibited	Permitted list	Annatto and carotene permitted	—	Potato flour (0·5%)
South Africa	80	10	16	A and D obligatory	Benzoic acid (0·2%)	—	Prohibited, except natural oil colour	Permitted list	Starch (0·025%)
Spain	70	Permitted	25	Permitted	Sorbic acid	Octyl gallate	Permitted list	Diacetyl permitted	Potato starch (0·2%)
Sweden	82	Permitted and declared	16	Permitted and declared	Permitted list	Permitted list	Permitted	Permitted list	None
Switzerland	84	Free	16	With special permission A optional	Prohibited	—	Permitted list	Prohibited	None
United States of America	80	Permitted	No statement	Permitted	Benzoic acid (0·1%); Sorbic acid	EDTA (0·0075%)	Permitted list	Diacetyl or other butter flavours permitted	None; Stearyl citrate permitted

India and Pakistan have special regulations for a vegetable margarine, *vanaspati*.
Emulsifiers, lecithin, and monoglycerides are generally permitted in most countries.

TABLE 4.2. Summary of legal requirements on main margarine ingredients.

safety grounds in margarine. In general, flavours that are permitted in other foods are allowed, or else no regulations exist—diacetyl is specifically permitted in a few countries. Indicators are still required in most countries, but now that chromatographic methods of analysis are generally available, their use is no longer really necessary.

In this chapter the greatest emphasis will be placed on the fats and oils in margarine, but some of the other ingredients have considerable nutritional importance. When each ingredient is considered, the general points of nutritional importance and the nutritional properties of each of the constituents will be discussed and possible interactions with other ingredients will be considered. The nutritional significance of the margarine ingredient will be compared with any comparable ingredient in butter where this is relevant and assessed in the context of the diet as a whole.

THE NUTRITIONAL PROPERTIES OF FATS AND OILS

The fats and oils which occur in margarine are essentially esters of fatty acids with glycerol—these are the common neutral fats widely distributed in both animal and plant tissues. Their nutritional properties will now be considered in greater detail.

The digestibility and assimilability of fats (4, 5)
When fats are ingested they pass into the small intestine, where they come into contact with the pancreatic juice. The enzyme, lipase, in this juice attacks the glycerides and liberates free fatty acids. Pancreatic lipase shows a marked preference for the links attaching the fatty acids to glycerol in positions 1 and 3 (i.e. not the one in the middle of the molecule). The main products of pancreatic lipolysis are di- and monoglycerides and free fatty acids; only small amounts of glycerol are usually liberated. The glycerides, longer-chain fatty acids, and bile salts present in bile, which are added to the intestinal contents at the same time as the pancreatic juice, bring about fine dispersion of the fat. This finely dispersed fatty material is absorbed into the intestinal cells. With ordinary dietary fats about 97 per cent or more is absorbed. A small amount of dietary fat remains unabsorbed and is passed out from the body in the faeces. If fat absorption is interfered with, the amount of fat in the stools may be greatly increased. This can occur because of lack of pancreatic lipase, lack of bile salts, or damage to the absorbing intestinal mucosa. The

digestibility of fats can be measured by feeding a known amount and by estimating the amount of fat passed in the faeces. Care must be taken not to be misled by fatty material in the faeces that is not of direct dietary origin.

Metabolism, transport, disposal, and utilization of fats (6) (see Fig. 4.2)
When the fatty material enters the intestinal cell, it may pass through into the body as fatty acid and become incorporated into the appropriate metabolic pool. This is certainly the fate of butyric acid. Other fatty acids, especially those with chains longer than ten carbons, become resynthesized into more complex lipid molecules. They may be resynthesized back into triglycerides, they may form phospholipids, especially phosphatidylcholine or lecithin, or they may link up to form esters with cholesterol. To transport the glyceride from the intestinal cells to the body tissues, complexes are formed with proteins—these lipoproteins contain protein, phospholipid, cholesterol, and glyceride. The lipoprotein molecules can also stabilize a fine emulsion of glycerides and these fine particles of fat, which may be up to 0·5 μm in diameter, are called chylomicrons. The chylomicrons leave the intestinal cell and pass in the lymph up the thoracic duct, which is a lymphatic channel that opens into the left jugular vein in the neck. The fatty material that passes by this route thus avoids the liver and enters the general circulation. When the fine emulsion of fat enters the circulation, it causes a visible milkiness of the plasma. The fat passes round the body in the blood stream and some of it is removed into the adipose tissue or fat depots, which are a store of glyceride fat. Within 3–5 hours all these fine fat particles will have disappeared; some of the fat will have been deposited in the fat depots, some will have been oxidized to produce energy, and some will have been used for making many other different sorts of molecules. Another lipase has been demonstrated in the body which plays a part in the clearing of these fine fat particles from the blood stream. This lipase acts on glycerides in chylomicrons and liberates fatty acids, which become attached to plasma proteins, especially albumen. These fatty acids can be readily used for energy production or broken down to building units from which other important molecules can be made. In a few people this lipolytic enzyme that helps to clear blood fat particles is deficient or ineffective; in such people the finely dispersed fatty material is not cleared from the blood and goes on accumulating until remarkably high blood fat levels are reached.

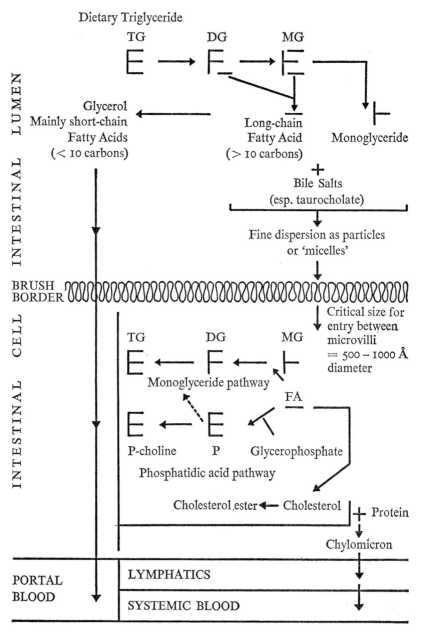

FIG. 4.2. Summary of digestion and absorption of fats.

The effects of fats on the body

Dietary fats are important nutrients in their own right, as they are a major source of energy. They also provide the suitable medium for the ingestion and absorption of fat-soluble vitamins and they help to make food more palatable. When taken in fairly large amounts, fats delay gastric emptying; in excessive amounts they may even cause vomiting. However, an adult human subject can tolerate 150 g or more of fat a day; the average fat intake in Britain and most comparable countries is 100 g or more daily. Fats have an effect on blood fat levels. As already described, the ingestion of fat gives rise to a marked increase of glyceride fat and other lipids in the blood for a period of 3–5 hours, with visible milkiness of the plasma. However, even when this lactescence has completely disappeared, the clear plasma still contains lipids as lipoprotein complexes. The amount of fat in the diet to some extent determines the level of β-lipoprotein retained in the clear blood plasma. This lipoprotein is rich in cholesterol, so the blood cholesterol level is also affected. These alterations in the levels of β-lipoprotein and cholesterol are related to the nature of the fat ingested; the significance of this in chemical terms will be more fully discussed later.

Lipids tend to accumulate in blood-vessel walls. This deposition may start early in life, and it progresses with age. All people of middle age or older have considerable lipid deposits in various blood-vessel walls. The lipids involved are the same as those found in lipoproteins: phospholipids, cholesterol, and glycerides. The deposits are referred to as atheromatous plaques. These plaques may be small and rather insignificant; however, they can become much more extensive and the surface of the blood-vessel over them may become damaged, may become the site of formation of blood clots, or may break down and ulcerate; at a later stage the atheromatous lesion may become calcified (7). People who have high blood levels of β-lipoprotein or cholesterol for any reason may also have advanced and severe atheromatous changes in blood vessels; however, all people showing advanced atheroma do not necessarily have a high level of β-lipoprotein and cholesterol. If the blood cholesterol and β-lipoprotein is high, the patient may have small yellow tumours in the skin—these are called xanthomas. They consist of phagocytes or scavenging cells that are heavily loaded with these same lipids. If a high level of β-lipoprotein and cholesterol is present, it can often be significantly reduced by the administration of appropriate fats; this may also cause the disappearance of some of the xanthomatous deposits. The ingestion of appropriate unsaturated fats caused a reduction of the atheromatous deposits in blood-vessel walls in animals (8), but it is not known whether such an effect occurs in man. The significance of atheromatous plaques in blood-vessel walls varies according to their site and their severity. If the plaques are confined to large vessels, such as the aorta, and if they are only of moderate extent, they may be of little importance. On the other hand, if the surface of the plaque is damaged so that further clotting may occur, and if the changes have occurred in smaller vessels in which blood flow may be affected, the effects can be serious. The function of the affected blood-vessel is important; if it is one of the coronary blood-vessels which supply the heart muscle with blood, interference with its functional efficiency might be fatal. Severe atheroma of the coronary arteries may be an important factor in some cases of coronary thrombosis; it must be emphasized, however, that marked atheromatous changes in the coronary vessels have not been found at autopsy in all people who have died from coronary thrombosis. Other factors are undoubtedly involved. There are some indications that dietary fats might have some effects on the many factors involved in blood coagulation and thrombosis, but nothing definite has yet emerged. It is a field that requires further exploration.

It may be concluded on present evidence that dietary fats undoubtedly affect blood lipids, both in the short term after a fatty meal and in the longer term. It is possible that modification of the blood lipids may play a part in the deposition of lipids in blood-vessel walls. However, if modification of atheromatous plaques occurs, this would not necessarily improve or prevent ischaemic heart disease, since the atheromatous changes may not be at relevant sites and other aetiological factors may be involved. It is not known whether ingestion of fats influences blood coagulation or thrombosis; more information on this subject is urgently needed.

The importance of the chemical and physical characteristics of fats in determining biological effects

The molecular characteristics of the fatty acids or glycerides must be considered in some detail, as they determine the biological effects of the fat. The main features include chain length, the presence of unsaturated double bonds, and the number and position of these double bonds and the configuration of the hydrogen atoms about them (see Fig. 4.3).

Saturated fatty acids

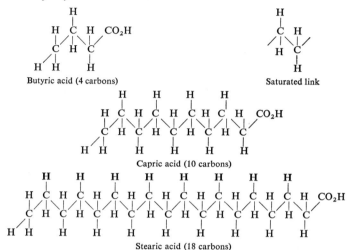

Unsaturated fatty acids

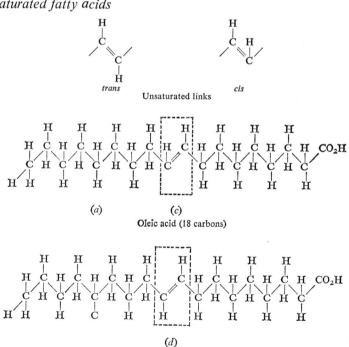

Polyunsaturated fatty acids

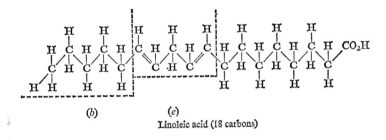

(b)   (e)
Linoleic acid (18 carbons)

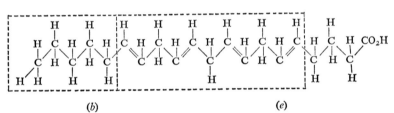

(a)   (e)
Eicosatrienoic acid (20 carbons)

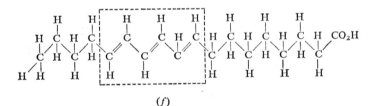

(b)   (e)
Arachidonic acid (20 carbons)

(f)
α Elaeostearic acid (18 carbons)

FIG. 4.3. Molecular characteristics of fats and oils of biological significance.
(a) Head group, which does not confer essential fatty acid properties.
(b) Head group associated with essential fatty acid properties.
(c) *Cis* configuration about the double bond.
(d) *Trans* configuration about the double bond.
(e) Two or more double bonds separated by methylene groups—a feature of essential fatty acids if configuration *cis* throughout.
(f) Conjugated double bonds—no essential fatty acid properties.

Each of the characteristics will be discussed separately.

Chain length. As the chain length of a fatty acid is increased, the melting point becomes higher, as illustrated in Table 4.3 (5). This

	Melting point (°C.)	Digestibility (per cent)
Mutton	50	88
Oleostearin	50	80·1
Venison	51·4	81·7
Trilaurin	49	97·3
Trimyristin	56	76·6
Tripalmitin	66·5	27·9
Tristearin	70	18·9
Hydrogenated cottonseed oil	46	83·8
	54	68·7
	63	24·0
Hydrogenated lard	55	63·2
	61	21·0

TABLE 4.3. Melting point and digestibility of fats and oils (after H. J. Deuel, Jr.)

affects digestibility. Fatty acids with a melting point well above body temperature are relatively poorly absorbed, unless there is an adequate amount of liquid oil present to act as a vehicle. This may partly account for the fact that a high proportion, often 40 per cent or more, of the fat that remains unabsorbed and is passed out from the body in the stools is stearic acid. Difficulty in the absorption of long-chain fatty acids is not entirely due to melting point, however, since erucic acid, which has a chain length of 22 carbons, but a melting point of 31 °C., also tends to be selectively rejected (8).

The common fatty acids have an even number of carbons in the chain; the number varies from 4 in butyric acid to 18 in stearic and up to 24 in other fatty acids found in nature. The chain length of saturated fatty acids affects their biological behaviour. The shorter fatty acids, with 10 carbons or less, are readily released from glycerides in the intestinal lumen, but they do not become resynthesized into glycerides in the intestinal mucosa. Consequently, they are transported mainly in the portal blood and add to the appropriate fatty acid pools in the liver. The fatty acids with a chain length of 12 carbons or more are resynthesized into glycerides in the intestinal mucosa, and are subsequently transported as chylomicrons. The chain length therefore determines the immediate fate of the absorbed fat (9, 10).

Fatty acids are broken down in the body into 2-carbon fragments which are used for the production of energy or for the construction of other molecules. From this point of view there are no important differences between the main dietary fatty acids. Fatty acids with an odd number of carbons, although much less common in the diet, present no special nutritional problem.

Degree of saturation of fatty acids. In saturated fatty acids hydrogen atoms are attached to all the available links on the carbon chain. In some fatty acids, however, carbons may be linked by a double bond, and the chain then contains two less hydrogen atoms. This double bond can be attacked by a halogen, such as iodine, so that the amount of iodine taken up by a fatty acid under standardized conditions is a measure of the number of unsaturated double bonds present. The number of double bonds present in a fatty acid may be as many as six. Oleic acid is one of the most widely distributed fatty acids; it has 18 carbons, like stearic acid. However, stearic acid is saturated, but oleic acid has one double bond. This affects its properties; for example, in its natural form it has a lower melting point than stearic acid, and it is liquid at body temperature. Its utilization in the body does not appear to differ greatly from that of the long-chain saturated fatty acids, especially when it is ingested in a mixture of fatty acids. Oleic acid can be hydrogenated and converted into stearic acid in the rumen in ruminant animals and in the lower parts of the small intestine in man; this reaction is carried out by the intestinal flora. Unsaturated fatty acids are preferentially selected for the esterification of cholesterol.

Polyunsaturated fatty acids—siting of double bonds and configuration (11). Double bonds can be distributed in many different ways in the carbon chain of a fatty acid. From a biological viewpoint this distribution is important. Generally speaking conjugated fatty acids in which double and single bonds alternate do not possess useful biological properties, and some of them may even be toxic. More useful to the body are fatty acids in which the double bonds are separated by a methylene group, as illustrated in Fig. 4.3. A classical example of such a fatty acid is linoleic acid. This is a dietary essential for many animals, and it may also be a necessary nutrient for man. Substances become dietary essentials if they are needed for some purpose in the body and cannot be synthesized in the cells or tissues in sufficient amounts. Linoleic acid is needed by the body because it is the starting material from which another important fatty acid, arachidonic acid, is made. Arachidonic acid has 20 carbons and 4 double bonds which are separated from each other by methylene groups. It is an important part of phospholipid molecules, which help to form the membrane structure of mitochondria. The mitochondria play a vital role in energy exchange mechanisms in every cell.

However, the presence of two or more double bonds separated by methylene groups is not the only requirement for an essential fatty acid. It is also necessary for the double bonds to be spaced correctly in relation to the methyl end of the fatty acid molecule. If the formulae for linoleic and arachidonic acids are studied in Fig.4.3, it will be seen that the first double bond is at the sixth carbon counting from the methyl group. This is an important characteristic of this family of essential fatty acids (12). If the structure of eicosatrienoic acid is examined in Fig.4.3, it will be seen that it also has double bonds separated by methylene groups, but the spacing in relation to the methyl group does not meet the specification for an essential fatty acid given above. This polyunsaturated fatty acid is formed from oleic acid instead of from linoleic acid; it is often found in the tissues in animals that have been deprived of linoleic acid, and is not effective as an essential fatty acid.

The specifications for the structure of an essential fatty acid are not yet complete; the configuration of the hydrogen atoms about the double bonds must also be taken into consideration. If the hydrogen atoms have the *cis* configuration (see Fig.4.3) the fatty acid has a lower melting point than the corresponding *trans* isomer. Thus, a change from *cis* to *trans* configuration can alter the digestibility of a fat. The form of linoleic acid that functions most effectively as an essential fatty acid is that with *cis cis* configuration; that is to say, the hydrogens of both double bonds must have the *cis* arrangement. *Trans* isomers of linoleic acid are much less effective as essential fatty acids. Some further molecular features of essential fatty acids have more recently been defined. Their relationship to prostaglandins is of physiological rather than nutritional interest and is fully discussed elsewhere (13).

Polyunsaturated fatty acids have another interesting biological property—they tend to lower the resting blood lipid levels, especially in those in whom relatively high values are found. This effect is illustrated in Fig. 4.4 which is taken from one of the classical studies of the late Dr. Bronte Stewart (14).

If there is a high proportion of saturated fats present in the dietary fat, there is a tendency for the levels of β-lipoprotein and cholesterol to increase; if the proportion of polyunsaturated fatty acids is increased, the amount of these lipids in the resting blood plasma is decreased. The linoleic acid series of fatty acids have this effect; so also do many marine fats that are not effective as essential fatty acids in the treatment of essential fatty acid deficiency in animals. In general, *trans* acids tend to have less effect, so that *cis* configuration may also be important in this context.

The position of the double bonds in the carbon chain and the *cis cis* configuration are therefore both important determinants of essential fatty acid function. The inclusion of the *cis cis* linoleic acid family of fatty acids is essential in the diet of the rat for maintenance of good health (15). There is evidence that it is also needed by infants and that abnormalities may develop if the intake is too low (16, 17). The requirement of adult human subjects for *cis cis* linoleic acid is more problematical, since a clear-cut deficiency syndrome could not be demonstrated after long periods of deprivation (18).

The effects of processing or storage on the chemical and physical properties of fats

The fats and oils selected as raw materials may be subjected to a number of processes in the course of margarine manufacture. Since the biological properties of the fats are closely related to their chemical and physical characteristics, the possible effects of these procedures will be briefly considered—more detailed information is provided in other chapters.

Refining. The fats and oils are subjected to the usual refining processes. These convert the crude materials into edible oils and fats. Various contaminants are removed. In the case of soya bean oil, special treatment is given to prevent flavour reversion. As might be expected, the general effect of these refining processes is to increase the acceptability of the fat or oil and to make it more wholesome. No significant changes in useful biological properties occur.

Fractionation. In the early days of margarine manufacture, beef tallow was extensively used. The value of this material could be improved by removing a proportion of the more saturated fatty acids.

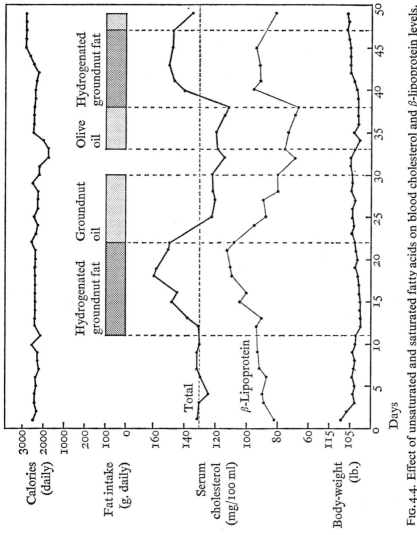

FIG. 4.4. Effect of unsaturated and saturated fatty acids on blood cholesterol and β-lipoprotein levels.

(From B. Bronte Stewart, *Brit. Med. Bull.* **14** (1958), 243. With permission.)

This was achieved by application of cold filtration. The alteration of the proportion of saturated and unsaturated fatty acids improved digestibility and assimilability; this material contained little poly-unsaturated fatty acid.

Hydrogenation (see p. 91). The introduction of hydrogenation as a means of modifying the physical properties of liquid oils to make them suitable for margarine manufacture was a major step forward. Hydrogenation, as its name implies, makes unsaturated fatty acids more saturated. If a mixture of unsaturated fatty acids is hydro-genated, the more unsaturated fatty acids are modified first. Not only is hydrogen introduced into the double bonds, thereby eliminating them, but the process of hydrogenation may also bring about other important structural changes. Thus, the position of the double bonds may be changed, and the configuration of the hydrogen atoms about the double bonds that remain may be altered from *cis* to *trans*. The actual number of double bonds saturated with hydrogen can be assessed from the change in the iodine value. The effect on the bio-logical properties of the polyunsaturated fatty acids may, however, be much greater than the change in iodine value indicates, as bio-potency may also have been reduced due to a shift of the double bonds in the carbon chain or to change of configuration from *cis* to *trans*. If hydrogenation is taken far enough, the effect on the propor-tion of saturated to unsaturated fatty acids and the consequent increase in melting point of the mixture could significantly affect digestibility of the fat. There have been extensive developments in the application of hydrogenation procedures to fats for margarine manu-facture. Careful choice of raw materials, catalysts, and conditions provide great flexibility. The complex technological aspects are not of special nutritional significance and are more fully discussed else-where (Chapter Three). In the manufacture of margarine the hydro-genation process is carefully controlled, so that the final product is acceptable to the consumer and readily digested and assimilated.

When hydrogenation was first introduced, manufacturers used the process mainly to obtain suitable physical properties in the finished product and not much attention was paid to preserving polyun-saturated fatty acids. Thus, the final *cis cis* linoleic acid content of many margarines at that time was of the order of 5–7 per cent, as compared to 1–3 per cent in butter. Over the last twenty years, however, the attitude has changed and methods have been developed which will allow the production of margarine containing up to 50 per cent or more of polyunsaturated fatty acids.

Considerable attention has been paid to the biological effects of *trans* fatty acids (19). At present there is no reason to suppose that they have any harmful effect; they are metabolized and utilized in the same way as other fatty acids, but they have little essential fatty acid function, nor do they exert the same effect as polyunsaturated fatty acids on blood lipid levels. *Trans* fatty acids are found in milk and butter (20); they probably arise from hydrogenation in the rumen. *Trans* acids are also found in human adipose tissue; where they are presumably derived from the diet.

Oxidative rancidity (21). In the presence of molecular oxygen, unsaturated fatty acids may undergo oxidative changes. Hydroperoxides are formed and they are potent oxidizing agents; they will destroy oxidizable substances in the diet, such as vitamins A and E, and they give rise to a large number of carbonyl compounds as secondary oxidation products. They may also assist in the formation of polymerized products. Oxidative rancidity is a chain reaction; once it has started to develop it is difficult to control. The changes are catalysed by various metals or metal-containing compounds. Fatty acids can be protected from these oxidative changes by the presence of anti-oxidants or sequestering agents that bind catalytic metals. Many oils contain natural anti-oxidants, such as tocopherols, and these may be useful in margarine manufacture; some marine oils are relatively deficient in anti-oxidants and are readily oxidized. The products of oxidative rancidity are toxic. Probably the most deleterious substances produced are the hydroperoxides, small polymers, and cyclic fatty acids, which are only formed under special circumstances. Carbonyls, due to secondary oxidation, and larger polymers appear to be relatively harmless. The polymerized oils are not readily absorbed. Oxidative rancidity is usually associated with an unpleasant taste and odour of the fat; however, when oils are used for deep frying the more volatile products may be lost, but potentially harmful compounds that are not readily detected by taste or smell may accumulate in the residue. However, this is not likely to occur with margarine, since it is not used for deep frying.

Effect of heating. The heating of oils containing hydroxy acids may result in the formation of lactones (22). These have been demonstrated in butter fat, and they are increased after heating. The biological properties of compounds of this nature require scrutiny. Lactones play an important part in flavour development, and those of importance in margarine manufacture have been shown to be harmless to the consumer. This is a complex subject that is only of marginal nutritional interest, but of great importance to margarine manufacturers. It is fully discussed elsewhere.

| | PERCENTAGE OF FATTY ACIDS | | |
| | Saturated | Unsaturated | |
		Oleic	Linoleic
Beef or mutton tallow	48	48	3
Pig lard	40	47	11
Coconut oil	90–2	8–10	—
Palm kernel oil	83	17	—
Palm oil	48	42	10
Shea butter	42	50	4
Olive oil	10	81–3	7
Groundnut oil	17–20	60	20
Cottonseed oil	25	45	30
Soya bean oil	12–15	25–30	50–5 (5–9 linolenic)
Safflower oil	10–14	25–35	55–65

TABLE 4.4. Proportions of saturated fatty acids, oleic and linoleic acids in fats and oils used in margarine manufacture.

Oils and fats chosen as raw materials for margarine manufacture

At one time it was common practice to classify fats as animal or vegetable, according to their origin, and to assume that the former would contain more saturated and the latter would contain more unsaturated fatty acids. This is fallacious, as can be seen from examination of Table 4.4. Beef and mutton fat are certainly saturated fats, but pig lard may contain a considerable amount of linoleic acid, depending upon the nature of the feed used. Many seed oils are highly unsaturated, but coconut and palm kernel oil are largely saturated fats. It is necessary to categorize oils and fats according to their chemical composition, irrespective of their origin (23). Those used in margarine manufacture can be grouped as follows:

(a) *Fats with high content of long-chain saturated fatty acids, and low linoleic acid*

This group includes beef and mutton tallow, which were extensively used in the early days of margarine manufacture. Ruminant animals consume large amounts of polyunsaturated fatty acids in grass and other feeds; however, the flora present in the rumen hydrogenate them. The tallows contained rather too much saturated long-chain fats, and a more useful material was made by cold filtration which removed some high melting point material. This material is useful in margarine manufacture, and is still occasionally used when it is available at an economic price. Beef fat is better than mutton fat because the latter is liable to impart an undesirable flavour to the margarine.

(b) *Oils with high content of medium-chain saturated fatty acids and low linoleic acid*

Included in this group are coconut oil and palm kernel oil. They contain large amounts of fatty acids with 12 or 14 carbon chains, and practically no linoleic acid. They are useful in margarine manufacture and are said to impart sweetness to the product.

(c) *Oils with a high content of unsaturated fatty acids and low linoleic acid*

Such fats as palm oil, olive oil, shea butter, and some pig lard may be placed in this group. They commonly contain a lot of oleic acid, but relatively little (less than 10 per cent) linoleic acid.

(d) *Marine oils*

This group includes whale oil and other fish oils. These contain large amounts of polyunsaturated fatty acids, but have a low linoleic acid content.

(e) *Oils with high content of unsaturated fatty acids and medium linoleic acid*

The main oils in this group are groundnut oil and cottonseed oil. Some pig lard may be included in the group. The linoleic acid may amount to 15–30 per cent.

(f) *Oils with high linoleic acid content*

This group includes soya bean oil, corn oil, and sunflower seed oil with a linoleic acid content of 50 per cent or more. Soya bean oil contains a considerable amount of linolenic acid, and it has to be specially processed to avoid giving an unpleasant taste and odour to the product.

The margarine manufacturer blends a selection of these oils with two main objectives. First, to provide an acceptable product with the properties wanted by the consumer, using those fats and oils which are suitable and available at an economic price. Thus, the margarine produced must have the right appearance, texture, spreadability, flavour, digestibility, and price. Secondly, the nutritional value of the margarine must be satisfactory. Vitamins A and D are added to the required level. The content of *cis cis* linoleic acid may be varied from about 5 to 50 per cent or more of the fatty acids present.

	Minimum percentage cis cis *linoleic acid*
Echo	4
Stork	4
Summer County	4
Tomor	15
Blue Band	15
Flora	30

TABLE 4.5. *Cis cis* linoleic acid content of some brands of margarine.

The fats and oils used have been varied considerably from time to time during the hundred years that margarine has been produced, and also from one manufacturer to another. In the early days, there was a tendency to use fats of animal origin, especially beef tallow or products from it. In Britain there has been a considerable swing away from these fats to marine oil and groundnut oil, but other oils are also used according to the market situation. In America there has always been a greater tendency to use vegetable oils. In Norway fish oils have been popular, while in India the special margarine, *vanaspati*, must be made from vegetable oils alone.

The nutritional significance of the fats and oils in margarine
In considering the nutritional significance of the end product it is necessary to distinguish between those margarines in the preparation of which no particular attempt has been made to retain a high *cis cis* linoleic acid content, and those in which this has been a definite objective (see Table 4.5).

The nutritional value of margarine as an energy source. A vast number of digestibility and other biological studies have been made on margarine (5, 21, 24). These have been carried through many generations of animals. All this evidence shows that margarine is readily digested and absorbed, that it supports health and growth as well as any comparable food material. It has no harmful effects on the animals or their offspring, even when eaten in large amounts over thirty to forty generations. Fats and oils in margarines are just as well utilized for energy purposes as those in the raw materials from which the margarine was manufactured.

The processes that have been used may, however, have modified the biological effects that the polyunsaturated fatty acids in the raw materials originally had. Thus, the margarine may have a relatively low essential fatty acid content and may have little effect on blood lipid levels; on the other hand, if the polyunsaturated fatty acids have been preserved, margarine is a good source of these nutrients.

The other constituents of margarine will not have any adverse effect on the digestion and assimilation of the fats and oils. The natural anti-oxidants present in the raw materials may help to delay oxidative changes.

In comparison with butter there are no significant differences so far as the digestibility, assimilability, and availability for energy production of the contained fats are concerned. From an energy point of view, the differences in fatty acid composition are not sufficient to warrant any comment. In the diet as a whole, margarine fats are a satisfactory alternative to butter fats on general nutritional grounds.

The nutritional significance of margarine as a source of cis cis *linoleic acid.* Margarines with a high *cis cis* linoleic acid content require special consideration. Provided that the linoleic acid present has retained its biopotency, it will contribute significantly to the dietary supply of essential fatty acids and may also cause some lowering of blood lipid levels, especially in those people in whom they are already elevated. This type of margarine is of great value in any therapeutic diet that aims to lower the consumer's blood cholesterol or β-lipoprotein level. Its use is clearly indicated in patients with raised blood lipid levels or other signs of hypercholesterolaemia, such as xanthomata. There would seem to be some basis for recommending the use of a margarine with a high linoleic acid content in patients with atheromatous lesions, irrespective of whether they show evidence of ischaemic heart disease. It certainly will not have any deleterious effect, and margarine is one of the more palatable ways of consuming polyunsaturated fatty acids in reasonable quantity.

It has been claimed that essential fatty acid deficiency is the basis for a number of disease states, including coronary heart disease (25). With the exception of the studies in babies already mentioned, no one has substantiated this claim. Investigation of the lipid pattern in groups of patients with severe atheroma and ischaemic heart disease did not reveal any accumulation of eicosatrienoic acid (26), which is found in animals deprived of *cis cis* linoleic acid. There would seem to be no adequate scientific case for recommending supplementation of ordinary diets as consumed in Britain and similar countries with extra *cis cis* linoleic acid in order to avoid essential fatty acid deficiency, since this deficiency state has not been shown to exist.

The administration of larger amounts of polyunsaturated fatty acids in the diet might lower the level of blood cholesterol and β-lipoprotein in consumers. It is already agreed that this might be worthwhile in any person with unusually high blood lipid levels. However, is this a sensible objective for the community as a whole? To assess this wide question of possible effect on the health of the whole community, it is necessary to review briefly the present status of knowledge about the aetiology of atherosclerosis and ischaemic heart disease.

There is adequate experimental evidence to show that replacement of saturated by appropriate polyunsaturated fats in the diet may reduce the blood cholesterol and β-lipoprotein level; it may also cause the disappearance of some xanthomata. The possibility that atheromatous changes are modified remains speculative so far as man is concerned. There is evidence that people with high blood cholesterol and β-lipoprotein levels, such as those with genetically determined hypercholesterolaemia, tend to suffer from severe ischaemic heart disease at an early age. However, many of these hypercholesterolaemic subjects do not respond well to dietary polyunsaturated fats. There has been an increasing interest in recent years in the possible relationships between a different group of lipids and ischaemic heart disease. These lipids may be more related to dietary carbohydrate than to dietary lipid. It may well be the case that the response to dietary fats or carbohydrates differs from one individual to another, according to genetic make-up.

Another line of argument that has been advanced to support the idea that diet plays a vital role in the aetiology of ischaemic heart disease is the view that the incidence of coronary thrombosis has greatly increased during the last fifty years, and that this can be linked to changes in dietary habits over the same period. The basic premise that there is a great increase in the incidence of coronary heart disease in this country over the last fifty years has, however, been challenged recently by Robb-Smith (27). He concludes that this view is not valid so far as Britain is concerned.

This is such an important conclusion in relation to the nutritional aspects of this problem that it deserves further examination. In the sixty years under consideration many things have happened; perhaps one of the most striking is the introduction of a great many effective chemotherapeutic agents, as a result of which deaths due to infective conditions have been greatly reduced. As a result of this and other factors, the over-all death rate has decreased. About as many people die each year now in Britain as 100 years ago, but the population has more than doubled. In 1900 44 per cent of deaths were in people over 45; in 1960 92 per cent were in this age category. The Registrar-General's returns only indicate a single cause of death for each person who dies. It is true that the number of people each year who are said to have died from coronary thrombosis has greatly increased since 1930. However, this is not necessarily due to an increased incidence of this disease. Several other factors might be involved— for example, there might have been a change in the age-pattern of the population so that more people are at risk, or there may have been changes in diagnostic methods or the diagnostic labels used for certification. Study of these possibilities reveals that there was indeed a striking change in the age pattern of the British community over the last 50–100 years. In recent years there has been a growing preponderance of middle-aged and older age-groups. Since coronary thrombosis particularly involves these groups, this change in the age pattern certainly contributes to an increased prevalence of this disease. Examination of the causes of death recorded by the Registrar-General reveals that the deaths per 100,000 recorded as due to degenerative heart diseases were 417 in 1900 and 445 in 1960. Between these two dates there were considerable fluctuations, especially between 1920 and 1939, but these changes can be explained by alterations in the method of recording adopted by the Registrar-General's department and they were predicted by the authorities when the changes were introduced. Another striking fact is that the proportion of these cardiac deaths attributed to coronary and arteriosclerotic heart disease has changed from 22 per cent in 1939 to 82 per cent in 1960, with a reciprocal decrease in deaths due to myocardial degeneration. If one seeks to explain the marked increase in coronary disease over this period, one must also explain the equally dramatic disappearance of death from myocardial degeneration. It may be concluded that ischaemic heart disease is of great importance in our community today; it is a major cause of death. The apparent increase in the incidence of coronary disease might be largely illusory and attributable to changes in the age pattern of the human community and alterations in the diagnostic labels used in death certification.

If Robb-Smith (27) is correct, then allegations that changes in dietary habits, whether affecting fats, carbohydrate, or the general level of caloric intake, have a causal relationship to ischaemic heart disease fall to the ground. This does not mean that dietary control may not be important in the management of patients with ischaemic heart disease, or that dietary factors may not contribute in various ways to these patients' problems. It does, however, considerably reduce the force of any argument for changes in the diet of the community as a wholesale preventive measure against ischaemic heart disease.

What is needed is a prospective study on an adequate scale which would show unequivocally any influence that supplementation of the diet with polyunsaturated fatty acids might have on the incidence of atherosclerosis and ischaemic heart disease. Such studies are extremely difficult to do and cost vast amounts of money; an investigation along these lines has been planned in the U.S.A. Studies in patients with myocardial disease have been carried out (28). Supplementation of the diet with polyunsaturated fatty acids appears to reduce the incidence of recurrent symptoms, but the response seems to be confined to subjective effects. Interpretation of such studies calls for great caution.

The factors concerned in the aetiology of ischaemic heart disease are complex. Conservative individuals are likely to agree with an authoritative committee set up in the U.S.A. to study this problem, who concluded (29) that there was not sufficient evidence to justify a recommendation that the community's dietary intake of linoleic acid required supplementation. People with a more experimental approach to life's problems, however, might think that increasing the daily intake of polyunsaturated fatty acids by consuming an appropriate margarine could do no harm and might eventually be found to be beneficial to health.

INGREDIENTS OF MARGARINE OTHER THAN
OILS AND FATS (3)

Margarine contains a number of other ingredients. Some of these may be present in the raw materials in small amounts, but it may be noted that refining removes the traces of polycyclic hydrocarbons or mycotoxins that might be present in some crude natural oils. The water content of margarine is controlled by law, as already noted. The ingredients that call for further comment are those that are added for technological or nutritional reasons. The most important groups are vitamins, preservatives, anti-oxidants, colouring agents, flavours, dispersing and stabilizing agents, and substances added to prevent spattering. Before considering these groups in detail, some of the broad principles involved in the use of food additives and the assessment of their safety-in-use will be discussed.

Some general principles governing the use of food additives

Effective control of the use of food additives is based on the acceptance of certain general principles which will be found discussed in the First Report of the Joint F.A.O.–W.H.O. Expert Committee on Food Additives (30). They are:

(i) The use of a food additive should be beneficial to the consumer. For example, it may help to provide a more acceptable product or one that keeps better; or it may improve availability or lower cost.
(ii) A food additive should not be used to mislead the consumer as to the nature or quality of food.
(iii) A food additive should be technologically efficacious and should not be used in greater amounts than are necessary to ensure that the technological objective will be achieved.
(iv) A food additive must be safe-in-use.

It is essential that all concerned with food production should understand and accept these general principles. Working on this basis, it is possible to establish controls without interfering unduly with the development of new ideas and techniques in the field of food science and technology.

Assessment of safety-in-use (31) (see Fig. 4.5). Certain features of the potential hazards that might arise from the use of a food additive call for comment. A food additive may be consumed every day for the whole life-span; it may be eaten by the young or the old, as well as by healthy adults; it may be consumed by pregnant or lactating women, and by the sick as well as the healthy. For all these reasons it is generally agreed that a large margin of safety is desirable.

In order to assess safety-in-use it is first necessary to have adequate specifications for the food additive, so that it can be readily identified and kept free from undesirable impurities. Secondly, the biochemical

M.—12

behaviour of the substance is studied: its digestion, absorption, metabolism, distribution, and eventual elimination from the body. These studies are made in appropriate laboratory animals. Any effects on the animals of a wide range of different dosage levels are noted and,

Chemical Specifications Identity Purity	Biochemistry Digestion Absorption Distribution Metabolism Utilization Elimination	Probable Use Daily Intake Effects on Food Nature of Residue Possible Toxic Products	Biological Effects Acute Studies Intermediate Studies Life-span Studies Animals Chosen From Metabolic Data	ADI Assessed Check by Human Studies Plan use to Conform to ADI Zoned Distribution

FIG. 4.5. Steps in assessment of safety of a food additive.

so far as possible, their nature and significance are evaluated. From these studies it is possible to determine a dosage level that causes no demonstrable effect—this is the no-effect level. This can be expressed in mg/kg body weight. This figure can then be extrapolated to man, using a 100-fold safety factor, in order to obtain the acceptable daily intake (ADI). Thus, if the no-effect level in rats has been shown to be 500 mg/kg body weight, the ADI in man using the 100-fold safety factor would be 5 mg/kg body weight. This safety factor is an arbitrary figure, but it has been found to work well in practice. In certain circumstances, for example if the first effects observed are not thought to be of any true toxicological significance, it may be considered reasonable to use a smaller safety factor. With all problems of this nature, the decision will mainly depend on the balance between benefit and risk. Having obtained an ADI, there is a further step required which takes into account the use of the additive; the uses and the levels of use permitted in individual foods must be such that the ADI will not be exceeded when they are all taken into account. A decision with regard to probable intake may be based on appropriate food surveys carried out on the community involved. It is wise to assume in these calculations that all the foods that might be treated with the additive are so treated. In order to keep the over-all intake within the limit set by the ADI, it may be necessary to restrict the use of the additive to particular foods. This approach requires a permitted list system and this is now employed by many countries. This system is relatively easy to apply to major food additives; there are difficulties, however, in applying it to substances that are used in very small amounts, such as many flavouring agents.

Since food additives are consumed over long periods, perhaps even the whole life-span, considerable attention has been paid to possible long-term effects. One of the most important of these is the possible induction of cancerous changes (32). It is known that certain substances can induce cancerous changes and it is necessary to assess the potential cancer risk of any new food additive. This is usually done by feeding the food additive at several levels, including the maximum tolerated dosage level, to laboratory animals over the major part of their life-span. The incidence of tumours in the experimental groups is compared with that in appropriate control groups. A statistically significant increase in the incidence of tumours is regarded as an indication of a possible cancer hazard. Unless this effect can be shown to be species- or strain-specific and not applicable to man, it is wise to reject any substance giving an increase of tumour incidence for use as a food additive. In Britain the studies are based on life-span feeding tests in rats and mice; in the U.S.A. the Food and Drug Administration accept life-span tests in rats and two-year tests in dogs; these dog studies only cover about 15 per cent of the life-span of the dog and it is doubtful whether a negative finding in such a study has much value in assessment of the cancer risk. It is important to know that the biochemical behaviour of the substance in the test animal used is reasonably comparable with that in human subjects. Parenteral administration can be used, but this may give rise to problems of interpretation. The occurrence of tumours at the injection site may have little, if any, significance in the assessment of cancer risk; such tumours may occur after the injection of many substances which certainly give rise to no cancer risk when taken by mouth.

When an additive is used it may cause changes in the food that are deleterious. For this reason it is always necessary to carry out biological tests on the treated food material as well as on the additive itself. It is often assumed that a substance of natural origin is inherently safer than a synthetic chemical; there is no scientific basis for such an assumption. Indeed, plants often synthesize molecules that are not easily dealt with in the animal body and that produce various effects on the body; many of these substances have been used in medicine for therapeutic purposes (33). All food additives require careful scrutiny regardless of their natural or synthetic origin.

The various additives used in margarine manufacture have been studied along the lines indicated and shown to be safe-in-use.

Vitamins in margarine

The raw materials used in margarine manufacture may contain significant amounts of vitamin E (α-tocopherol), but they tend to be deficient in vitamins A and D. These three fat-soluble vitamins require detailed consideration.

Vitamin A. Vitamin A can be formed in the intestinal mucosa from β-carotene, or it may be consumed in the diet as pre-formed vitamin A. The daily requirement for an adult is 5,000 international units, of which one-third should be as vitamin A itself, while the remainder may be β-carotene. An increased daily supply up to 6,000 i.u. is desirable in pregnancy and up to 8,000 i.u. during lactation. Vitamin A is important for the welfare of many cells, especially those that maintain the normal integrity and functional efficiency of the skin and mucous membranes. There is no satisfactory evidence at the present time that vitamin A intake affords any protection against infections such as the common cold. The anti-infective action of vitamin A that has been claimed is probably secondary to its effect on skin and mucous membranes. An ordinary mixed diet usually contains a sufficient amount of vitamin A and β-carotene for normal needs. The vitamin is found in milk, butter, cheese, egg-yolk, liver, and some fish; fish-liver oils are an exceptionally rich source. β-carotene is found in green vegetables, many red and yellow fruits, and vegetables. If red palm oil is used in the manufacture of margarine, a significant amount of β-carotene may be present in the end-product; however, taste problems may arise. Synthetic vitamin A and β-carotene is added to margarine in most countries nowadays. In Britain (34) the addition of vitamin A (760–940 i.u. per oz) is required by law. This makes the vitamin A content of margarine comparable to that of good quality summer butter. The consumption of margarine reported in the National Survey (35) indicates that margarine might contribute about 10 per cent or more of the daily requirement of vitamin A.

It is possible to take too much vitamin A, but the dosage level that causes toxic effects is massive and there are no risks involved in the amounts added to margarine.

Vitamin D. Vitamin D may be consumed in the diet or it may be formed in the skin by the action of ultra-violet light on cholesterol and some related substances. The irradiation opens the ring structure and confers new biological properties on the molecule. Vitamin D affects calcium absorption; if it is deficient there is a lack of calcium and phosphate needed for the calcification of bone, and consequently the bones may be soft and may become deformed due to gravitational effects or other stresses. The deficiency state is called rickets in children and osteomalacia in adults. Vitamin D is of special importance in growing children and in pregnant women; it may also be needed in the diet of old people who do not get much exposure to sunlight. The daily requirement is 400 i.u. and this should be increased to 700 i.u. in pregnancy and 800 i.u. during lactation. A dietary intake of vitamin D may not be important for adults so long as they are exposed to sunlight and not subjected to any special metabolic demands. The best natural source of vitamin D is fish oils, especially liver oils, but fatty fish, such as herrings, contain significant amounts. It is also found in eggs and butter; very small amounts are present in cheese and milk. The diets of children, pregnant and lactating women, and perhaps old people, require supplementation. The raw materials used in margarine manufacture usually contain no vitamin D. For this reason synthetic vitamin D is added to margarine.

The addition of vitamin D (80–100 i.u. per oz) is a legal requirement in Britain (34) and several other countries. The amount of margarine commonly consumed, according to the National Survey (35), might supply about 15 per cent of the daily vitamin requirement.

Undesirable effects may result from an excessive dosage of vitamin D. The quantity that has to be taken to bring about deleterious effects is large, and the addition of vitamin D to margarine in the amounts recommended carries no risk.

Vitamin E. There are several isomers of tocopherol, all of which are potent anti-oxidants, but only α-tocopherol has full potency in relieving the signs of vitamin E deficiency in rats. The anti-oxidant action of tocopherols has undoubted nutritional importance. It delays the development of oxidative rancidity and the formation of undesirable oxidation products. Its anti-oxidant activity may continue after absorption into the body, since tissues of tocopherol-deficient animals autolyze more rapidly than those from normal animals; this autolysis in deficient animals may be accelerated by ingestion of polyunsaturated fats. Vitamin E is important for normal reproduction in rats and appears to be a dietary essential for several species; a well-defined deficiency syndrome has been described in the rat. The situation in man, however, remains obscure. Many effects have been attributed to vitamin E deficiency, but none has been unequivocally substantiated and no deficiency syndrome has been adequately characterized. From analogy with other species, the daily requirement is likely to be in the region of 10 mg. The dietary tocopherols are found in cereals, vegetable oils, and eggs. Wheat-germ oil is a rich source, but the milling process reduces the tocopherol content of flour; only a relatively small part of the total tocopherols in flour is α-tocopherol. Furthermore, these flour tocopherols are labile and readily destroyed by storage, treatment of the flour with oxidative maturing agents, aeration, or baking. No significant differences in blood tocopherol levels were found between people who habitually consumed bread made from untreated flour and those who ate bread made from flour treated with chlorine dioxide (36). There is no evidence to suggest that an ordinary mixed diet does not contain an adequate supply of α-tocopherol. Some margarines are a good source of α-tocopherol; this depends on the oils used in manufacture. If it was ever found necessary to supplement the α-tocopherol content of the diet, margarine would be a useful vehicle for this purpose. The tocopherols in margarine also have a useful anti-oxidant function in the product, which will be further discussed later.

Food additives

Preservatives. The need for anti-microbial preservatives arose from the occurrence of deteriorative changes, such as hydrolytic rancidity, brought about by micro-organisms. A considerable number of preservatives have at one time been used. These include sodium fluoride, salicylates, formaldehyde, boric acid, benzoic acid, and sorbic acid. Of these, 0·2 per cent benzoic acid and sorbic acid are still permitted in several countries. Benzoic acid is found in a number of natural products; it is readily metabolized in the body and excreted as hippuric acid. At the level permitted benzoic acid in margarine is unlikely to exceed 10 per cent of the F.A.O.–W.H.O. recommended ADI (37, 40); it is said to affect margarine flavour to some extent. Sorbic acid is recommended for use at 500 ppm, or sometimes rather more. At this level the amount in margarine would be unlikely to contribute more than 2 per cent of the F.A.O.–W.H.O. recommended ADI (37, 40). Boric acid is generally considered undesirable (37); it is not particularly effective and it sometimes causes toxic effects. The development of closed processes of manufacture has made it possible to avoid many of the problems of microbial contamination without recourse to the use of preservatives other than sodium chloride, which has some preservative action. In many countries no other preservative is permitted in margarine.

Anti-oxidants. Natural anti-oxidants are present in many vegetable oils. Some of them may have undesirable or even toxic properties; these are got rid of in the refining process. Others, such as tocopherols, are acceptable. They delay the onset of oxidative rancidity. There are a number of other anti-oxidants found on most permitted lists of food additives; these include gallates, butylated hydroxyanisole (BHA), and butylated hydroxytoluene (BHT). These may be permitted in margarine in some countries, including Great Britain. The available biological evidence indicates that BHT or BHA could be safely used in the diet up to a level of 50 ppm on the whole diet. The levels of anti-oxidants that may be present in margarine would not be likely to contribute more than 10 per cent of the ADI recommended by the Joint F.A.O.–W.H.O. Expert Committee on Food Additives (40). There seems to be no need to prohibit the use of anti-oxidants in margarine on safety grounds. Anti-oxidants also protect vitamin A and other oxidizable ingredients.

Colouring agents. Many margarines are white, and this is not generally acceptable to the consumer for ordinary household use; it would not matter in margarine used for other purposes, such as pastry-making. A cream or yellow colour may be obtained by using red palm oil as one of the ingredients of the margarine; the colour is due to carotenes. However, it has been found difficult to avoid taste problems when these palm oils are used. Alternatively, a suitable colouring agent, such as synthetic β-carotene, can be added. At times various aniline dyes have been used in some countries, but this is not generally favoured as some compounds of this type have been found to have undesirable biological effects; a few are still used in one or two countries. The two colourants most widely used nowadays are synthetic β-carotene and annatto. The former is a provitamin A and a recognized nutrient; the amount required to give the necessary colour does not provide more than about 15 i.u. of vitamin A activity per ounce. It is entirely safe at the level required in margarine. Annatto is a natural colour obtained from the fruit of a shrub, *Bixa orellana*, which has been widely used as a colourant in food. The Joint F.A.O.–W.H.O. Expert Committee on Food Additives have asked for further scientific information on the biological effects of annatto, so that a toxicological evaluation can be made (39). There is no reason to suppose that the amounts used in margarine are not safe-in-use; it is permitted for this purpose in several countries.

Flavours. The general situation with regard to flavouring additives is not satisfactory. Extremely small amounts of many substances are used in flavour formulations. Consequently, because of the relatively limited commercial potential, it is often not economically feasible to subject each of these flavour ingredients to extensive biological testing. Various methods of dealing with this situation have been adopted. Some people have suggested that flavouring substances of natural origin are safe and might be accepted without testing, but that synthetic flavouring agents should be tested. As already pointed out, the opposite policy would be more logical; toxic effects are more likely to arise from complex plant products than from many of the substances of synthetic origin used in flavours. In the U.S.A. many flavouring substances have been categorized as 'Generally recognized as safe' (GRAS) and they are then exempted from testing. This is a useful expedient, but it is difficult to see on what grounds it is possible to predict the harmlessness of many of these substances without any appropriate scientific evidence upon which to base such a conclusion. However, the essential point with flavouring ingredients is that they are commonly consumed in extremely small quantities, so that the cumulative dosage level is likely to remain very small. It seems possible that some approach might be based on the expected cumulative dosage level; thus an ingredient might be given clearance on relatively little toxicological evidence for certain uses and for a period of time that would keep the cumulative dose ingested within appropriate limits. With such a scheme, adequate testing would be required for all ingredients that would be used for flavouring foods that might be consumed in quantity, especially by children. However, the problem so far as margarine is concerned is relatively simple. The main requirement is provision of a butter flavour.

Butter-like flavours have been produced by using cultures of various micro-organisms derived from milk; this would appear to be a safe procedure. Certain lactones formed from hydroxy fatty acids (22), which occur naturally in butter, contribute to it, but the main substance that imparts a butter-taste is diacetyl. The diacetyl is commonly added with a number of organic acids, such as lactic, citric, and acetic acid in small amounts. The quantity of diacetyl required is of the order of 1–3 ppm. Acetoin helps to develop and maintain flavour. The extremely small amounts of these various substances, which occur naturally in butter, are considered to be safe-in-use.

Dispersing agents, emulsifiers, stabilizers, and fillers. A wide range of substances have been used to assist in obtaining the most appropriate physical properties of margarine, such as consistency, spreadability, and texture (3). Many of them have been chosen empirically and their use may have several effects; for example, milk products may affect taste as well as texture, and soya flour has an anti-oxidant effect as well as influencing consistency. Those substances that are food materials in their own right, such as egg-yolk, milk products, starches, or dextrins, require no further comment from a safety point of view. Their nutritional contribution is slight, since they are only added in small amounts. Other additives that have been used for these purposes include alginates, carboxymethyl cellulose, gums, lecithin, and various glycerol esters and glycol derivatives such as glyceryl monostearate, stearyl tartrate, stearyl citrate, and brominated vegetable oil. Many of these have been evaluated by the Joint F.A.O.–W.H.O. Expert Committee on Food Additives and the amounts proposed for use in margarine represent only a small contribution towards the recommended ADIs for these various substances (37, 38). It is important that only those substances that have been thoroughly studied and generally approved should be used in margarine. Of those mentioned above, adequate specifications are still awaited for some and brominated oil has not yet been satisfactorily cleared.

The state of dispersion of oil and water in margarine is extremely important for acceptability and for giving the margarine many desirable characteristics. It does not appear to have much influence on digestibility or utilization of the margarine. As already described, the physical state of the fats and oils changes during the course of digestion to the form that is most appropriate for digestion and assimilation, and this involves the breakdown of the dispersion systems used in manufacture.

Anti-spattering agents. When margarine is used for frying, the water particles enclosed in the fats and oils soon reach boiling point and the water vapour escapes from the oil phase; this may give rise to spattering. Spattering can be reduced by using certain types of dispersion system in the manufacture of the margarine, or by the inclusion of lecithin or other anti-spattering agents. Some anti-spattering agents, however, have not been so satisfactory, especially one used in Planta margarine in 1960. The substance used was a maleic anhydride derivative of isomerized soya bean oil (ME-18). Soon after its introduction on the market, it was alleged that this margarine was giving rise to a severe skin reaction in consumers (41). The observation was given considerable publicity, and the margarine was withdrawn. It was first stated that there was close correlation between the intake of the margarine and the occurrence of the skin effects and improvement on withdrawal of the margarine; further studies also showed a skin reaction in animals (42). Later on, however, it was pointed out that the skin reaction was closely similar to exudative erythema multiforme (43), which occurs in epidemics in Holland at the same time of the year as the margarine episode; furthermore, these outbreaks affect women more than men, which was a feature noted in the alleged response to Planta margarine. The skin lesions reported in pigs were also found to occur without ingestion of the substance under test. It was finally concluded that neither the margarine nor the anti-spattering agent it contained was responsible for the alleged skin reactions in those who had consumed it.

Indicators. Various indicators are required in some countries. They are normal food constituents that call for no comment here. However, modern analytical methods make their use for detection of margarine quite unnecessary.

SUMMARY OF THE OVER-ALL NUTRITIONAL SIGNIFICANCE OF MARGARINE

Digestion and assimilability. Any good-quality household margarine appears to be a readily digested and assimilated food. It consists mainly of oils and fats, 97 per cent or more of which are absorbed from the gastro-intestinal lumen. The other ingredients present in any significant quantity are also readily absorbable substances. In these respects margarine is completely comparable with butter.

With regard to speciality margarines made for other purposes, such as pastry-making, less information is available. There is no reason to suppose, however, that these products are not equally well digested and assimilated. The only feature that might result in a lowering of digestibility would be the inclusion of a large amount of highly saturated fats or excessive hardening of liquid oils by hydrogenation. Such procedures would be likely to produce a generally unacceptable product.

Energy production. The oils and fats in margarine have been shown to be available for maintenance of normal growth, health, and fertility in laboratory animals through many generations. They are, so far as can be judged by the methods available, comparable with other dietary sources of fat so far as energy production is concerned.

Vitamin content. The vitamin A and D content, as required by law in Britain and some other countries, makes a useful contribution to the dietary supply of these vitamins.

Polyunsaturated fatty acid and linoleic acid content. Some forms of good-quality household margarine may not differ greatly from butter in polyunsaturated fatty acids or linoleic acid content. Although the raw materials chosen may have had a relatively high content of these unsaturated fats, these may have been modified by the hardening process applied in margarine manufacture.

However, many margarines nowadays may contain large amounts of *cis cis* linoleic acid or other biologically active polyunsaturated fatty acids. The amount present may be as high as 50 per cent or more of the contained fat. Such margarines add significantly to the polyunsaturated fatty acid content of the diet. This is of undoubted value in therapeutic diets designed to cause a reduction of the blood cholesterol or β-lipoprotein level in the consumer. In patients in whom these blood lipids are raised above the expected level for age, an increased proportion of polyunsaturated fats in the diet may be desirable. It is possible that the community as a whole might benefit from an increased intake of polyunsaturated fatty acids, although there is no evidence at the present time that essential fatty acid deficiency occurs in adult human subjects, or that an increased polyunsaturated fatty acid intake will prevent an increase of blood lipid levels as age advances, or the development of atherosclerosis or ischaemic heart disease. The consumption of these margarines containing large amounts of *cis cis* linoleic acid will certainly do the consumer no harm; only extensive prospective studies, not yet undertaken, can demonstrate whether eating these margarines may make any positive contribution to good health.

NOTES AND REFERENCES

The references are mainly to standard works in which more detailed information can be found.

1. BERNARD, C. *Mémoire sur le pancréas et sur la rôle du suc pancréatique dans les phenomènes digestifs, particulièrement dans la digestion des matières grasses neutres* (*A note on the pancreas and on the role of pancreatic juice in digestive processes, especially in the digestion of neutral fats*) (Paris, 1956).

2. FRAZER, A. C. *British medical bulletin*, **14** (1958), 212.

3. ANDERSEN, A. J. C., and WILLIAMS, P. N. *Margarine* (Oxford, 1965).

4. BELL, G. H., DAVIDSON, J. N., and SCARBOROUGH, H. *Physiology and biochemistry* (Edinburgh, 1965).

5. DEUEL, H. J., JR. *The lipids* (New York, 1955).

6. *Proceedings of the international symposium on lipid transport, Vanderbilt University* (Springfield, U.S.A., 1964).

7. MITCHELL, J. R. A., and SCHWARTZ, C. J. *Arterial disease* (Oxford, 1965).

8. FRAZER, A. C. *Advances in clinical chemistry*, **5** (1962), 69.

9. —— *Physiological reviews*, **26** (1946), 103.

10. —— *British medical bulletin*, **14** (1958), 197.

11. BLOCH, K. *Lipide metabolism* (New York and London, 1960).

12. THOMASSON, H. J. *Review of vitamin research*, **25** (1953), 1.

13. See Chapter Five by J. Boldingh in this volume.

14. BRONTE STEWART, B. *British medical bulletin*, **14** (1958), 243.

15. BURR, G. O., and BURR, M. M. *Journal of biological chemistry*, **82** (1929), 345.

16. HANSEN, A. E., ADAM, D. J. D., WIESE, H. F., BOELSCHE, R. N., and HAGGARD, M. E. *Proceedings of the fourth international conference on the biochemistry of lipids* (London, 1958), p. 216.

17. PIKAAR, N. A., and FERNANDES, J. (with SCHIPPERS, F.) *American journal of clinical nutrition*, **19** (1966), 194.

18. Brown, W. R., Hansen, A. E., Burr, G. O., and McQuarrie, I. *Journal of nutrition*, **16** (1938), 511.

19. Ahrens, E. H., jr., Tsaltas, T. T., Hirsch, J., and Insull, W., jr. *Journal of clinical investigation*, **34**, (1955), 918.

20. Hartman, L., McDonald, I. R. C., and Shorland, F. B. *Nature*, **174** (1954), 185.

21. Morton, I. D. *Food processing and marketing* (1967), p. 303.

22. Boldingh, J., and Taylor, R. J. *Nature*, **194** (1962), 909.

23. Hilditch, T. P., and Williams, P. N. *The chemical constitution of natural fats* (London, 1964).

24. Thomasson, H. J., and Gottenbos, J. J. *Proceedings. Koninklijke Akademie van Geneeskunde*, **19** (1967), 369.
 —— —— *Bibliotheca 'Nutritio et Dieta'*, **7** (1965), 110.

25. Sinclair, H. M. *Lancet*, **1** (1956), 381.

26. Botcher, C. J. F., Boelsma van Houte, E., ter Haar, R., Watcher, C. Ch., Woodford, F. P., and van Gent, C. M. Ibid. **2** (1966), 1162.

27. Robb-Smith, A. H. T. *The enigma of coronary heart disease* (London, 1967).

28. Leren, P. *Acta Medica scandinavica, Supplement, 466* (1966).

29. *Report of the Food and Nutrition Board. National Academy of Sciences, National Research Council, publication no.* **1147** (1966).

30. First report of the Joint F.A.O.–W.H.O. Expert Committee on Food Additives, *W.H.O. technical reports series* **129** (1957), *F.A.O. Nutrition Meetings report series* **15** (1957).

31. Second report of the Joint F.A.O.–W.H.O. Expert Committee on Food Additives, *W.H.O. technical reports series* **144** (1958), *F.A.O. Nutrition Meetings report series* **17** (1958).

32. Fifth report of the Joint F.A.O.–W.H.O. Expert Committee on Food Additives, *W.H.O. technical reports series* **220** (1961), *F.A.O. Nutrition Meetings report series* **29** (1961).

33. Davidson, S., and Passmore, R. *Human nutrition and dietetics* (Edinburgh, 1961).

34. *Margarine regulations* (Her Majesty's Stationery Office, London, 1968).

35. *Domestic food consumption and expenditure* (Her Majesty's Stationery Office, London, 1964).

36. Frazer, A. C., and Lines, J. *Journal of the science of food and agriculture*, **18** (1967), 203.

37. Sixth report of the Joint F.A.O.–W.H.O. Expert Committee on Food Additives, *W.H.O. technical reports series* **228** (1962), *F.A.O. Nutrition Meetings reports series* **31** (1962).

38. Seventh report of the Joint F.A.O.–W.H.O. Expert Committee on Food Additives, *W.H.O. technical reports series* **309** (1965), *F.A.O. Nutrition Meetings report series* **35** (1964).

39. Eighth report of the Joint F.A.O.–W.H.O. Expert Committee on Food Additives, *W.H.O. technical reports series* **309** (1965), *F.A.O. Nutrition Meetings reports series* **38** (1965).

40. Ninth report of the Joint F.A.O.–W.H.O. Expert Committee on Food Additives, *W.H.O. technical reports series* **339** (1966), *F.A.O. Nutrition Meetings report series* **40** (1966).

41. HUISMANS, J., DOEGLAS, H. M. G., BUREMA L., and HERMANS, E. H. *Nederlands tijdschrift voor geneeskunde*, **104** (1960), 1828.

42. MALI, J. W. H., MALTEN, K. E., and VAN NEER, F. C. J. *Hautartzt*, **4** (1962), 13.

43. SIMONS, R. D. C. *Deutsche medizinische Wochenschrift*, **7** (1962), 291.

I am grateful to Dr. P. W. M. van der Weijden for checking the information in Table 4.2; to Mr. P. M. A. Codd for providing that given in Table 4.5; to Dr. H. J. Ringers for collecting many relevant facts for me and to Dr. J. Boldingh for useful criticism and advice.

CHAPTER FIVE
Research

J. BOLDINGH

GROWTH OF THE INDUSTRY 1870–1900

SOON after its introduction margarine had gained sufficient importance for the Conseil d'Hygiène officially to authorize its sale on condition that in any reference to it the name 'butter' be avoided.

By 1889 there were ten margarine factories in France, the most important being that of the Société Anonyme d'Alimentation at Aubervilliers.

The new product also attracted attention in other countries. In 1874, at Liesing near Vienna, a factory was built for the production of margarine, the sale of which was officially approved by the municipal authorities of Vienna.

Mège Mouriès applied for patents on the process in England, in the U.S.A., in Germany, and in a number of other countries. In the U.S.A. the United States Dairy Company acquired the rights and passed them on under licence to the Commercial Manufacturing Company, New York.

The biggest buyer of the new product was the Netherlands, from which country the margarine, partly mixed with butter, was re-exported. That country also imported margarine from the U.S.A.; in 1879, the total registered export from the U.S.A. was about 6,000 tons (1).

It was not long, however, before the main margarine production came to be centred in those countries which were themselves foremost in the production of butter, namely, the Netherlands, Denmark, and Germany. At first sight, this might sound illogical, but in fact the reason is not far to seek. It was precisely in these countries that large amounts of skim milk, a by-product of butter-making, were available. This development later even went so far that, before the Second World War, Denmark exported its butter almost entirely to England

and became, at that time, the country with the highest *per capita* consumption of margarine.

Fat chemistry in the nineteenth century

In the technology, chemistry, and biochemistry of fats and their physiological significance, by far the greater part of our now extensive knowledge has been gained only in the last two or three decades. Scientific research has enabled margarine to attain the place it now occupies in the daily diet of many countries in Europe, Africa, North America, and Australia. For economic reasons alone, in these areas, the non-existence of this product is unthinkable.

Nevertheless, even in the early years, the margarine-making process as first applied by Mège Mouriès had undergone important changes. In the period 1870–90 many workers had become interested in margarine processing and the pretreatment of beef tallow, and one result was that the use of organs as an ingredient was stopped. Mège Mouriès himself had also quickly realized that the addition of milk was in itself sufficient to ensure the desired result, and this for hygienic reasons was far preferable to the use of milk-gland extract as emulsifier. Still later, the use of emulsifiers derived from fats was introduced. As early as 1873, vegetable fats and oils began to be used, in addition to beef tallow, as raw materials for margarine, and a start was made on improving the refining methods of such fats (see Chapter Three).

The question inevitably arises as to how far these first developments were based on real insight, however elementary, into the chemistry of oils and fats, or how far they were the results of purely empirical experimentation. It is therefore interesting to recapitulate what the chemist knew about the structure and properties of oils and fats at the time of the birth and infancy of margarine. Although fat chemistry had then existed for fifty years, knowledge of the subject was very limited. In 1823, the Frenchman M. E. Chevreul (Pl.33) described, in his *Recherches chimiques sur les corps gras d'origine animal*, experiments in which for the first time fatty acids such as butyric acid, caproic (hexanoic) acid, stearic acid, and oleic acid, which Chevreul had succeeded in isolating, were defined as the building stones of fats. In the first half of the nineteenth century, fat chemistry was the province mainly of French investigators who continued to work along the lines laid down by Chevreul. Berthelot in particular should be named here; in 1854 (2) he had established the structure of the other building stone of fats, glycerol—which had been discovered much earlier (1779) by Scheele—and was thus able to deduce that the main constituent of fats was formed by a combination of three fatty acid molecules with one molecule of glycerol, that is, the triglycerides.

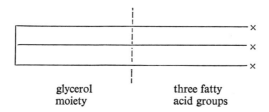

glycerol
moiety

three fatty
acid groups

He also prepared monoglycerides and diglycerides, compounds which were later to occupy such an important place as emulsifiers in margarine processing.

Probably, then, it was not merely a matter of chance that it was a French scientist who shortly afterwards invented margarine: the ground had been well prepared and a keen interest in fats was also shown in French academic circles. But there can be no question of an invention based on scientific insight into the structure and properties of fats. Neither was there the slightest knowledge of the physico-chemical interaction between water, fat, and protein, which to a very large extent is determinative for the properties of margarine as water-in-oil emulsion.

The raw material problem

So rapidly did the margarine industry expand, that even towards the turn of the century it was realized that an acute shortage of solid fats required to give the necessary body to margarine would shortly have to be faced. This gave rise to the enormous increase in the export of American oleo-oil (i.e. the liquid fraction of tallow) to Europe: in 1884, the export was 17,000 tons (chiefly to the Netherlands); in 1908 it had risen to about 100,000 tons.

An alternative was the incorporation of coconut oil, which had first been made possible in 1887 when F. W. Loder developed a suitable refining method to remove the sharp, unpleasant taste from this oil (3). At first, this refined coconut oil found an outlet only in the confectionery industry, but when, around the turn of the century, margarine production came into its own in England, the product found a ready market there. This was also true of the continent where, in France, Rocca, Tassy & de Roux built the largest coconut oil

M.—13

refinery of that time (1885), with many subsidiary companies in other countries, and with a production which by 1914 had risen to 75,000 tons.

Despite this important development, the supplies of raw materials to the margarine industry remained a limiting factor until with the development of hydrogenation an advance was made which enabled almost unlimited quantities of liquid oils (e.g. cottonseed oil, ground-nut oil, and especially whale oil) to be converted into solid fats at reasonable cost. This process has contributed greatly to the rapid growth of the margarine industry during the last fifty years.

1913	0·6
1938	1·3
1967	c. 4·0

TABLE 5.1. World production of margarine (in millions of tons).

HYDROGENATION OF FATS: THE INDUSTRY AFTER 1900

Two French chemists, Sabatier and Sendérens (4), defined the basis of this new process when they discovered catalytic hydrogenation with the aid of metal catalysts. Its application to oils was patented a year later by the German scientist W. Normann (Pl. 35), in England under his own name and in Germany under the name of Herforder Maschinenfett-und Oelfabrik Leprince & Sieveke (5). In England the possession of the patent was transferred to Joseph Crosfield & Sons Ltd., Warrington, where, in 1906, the process was put into practice. The patent rights were acquired from Crosfield's by the Dutch firm of Anton Jurgens N.V., who founded the Oelwerke Germania at Emmerich, Germany.

Here, in 1911, the production of hardened fats was begun, with whale oil as the main starting material. After a short warming-up period the annual production of hardened fat produced here soon reached 50,000 tons. A few years later, fat hydrogenation was intro-duced into the U.S.A. by Procter & Gamble in Cincinnati.

In England a hard battle for patent rights was fought between the Crosfield group and Lever Brothers, Port Sunlight; the latter already had other (including Russian) patents at its disposal. Finally the Normann patent was ruled to be null and void in England, and the two parties reached an agreement for joint operations in this field.

In America, meanwhile, six firms had been working since 1915 according to the patents of C. E. Kayser (1910) and Carleton Ellis

(1912), and with a number of other processes, most of which have never been published. These processes were mainly concerned with the hydrogenation of American cottonseed oil.

It can be said without exaggeration that the invention of the hydrogenation process was an indispensable complement to the invention of margarine. It was a milestone in the development of the oils and fats processing industry; it marks the point at which the margarine manufacturer got the tools which were to ensure for him not only a sufficiency, but also a greater choice of raw materials. Moreover, it was about this time that scientific interest in fat chemistry strongly increased.

Fat chemistry at the beginning of the twentieth century

It is surprising that in the period immediately following Mège Mouriès's invention, interest in fat chemistry in France waned almost to disappearing point; elsewhere too, it was not until the early years of the twentieth century that this branch of science acquired new momentum.

In retrospect, this can be explained. Nature produces fats with so very many types of fatty acids and with so many combinations of these fatty acids with glycerol, that the chemist of that time was faced with an almost insoluble analytical problem. In nature, the lipids occur in multicomponent systems which are so complicated and confusing that their elucidation imposed too great a demand on the analytical aids then known. This was also the reason why the technological processing of oils and fats at that time had to base itself largely on empiricism. It is remarkable that no way out of this impasse was found until the years after 1950, when lipids became accessible for really detailed investigation, long after this had been accomplished for carbohydrates and proteins, the other two main components of our diet.

Characteristic constants. Nevertheless, we should have the greatest admiration for the results achieved in this empirical stage. The entire oil and fat processing industry, now annually converting more than 30 million tons of fats into margarine, shortenings, table dressings, and other fat-containing food products, owes much to the technological adaptations of that period, in which oils and fats could be characterized solely by means of physical and chemical constants (6). Examples of such constants include the iodine addition number as a

measure of the unsaturation, developed by Wijs (7), use of the saponification value for further classification of the type of fat (8), the Lea-
value as a measure of the degree of oxidation (9), the crude measure
of the amount of crystalline solid phase in a fat, obtained from the
measurement of its slip point, which is later followed by the more
accurate determination by measurement of the coefficient of expansion of the fat during melting, the dilatation determination, developed
in the Netherlands in 1920 by Adriani and Bertram and first published
by Normann (10), the Lovibond colour measurement, and the determination of the amount of unsaponifiable constituents. In many works
laboratories all these are still used, even though from a scientific
point of view they are not particularly inspiring. We may justifiably
call this the period of the *Schmierchemie* (11). In this period, many of
those who tried to put fat chemistry on a higher plane must have
thrown up their hands in despair when faced with the great diversity of
the combinations of building stones, often differing only slightly in
properties, and the complete lack of suitable methods for their analytical characterization. The separation of a large group of very closely
related fatty acids, representatives of a number of homologous series,
still remained a very difficult problem before 1950, yet we may again
feel astonishment when we see how much had already become known
thanks to a chain of chance discoveries. For example, rucic acid, a
fatty acid which occurs in considerable amounts especially in rape-
seed oil and mustard oil, was isolated by Darby (12) as early as 1848;
in 1886 Peters (13) gave the structural formula of linoleic acid, yet it
was not until half a century later that this fatty acid, with its 18
carbon atoms and two double bonds, was recognized by Burr and
Burr (14) to be an essential nutrient for man; not until 1909 was the
structure of linolenic acid elucidated (15), although the acid itself,
which is closely related to linoleic acid and forms one of the main
constituents in, for instance, linseed oil, had been isolated as early
as 1887.

Among those who occupied themselves with this type of investigation we come across a name which is honoured by all fat chemists:
T. P. Hilditch (Pl. 36), the scientist who devoted his professional
career largely to the study of oils, fats, and waxes, originally from
1911 onwards as a research chemist of Joseph Crosfield & Sons Ltd.,
Warrington (U.K.) and later as Professor of Industrial Chemistry at
Liverpool University (1926–51). By him and his students, the fatty
acid composition and, as far as it was possible in those days, the

glyceride composition, of an impressive number of naturally occurring fats and oils were established. The results of this work were published for the first time in book form in his *Chemical Constitution of Natural Fats and Oils* (16), a standard work which was reprinted in 1964, in a greatly expanded version, and included data on 1,450 fats and oils. It contains entries on fats of the most varied origin from the higher and lower forms of life in both the vegetable and animal kingdom.

His own publications and those of his assistants and students, in which newly discovered fatty acids are described and characterized, are innumerable. When fat chemistry stood on the threshold of a remarkable analytical breakthrough, at the time of Hilditch's retirement in 1951, the identity of some hundreds of fatty acids as building stones of natural fats had already been established. For those who took their first steps along the interesting path of fat or lipid chemistry after 1950 and for whom, with the help of the analytical methodology developed in the past two decades, a detailed lipid analysis is now but a matter of days, if not hours, it is useful and instructive to note how earlier workers, with the considerably more primitive methods—little more than fractional distillation and crystallization, followed by determinations of the characteristic constants of the resulting fractions—were still able to penetrate fairly deeply into the essence of the matter.

Hilditch's interest in lipids was awakened, immediately after his university education, at Joseph Crosfield & Sons Ltd., largely by the fat hydrogenation plant which had been successfully installed there shortly before. Also employed in this plant was Normann, the previously named inventor of catalytic fat hydrogenation.

Because of the many changes that the fatty acids may undergo during hydrogenation, the number of components with which the analyst is finally confronted is many times greater than that of the components in the original oil. In his time, Hilditch was certainly well aware of the serious shortcomings of the available aids in the analysis of oils and fats, and he devoted himself wholeheartedly to this problem throughout the later years of his life.

Despite the enormous progress made, the formidable analytical problem is still not entirely solved; but thanks to the introduction of chromatographic separation techniques, coupled to methods of spectrophotometric structure identification, the ultimate goal is rapidly being approached.

Early biochemical developments

Before we go further into these analytical developments, it is useful again to look into the past to ascertain what early contributions had been made to our knowledge of the biochemistry of fats. Here again the important discoveries are found to have been extremely scarce in the last century. No facts at all were unearthed on lipid biochemistry in its strictest sense, that is, of ascertaining what precisely happens chemically to the building stones of fats in various metabolic processes. In the nineteenth century, such studies were restricted to a number of crude observations of a physiological nature. Nor is this surprising. In a period in which the ultimate differentiation of the lipid building stones was still completely impossible, the biochemist could fasten his hopes only on very obvious macro-effects observed during nutrition studies on experimental animals. For the chemist in lipid biochemistry, it was at that time impossible to experiment on a cellular level.

The amounts of lipid material which such experiments may make available (in the order of no more than a few milligrammes, or even microgrammes) were, in general, much too small to admit of detailed analytical differentiation with the then available aids. During the entire Hilditch era until the beginning of the 1950s, at least several hundred grammes of fatty material were necessary for a detailed lipid analysis, and such an analysis took, in the most favourable case, several weeks of intensive work.

The fat chemist and the physiologist first met professionally in the field of fat absorption in the alimentary tract. It was notably Bernard (1856) (17) who established that, during metabolism, fats were resorbed in the duodenum, but the question as to how far fats were (enzymatically) split in this way and the actual mechanism of fat absorption remained a controversial issue until far into the twentieth century (see Chapter Four).

A striking example of an early development in the true biochemical sense is to be found in the experiments of Knoop (18). These were concerned with the role of fats—and particularly of the fatty acids—in the metabolic energy supply of man, in respect of which Knoop regarded the fatty acids as one of the most important biological fuels. His investigation was designed to ascertain what metabolic changes the fatty acids are subjected to in the biochemical degradation process. In his feeding experiments with dogs, he replaced the dietary fatty acids (which in nature are built up from long, unbranched carbon chains that can be broken up completely into small fragments) by fatty acids having at the end of the carbon chain an easily recognizable ring structure that is not readily broken down biologically (the so-called terminal phenyl-substituted fatty acids). From the urine of the test animals he succeeded in isolating a number of metabolites with this end-structure. Structural relations enabled him to postulate that

Phenylvaleric acid

Benzoic acid   Acetic acid

during the biological breakdown process fatty acids lose fragments stepwise and each fragment contains two carbon atoms. This would mean the repeated oxidative splitting off of one molecule of acetic acid, so that finally the fatty acids, which generally have an even number of carbon atoms, are completely broken down. The fragments (acetic acid) would then—so Knoop reasoned—be used as part of the biological energy supply of the body, by further oxidation. Later it was demonstrated from many examples that acetic acid is also used by the body for the building up of many substances required by the organism.

With this hypothesis of the β-oxidation Knoop was fifty years ahead of his contemporaries. A milestone on the road to a more detailed understanding of fatty acid metabolism was the discovery of coenzyme A, by Lipmann and Tuttle (19), as a cofactor in the β-oxidation of fatty acids. By an enzymatic process, with the aid of the energy-rich adenosine triphosphate (ATP), coenzyme A brings the fatty acids into an activated state, which is essential for β-oxidation.

Moreover, coenzyme A has been found to be necessary for the utilization of acetic acid in many biosynthetic processes (20).

It was not until 1953 that a start was made on an extensive biochemical investigation of β-oxidation of fatty acids, notably by Lynen (21) and by Green (22), and in subsequent years they have been followed by an ever-increasing number of lipid biochemists. Knoop's theory was fully confirmed. The way in which the breakdown occurred, what intermediate steps take place between the splitting off of one molecule of acetic acid and the next, which enzymes are involved in the process, which cofactors are necessary to assist these biochemical conversions and, finally, how the liberated energy is utilized during the metabolism of the acetic acid formed in the tissues; all this is now known in extensive detail. Again we see how, in this field, the greatest advance has been made in the last two decades.

In 1932 Verkade (23, 24) discovered an alternative but less frequently occurring pathway of the biochemical breakdown of fatty acids; the ω-oxidation, in which oxidation of the fatty acid at the terminal methyl group is the initial step. The dicarboxylic acid thus formed is again broken down by the splitting-off of acetic acid groups, now starting from both ends of the chain at the same time.

Another example might well be given here, one that dates back to the early days, to the time when the exceptionally large and richly varied group of naturally occurring unsaturated fatty acids—of which some 200 are now known—could be differentiated only as a category from the group of the saturated fatty acids of which a few score have now been identified. The unsaturated fatty acids could be separated from the saturated fatty acids by means of lead salt precipitation of the latter. Before that time only a few representatives of the group of the unsaturated fatty acids had been identified; oleic acid, linoleic acid, linolenic acid, erucic acid, and a few others. This was the situation in the first quarter of the twentieth century.

In 1929, Burr and Burr (14) made a discovery which was to prove of great significance. They found that when put on a strictly fat-free diet animals began to show serious physiological abnormalities, including poor growth, loss of hair, poor skin condition, and sterility resulting from degeneration of the reproductive organs.

But when fats were again fed, all these abnormalities were promptly corrected, provided the deficiency level had not dropped too low. The surprising discovery of Burr and Burr was that these fat deficiency symptoms were not caused by the absence in the diet of fats in

33. M. E. Chevreul (1786-1889). Medal struck on the occasion of his hundredth birthday.

N° 1515  A.D. 1903

Date of Application, 21st Jan., 1903

Complete Specification Left, 20th Oct., 1903—Accepted, 26th Nov., 1903

PROVISIONAL SPECIFICATION.

Process for Converting Unsaturated Fatty Acids or their Glycerides into Saturated Compounds.

I, WILHELM NORMANN, Doctor of Philosophy, of Herford, Westphalia, in the German Empire, do hereby declare the nature of my invention to be as follows: —

The property of finely divided platinum, to exercise a catalytic action with hydrogen, as it does with oxygen, is already known. For instance, Wilde

5 observed the following reaction taking place in the presence of platinum black:

$$C_2H_2 + H_4 = CH_3 - CH_3$$
$$C_2H_4 + H_2 = CH_3 - CH_3$$

and Debus noticed the reaction:

$$HCN + H_4 = CH_3.NH_2$$

10 Recently Sabatier and Senderens, of Paris, have discovered that other finely divided metals will also exercise a catalytic effect on hydrogen, *viz.* iron, cobalt, copper and especially nickel.

By causing acetylene, ethylene, or benzene vapour in mixture with hydrogen gas to pass over one of the said metals (which had just been reduced in a

15 current of hydrogen) the said investigators obtained from the unsaturated hydrocarbons saturated hydrocarbons, partly with simultaneous condensation.

I have found, that by this catalytic method it is easy to convert unsaturated fatty acids into saturated acids.

This may be effected by causing fatty acid vapours together with hydrogen

20 to pass over the catalytic metal, which is preferably distributed over a suitable support, such as pumice stone. It is sufficient, however, to expose the fat or the fatty acid in a liquid condition to the action of hydrogen and the catalytic substance.

For instance, if fine nickel powder obtained by reduction in a hydrogen cur-

25 rent, is added to chemically pure oleic acid, the latter heated over an oil bath and a strong current of hydrogen is caused to pass through it for a considerable time, the oleic acid may be completely converted into stearic acid.

The quantity of the nickel thus added and the temperature are immaterial and will only affect the duration of the process. Apart from the formation of

30 small quantities of nickel soap, which may be easily decomposed by dilute mineral acids, the reaction passes off without any secondary reaction. The same nickel may be used repeatedly. Instead of pure oleic acid, commercial fatty acids may be treated in the same manner. The fatty acid of tallow which melts between 44 and 48° C, has an iodine number 35.1 and a yellow colour,

35 will after hydrogenation, melt between 56.5 and 59°, while its iodine number is 9.8 and its colour slightly lighter than before, and it will be very hard.

The same method is applicable not only to free fatty acids, but also to the glycerines occurring in nature, that is to say, the fats and oils. Olive oil will yield a hard tallow-like mass; linseed oil and fish oil will give similar results.

40 By the new method, all kinds of unsaturated fatty acids and their glycerides may be easily hydrogenised. It is not necessary, to employ pure hydrogen for

[Price 8d.]

34. The patent for the hardening process, a decisive invention in this field, was granted to Wilhelm Normann on 26 November 1903.

35. Wilhelm Normann (1870-1939).

36. T. P. Hilditch (1886-1965) devoted a great deal of his scientific career to the study of oils, fats, and waxes.

general, but were closely connected with the absence from the dietary fat of linoleic acid, a fatty acid with 18 carbon atoms and two double-carbon bonds.

$$\begin{array}{ccccccccc} CH_2 & CH_2 & CH=CH & CH=CH & CH_2 & CH_2 & CH_2 & CO_2H \\ {}_{17} & {}_{15} & {}_{13}\ \ {}_{12} & {}_{10}\ \ \ {}_{9} & {}_{7} & {}_{5} & {}_{3} & \\ CH_3 & CH_2 & CH_2 & CH_2 & CH_2 & CH_2 & CH_2 & CH_2 \\ {}_{18} & {}_{16} & {}_{14} & {}_{11} & {}_{8} & {}_{6} & {}_{4} & {}_{2} \end{array}$$

Linoleic acid

Linoleic acid occurs in large amounts in a number of vegetable oils (soya bean oil and corn oil 55 per cent, sunflower seed oil 65 per cent). Opinions on the role played by this acid in the body were, at first, rather contradictory; nor was there agreement on whether or not the deficiency symptoms indicated that the animal itself was entirely incapable of producing this acid. We now know with certainty that higher animals are not able to make this acid themselves. Both the higher animals and man are dependent on the linoleic acid obtained from food for the maintenance of an optimum physiological condition.

At that time it was quite impossible to say on what the physiological effects of linoleic acid were based, yet despite the serious analytical handicap, within ten years the conclusion was reached that linoleic acid underwent chain elongation and further desaturation in the body to form an even more strongly active essential fatty acid, arachidonic acid (25).

$$\begin{array}{cccccccc} CH_2 & CH_2 & CH=CH & CH=CH & CH=CH\ \ CH=CH & CH_2 & CO_2H \\ {}_{19} & {}_{17} & {}_{15}\ \ {}_{14} & {}_{12}\ \ {}_{11} & {}_{9}\ \ {}_{8}\ \ \ {}_{6}\ \ {}_{5} & {}_{3} & \\ CH_3 & CH_2 & CH_2 & CH_2 & CH_2 & CH_2 & CH_2\ \ CH_2 \\ {}_{20} & {}_{18} & {}_{16} & {}_{13} & {}_{10} & {}_{7} & {}_{4}\ \ \ {}_{2} \end{array}$$

Arachidonic acid

In those days linoleic acid and arachidonic acid were sometimes referred to as vitamin F, a term now no longer used, partly because, after 1950, yet other fatty acids with similar activity were discovered, and partly because the amount needed by an adult in the diet is several grammes a day, an amount which is out of all proportion to the requirements of the many vitamins now known, the former being higher by a factor ranging from 1,000 to several millions. The term *essential fatty acids* (EFA) is now in general use. It was not until 1964 that the extreme importance of the physiological effect tracked down by Burr and Burr in 1929 was fully realized. In this field biochemistry has recently advanced by leaps and bounds until it can now be safely said that the role of the polyunsaturated fatty acids, and in particular that of the sub-class of the EFAs, is of primary importance in the study of heart and vascular diseases. We shall return to this in more detail later.

Refinement of techniques

A very important development was undoubtedly the fact that isotopes became available, namely, the radioactive carbon isotope (^{14}C) and the non-radioactive hydrogen isotope deuterium, obtained from heavy water, with the atomic weight of 2. The introduction of isotopes as an analytical tool led to new techniques which enabled rapid progress to be made in the study of the biochemistry of lipids, as well as in many other fields.

This principle was applied by Schoenheimer and Rittenberg (26) as early as 1936. By the use of deuterium-labelled stearic acid in feeding experiments with animals they succeeded in demonstrating with a high degree of certainty the direct conversion of the stearic acid into oleic acid. It was not until much later that Bloch (27) was able to establish the exact biochemical mechanism of this conversion:

$$CH_3\!-\!CH_2\!-\!CH_2\!-\!CH_2\!-\!CH_2\!-\!CH_2\!-\!CH_2\!-\!CH_2\!-\!CH_2\!-\!CH_2\!-\!CH_2\!-\!CH_2\!-\!CH_2\!-\!CH_2\!-\!CH_2\!-\!CH_2\!-\!CH_2\!-\!CO_2H$$

Stearic acid

oxygen $\downarrow$ (-2H)

$$CH_3\!-\!CH_2\!-\!CH_2\!-\!CH_2\!-\!CH_2\!-\!CH_2\!-\!CH_2\!-\!CH_2\!-\!CH\!=\!CH\!-\!CH_2\!-\!CH_2\!-\!CH_2\!-\!CH_2\!-\!CH_2\!-\!CH_2\!-\!CH_2\!-\!CO_2H$$

Oleic acid

For some years now we have known various biochemical pathways which can lead to the introduction of unsaturated carbon–carbon double bonds, and we know it is by no means certain that a double bond will result from dehydrogenation of pre-formed saturated fatty acid.

The double bond of a large number of mono-unsaturated fatty acids is often introduced at an early stage during biosynthesis; further chain elongation causes the double bond to 'move up' more and more in the chain.

When the deuterium-labelling technique was first applied, relatively large amounts of deuterium had to be introduced into the preparations. However, the introduction and perfection of the mass spectrograph after 1945 made it possible to work with very minute samples.

The introduction of radioactive carbon and the rapidly refined technique which enabled it to be introduced at the desired position in model substances (in this case, in various fatty acids) meant that it became possible to work on the microscale, as radioactive labelling is easily determined in exceptionally low concentrations. The same is also true for the radioactive hydrogen isotope tritium, with atomic weight 3, which can replace hydrogen atoms in organic compounds without appreciably changing their chemical behaviour in most reactions.

Chromatography: the great breakthrough

Before 1950 much had been accomplished, but had it not been for a radical innovation in separation techniques, which really 'bust everything wide open', lipid biochemistry could never have made such rapid advances.

Formerly it was possible by distillation, crystallization, and precipitation on a macroscale (some hundreds of grammes) to detect a few rough and ready differentiations between fats and fatty acids; it is now possible, at the flick of a switch, to separate minute amounts (1 mg) of a complicated mixture of fatty acids—nature rarely makes simple mixtures—into its individual components, and to isolate these for further structure investigation.

The first step towards this new separation technique was the work of the Polish botanist Tswett (28), who in 1906 (about the same time as Normann invented fat hydrogenation) published details of the first chromatographic separation of pigments from green leaves.

Tswett passed a benzene solution of these pigments through a glass tube filled with castor sugar. Because of the differences in absorption equilibria of the dissolved pigments relative to the castor sugar, they moved through the tube at different speeds and could be collected by elution as separate fractions. The green leaf extract was thus broken down into a number of colours, including chlorophylls and carotenoids.

A surprisingly long time elapsed before this new principle attracted general attention. It was not until the late 1930s that the Hungarian Zechmeister (29) and many other investigators revived the technique, and it soon found an impressive number of applications in chemistry. The castor sugar was replaced by more effective adsorbents, such as aluminium oxide, silica gel, and active carbon. The term chromatography was retained as a collective name for these techniques even when colourless compounds were separated.

However, this method of separation was in this form not sensitive enough to separate completely all members of the large family of fatty acids, which because of the often subtle differences in structure, differ only very slightly in physical properties. Some means had therefore to be found which would make more sensitive use of these slight

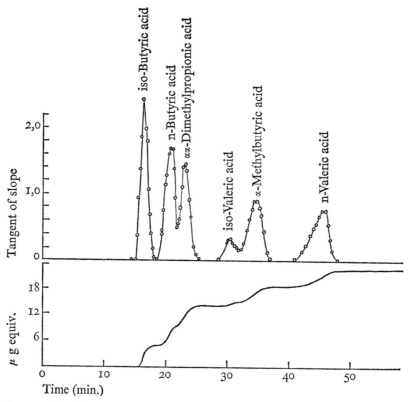

FIG. 5.1. Gas-chromatographic analysis of a number of short-chain fatty acids according to James and Martin (33).

differences. The breakthrough came in 1941 when Martin and Synge (30) introduced a new version of the chromatographic technique. This was based on the distribution of substances between two mutually immiscible liquid phases. The solid adsorbent of the chromatographic column was now replaced by a second liquid phase (the immobile liquid phase), which is immiscible with the mobile liquid phase and is secured in the column on a finely dispersed carrier. This method is known as liquid–liquid partition chromatography. In a variation of this method, paper chromatography (31), the column filled with carrier material is replaced by a strip of filter paper which sucks up the liquid phase.

This invention, which in 1952 was honoured with a Nobel prize, was quickly developed into a form useful for fatty acid separation (32). Even so, protein chemistry and sugar chemistry were to benefit much

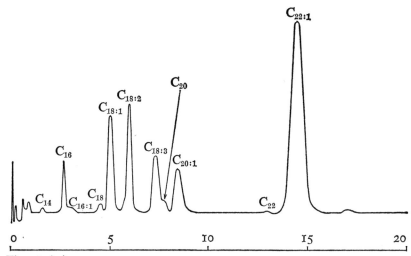

Time (min.)

FIG. 5.2. Gas-chromatographic analysis of the fatty acids from rape-seed oil.

more from the new technique than fat chemistry did. It remained a difficult, time-consuming business to separate a fatty acid mixture into its components in this way, until Martin, then working with James (33), introduced a new method in 1952. The mobile liquid phase was replaced by a gas which was passed through a long tube. This was packed with a finely dispersed carrier on which a non-volatile liquid, e.g. silicon oil, formed the immobile phase. Gas–liquid chromatography (GLC) has since taken almost every branch of chemistry by storm. This is due especially to the ingenious apparatus developed by James and Martin which enabled the fractions being eluted from the column in the form of vapour to be determined quantitatively. This made it possible for GLC to be rapidly developed into a fully automated analytical process, in which the results were also automatically recorded.

Within a few years GLC proved to be the key to lipid research. Half a century after Tswett's initial chromatographical experiment, it was possible to separate almost unimaginably small amounts of lipid mixtures (a few hundred thousandths of a gramme) and to study chemical conversions of lipids subcellular particles such as microsomes and mitochondria, where a very wide range of conversions are now known to occur. Moreover, the new technique proved to be highly time-saving (see Table 5.2).

	1945	*1960*	*Increase in efficiency*
Amount needed	500–1,000 g	I mg	10^6
Time required	2–4 manweeks	2–4 manhours	40

TABLE 5.2. Gain in efficiency of fat analysis.

Even so, this microscale method of separating lipids would have been of relatively little value to biochemical research had not methods also been available for establishing the structure of the micro-amounts of lipids so separated. This had been made possible by the development of various spectroscopic methods designed to give exact data on the molecular structure of organic compounds. One such method, colorimetry—the measurement of colour absorption—dates back to the nineteenth century and does give some information about certain structure elements, but the technique is limited to coloured compounds. This technique was extended in the twentieth century to absorption measurements of ultra-violet light (UV) of various wavelengths. To these methods were rapidly added, especially after 1945, several other 'fingerprint' techniques.

Mass spectrometry (MS), infra-red (IR) absorption measurements, nuclear magnetic resonance (NMR) spectroscopy; all these are powerful tools for the elucidation of chemical structure. Close co-operation now exists between the biochemist and the firms which manufacture the apparatus for these methods and it is essential that such equipment must be able to analyse the minute amounts of material normally obtained from GLC. This co-operation has undoubtedly paid high dividends: it is this combination of GLC and spectroscopy that has enabled biochemical lipid research to flourish.

FLAVOUR

It is by no means only in biochemistry that these modern techniques have proved of great importance in lipid research. Their first major application to margarine was in the study of taste and aroma factors.

Little imagination is needed to conjure up an impression of how Mège Mouriès's first margarine must have tasted. Once production had increased sufficiently to give margarine its own place on the market, no efforts were spared to improve the taste. In the first instance, the aim was to approximate to the flavour of butter.

Both in the tracing of flavour components in butter and in the isolation and identification of undesirable odorous substances in oils and fats, whether occurring naturally or induced by oxidation, we have to deal with compounds in such minute quantities that classical chemical methods of analysis are entirely inadequate.

It was in the investigation of volatile components liable to influence the flavour of fats and margarine that the combination of isolation by GLC and identification by spectroscopy first bore fruit.

The first attempts to match the aroma of butter were purely empirical. In the first half of this century many firms specializing in flavours did their best, but with only moderate success. The aroma of butter which, of course, is of animal origin, was in general outside the scope of the conventional perfumer and flavour blender, who, apart from musk and ambergris, worked traditionally with essential oils of botanical origin. Only butyric acid was recognized as an important component of the aroma of butter. Butyric acid, once made by a fermentation process but now via purely synthetic routes, has been used in margarine since the turn of the century.

In 1929 van Niel, Kluyver, and Derx (34) discovered diacetyl, which is formed during the souring of milk. As early as 1874 Mott (35) pointed out the favourable effect that the use of sour milk could have on the aroma of margarine, so that in fact the effect of diacetyl was utilized although the compound itself was still unknown.

Before diacetyl became commercially available, much use had been made of microbial fermentation methods for its production. The micro-organism which is commonly used is *Leuconostoc citrovorum*. Its growth in milk is promoted by other lactic acid bacteria such as *Streptococcus lactis* and *S. cremoris*. Together these bacteria constitute a lactic acid 'starter'.

At relatively low pH (5·0–4·3) *L. citrovorum* converts citric acid via pyruvic acid and α-acetolactic acid into diacetyl in the presence of oxygen. Citric acid normally occurs (0·13 per cent) in milk.

$$CH_3 \cdot \overset{\displaystyle CO_2H}{\underset{\displaystyle \underset{OH}{|}}{\overset{|}{C}}} \cdot \underset{\displaystyle \underset{O}{\|}}{C} \cdot CH_3 + \tfrac{1}{2}O_2 \rightarrow CH_3 \cdot \underset{\displaystyle \underset{O}{\|}}{C} \cdot \underset{\displaystyle \underset{O}{\|}}{C} \cdot CH_3 + CO_2 + H_2O$$

α-acetolactic acid   diacetyl

In the absence of oxygen only acetylmethylcarbinol is formed:

$$CH_3 \cdot \underset{\displaystyle \underset{OH}{|}}{CH} \cdot \underset{\displaystyle \underset{O}{\|}}{C} \cdot CH_3$$

Once formed, acetylmethylcarbinol cannot be converted into diacetyl, for instance, by aeration of the milk, as α-acetolactic acid is the only precursor of diacetyl. The same reaction scheme is followed when the lactic acid starter contains mainly *S. diaceti lactis*.

The concentration of diacetyl formed is relatively low, 7–14 ppm. Aeration of the milk during lactic acid fermentations will induce the formation of higher concentrations: 60–100 ppm. The aeration method, however, is uneconomic and cumbersome because measures have to be taken to forestall bacterial and mould infections during the process.

In 1952 Kneteman (36) described the enrichment of the micro-organism *S. citrophilus* which ferments high concentrations of citrate (7·5 per cent). If sufficient oxygen is present, up to 500 ppm of diacetyl may be formed by the culture.

After the Second World War fermentation processes for the production of diacetyl were replaced by a chemical method, the oxidation of ethyl methyl ketone. Diacetyl is commonly added to margarine in a concentration of a few parts per million.

However, artificial flavour additives to margarine made no really important contribution until the early 1950s, when Unilever research workers developed synthetic aroma components from an intensive study of the flavour of butter. Many naturally occurring compounds were found to influence butter flavour, even in extremely low concentrations.

Careful analysis of butters from various sources revealed that the higher homologues of butyric acid, with 6, 8, and 10 carbon atoms, also occur in substantial amounts as free acids in butter. Moreover, it was found that in sour cream butters, besides lactic acid, the volatile acetic acid occurs in such amounts that it appreciably influences the flavour, especially during cooking. This means that the entire homologous series of fatty acids with straight chains and an even number of carbon atoms ranging from 2 to 10 contribute to butter flavour. The still higher homologues, such as lauric acid, myristic acid, etc., have little influence on flavour because of their slight volatility. The amounts involved range from 1 to perhaps 50 ppm (mg/kg).

General formula:	$CH_3 \cdot [CH_2]_n \cdot CO_2H$
Acetic acid:	$n = 0$
Butyric acid:	2
Caproic acid:	4
(Hexanoic acid)	
Caprylic acid:	6
(Octanoic acid)	
Capric acid:	8
(Decanoic acid)	

TABLE 5.3 Homologous series of the lower fatty acids.

The fatty acids with 6–10 carbon atoms form constituents of coconut and palm kernel oil, and in general the acids used for aromatizing are obtained from the first runs in the fractional distillation of technical fatty acids from these oils. In recent years some of them have been prepared synthetically.

Branched-chain fatty acids also occur in butter, but they play no appreciable role in the aroma, as they are present at extremely low concentrations.

In the early 1950s, a Unilever team in Vlaardingen, working in co-operation with their English colleagues in Port Sunlight, discovered an extremely important class of butter aroma components. These also were lipids.

If butterfat is extracted with a dilute lye solution a fraction is obtained which, when subjected to gas chromatography, is found to contain, apart from the above-named fatty acids, other substances which are characterized by a rather heavy sweetish smell. Such a concentrate can more easily be obtained with the aid of a high-vacuum degassing procedure, which enables the volatile components to be separated from the fat. This procedure was developed specially for the investigation by Schogt and de Bruijn (37).

It soon became clear that the flavour fraction thus obtained consisted of a group of closely related compounds. Gas chromatography

M.—14

and infra-red absorption measurements led to their classification as δ-lactones, members of a homologous series with 6–16 carbon atoms.

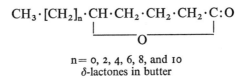

n = 0, 2, 4, 6, 8, and 10
δ-lactones in butter

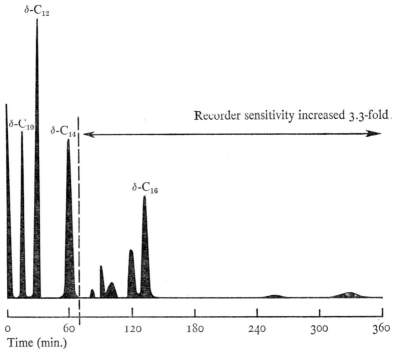

FIG. 5.3. Gas-chromatographic analysis of lactones from butter.

They occur in butter in amounts of only up to 50 or more ppm. In an aqueous medium the lactones are in equilibrium with the open-chain form, the corresponding δ-hydroxy acids,

$$CH_3 \cdot [CH_2]_n \cdot CHOH \cdot CH_2 \cdot CH_2 \cdot CH_2 \cdot CO_2H \rightleftharpoons$$
$$CH_3 \cdot [CH_2]_n \cdot CH \cdot CH_2 \cdot CH_2 \cdot CH_2 \cdot C{:}O$$

δ-hydroxy acids

The acids, especially in the lower homologues, are more readily water soluble than the δ-lactones; this explains why these aroma substances are also partly found in the water-phase of butter.

From 1952 onwards Unilever acquired the patent rights in many countries for the application of these lactones in margarine and other fat products.

In the U.S.A. Patton's group (38) reported, a few years later, the occurrence of δ-lactones in milk fat.

Fat phase	C_{10} lactones Before heating	After heating	C_{12} lactones Before heating	After heating
Fresh butter	5	10		
	4	10	10	25
	3	10	5	28
	9	14	16	30
Non-pasteurized cream (fresh)	3	20	4	27
Non-pasteurized cream (soured)	3	19	5	31
Pasteurized cream (fresh)	6	19	11	38
Pasteurized cream (soured)	6	18	13	35
Beef tallow	0·2	0·5	0·6	2·3

TABLE 5.4. Lactone content (mg/kg) of various fats before and after heating at 140 °C.

There was a remarkable discrepancy in the approach of the two laboratories to the role of these δ-lactones: the American investigators attributed certain off-flavours of whole milk to them, whereas Unilever recognized them as positive aroma constituents of natural butters.

The explanation of this was published in 1962 (39). It is based on the exceptional state in which the hydroxy-acids occur in the milk fat of the cow. It had been observed, that when butter fat that had been melted at a low temperature (40 °C.) was analysed, it was found to contain significantly fewer δ-lactones than butter fat that had first been heated for some time at a higher temperature (120–40 °C.). This was also found to be the case with cream fat, as appears from Table 5.4 for δ-decalactone (C_{10}) and for δ-dodecalactone (C_{12}).

From the table it will be seen that these lactones behave analogously in beef fat when it is heated, although in much smaller concentrations than in the other fats. There can be no doubt therefore that the δ-hydroxy acids occur in some bound form and that it is in this form that they occur in completely fresh milk, the aroma of which is therefore not determined by δ-lactones. This then is the reason why Patton characterized the δ-lactones as milk off-flavours; in butter, however, they always occur in a free state, as an actual component of the aroma.

The most logical assumption was that the δ-hydroxy acids, in combination with normal fatty acids, are built into the triglycerides of milk fat, and that they are split off by heating and also to some extent by prolonged contact with the water droplets contained in the butter.

Synthetically prepared triglyceride models of this kind actually show the expected behaviour. Heating them for 1·5 h at 120 °C. or 1 h at 145 °C. results in almost a 100 per cent conversion into the free δ-lactones.

It is only recently that these lactone precursors have been actually isolated as such from milk fat (40); this gave the final proof. In butter, owing to the presence of a water phase, the precursors are partly hydrolyzed after the formation of the lactones.

The occurrence of the homologous series from C_8 to C_{16}, which so closely parallels the occurrence of a similar homologous series of the normal fatty acids, suggests a common biochemical origin.

It was soon discovered that the δ-lactones show optical activity (the property of rotating the plane of vibration of polarized light); this indicates that they are formed by a biochemical process in the cow, either in its own lipid metabolism system or in the rumen by bacterial activity. (If they were chemically synthesized a racemic mixture would be formed.)

It is still not possible to give a definite account of the origin of the lactones; a possibility is that during very active fatty biosynthesis in the mammary gland of the cow some intermediates escape conversion to normal fatty acids and are built into triglycerides before they have reached the end stage of the fatty acid cycle.

Almost at the same time as the discovery of the lactones yet another group of lipid flavour compounds was found by the Unilever group of investigators, methyl ketones of the general formula:

$$CH_3 \cdot [CH_2]_n \cdot CO \cdot CH_3$$
$$(n = 2, 4, 6, 8, 10 \text{ or } 12)$$

Again a regular homologous series, each member differing by 2 carbon atoms from its neighbours, precisely as in the case of the normal fatty acids and the δ-lactones.

These substances, which have long been known to occur in, for example, cheeses of the Roquefort type, were detected in butter by degassing and subsequent GLC analysis, in amounts of a few parts per million. However, far greater amounts are present in a bound form, as was revealed by subsequent steam distillation of the degassed butterfat at 180 °C. (see Table 5.5).

C_{15}	Methyl tridecyl ketone	42
C_{13}	Methyl undecyl ketone	22
C_{11}	Methyl nonyl ketone	13
C_9	Methyl heptyl ketone	9
C_7	Methyl pentyl ketone	12

TABLE 5.5. Methyl ketones obtained from butterfat by steam distillation at 180 °C. (in ppm).

The nature of the precursor in this case was obvious. It is well known that β-keto acids cannot withstand heat treatment; they lose a 1-carbon fragment, as carbon dioxide, and form the corresponding methyl ketones.

$$CH_3 \cdot [CH_2]_n \cdot \overset{\beta}{CO} \cdot \overset{\alpha}{CH_2} \cdot CO_2H \rightarrow CH_3 \cdot [CH_2]_n \cdot CO \cdot CH_3 + CO_2$$
β-keto fatty acid　　　　Methyl ketone　　　　Carbon dioxide

Hence it was to be expected that butterfat triglycerides would contain β-keto fatty acids which split off the free acid during steam treatment, frying, baking, etc.

Triglycerides containing a β-keto fatty acid instead of a normal fatty acid were in fact identified at a later stage of the investigation. Again a parallel with fatty acid synthesis in the cow is evident. β-keto fatty acids are a normal intermediate product in both the biochemical synthesis of normal fatty acids and in biodegration during the β-oxidation cycle, already mentioned in connection with Knoop's investigations in 1904 (18). This is a very clear example of the escape from the fatty acid cycle of a biochemical intermediate which becomes prematurely incorporated into a triglyceride.

The use of the free δ-lactones and methyl ketones and their precursors in margarines, bakery fats, and shortenings has resulted in products that show exactly the same flavour-release as butter during heating, baking, and frying. But simply adding such a quantity of lactones and methyl ketones in the free state would impart too strong a flavour to margarine when eaten cold.

Apart from these flavouring compounds, which are so clearly related to fat metabolism, a great many other flavour compounds have been identified by various investigators. Among these compounds aldehydes occupy an important place. Quite a number of these are not specific for butterfat: they are generated from unsaturated fatty acids in butter, but also in many other oils and fats as a normal result of autoxidation in air. Most fats also contain minute amounts of unsaturated compounds which are typical for that typical fat. It is the aldehydes derived from these trace amounts of precursors that determine the reversion flavour, which is characteristic of each type of oil or fat. It is remarkable that a typical creamy-flavour note in butterfat is, in fact, due to an aldehyde thus formed, 4 *cis*-heptenal (41):

$$CH_3 \cdot CH_2 \cdot CH:CH \cdot CH_2 \cdot CH_2 \cdot CHO$$

This is generated in butterfat when in contact with air; it is derived from an isolinoleic acid in which the two double bonds are in such positions in the chain that, by autoxidation, the above aldehyde is formed. This aldehyde is one of the most potent of all odoriferous substances and it can be detected even when added to margarine in a concentration of only a few parts per 1,000 million (milligrammes per ton).

The proper combination of a number of aroma compounds has, since about 1952, greatly contributed to the improvement of the flavour of margarine. The application of precursors has also added extra features to the margarine for use in the kitchen, for spreading on hot toast, etc. Thus the empirical flavour-compounding of margarine has been replaced by a rational scientific approach.

Autoxidation

Because of the ever-increasing sophistication of the improvement of margarine by the addition of aroma components the product became more and more sensitive to factors which could spoil the effects of such additions, particularly to off-tastes and off-flavours that might arise from the oil blends used in its manufacture. In consequence, the phenomenon generally known as flavour reversion in oils and fats became a critical factor.

Many substances that become evident in flavour reversion originate from precursors present in the various types of oils and fats, as was explained when butter flavour was discussed. Although certain natural off-flavour precursors have now been identified, it is still a formidable task to eliminate them. For example, particular attention is paid nowadays to the elimination of unwanted flavour substances which tend to develop in soya bean oil, one of the most abundantly available vegetable oils, which quickly develops a smell of freshly cut green beans.

Flavour reversion of oils by autoxidation takes place when un-saturated oils are in contact with air, and is promoted by light and by traces of heavy metals. The nature of the fatty acids in the oils deter-mine the degree of sensitivity to autoxidation; for instance, soya bean oil, which contains polyunsaturated fatty acids such as linoleic and linolenic acid, is more prone to autoxidation than coconut oil, which is of a more saturated type. Autoxidation can be hampered to a cer-tain degree by substances known as anti-oxidants, which most vegetable oils contain naturally in considerable amounts in the form of tocopherols (see Chapter Four)

Much has become known about the mechanism of the oxygen attack on unsaturated fatty acid chains in fats and oils According to Farmer (42) it leads to the formation of labile hydroperoxides by a radical type of chemical reaction, in which each radical can start a chain of events resulting in the formation of still more hydroper-oxides and, in turn, more radicals, and so on: hence the term autoxi-dation. Anti-oxidants are capable of interfering with such chain reactions, thus delaying the onset of rancidity owing to a slower for-mation of hydroperoxides and their volatile decomposition products. However, the anti-oxidants normally present in refined oils are not capable of blocking oxygen attack completely. Volatile flavour reversion compounds will, therefore, still be formed and, owing to the incredible sensitivity of olfactory perception, can be detected even a few hours after the final refining step (deodorization by steam stripping *in vacuo*), and long before the oil is considered to be truly rancid.

It was a challenge to research to ascertain exactly what precursors were responsible for these reversion flavours and then find means for their elimination.

KEEPING PROPERTIES

Here we return to one of the main conditions laid down in Mège Mouriès's commission, namely, that the product should have good keeping properties. This should certainly not be seen as a hobby-horse of Napoleon III, but rather as a universal requirement that should be met by every high-quality food.

In a century of margarine research much has been accomplished, but it is not an exaggeration to say that no sector of this research has been so successful as that directed to the improvement of the keeping properties by the elimination of spoilage by bacteria and flavour deterioration due to chemical flavour-reversion in the fat base.

It will be obvious that a first essential is the thorough refining of the raw material to remove or neutralize all the disagreeably tasting and smelling compounds which naturally occur in the crude oils.

First of all, the mucilage always present in crude oil must be removed by degumming before the oil is subjected to high temperatures. Otherwise—especially if the oil becomes dry during the treatment—the mucilage would settle on the walls of the refining apparatus where it would char and cause flavour deterioration, besides fouling the equipment. This also holds good for the phosphatides, such as lecithin and related compounds which, although not actually fat-soluble, can still occur in a dispersed state in dry or almost dry oil. These phosphatides are then present in the form of micelles which, if they are not first removed, may be disturbed and as a result settle on the walls of the apparatus. Moreover, phospholipid micelles may contain heavy metals, which when liberated can greatly accelerate autoxidation.

The subsequent lye treatment for the removal of free fatty acid in the oil also has the result that any heavy metals still present—provided they are not bound in complexes—are entrained with the soap formed. Moreover, many pigments that usually impart a reddish-brown tint to the oil are also washed away with the soap. Other pigments, including chlorophylls and carotenoids, can be satisfactorily removed by a bleaching treatment, which cannot have the optimum effect until the oil has been neutralized, as fatty acids greatly reduce the adsorptive capacity of the bleaching earth. Water, too, has an unfavourable influence; it is therefore necessary to dry the oil well, either before or during bleaching.

These empirically developed methods are still applied on a large scale, and the refining procedure is always completed by the deodorization treatment during which citric acid or other metal-complexing agents are often added to improve still further the quality of the refined product.

During deodorization any volatile odour components still in the oil are removed by steam distillation at reduced pressure (see Chapter Three). In some oils at least the purely physical changes during deodorization are accompanied by a chemical conversion; to ensure that this conversion proceeds to completion it is necessary either to deodorize for quite a long time at a relatively high temperature (180 °C.) or for a short time at a still higher temperature (200–40 °C.), as, for instance, in the Girdler deodorizer. This final step, then, is concerned with the removal of volatile off-flavours. If the refining is properly carried out, many oils and fats can be stored in the dark for considerable periods, without deterioration of taste, especially if kept in tanks under a layer of inert gas (usually nitrogen).

As soon as refined oils containing polyunsaturated fatty acids again come in contact with oxygen, however, they quickly develop new volatile off-flavours owing to autoxidation, resulting in a flavour reversion which is inherent in the highly unsaturated compounds occurring in the particular oil. This cannot be prevented by the use of anti-oxidants, nor can the basic cause be removed by conventional refining methods; for this, completely different remedies had to be used.

For this seemingly insoluble problem, which particularly hampered the use of marine oils in margarine manufacture, hydrogenation provided at least a partial answer.

Because of its highly unsaturated nature, whale oil has an extremely strong flavour reversion which no refining process is able to reduce to anything like an acceptable level.

As catalytic hydrogenation is specially designed to saturate double bonds in the fatty acids with hydrogen, it is not surprising that its effect on the flavour reversion of marine oils proved to be spectacular. For this reason, the use of hardened whale oil in margarine and in a number of other fatty products began to increase progressively soon after the introduction of catalytic hydrogenation.

Nevertheless, as the demands made upon the quality of the flavour of margarine became more and more exacting, another type of flavour reversion proved to be a stumbling-block in the production of premium brand margarine. Hydrogenation very often not only eliminates the natural reversion flavours, but also introduces new precursors—and this is true by no means only in the case of whale oil. From these precursors which were not present in the original oil are formed, by autoxidation, the so-called *hardening reversion flavours*.

An exceptionally clear example of this is found in conventionally hardened soya bean oil, an example which we cite here as it elegantly demonstrates what can be achieved, by the use of modern analytical techniques, to improve quality.

American as well as European investigators had tried in vain for years to eliminate empirically the reversion of hardened soya bean oil. But it was not until modern separation and identification techniques were applied that the volatile component formed by this reversion could be identified as 6-trans-nonenal (43)

$$CH_3 \cdot CH_2 \cdot \overset{t}{CH} \colon CH \cdot [CH_2]_4 \cdot CHO$$

It was then immediately obvious that an isolinoleic acid

$$CH_3 \cdot CH_2 \cdot \overset{t}{CH} \colon CH \cdot [CH_2]_4 \cdot \overset{c}{CH} \colon CH \cdot [CH_2]_7 \cdot CO_2H$$

formed during hydrogenation from linolenic acid, was the precursor (44).

In the fatty acids in whale and fish oils too, this compound is readily formed during hydrogenation. 6-trans-nonenal is organoleptically perceptible in oil in amounts as small as 1 part in 1,000 million (1 mg/ton), which explains why it is detectable almost immediately after even the most perfect deodorization of the hardened oil. One might conclude that the hydrogenation process would have to be studied with the direct objective of preventing the formation of these precursors. To this end, it was essential first to get a much clearer insight into what actually happens during the hydrogenation process, both on the catalyst surface and in its pores.

CATALYTIC HYDROGENATION

Research in this field, especially since the Second World War, has developed enormously in many industrial research laboratories, state research institutes, and academic research centres. It is not within the scope of this chapter to give a complete account of this work, and we will limit ourselves to those factors that have proved of importance in the development of margarine processing.

Catalytic hydrogenation is based on the chemisorption of the reactants (hydrogen and triglycerides) on the metallic nickel surface of the catalyst, whereby they are brought into an activated state, causing reactions which at the prevailing temperature would normally occur only very slowly, if at all, to take place rapidly. However, the molecules of the reactants may leave the surface prematurely (retention times are in the order of microseconds). In the case of triglycerides adsorbed to the catalyst, there can be no question of any definite location of the double carbon bond in the fatty acid chains. If these triglyceride molecules leave the catalyst surface without having reacted with hydrogen, it may be found that the fatty acid has its reformed¯double carbon bond at a different place than was originally the case ; that is, that isomerization has taken place. Moreover, the resulting⸍double bond may be either in the original *cis* form or in the reversed *trans* configuration. This was first reported by Twigg in 1941 (45).

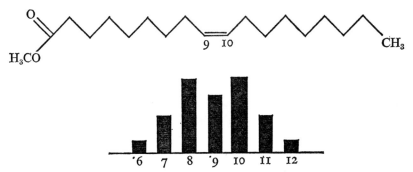

FIG. 5.4. Distribution of the double bond after isomerization of methyl oleate with nickel catalyst

In the Hilditch period it would have been impossible to follow in detail these subtle changes occurring during fat hydrogenation. But thanks to chromatography in its various forms and mass spectroscopy this has now been made possible. Of particular importance has been the development of elegant micro-methods for determining the position of double bonds in fatty acids (46). In one such method the fatty acids are oxidized by osmium tetroxide at the double bond, and then split by potassium periodate.

The resulting aldehydes can then again be separated by chromatography (47–51), and identified, which enables the position of the double bond or bonds in the original fatty acid to be established. In the course of the years further refinements have been added to this method. Furthermore, it was found that the percentage of double bonds having the *trans* configuration can easily be determined by the use of infra-red spectrometry.

Even in the 1920s it was known empirically that hydrogenation with a catalyst poisoned by sulphur is powerful in suppressing the reaction with hydrogen, and promotes an extremely strong *cis–trans* isomerization. An increased *trans* content leads, as does also saturation of the double bond with hydrogen, although in a less-marked degree, to a rise in the melting point of the oil. This principle is very often applied to whale oil. As whale oil contains relatively large amounts of sulphur compounds, a nickel catalyst, even though fresh initially, is heavily loaded with sulphur, after having been in contact several times with this oil, so that no extra sulphur has to be added in the catalyst preparation. This catalyst can be used subsequently for the treatment of other oils, groundnut oil and soya bean oil, for example. The fats so obtained have a very favourable melting behaviour for use in margarine but, as has been previously indicated, the resulting isomerization leads to the hardening off-flavour reversion problem in soya bean and marine oils.

Even with an entirely fresh catalyst there is still some chance that isomerization will occur; this is highly dependent on the way in which the reactants come in contact with each other. Unless the surface of the catalyst is entirely covered with adsorbed hydrogen atoms the chance of saturation of the double bonds is reduced, and isomerization will again prevail. Such an effect can be observed when the hydrogen and the catalyst are not brought into extremely close contact with the oil, owing to insufficient stirring or an inadequate hydrogen supply. Moreover, the probability of isomerization rapidly increases at higher temperatures. It will be obvious that, even with such empirical data, it was possible to direct the process.

When it became necessary to prevent the formation of hardening off-flavour precursors, it was necessary to follow the course of the isomerization in a more subtle way, by means of modern methods for fatty acid analysis and location of the double bonds. It became apparent that the way in which the catalyst is prepared and the structure of the catalyst particles play an important part in the course of the hydrogenation and isomerization.

Both the activity of the catalyst (the rate at which a certain hydrogenation effect is reached under standard conditions) and its selectivity, (the preference of the hydrogen to react only with certain fatty acids), are very closely dependent on the structure of the catalyst, especially the size of the nickel crystallites on the support and the average pore diameter and pore length of the catalyst particles. This meant that methods for the direct measurement of these structure characteristics had to be developed to make it possible to investigate the influence of the method of preparing the catalyst on the catalyst structure, on the one hand, and to correlate the hydrogenation behaviour with the structure on the other.

One method for the determination of the total surface area of solids, which was developed by Brunauer, Emmet, and Teller (52) in

1938, is based on the measurement of the amount of gas (e.g. nitrogen) which can be adsorbed as a monomolecular layer to the surface of the solid at a low temperature (the B.E.T. method).

This and similar procedures have provided a great deal of information on the area of the metal surface as well as on the catalyst's

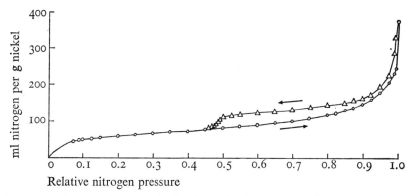

FIG. 5.5. Nitrogen adsorption in the determination of the surface area and pore structure of a nickel catalyst.

carrier material. In this way, and by the use of electron-microscopy and X-ray diffraction analysis (53), exceptionally good insight has been gained into the extremely complicated structure of individual catalyst particles and the dimensions of the metal crystallites present on the carrier. A nickel-on-silica catalyst consists of a conglomerate of flat silica plates on which the metal crystallites are 'stuck' (Pl.38).

To give the reader some idea of the complicated 'cave' structure, Pl.37A shows a photograph of a model of a catalyst particle.

In 1 g of catalyst with a particle size of 2–10 μm a total pore volume of 0·75 cm³/g and an average pore diameter of 5 nm (1 nm = 10⁻⁹ m) there is so much capillary cavity that if the total capillary length were added up, a plane flying at a speed of 1,000 km/h would take about 4½ years to cover the distance (i.e. about 40,000,000 km!) (54).

The way in which the catalyst precipitation and reduction of the green cake to an active nickel catalyst (see Chapter Three) are carried out has an enormous influence on the structure of the catalyst. Both the average pore diameter and the size of the metal crystallites can be widely varied by the method of preparation.

The degree to which the oil molecules are able to penetrate into the catalyst is dependent on the dimensions of the capillaries; this also determines the average time during which the triglycerides stay in contact with the metal surface. This average contact time, in turn, largely determines the selectivity. If we wish to hydrogenate only the most reactive components, for instance the triple-unsaturated linolenic acid in soya bean oil, and leave the linoleic acid and oleic acid undisturbed, we must try to ensure that the molecules stay in contact with the metal for as short a time as possible, as otherwise even the less strongly saturated fatty acids—which are not so readily adsorbed on the nickel surface—will also have time to react and become saturated. Thus the catalyst must have wide pores in which free movement of the triglyceride molecules can occur (in narrow pores, the molecules are retained longer). The activity of the catalyst is determined by the size of the total metal surface per unit of weight of the catalyst, which means that for a high activity very many small metal crystallites are necessary. This, too, is largely determined by the catalyst precipitation; it depends on the formation primary plate-like nickel silicate, which on subsequent reduction partially converts to silica with islands of metallic nickel.

How all these factors can be attuned to specific applications is a matter for the skill of the catalyst manufacturer. There is a wealth of patent literature on this subject, which in general, however, gives little information about background research.

The selectivity of a catalyst is a property which may take one of several forms.

(i) The property of causing little hydrogenation but much isomerization.

(ii) The property of hydrogenating for preference and isomerizing as little as possible.

(iii) The property of hydrogenating only polyunsaturated fatty acids (linoleic and linolenic acids and higher unsaturated fatty acids such as occur in fish oils) while leaving the mono-unsaturated untouched.

(iv) Triglyceride selectivity (see p. 200).

It can safely be postulated that, at least in the case of the nickel catalyst, selectivity is never absolute, most certainly not if the hydrogenation conditions are kept constant in all cases. But if various methods of preparation of the catalyst are combined with adequate hydrogenation conditions (temperature, hydrogen supply, stirring, continuous process design, etc.) it is possible to achieve very high selectivity in each of the categories mentioned above.

The great advances made in modern hydrogenation technique not only enable us to produce tailor-made fats, with predetermined consistency properties, but also to suppress completely the formation of the specific hardening off-flavour precursor (e.g. in soya bean oil) and to eliminate at the same time the originally present precursors of the natural reversion off-flavour. In this highly sophisticated process, known as hydro-refining, the formation of high-melting fat components is no longer the primary aim.

About 1960 it was found that, for public health reasons, it was highly desirable to conserve as far as possible the natural linoleic acid which occurs in many vegetable oils (see p. 177). This meant that the hardening process had to meet even stricter demands than before. Previously no particular attention had been paid to the loss of linoleic acid that occurred when oils were subjected to hydrogenation or hydro-refining to modify their consistency or improve their keeping properties. In the last decade, however, the application of a completely new type of selectivity, whereby only the more than double-unsaturated fatty acids (e.g. linolenic acid) are hydrogenated, leaving the linoleic acid unaffected, has become imperative.

$$CH_3\!-\!CH_2\!-\!CH_2\!-\!CH=CH\!-\!CH_2\!-\!CH=CH\!-\!CH_2\!-\!CH_2\!-\!CH_2\!-\!CH_2\!-\!CH_2\!-\!CO_2H$$

Linoleic acid c. 54 per cent in soya bean oil

$$CH_3\!-\!CH_2\!-\!CH=CH\!-\!CH_2\!-\!CH=CH\!-\!CH_2\!-\!CH=CH\!-\!CH_2\!-\!CH_2\!-\!CH_2\!-\!CH_2\!-\!CO_2H$$

Linolenic acid c. 8 per cent in soya bean oil

For the hydrogenation specialist this was a hard nut to crack. Nevertheless, the problem was solved in a relatively short time, thanks to the intimate knowledge of catalyst structure and behaviour built up over the years. This led, in a number of countries (U.S.A., Japan, and the Netherlands), to the development of an entirely new catalyst for use in fat hydrogenation in which the nickel was replaced by copper (55-7).

This new copper catalyst shows extremely high selectivity in the removal of the triple-unsaturated linolenic acid and gives very little double-bond migration. It does not affect oleic acid, and also leaves the linoleic acid largely undisturbed. Soya bean oil up-graded in this way is completely liquid at room temperature, contains a very high percentage of natural *cis cis* linoleic acid, and has good keeping properties. This provides an inexpensive way of increasing the linoleic acid content of margarine. Compared with corn oil and sunflower seed oil, which could be used as alternative sources of linoleic acid without needing to be hydro-refined, soya bean oil has the advantage of being relatively cheap.

Safflower seed oil	75
Sunflower seed oil	65
Soya bean oil	55
Corn oil	50
Cottonseed oil	50
Groundnut oil	20–45
Lard	8
Beef fat	3
Butterfat	1–2

TABLE 5.6. Average linoleic acid content of various oils (per cent).

Triglyceride composition

Should a combination of saturated and unsaturated fatty acids occur in the triglycerides of a fat, the melting point, and still more the melting range, of the fat depend very largely on the structure of the triplets. Should the saturated fatty acid, for instance stearic acid, be present solely as the very high-melting tristearin, together with triplets consisting exclusively of unsaturated fatty acid, for instance liquid triolein, the last solid components will liquefy only at a high temperature. If this is higher than body temperature, the fat gives a thick, slow-melting, even a warm and sandy impression on the palate. If, on the other hand, the saturated fatty acids are distributed, in the same relative amounts but more at random, in mixed triplets, over the triglycerides, the fat is much thinner, is quick on the palate.

Where formerly the melting behaviour could be predetermined only by a correct combination of fats containing natural solid constituents, it is now possible to manipulate the process during hydrogenation to give any desired result.

For hydrogenation purposes therefore, it is not sufficient to know to what degree the fatty acids are saturated; the way in which the saturated fatty acids are distributed in the triglyceride molecules must be controlled.

We have seen that catalytic fat hydrogenation must be regarded as a dynamic molecular process in which the triglyceride molecules are one moment adsorbed to the surface of the catalyst and the next moment are replaced by other triglyceride molecules. A critical factor is the retention time, the time during which a triglyceride molecule remains in contact with the catalyst surface. If the average retention time is long, as in a catalyst with small pores, it is more likely that the three fatty acid chains will all become saturated to form tristearin.

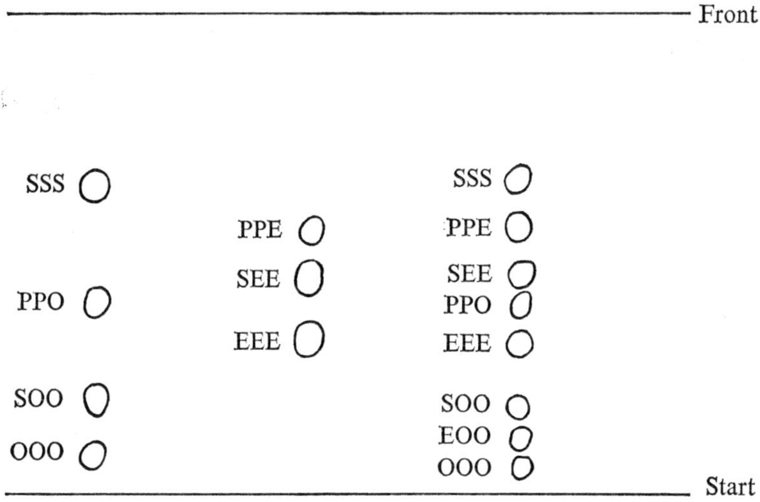

———————————————————————————————————— Front

SSS ◯   SSS ◯

                PPE ◯   PPE ◯

                SEE ◯   SEE ◯

PPO ◯   PPO ◯

                EEE ◯   EEE ◯

SOO ◯   SOO ◯

                        EOO ◯

OOO ◯   OOO ◯

———————————————————————————————————— Start

E = elaidic acid.   O = oleic acid.   P = palmitic acid.   S = stearic acid.

FIG. 5.6. Thin-layer chromatogram of triglycerides.

Other triglyceride molecules then do not get enough opportunity to come in contact with the catalyst surface and remain completely un-saturated. The result is a fat that is slow or thick on the palate. On the other hand, if the average contact time of the molecules with the catalyst is very short, the saturated fatty acids will be distributed more at random over all the triglyceride molecules, and the resulting fat will be quick on the palate.

For the catalyst specialist it is therefore necessary to have available a sensitive method of triglyceride analysis that enables him to follow the hydrogenation process through its various stages and so guides him in the development of catalysts with the desired structure. For this purpose vapour-phase separation (GLC) is unsuitable because of the very slight volatility of triglycerides, and a completely new technique had to be evolved.

This analytical goal was reached in 1962 when de Vries (58) found that silica gel impregnated with silver nitrate is an excellent adsorbent for the separation of triglycerides with only very subtle differences in structure. Applied in the form of thin-layer chromatography

M.—15

(TLC), which for other separations was first described in 1938 and was later further developed by Stahl (59), the method has proved to be of great importance in triglyceride analysis. Even a difference in molecular weight of only two units (the presence or absence of one

Triglycerides with 0 double bond		Triglycerides with 1 double bond		Triglycerides with 2 double bonds		Triglycerides with 3 double bonds		Triglycerides with 4 and more double bonds	
SSS	6·6	SOS	33·0	SOO	22·4	OOO	2·7	OOL	1·8
		SSO	5·1	OSO	1·3	SOL	4·8	OLO	1·4
				SSL	0·5	SLO	5·4	SLL	2·5
				SLS	10·8	OSL	0·4	LSL	0·6
						SLeS	—	SOLe⎫	
								SLeO⎬	0·7
								OSLe⎭	
								LOL	—
								OLL	—
								LLL	—
Totals	6·6		38·1		35·0		13·3		7·0

S = saturated fatty acids (mainly palmitic acid).   O = oleic acid.   L = linoleic acid.
Le = linolenic acid.

TABLE 5.7. Triglyceride composition (mole per cent) of Congo palm oil (60).

double bond) in a triglyceride of molecular weight of about 800, is sufficient to give a clear-cut separation.

A number of fats of relatively simple composition, such as palm oil, coconut oil, and some liquid vegetable oils, have been analysed by means of this method, and we now have a very clear picture of their glyceride compositions; for instance which triplets of fatty acids bound to glycerol occur and in what proportions. This knowledge has been of great value for improving the consistency of margarine.

The information obtained from the glyceride analyses indicated how the glyceride composition of fat compositions could be adjusted in a predetermined way, either by mixing of various raw materials or by controlled hydrogenation. Moreover, it is possible to modify the triglyceride composition, and thereby the melting behaviour, by re-arrangement of an unfavourable triplet composition with the aid of yet another catalytic reaction known as interesterification. By heating fats for some time at temperatures of 100–200 °C. with sodium ethylate or stannous hydroxide as catalyst, a non-random fatty acid distribution is modified towards a random distribution—rather like shuffling a new deck of cards. Later these catalysts were replaced by others, including potassium glycerolate and sodium methylate. The catalyst can also be formed in the oil by the addition of the liquid alloy of sodium and potassium (61). The method was applied in the fat-processing industry (62) long before the analytical tools for precise triglyceride analysis were invented.

PHYSICO-CHEMICAL INVESTIGATION INTO THE STRUCTURE OF MARGARINE

The consistency of margarine is of importance not only in so far as it determines the oral behaviour on the palate. The consumer most certainly looks for other properties. A criterion such as the ease of spreadability may be an important factor; this has gained weight since refrigerators have become popular in the home.

By making a correct choice of fat composition the modern producer can now adjust his products to meet current consumer habits by giving a wide spreadability range; in other words avoiding excessive hardness and brittleness at low temperature and too soft a product at room temperature. This is a great advantage which is not available to the butter producer.

Just as there is a great difference between a pebble beach where the water runs freely in and out of the stony layers, and a sandy shore that holds the water tightly within its fine structure, the consistency of a particular fat blend depends largely on the shape and size of the solid fat particles embedded in the liquid oil phase. A coarse, solid, fat phase may result in a soft, oil-exuding material, whereas with the same amount of solid phase more finely divided, a stiff, consistent, solid-looking product may be obtained which does not exude its oil phase during storage and transport. The amount of solid fat phase and the triglyceride composition are, therefore, only part of the story of consistency of margarine. The size and shape of the solid fat crystals are also of paramount importance.

In order to be able to adjust these factors as required, the following are necessary:

(i) Methods for determining the amount of solid phase present at any given temperature.

(ii) Methods for determining in what form the solid phase is present (shape and size of the fat crystals).

(iii) Methods for influencing the crystal shape, growth, and recrystallization.

The margarine manufacturer has long known from experience that the rate of cooling of the fat emulsion greatly influences the consistency of the product.

The formerly much-used churn–drum margarine excelled— especially when beef tallow oleo-oil was used—in its rather tough, butter-like consistency. The modern votator process, which for hygienic reasons is greatly preferable to the churn–drum method (see Chapter Three), gives a product which, by contrast, readily displays consistency defects such as brittleness and oily exudation unless special precautions are taken during the cooling stage of the liquid margarine emulsion, especially since the oleo-oil prepared from beef tallow is very little used nowadays.

The votator also has the disadvantage that the fat tends to form large, coarse crystals as a result of supercooling phenomena, so that the margarine post-crystallizes after it is packed. This causes the formation of a solid network of crystals; the margarine stiffens and assumes the property of so-called structural hardness.

On spreading the margarine with a knife the network is disrupted; this can be felt as a resistance to spreading.

In recent years the electron-microscope has taught us a great deal about the form of triglyceride crystals, and about the way in which they can grow together (see Pl. 37B). It is now possible to measure the structural hardness precisely by means of a consistency measurement known as work softening. The difference in hardness before and after kneading the margarine is measured. This difference in hardness is a measure of the extent to which the crystals in the product during post-crystallization have formed a crystal network (see Pl. 39A, B). In Chapter Three an account is given of how the unwanted structural hardness can be prevented to some extent by, for instance, a recirculation system. From as early as 1920, dilatation measurements have been used to determine the amount of solid phase. This is done by measuring, in a dilatometer, the difference in the volume occupied by oil and the same weight of fat crystals at the same temperature; in other words, to determine the volume increase (the dilatation) during melting.

The dilatation curve, from which the amount of solid phase at any temperature can be calculated, is a universally accepted criterion in margarine processing. Fortunately, identical or at least closely similar dilatation lines can be obtained with different fat compositions, and this gives the necessary flexibility in the choice of raw materials. The required melting behaviour is dictated by the conditions under which the product is to be used. If a quick-melting product is needed for a moderate climate, the aim will be for a steep dilatation curve. When, however, a product is for use in the tropics, it will need

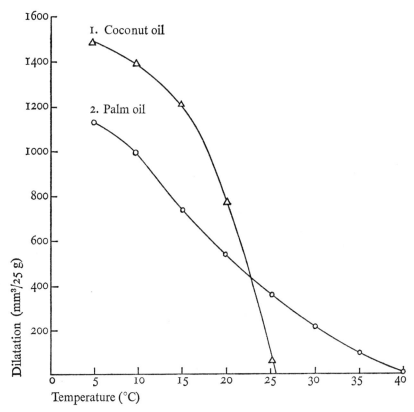

FIG. 5.7. Dilatation curves of coconut oil and palm oil.

to have a certain 'body'; a sufficient amount of solid phase, even at higher temperatures. The aim will then be for a rather flat dilatation curve (see Fig. 5.7).

Between these two extremes, many intermediate melting behaviours can be achieved. For a soft margarine to be kept in refrigerators for use in a moderate climate the ideal dilatation curve is one that is at first flat and then falls steeply at higher temperatures; otherwise the margarine would be thick on the palate as a result of too large an amount of high-melting triglycerides. Many attempts have been made to evolve a method for calculating the melting behaviour of complicated fat mixtures, on the basis of measurements made on simple, well-defined, triglyceride mixtures. However, a complication is introduced by the solubility of the fat crystals in the liquid oil phase. At present it is not possible to replace the empirical method of fat compounding, based on the dilatation properties of the individual components, by a more rational method based purely on triglyceride composition. Thus the use of the dilatation method is still indispensable. However, it has the disadvantage of giving no information at all about the state of the fat crystals (e.g. whether there are a few coarse or many fine crystals).

When only a few types of triglycerides are present, the tendency for large crystals to form is much greater than when the high-melting fatty acids are distributed at random over the triglycerides. This is one of the reasons why the formerly much-used oleo-oil, with its fatty acids distributed almost entirely at random, gives a product with a tough, somewhat springy consistency. In this connection, interesterification has become an important means of approximating to such a consistency when other raw materials are used.

It has already been explained that the hydrogenation specialist also has something to contribute to this.

The consistency defects which were experienced when the votator process was first introduced in the factories, were gradually overcome as a result of all these investigations.

Emulsifiers

Up to now we have spoken only about the state in which the fats occur in margarine; the solid–liquid ratio and the size, shape, and cohesion of the fat crystals. However, in addition to a fat phase, margarine also has a water phase (about 16 per cent by weight). Margarine is a water-in-oil emulsion in which the water, with milk solids dissolved in it, is distributed throughout the fat phase in the form of microscopically small droplets.

In order to prepare such an emulsion and give it the necessary stability, the use of emulsifiers is essential. The action of these substances rests on their dual character, their mixed lipophilic–hydrophilic structure, which tends to cause the molecules of the emulsifier to move for preference into the interface between the oil phase and the water phase. When a two-phase system consisting of an oil phase and a water phase to which such a substance has been added is mechanically treated, the emulsifier molecules facilitate the formation of a large interfacial area between oil and water. With the choice of a suitable emulsifier, a very fine distribution of the water phase through the oil phase can be achieved.

For this purpose, the margarine manufacturer has, apart from skim-milk protein, a number of other emulsifiers at his disposal. Among the most widely used emulsifiers are the mixtures of phospholipids which occur in vegetable oils, and usually consist of lecithin, cephalin, and a few others including inosities. They are mixtures of lipids which are derived from triglycerides, but with one of the fatty acids replaced by a substituent containing phosphoric acid.

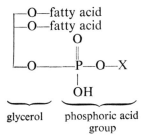

glycerol   phosphoric acid
            group

Lecithin: X = cholin.
Cephalin: X = ethanolamine.
Inositide: X = (myo)inositol.

The separation of these substances from the oil during refining and their subsequent purification are described in Chapter Two.

The effect of protein and lecithin can be boosted by the addition of monoglycerides—long since described by Berthelot (2)—which are known as strong water-binders. The preparation of these compounds is again based on the interesterification principle; fat is treated with an excess of free glycerol, which causes the fatty acids to distribute themselves over all glycerol molecules under the influence of a catalyst. Thus a mixture of mono- and diglycerides is formed, which is normally used, as such, as an emulsifier.

The effect of lecithin is unfavourably influenced by milk proteins which may be present. Lecithin is adsorbed by these proteins, and this impairs its emulsifying action. The addition of salt, however, can partially break the protein–lecithin association and restore the emulsifying action.

Just how phospholipids associate with proteins is not yet completely clear, but it seems likely that important information on this will become available from biochemical studies in the near future. We are

referring here to the problem of the structure of the so-called biomembranes (63), which is currently being studied in laboratories all
over the world. These biomembranes are an essential feature of every
living cell, and it has been established that they consist mainly of a
combination of proteins and phospholipids, in animal cells often
further combined with cholesterol.

The biochemical investigation of these structures, which are of the
utmost importance for the function of the cell, repeatedly comes up
against great difficulties. It is definitely known that the association is
partly dependent on an interaction between the fatty acid chains of
the phospholipids and certain non-polar groups of the membrane
proteins. It is not inconceivable that such interactions also occur
between lecithin and milk proteins.

Knowledge of these phenomena is important for the further improvement of the behaviour of margarine when used for shallow
frying. Unless the lecithin can continue, during frying, to exercise its
stabilizing influence, the water phase will quickly precipitate in large
droplets as the margarine melts. This may give rise to excessive spattering, a problem which is serious in some European countries where
saltless margarine is preferred.

Many attempts have been made to improve the emulsion stability
of saltless, milk-containing margarine. However, the additives recommended for this purpose often have the disadvantage that they consist of poorly defined mixtures, the physiological effect of which is
far from being established. In most countries their use is therefore
forbidden, and the choice of emulsifier is limited to lecithin, monoglycerides, and milk proteins. In some cases egg-yolk is also added,
but a disadvantage is its strong, characteristic taste.

MILK SOURING

A water phase containing milk solids (proteins, lactose, salts) is by
its very nature an exceptionally good medium for the growth of
micro-organisms.

We have now come to the previously named second aspect of the
keeping properties of margarine, the resistance to microbial spoilage.

The preservation of margarine, that is, the prevention of the growth
of undesirable micro-organisms, can be achieved by the deliberate
addition of other micro-organisms. From time immemorial, people
have made use of the bacterial souring of milk and cream as a

37A. Model of a nickel-on-silica catalyst.

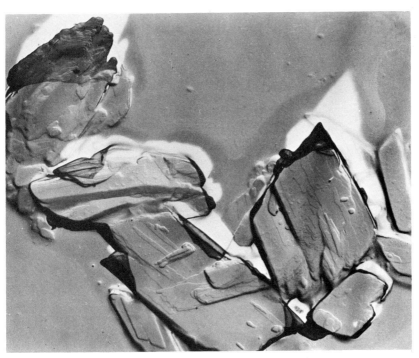

37B. Electron micrograph of fat crystals.

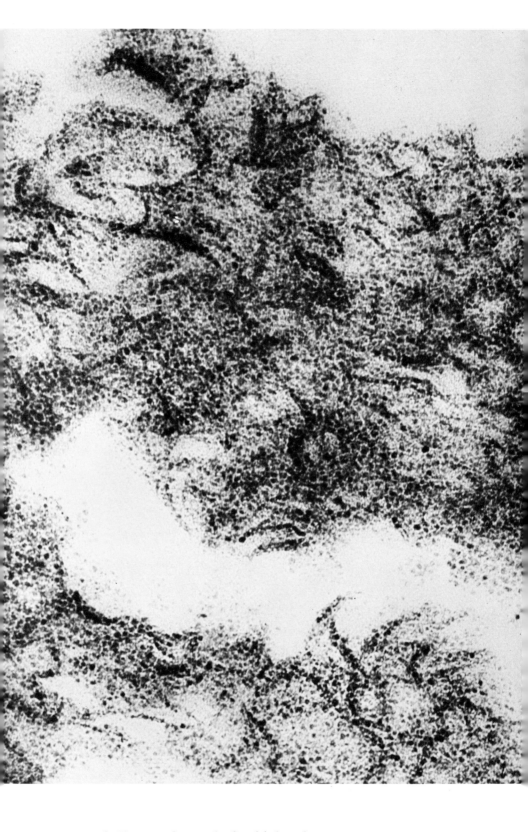

38. Electron micrograph of a nickel catalyst.

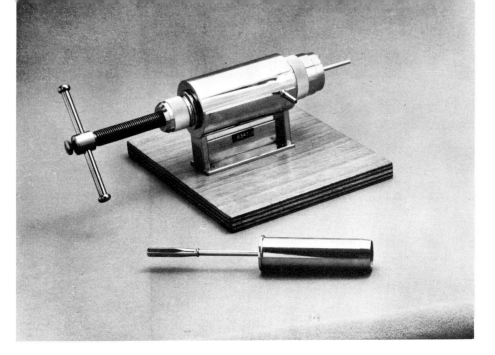

39A. Kneader used for measuring the consistency of margarine.

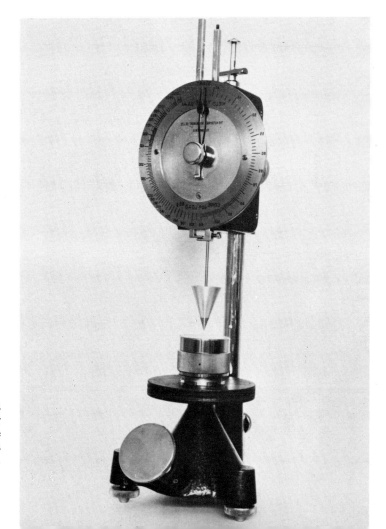

39B. Hutchinson's penetrometer for measuring the hardness of margarine.

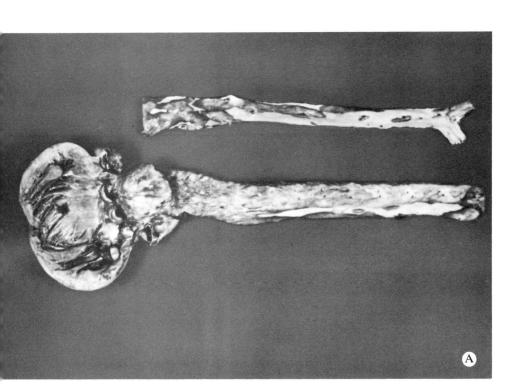

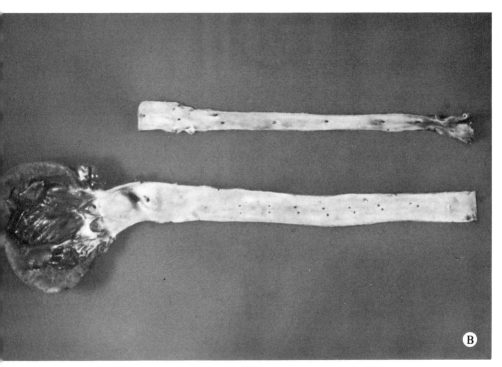

40. Rabbit aortas: (A) affected by, and (B) unaffected by, atherosclerosis.

reliable way of preventing growth of unwanted micro-organisms. Without knowing what was happening, they thus made use of the ability of lactic acid bacteria to form lactic acid from lactose. This created a medium which, partly because of its low pH, prevented the growth of taste-deteriorating and pathogenic micro-organisms.

In 1890, Storch and Weigmann introduced the use of pure cultures of *Bacterium lactis acidis* Leichmann in the preparation of butter, 'to induce and control the desired ripening and thus to obtain a well-flavoured butter' (35). This principle was soon applied to the souring of the milk phase for the preparation of margarine. Pure cultures became commercially available under the name of 'starters'; yet even today, many margarine producers still use pure cultures that they have developed themselves. It is essential for a satisfactory souring process that the skim-milk is first pasteurized, in order to suppress the influence of other micro-organisms in the initial stages of the process.

Originally the souring process was prompted by the desire to impart a butter-like aroma to the margarine. But from what has already been said about butter aroma, it may have become evident that such attempts were only partially successful as far as the formation of diacetyl was concerned. Other aroma components could not be obtained in this way. The main importance of milk souring in the preparation of margarine—now that all the important components of butter aroma are known and can easily be added—lies not in the improvement of the aroma of the product, but in the possibility of producing margarine with an almost unlimited microbiological keeping property without the addition of artificial preserving agents.

In those countries where consumer preference tends towards a less acidic or a completely neutral-tasting margarine—similar to sweet cream butter—the lactic acid formed in the soured milk is neutralized with bicarbonate. With this type of product special precautions must be taken to ensure a reasonably long shelf-life, since a neutral protein- and lactose-containing water phase cannot function as a preserving medium. That is why milk solids are either omitted altogether (water margarines) or, provided this is in line with the preference of the consumer, salt is added to the milk phase as a preserving agent. Such salted milk margarines are in demand in many countries, including England, Sweden, the U.S.A., and Canada.

Up to about 1960, however, use was often made of benzoic acid (about 0·1 per cent) where this was permitted as a preserving agent, to act as an extra precaution against possible infections. But in the last twenty years hygienic standards generally, and control of the cleanliness of the apparatus (made easier by the introduction of votators) have gradually made the use of benzoic acid as a preserving agent superfluous. This is important as it eliminates an additive which is not entirely without influence on the taste of the final product and which impeded the recent work on flavour improvement.

The complete suppression of the growth of undesirable bacteria and mould in sour margarines, without the use of extra preserving agents, is partly due to better control of the water distribution in margarine. If it is ensured that the size of the water droplets is of the order of 10 μm, and the amount of milk solids is correctly adjusted by the choice of the milk–water ratio, it can easily be calculated that, per droplet, there is simply not sufficient nutrient present for any appreciable growth of bacteria, even if there should be reinfection in the individual droplets. Should growth occur in a limited number of droplets, it will quickly cease for lack of nutrients. The emulsion stability now attainable is a guarantee that during transport and storage the droplets will not coalesce to form larger droplets, and therefore will not form free moisture on the surface of the margarine. This prevents mould growth on the surface.

In a number of European countries (Germany, Austria, the Netherlands, Belgium), low-salt, or saltless, acidic margarines have been in favour since the Second World War. This is partly because the consumers in these countries had grown accustomed to saltless butter; in the latter years of the war the salt content in this product had been drastically reduced, because of oxidative flavour-deterioration during cold storage. Experience has shown that oxidative spoilage in oils and fats is promoted by chlorine ions from kitchen salt as well as by acidity. Because of the modernization of distribution techniques (cold storage and transport) it has in the past few years been possible to market less acidic, or even neutral, saltless margarines which strongly resemble, for instance, the *Süssrahm* butter produced in Germany. The rapid acceptance of these margarines must be at least partly attributed to the appearance of the refrigerator in so many households. When, despite this, salt is added for reasons of taste preference, microbial control becomes much easier; but then one has the disadvantage of flavour reversion in the fat component. That is why it has proved so important to subjugate the oxidative flavour reversion completely by eliminating the precursors of the flavour reversion from the raw materials. Here again, the introduction of cold transport and storage has helped, as the rate of chemical oxidation slows down at lower temperatures. The advent of the refrigerator in the home in most countries of Europe since the Second World War has, moreover, enabled the margarine manufacturer to gain a formidable lead over the butter producer. By making full use of the knowledge of consistency as influenced by fat blending and processing which had meanwhile been accumulated, it was possible to market in rapid succession a whole new range of margarines, whose most important assets were good consistency and spreadability straight out of the refrigerator. Compared with conventional margarines these ice-box types contain, of course, a higher proportion of liquid oil.

It was certainly a kind turn of fate that the introduction of more liquid oil phase in modern margarines went hand-in-hand with surprising developments in the field of the physiology and biochemistry of fats, as we shall now see.

Essential fatty acids

For reasons given earlier, it was not until about 1950 that an intensive study of the biochemical and physiological role of lipids could really get off the ground. Let us have another look at the essential fatty acids and review what has come to light in the past two decades about the essential fatty acids, linoleic acid and arachidonic acid.

Especially the investigations of Thomasson (1953, the Netherlands) (64) and of Mead and Howton (1957, U.S.A.) (65) revealed many new data.

It was Thomasson who, using fatty acids which were either isolated from natural sources or had been prepared synthetically, first investigated the relation between the structure of the fatty acids (chain length and number and location of the double bonds) and their biological activity. By means of his rapid bio-assay method the biopotencies of a large number of fatty acids were determined.

From the values of the biopotencies, Thomasson made the interesting discovery that all fatty acids with an even number (18 or 20 carbon atoms), having at least two double bonds, located in the 6 and 9 positions, counted from the terminal methyl group of the fatty acid chain (for which he introduced the $\omega 6, 9$ notation),

$$CH_3-(CH_2)_4-\overset{\overset{\displaystyle H}{|}}{C}=\overset{\overset{\displaystyle H}{|}}{C}-CH_2-\overset{\overset{\displaystyle H}{|}}{C}=\overset{\overset{\displaystyle H}{|}}{C}-(CH_2)_n-CO_2H$$

(in which n = 7 or 9)

possess EFA activity, provided both double bonds are in the *cis*-configuration.

If, in the right-hand half, the proximal part of the chain, another one or two double bonds occur in the same sort of arrangement, the activity is generally further increased.

Structural formula of the acid (counted from terminal CH₃-group)	Biological activity
CH₃ CH₂ CH₂ — CH₂ — CH₂ CH₂ CH₂ CH₂ / CH₂ CH₂ CH=CH(6,7) CH=CH(9,10) CH₂ CH₂ CH₂ CO₂H(18)	100
CH₃ CH=CH(3,4) CH=CH(6,7) CH=CH(9,10) CH₂ CH₂ CH₂ CO₂H(18) / CH₂ CH₂ CH₂ CH₂ CH₂ CH₂ CH₂	9
CH₃ CH₂ CH₂ — CH₂ — CH₂ — CH₂ CH₂ CO₂H(18) / CH₂ CH₂ CH=CH(6,7) CH=CH(9,10) CH=CH(12,13) CH₂ CH₂	115
CH₃ CH₂ CH₂ — CH₂ — CH₂ CH₂ CH₂ CH₂ CO₂H(19) / CH₂ CH₂ CH=CH(6,7) CH=CH(9,10) CH₂ CH₂ CH₂ CH₂	9
CH₃ CH₂ CH₂ — CH₂ — CH₂ — CH₂ CH₂ CH₂ / CH₂ CH₂ CH=CH(6,7) CH=CH(9,10) CH=CH(12,13) CH₂ CH₂ CO₂H(19)	6
CH₃ CH₂ CH₂ — CH₂ — CH₂ CH₂ CH₂ CH₂ CH₂ / CH₂ CH₂ CH=CH(6,7) CH=CH(9,10) CH₂ CH₂ CH₂ CH₂ CO₂H(20)	46
CH₃ CH₂ CH₂ — CH₂ — CH₂ — CH₂ CH₂ CH₂ CO₂H(20) / CH₂ CH₂ CH=CH(6,7) CH=CH(9,10) CH=CH(12,13) CH₂ CH₂ CH₂	102
CH₃ CH₂ CH₂ — CH₂ — CH₂ — CH₂ — CH₂ CH₂ / CH₂ CH₂ CH=CH(6,7) CH=CH(9,10) CH=(12) H(13) CH=CH(15,16) CH₂ CO₂H(20)	130

TABLE 5.8. Biological activity of polyunsaturated fatty acids.

If, on the other hand, in the left-hand part of the chain, the terminal part, a double bond occurs at the terminal ω3 position, the activity decreases to such an extent that it must be strongly doubted whether the activity measured comes from the acid itself or is not rather the result of a slight contamination with one of the strongly active ω6 acids. This can also be said of the ω6 acids with an uneven number of carbon atoms, which have proved to be very weakly active. A comparison of the activities of the following ω6, 9 acids, containing an even number of carbon atoms:

	Activity/g
Linoleic acid (ω6, 9 with 18 carbon atoms)	100
Dihomo-linoleic acid (ω6, 9 with 20 carbon atoms)	46
γ-linolenic acid (ω6, 9, 12 with 18 carbon atoms)	115
Dihomo-γ-linolenic acid (ω6, 9, 12 with 20 carbon atoms)	102
Arachidonic acid (ω6, 9, 12, 15 with 20 carbon atoms)	130

has led to a hypothesis of the biochemical pathway by which arachidonic acid is formed from linoleic acid both in man and in animals. In the conversion of linoleic acid into arachidonic acid, during which the activity on the same weight basis does after all increase by some 30 per cent, we may reasonably proceed from the premiss that the intermediate products in the biochemical reactions have at least the activity of linoleic acid.

From the scheme of possible pathways given below (66), it will be clear that route *a* is the most probable one.

$$\begin{array}{ccc}
& b & \\
\text{linoleic acid} & \rightleftharpoons & \text{dihomo-linoleic acid} \\
a\downarrow & c & \downarrow b \\
\gamma\text{-linolenic acid} & \rightarrow & \text{dihomo-}\gamma\text{-linolenic acid} \\
& a & \downarrow \\
& & \text{arachidonic acid}
\end{array}$$

($\rightarrow$ chain elongation: $\downarrow$ desaturation)

According to route *a*, a third double bond is first introduced into the linoleic acid, after which the proximal end of the carbon chain is lengthened by two carbon atoms and finally this acid, now having 20 carbon atoms, is desaturated, again proximally, to arachidonic acid.

Route *b* is also conceivable but, in view of the low activity (64) of dihomo-linoleic acid, is less probable. When administered to test animals, this acid is likely to be converted to arachidonic acid along route *c*, followed by *a*, which means that an extra bio-conversion step is involved.

Shortly afterwards the high activity of dihomo-γ-linolenic acid was confirmed by Mead and Howton; they formulated the same sequence of events, and moreover, succeeded in demonstrating with the aid of radioactive labelled γ-linolenic acid, the direct conversion of this acid into arachidonic acid.

Still later, the intermediate products of route *a* were isolated and identified by Nugteren (67) and by Stoffel (68), during experiments concerning the *in vitro* conversion of linoleic acid by means of liver cell fractions. This confirmed the conversion route outlined above.

Meanwhile Mead had concentrated his attention on a peculiar fatty acid that had been described by Nunn and Smedley-Maclean as early as 1936. They found this fatty acid in abnormally high concentrations in animals deficient in linoleic acid. This eicosa-ω9, 12, 15-trienoic acid with 20 carbon atoms has one double bond less than arachidonic acid, also with 20 carbon atoms, which is found in non-deficient animals. The eicosatrienoic acid has no EFA-activity at all, this being in agreement with the absence of the ω6 double bond which has been found necessary for this activity in acids with an even number of carbon atoms. More than twenty years after Smedley-Maclean had suggested the biochemical origin of this acid, Fulco and Mead (69) demonstrated that it is formed in the deficient animal from the non-essential oleic acid, the most abundantly occurring fatty acid in nature, which the animal itself can produce from carbohydrates.

Apparently, the enzymes, whose function it is to convert linoleic acid to the more potent tetra-unsaturated arachidonic acid, will, in the absence of linoleic acid, accept oleic acid as a substitute, in a vain attempt to produce arachidonic acid. We have already referred to the phospholipids of biomembranes. It has been found that these phospholipids contain large amounts of essential fatty acids, and in particular, of arachidonic acid, which appears to accumulate at a specific position in the molecular structure. In the EFA-deficient test animal, the inactive eicosatrienoic acid takes up precisely this position instead of the arachidonic acid.

Although this biochemical trick may enable the animal to form cell membranes of apparently normal structure, the animal nevertheless shows a reduced growth-rate, abnormally high water evaporation through the skin, and all the other known EFA-deficiency syndromes.

PROSTAGLANDINS

No further clue to the specific role of arachidonic acid (see p. 177) was obtained until the spectacular discoveries, made in 1964 independently of each other, by van Dorp (70) (Unilever Research Laboratory, Vlaardingen, The Netherlands) and Bergström (71) (Karolinska Institute, Stockholm), which established the link between the essential fatty acids containing 20 carbon atoms (arachidonic acid and dihomo-γ-linolenic acid) on the one hand, and a substance known since 1930 to occur in human seminal plasma (Kurzrok and

Lieb (72) and referred to by the term of prostaglandins (Goldblatt (73), van Euler (74)), on the other. The study of the chemical nature of prostaglandins was revived by Bergström *et al.* (75) in 1967; their structure was defined as centrally cyclized fatty acids in which 3 oxygen atoms have been introduced at specific positions (two in the 5-membered carbon ring and one in the terminal side chain).

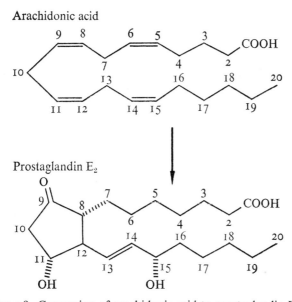

FIG. 5.8. Conversion of arachidonic acid to prostaglandin E_2.

In 1964 it was shown that a particular animal tissue (one vesicular gland of the ram) contains an enzyme system capable of converting these essential fatty acids into certain, by then identified, prostaglandins (PGE_1, PGE_2, PGF_1, PGF_2). It was soon found that such enzymes also occur in other animal, as well as human, tissues and organs, and at present there is evidence that the enzyme is distributed very widely indeed (brain, kidney, liver, lung, intestine, smooth muscle, iris).

In the subsequent two years, the research teams in Stockholm and Vlaardingen succeeded in elucidating the mechanism of this type of bioconversion. In addition, the Swedish group added greatly to the analytical refinement and was highly successful in relating the prostaglandins, of which at present sixteen species are known, to physiological effects, such as the reduction of fat mobilization from adipose tissue and the lowering of the blood pressure in arteries.

The Dutch group have studied the enzyme substrate specificity and found a highly significant correlation between essential fatty acid activity and the case of bioconversion of the precursor acids into prostaglandins on the one hand, and the physiological activity of the prostaglandins thus formed, on the other. On this basis they developed a wider concept of the relationship between EFA-activity and molecular structure in which the proximal chain structure of the acid proved to be essential. Their definition of essential fatty acid structure covers the natural even-numbered, as well as some odd-numbered, fatty acids with chain lengths of 19, 20, and 21 carbon atoms.

Physiological studies carried out in the same laboratory revealed the interesting phenomenon that prostaglandin E_1 has a strong inhibiting effect on human blood platelet aggregation (76). Moreover, a marked influence on heart activity was observed. An appreciably increased coronary flow is induced by PGE_1 and PGE_2, whereas the PGF series is inactive in this respect. The reverse sequence being observed in measurements of the heart contractility: the F-series is active and the E-series shows no activity at all (77). Activities are observed at concentrations of $1-10$ $\mu m/kg$ bodyweight. At the time of writing, many laboratories are contributing to this 'boom' in lipid biochemistry and the staggering number of publications reflects the great importance which is being attached to this subject.

Health aspects

Let us see what, in the context of this chapter on margarine, is the significance of these scientific findings. For this we again turn to the early 1950s. In those days, medical circles were becoming increasingly concerned about the very high incidence in western countries of cardiovascular diseases. Of the total number of deaths in men of the age-group 45–65 in these countries (U.S.A., Britain, Scandinavia, and some other European countries) about 50 per cent is due to these diseases. The most common cause is atherosclerosis, a degeneration of the blood vessel walls.

Sudden death by heart failure (heart infarct) is one of the most dramatic consequences.

A strong correlation between heart infarct and a high level of blood cholesterol as well as total blood lipids was found; and in the same period it was mentioned in the literature that highly unsaturated oils exert a lowering effect on blood cholesterol and blood lipids, whereas saturated type fats have the opposite effect (79). One group of investigators argued that an intake of unsaturated oils would therefore have a beneficial effect by reducing the risk of blood vessel lesions, whereas others (correctly) opposed this view becauᴐe of lack of proof of causality with respect to the effect of blood cholesterol on the development of atherosclerosis. The literature of this period is full

	Figures (per cent) of all deaths in each age-group			
	35–44	45–54	55–64	65–74
U.S.A.	37	51	57	62
United Kingdom	34	42	45	52
Scandinavia	21	37	48	55
Netherlands	25	33	39	48

TABLE 5.9. Mortality from cardiovascular diseases in males (1958–60) (78).

of rather contradictory statements, and the problem became a controversial issue in the U.S.A. and in some European countries between the dairy and the oils and fats industries. The problem has by now gradually been settled owing to the straightforward observation, made in a number of institutes, of a direct relationship between the type of fat and the development of atherosclerotic blood vessel lesions, which has been reported for five animal species. Lambert (80) (1958), Gottenbos (81) (1959), and Malmros (82) (1959) were first to observe this relationship in rabbits, and these observations ran parallel to those made by Wigand (83) (1959), Krogh (84) (1961), Funch (85) (1962) (rabbits); Roswell (86) (1958) (pigs); Hegsted (87) (1960) (chickens); (Clarkson (88), Lofland (89) (1961) (pigeons); and by Wissler (90) (1960–1) on primates. In short, the results of these animal experiments are: a distinct inhibiting effect on the development of atherosclerosis was observed with oils containing linoleic acid (corn oil, sunflower oil, soya bean oil), whereas a severe atherosclerosis had developed in the animals that had received diets containing saturated type fats (e.g. coconut oil) at a level of about 40 calories per cent (20 per cent by weight). A neutral effect was observed with mono-unsaturated fats. Moreover, Thomasson (81) demonstrated that a fat-free diet induced a moderate atherosclerosis under the same test conditions (see Pl. 40).

Positive evidence justifying the extrapolation of these findings to humans was obtained from long-term statistical studies on large population groups, and meanwhile about a dozen such investigations have been carried out in the U.S.A., Britain, and Scandinavia. In these studies, a population group on a normal dietary regime was compared with a group which volunteered to use a diet in which a high level of polyunsaturated oil had been incorporated. In most of these studies, men were chosen who had already suffered a non-fatal coronary infarct. In a thesis by Leren (91), an analysis is given of the results obtained so far. It leads to the important conclusion that in the majority of these studies the polyunsaturated diet had a significantly beneficial effect, as judged by the difference in incidence of reinfarction between the groups of participants during the test periods. Only a few tests were inconclusive, and none of the studies showed the opposite effect. Margarine manufacturers in the U.S.A. were among the first to recognize the importance of incorporating fats with a high content of polyunsaturated fatty acids in their products. There has been in the U.S.A. a gradual shift towards the production of margarine with a high content of linoleic acid, a development which is also manifest in Europe, where several brands have become available in both the 25 per cent and the 50 per cent linoleic acid range.

There is every reason for the margarine manufacturer to aim at the maximum percentage of linoleic acid and as low a percentage of saturated fatty acids as attainable in practice, the more so since it is necessary to over-compensate for the saturated fatty acids occurring in 'invisible' fats contained in many common foods (e.g. meat, milk, cheese, chocolate, ice-cream, biscuits). The obvious way to achieve this extra supply of linoleic acid is through margarine or salad oil. The former is by far the most effective because of the amounts which are consumed. In a number of western countries, an appreciable percentage of the daily fat intake is derived from margarine. In the Netherlands this is between 40 and 50 per cent.

It is interesting to see how the role of polyunsaturated fatty acids can be related to prostaglandins. At present it is known that some of the prostaglandins are generated in most parts of the human body. When a smooth muscle contracts, prostaglandins E_1 and E_2 are formed (92). They promote the widening of the peripheral blood vessels, thus stimulating the blood oxygen supply. The same activity presumably occurs in the heart muscles, and one might speculate that the essential fatty acids in the cell biomembranes, as the precursors of the prostaglandins, are the promoters of a very intricate local regulation mechanism. Once the prostaglandins are in the blood stream they are quickly eliminated. Supply of prostaglandins as such, by food or by injection, cannot cure EFA deficiency (93). This suggests that the prostaglandins must be generated *in situ* at cellular level in various parts of body tissue and organs in order to exert their physiological functions.

The counteraction of blood platelet aggregation (stickiness) by certain types of prostaglandins suggests a possible mechanism against the onset of thrombosis, which is, among other things, so closely linked to heart infarct and possibly also to the deposition of platelets on blood vessel walls as the initial stage of atherosclerosis.

At the time of writing it is certainly premature to draw any definite conclusion from these observations, but it is not over-optimistic to assume that this most recent offspring of biochemical lipid research may, in the end, contribute to an understanding of the beneficial role of polyunsaturated fats in combating atherosclerosis.

SUMMARY

Finally, let us review in broad outline these first 100 years in the history of margarine.

The first conspicuous and highly unusual fact is that, in contrast to so many inventions that have been shelved sometimes for decades, the invention of Mège Mouriès was immediately put to practical use; and not only in France, but in most western countries and even outside Europe. From the very beginning production rose steeply; one must therefore draw the conclusion that the invention fitted exactly into the social and economic pattern of those days, and proved to have a much wider application than that envisaged in Napoleon III's original assignment. From the moment that the product made its début on the open market, its quality aspect became the focal point in further development. It is in this field, in its broadest sense, that first factory development units and, at a later stage, research laboratories occupied themselves.

In the furtherance of the scientific research designed to improve the quality of margarine, many disciplines have gradually become involved. Hydrogenation came just in time to correct a situation in which a shortage of solid fats was becoming acute, and enabled hitherto unsuitable raw materials to be used in margarine production. Later, of course, the original hydrogenation process underwent improvement after improvement, resulting in a shift from the mere hardening of fats to the production of oil–fat mixtures with very subtle differences in melting behaviour which could be adjusted at will. This led to close co-operation being established between the hydrogenation specialists and those engaged in the study of crystallization behaviour.

It is especially due to the efforts of these two groups that the present-day margarine manufacturer has at his disposal many sophisticated means of varying, as required, the consistency and flavour of the product.

Hygiene during production has also been of immense importance in the development of the margarine industry. In 1861, only eight years before Mège Mouriès made his first margarine, his compatriot, the chemist Louis Pasteur, published the historic paper rejecting the doctrine of *generatio spontanea*, which was to spark off a controversy that raged for at least ten years. Not until much later were hygienic precautions, such as sterilization and pasteurization, developed on a rational basis for use in food manufacturing. Pasteurization of the milk phase to prevent undesirable infections has now become a universally applied principle in margarine processing.

The deliberate application of milk-souring to improve the aroma of margarine played only a transient role, yet even today it contributes largely to the good microbiological keeping property of the final product. It has also reduced the necessity of adding preservatives, a trend further assisted by increased knowledge in the field of emulsifiers, which has enabled very stable emulsions with an extremely fine water-droplet distribution to be made.

The introduction, in 1952, of gas-chromatographic and spectro-photometric methods of separation and identification enabled the organic chemist to replace the originally used empirical procedure of the flavour blender by a rational approach based on exact knowledge of the components responsible for the butter aroma. The same analytical methods have made it possible to investigate the biochemical and physiological role of fats. Only forty years ago, fats were regarded merely as a constituent of our diet having a high calorific value, without any appreciation of the differences between the building stones of the various fats. It was, however, recognized after the discovery of the fat-soluble vitamins A and D, that margarine was an excellent vehicle for introducing these indispensable nutrients into the daily diet.

Margarine has achieved a new dimension from the point of view of public health, and has established its difference in a positive sense from the original concept, which was aimed solely at the imitation of butter.

Today the natural sciences are advancing very rapidly; large groups of investigators are now occupying themselves with the problem of the origin of life and are approaching the point at which they almost understand the various chemical mechanisms concerned. This has been accompanied by a regrouping of scientific disciplines in the so-called molecular biology. In this the lipids originally played a subordinate role; yet they too will undoubtedly assume a position of increasing importance. We can appreciate how comprehensive the lipid investigations undertaken in the research laboratories on behalf of the margarine industry have now become.

NOTES AND REFERENCES

1. CLAYTON, W. *Margarine* (London, 1920).

2. BERTHELOT, M.P.E. *Annales de chimie et de physique*, **41**, 3 (1854), 216.

3. See SCHWITZER, M.K. *Margarine and other food fats* (London, 1956), p. 65.

4. SABATIER, P., and SENDERENS, J.B. *Comptes rendues*, **132** (1901), 210.

5. NORMANN, W. Verfahren zur Umwandlung ungesättigter Fettsäuren und deren Glyzeride in Gesättigte Verbindungen. German Patent 139 457 (1902) (Process for converting unsaturated fatty acids or their glycerides into saturated compounds). British Patent Application 1515 (1903).

6. BOEKENOOGEN, H.A. *Analysis and characterisation of oils, fats, and fat products* (London, 1964), vol. i.

7. WIJS, J.J.A. *Berichte*, **31** (1898), 750.

8. KÖTTSTORFER, J. *Zeitschrift für analytische Chemie*, **18** (1879), 199.

9. LEA, C.H. *Proceedings of the Royal Society of London*, B **108** (1931), 175.

10. NORMANN, W. *Chemie Umschau Gebiete Fette, Oele, Wachse, und Harze*, **38** (1931), 17.

11. BLOCH, K. *Lipide metabolism* (New York and London, 1960).

12. DARBY, S. *Annales*, **69** (1849), 1.

13. PETERS, K. *Monatschrift*, **7** (1886), 522.

14. BURR, G.O., and BURR, M.M. *Journal of biological chemistry*, **82** (1929), 345.

15. ERDMANN, E., BEDFORD, F., and RASPE, F. *Berichte*, **42** (1909), 1334.

16. HILDITCH, T.P., *et al. Chemical constitution of natural fats and oils* (London, 1940).

222 J. BOLDINGH

17. BERNARD, C. *Leçons de physiologie expérimentale appliquée à la médicine* (Paris, 1856).

18. KNOOP, F. *Beiträge zur chemischen Physiologie und Pathologie*, **6** (1904), 150.

19. LIPMANN, F. *Journal of biological chemistry*, **160** (1945), 173.
—— and TUTTLE, L. C. *Biochimica et biophysica acta*, **4** (1950), 301.

20. LYNEN, F., and REICHERT, E. *Angewandte Chemie*, **63** (1951), 47.

21. See LYNEN, F., *et al.* Ibid. **71** (1959), 481.

22. GREEN, D. E. in *Biochemical problems of lipids* (ed. POPJÁK, G., and LE BRETON, E.) (London, 1956), p. 233.

23. VERKADE, P. E., ELZAS, M., VAN DER LEE, J., DE WOLFF, H. H., VERKADE-SANDBERGEN, A., and VAN DER SANDE, D. *Proceedings. Koninklijke Nederlandse Akademie van Wetenschappen*, **35** (1932), 251.

24. —— and VAN DER LEE, J. Ibid. **36** (1933), 314.

25. NUNN, L. C. A., and SMEDLEY-MACLEAN, I. *Biochemical journal*, **32** (1938), 2178.

26. SCHOENHEIMER, R., and RITTENBERG, D. *Journal of biological chemistry*, **114** (1936), 381.

27. BLOOMFIELD, D. K., and BLOCH, K. Ibid. **235** (1960), 337.
BLOCH, K., *et al. Federation proceedings*, **20** (1961), 921.
LENNARZ, W. J., LIGHT, R. J., and BLOCH, K. *Proceedings of the National Academy of Sciences*, **48** (1962), 840.

28. TSWETT, M. *Berichte der deutschen Botanischen Gesellschaft*, **24** (1906), 316.

29. ZECHMEISTER, L., and VON CHOLNOKY, L. *Die chromatographische Absorptionsmethode* (*Chromatographic absorption methods*) (Vienna, 1937).

30. MARTIN, A. J. P., and SYNGE, R. L. M. *Biochemical journal*, **35** (1941), 1358.

31. —— *et al.* Ibid. **38** (1944), 224.

32. BOLDINGH, J. *Recueil des travaux chimiques*, **69** (1950), 247.
HOWARD, G. A., and MARTIN, A. J. P. *Biochemical journal*, **46** (1950), 533.

33. JAMES, A. T., and MARTIN, A. J. P. Ibid. **50** (1952), 679.

34. VAN NIEL, C. B., KLUYVER, A. J., and DERX, H. G. *Biochemisches Zeitschrift*, **210** (1929), 234.

35. See LEBBIN, G. *Margarine* (Leipzig, 1926), p. 237.

36. KNETEMAN, A. *Antonie van Leeuwenhoek*, **18** (1952), 275.

37. SCHOGT, J. C. M., and DE BRUIJN, J. *Journal of the American Oil Chemists Society*, **37** (1961), 40.

38. PATTON, S., and KEENEY, P. G. *Food research*, **22** (1957), 524.
—— —— *Journal of dairy science*, **42** (1959), 791.

39. BOLDINGH, J., and TAYLOR, R. J. *Nature*, **194** (1962), 909.

40. JURRIENS, G., and OELE, J. M. Ibid. **207** (1965), 864.
—— —— *Journal of the American Oil Chemists Society*, **42** (1965), 857.

41. HAVERKAMP BEGEMANN, P., and KOSTER, J. C. *Nature*, **202** (1964), 552.

42. FARMER, E. H. *Transactions of the Faraday Society*, **38** (1942), 340.
—— *et al. Journal of the Chemical Society*, (1942), 121.
—— *et al. Transactions of the Faraday Society*, **38** (1942), 348.

43. KEPPLER, J. G., *et al. Journal of the American Oil Chemists Society*, **42** (1965), 246.

44. —— Ibid. **44** (1967), 543.

45. TWIGG, G. H. *Proceedings of the Royal Society of London*, A **178** (1941), 106.

46. DE JONG, K. *Fette, Seifen, Anstrichmittel*, **69** (1967), 277.

47. KLEIN, F., and DE JONG, K. *Recueil des travaux chimiques*, **78** (1959), 275.

48. HAVERKAMP BEGEMANN, P., and DE JONG, K. Ibid. **78** (1959), 275.

49. DE JONG, K., MOSTERT, K., and SLOOT, D. Ibid. **82** (1963), 837.

50. MEIJBOOM, P. W. *Journal of chromatography*, **24** (1966), 427.

51. BADINGS, H. T., and WASSINK, J. G. *Netherlands milk and dairy journal*, **17** (1963), 132.

52. BRUNAUER, S., EMMETT, P. H., and TELLER, E. *Journal of the American Chemical Society*, **60** (1938), 309.

53. COENEN, J. W. E. Thesis (Delft, 1958).

54. OKKERSE, C. in *2de lustrum Unilever chemie prijs* (Rotterdam, 1966), p. 54.

55. KORITALA, S., and DUTTON, H. J. *Journal of the American Oil Chemists Society*, **42** (1965), 144a; **43** (1966), 86.

56. NIKKI KAGAKU KABUSHIKI KAISHA—British Patent 973 957 (1964).

57. UNILEVER N.V. Dutch Patent Application 295 863 (1963).
OKKERSE, C., DE JONGE, A., COENEN, J. W. E., and ROZENDAAL, A. *Journal of the American Oil Chemists Society*, **44** (1967), 152.

58. DE VRIES, B. *Chemistry and industry*, (1962), 1049.

59. STAHL, E., *et al. Pharmazie*, **11** (1963), 633.

60. JURRIENS, G., DE VRIES, B., and SCHOUTEN, L. *Journal of lipid research*, **5** (1964), 366.

61. HAWLEY, H. K., and HOLMAN, G. W. *Journal of the American Oil Chemists Society*, **33** (1956), 29.
PLACEK, C., and HOLMAN, G. W. *Industrial and engineering chemistry*, **49** (1957), 162.

62. VAN LOON, C. (N.V. Anton Jurgens Margarine Fabrieken) British Patent Application 249 916 (1924); Dutch Patent Application 16 703 (1927).

63. See, for example, VAN DEENEN, L. L. M. *Progress in the chemistry of fats and other lipids* (Oxford, 1965), vol. viii.

64. THOMASSON, H. J. *Review vitamin research*, **25** (1953), 1.

65. MEAD, J. F., and HOWTON, D. R. *Journal of biological chemistry*, **229** (1957), 575.

66. BEERTHUIS, R. K., NUGTEREN, D. H., PABON, H. J. J., and VAN DORP, D. A. *Recueil des travaux chimiques*, in press.

67. NUGTEREN, D. H. *Biochimica et biophysica acta*, **60** (1962), 656; idem, *Biochemical journal*, **89** (1963), 28.

68. STOFFEL, W. *Biochemical and biophysical research communications*, **6** (1961), 270.

69. FULCO, A. J., and MEAD, J. F., *Journal of biological chemistry*, **234** (1959), 1411.

70. VAN DORP, D. A., BEERTHUIS, R. K., NUGTEREN, D. H., and VONKEMANN, H. *Biochimica et biophysica acta*, **90** (1964), 204.
——————— *Nature*, **203** (1964), 839.

71. BERGSTRÖM, S., DANIELSSON, H., and SAMUELSSON, B. *Biochimica et biophysica acta*, **90** (1964), 207.

72. KURZROK, R., and LIEB, C. C. *Proceedings of the Society for Experimental Biology and Medicine*, **28** (1930), 268.

73. GOLDBLATT, M. W. *Chemistry and industry*, **52** (1933), 1056.

74. VAN EULER, U. S. *Archiv für experimentelle Pathologie und Pharmakologie*, **175** (1934), 78.

75. BERGSTRÖM, S. *Science*, **157** (1967), 382.

76. KLOEZE, J., in 'Prostaglandins', *Proceedings of the second Nobel symposium* (Stockholm, 1967), p. 211.

77. VERGROESEN, A. J., DE BOER, J., and GOTTENBOS, J. J., Ibid.

78. DE HAAS, J. H. *Changing mortality patterns and cardiovascular diseases*, Department of Health, Netherlands Institute for Preventive Medicine (Haarlem, 1964).

79. KEYS, A., ANDERSON, J. T., and GRANDE, F. *Metabolism*, **14** (1965), 747.

80. LAMBERT, G. F., *et al. Proceedings of the Society for Experimental Biology and Medicine*, **97** (1958), 544.

81. GOTTENBOS, J. J., and THOMASSON, H. J. *Colloques Internationaux du CNRS*, **99** (1961), 221.

82. MALMROS, H., *et al. Arteriosklerose und Ernährung*, **3** (1959), 92.

83. WIGAND, G. *Acta medica scandinavica*, **166** (1959), 5.

84. KROGH, B., FUNCH, J. P., and DAM, H. *British journal of nutrition*, **15** (1961), 481.

85. FUNCH, J. P., KRISTENSEN, G., and DAM, H. Ibid. **16** (1962), 497.

86. ROSWELL, H. G., DOWNIE, H. G., and MUSTARD, J. F. *Canadian Medical Association journal*, **79** (1958), 647.

87. HEGSTED, D. M., *et al. American journal of clinical nutrition*, **8** (1960), 209.

88. CLARKSON, T. B., and PRITCHARD, R. W. *Federation proceedings*, **20** (1961), 96.

89. LOFLAND, H. B., CLARKSON, T. B., and GOODMAN, H. O. *Circulation research*, **9** (1961), 919.

90. WISSLER, R. W., *et al. Federation proceedings*, **19** (1960), 17; **20** (1961), 94.

91. LEREN, P. 'The effect of plasma cholesterol lowering diet in male survivors of myocardial infarction', *Acta medica scandinavica, Supplement 466* (1966).

92. RAMWELL, P. W., and SHAW, J. E. *Science*, **149** (1965), 1390.

93. GOTTENBOS, J. J., BEERTHUIS, R. K., and VAN DORP, D. A., in 'Prostaglandins', *Proceedings of the second Nobel symposium* (Stockholm, 1967).

CHAPTER SIX

Marketing

R. D. TOUSLEY

INTRODUCTION

MARGARINE was originally developed to provide an additional source of fat in the diet. The recurring shortages in the supply of butter and the resulting high prices in Europe in the 1860s were the factors that set the stage for the development of the margarine industry. And since margarine sold at a lower price than butter, its principal markets were originally to be found among the lower income population groups of the industrialized countries of Europe. Thus margarine was immediately designated as the 'poor man's butter', and despite the subsequent extension of its markets to include all income groups, it has continued to carry this image among some people.

The normal development of the margarine industry has also been held back in most countries by adverse government regulations (see Chapter Seven). Discriminatory taxes, colouring prohibitions, and many other restrictions have been applied to margarine in an effort to restrict its sale. Even in the industrialized countries of Western Europe, where margarine has its highest *per capita* consumption, there has been some adverse regulation from time to time. In the U.S.A. it was not until 1950 that the federal government repealed its discriminatory taxes and permitted, subject to the laws of the individual states, a relatively free marketing system for margarine.Even today, there are many countries in the world which have significant discriminatory laws against the manufacture and sale of margarine.

These two characteristics, the product image and the high degree of government regulation, have affected the marketing of margarine a great deal; but not always in a uniform way. So long as the obstacles were not insuperable, aggressive marketing has been encouraged. Continual improvement of the product, the use of direct channels of distribution, large expenditures for selling and advertising, and at times severe price competition have constituted the marketing mix for margarine in those countries where the industry has been given a reasonable opportunity to develop.

In those countries, however, in which product prejudice and dietary habits are firmly fixed, or in which government regulations are unduly restrictive, margarine marketing has lacked these dynamic qualities. The difference is well illustrated by the situation in the U.S.A. before and after 1950. In much of the earlier period, government regulation was so severe and the market so restricted that there was little incentive for dynamic and aggressive marketing. Since 1950, however, significant changes have taken place, and aggressive marketing has become the normal, rather than the exceptional, situation.

In this chapter, after some general comments about the markets for margarine, we shall examine the history of the marketing mix: product development and brand policy, the use of distribution channels, selling and advertising, and pricing. Since it has been impossible to obtain this information for every country in the world, attention has been concentrated on the United Kingdom, Germany, the Netherlands, and the U.S.A. These countries constitute, or appear to be representative of, the major markets for margarine.

THE MARKETS

Consumer markets and industrial markets

Historically margarine has been a product largely consumed in the home and purchased by the ultimate consumer. In addition, however, margarine has been purchased by bakeries for use as a raw material, and to a lesser extent by hotels, restaurants, and similar business firms. 'Industrial market' is the term customarily used in the U.S.A. to designate these commercial buyers. In the United Kingdom the term 'non-domestic' is used whereas on the continent of Europe the term 'non-distributive' is the appropriate one.

This business market, as distinguished from the consumer market, has always been of some importance to the margarine industry. Special products or brands for the bakery industry were available in the Netherlands as early as 1894, and there is a record of a special hospital price-list in the same country in the 1880s. Some firms in almost every country even specialized from time to time in selling to certain types of commercial buyers, often making little effort to sell also to the regular consumer market.

Before 1950 the importance of the industrial market varied widely from country to country. Although exact figures are not available, sales to business buyers in the United Kingdom and the Netherlands appear to have been considerably larger as a proportion of total margarine sales than was true in Germany and the U.S.A. Since 1950 the proportion has been rising in all countries, and particularly in Germany and the U.S.A. In 1965 the ratio of commercial sales to the total margarine market was approaching 20 per cent in these countries.

This increase in the relative importance of the industrial market reflects more a decline in sales to ultimate consumers than a real rise in industrial sales, although some increase has undoubtedly taken place in the latter. Since 1950, more and more women have been employed outside the home in all of the major developed countries. Accordingly, fewer meals are being prepared in the home and more meals are being consumed in restaurants. On balance, this tends to reduce the *per capita* consumption of margarine, since more of it is likely to be used in the home than by restaurants. This is certainly an important factor in the lack of growth shown by the margarine industry in recent years in many of its traditional markets.

Export markets

Today there is very little international trade in margarine. Considering the fact that the industry was started in the Netherlands as an export industry and that the original Dutch manufacturers, Jurgens and Van den Bergh, sold margarine for at least a decade in the United Kingdom and Germany before they attempted to enter the Dutch market, it may be interesting to examine the history of international trade in margarine and the reasons for its decline. The barriers to this trade are partly artificial and partly natural.

The principal artificial barrier, of course, is the tariff; this was used almost from the start to create and promote a domestic margarine industry. Two examples should be sufficient. The Dutch companies began exporting margarine to Germany in the 1870s, were subjected to a tariff in 1887, and as a result built factories in Germany. They entered Belgium in 1884 on an export basis, but had to build factories in Belgium after a tariff was imposed in 1896 (1). This story was repeated on numerous occasions as each consuming country attempted to encourage the creation of its own margarine industry.

The United Kingdom was an exception to the general rule, since it was committed to a free-trade policy. Although some margarine factories were constructed in the United Kingdom by English firms at an earlier date, the Dutch companies continued to serve the United Kingdom by exporting from the Netherlands and did not begin to erect factories there until 1918. As a result, margarine exports from the Netherlands to the United Kingdom between 1893 and the beginning of the First World War regularly amounted to some 40,000–50,000 tons per year (2). These quantities constituted 90–5 per cent of all Dutch exports of margarine during the period.

Dutch exports to the United Kingdom increased to almost 160,000 tons per year during the period of the First World War but fell to less than 20,000 tons in 1918 when the Dutch government banned margarine exports for a time because of a shortage of supplies (3). During the 1920s, the Dutch exports ranged from 60,000 to 90,000 tons annually, about three-quarters to the United Kingdom and most of the remainder to Germany. The Scandinavian countries were net importers of small amounts of margarine during the 1920s, as were several other European countries. During the 1930s, however, there was little international trade in margarine, and Dutch exports amounted to less than 10,000 tons annually.

The U.S.A. was also an exporter of margarine during the early days of the industry. Some 30,000 tons were exported in 1904, more than 10 per cent of total production, but in most years between 1900 and 1920 exports amounted to about 5 per cent of production. During the postwar year of 1920 over 100,000 tons were exported, but this was still only 5 per cent of production. After 1920 there was a rapid decline in export trade, and only negligible amounts were involved (4).

Since 1930 there has been a minimum of international trade in margarine, and today there is very little. From time to time margarine is introduced into a new market as an imported commodity, but as soon as consumption reaches a moderate level a factory is built in the country. One reason, of course, is that every developing country likes to have as much manufacturing as possible, and there is still, as there was in the late nineteenth century, a constant threat of tariff imposition. Aside from this, however, there are a number cf logical reasons for manufacturing margarine in the country in which it is consumed.

For one thing, there are important differences from country to country in consumer tastes and product preferences. The German market prefers a higher quality product than does the Dutch market, and is willing to pay a higher price for it. The principal raw materials used in making American margarine are less used in Europe, and the vegetable ghee produced in India is a different product again. On the whole, it is advantageous to import raw materials for the local manufacture of margarine rather than to import the finished product. In addition, margarine is a perishable product. Although it has a longer life now than was true half a century ago, it still requires prompt distribution to the consumer if quality and freshness are to be maintained. Manufacturers still inspect retail stocks to be certain that the product being sold is in good condition. In export trade, they lose much of the control now being exercised over product quality and condition.

Finally, there are still a number of artificial barriers to international trade in margarine. Each country has its own regulations for product and package specifications and labelling requirements. It is therefore virtually impossible to produce and package a product that can be marketed without change in more than one or two countries.

Interestingly enough, the European Economic Community is currently investigating the problem of margarine trade among its members. This investigation is designed to determine the reasons for the lack of international trade in margarine, and the obstacles to greater product uniformity. In all developed countries, the trend in recent years in all products has been toward market segmentation; that is, the production and marketing of more products with special appeal to certain segments of the market rather than a single product for the mass market. Products are thus more closely adapted to the tastes and wants of particular groups of consumers, and consumers are better served in the market-place. At the same time, the great increase in market demand that has taken place since the Second World War has made the practice of market segmentation economically possible. It appears that any E.E.C. effort to accomplish great product standardization will be difficult to achieve in view of the general trend towards market segmentation.

Regardless of what happens in the E.E.C., it does not appear that there will be any significant permanent growth in other export markets for margarine in the foreseeable future. Margarine is too well established as a domestic industry serving domestic markets for the situation to change significantly. Differences in consumer tastes and desires in different markets also favour maintenance of the present structure. Some of these differences will be shown in the following discussion of the history of the marketing mix.

PRODUCT POLICY: DEVELOPMENT AND IDENTIFICATION

The quality of margarine is difficult to measure objectively. Taste, flavour, and odour are important characteristics in the consumer's judgement of quality, but different consumers obviously have different tastes. Consistency of texture and resistance to deterioration are important attributes of quality which can be measured more objectively. The nutritional benefits to be derived from the product are important considerations in measuring quality, as is the general effect of the product on the user's health. Much of our knowledge of nutrition and health is, of course, very recent (see Chapters Four and Five).

In general, the quality of margarine depends upon the manufacturing technology employed and the raw materials used. Since it is a manufactured product, different raw materials can be used; and missing ingredients, such as vitamins, can be added for their nutritional value. Other chapters in this book treat the subjects of raw materials, nutritional value, and manufacturing technology. Some of the main points will be repeated here to show their relationship to the marketing process.

Product development: the first fifty years

The principal raw material utilized in the original margarine-making process was beef fat derived from oleo oil. Thus margarine was originally an animal-fat product. Because of occasional shortages in the supply of raw material, however, some vegetable oil was soon introduced into the product. This caused a lack of stability in the finished product because of the lower melting point of the vegetable oils, a problem which was overcome by the discovery of the hydrogenation process in the early 1900s. By 1906 one large-scale hydrogenation plant was in operation in Europe, and by 1910 a plant had been established in the U.S.A. (5). Nevertheless, it was not until after 1920 that hardened vegetable oils were generally used in margarine.

During the first half-century of its existence, therefore, margarine was not generally a high-quality product, as judged by modern standards. Until 1900 it was made largely of animal fat, including neutral lard in the U.S.A., and from 1900 to 1920 from various combinations of animal fat and hardened and unhardened vegetable oils. There were a few brands, introduced in the late 1890s, that were good products: Van den Bergh's Vitello and Jurgens's Solo in Europe (6) and Jelke's Good Luck in the U.S.A. (7). But on the whole, product quality was not maintained at a high and consistent level.

In the U.S.A., product development was greatly handicapped during this period by government regulation. The severe restrictions imposed limited the market so much that few large firms entered the industry; and for those that did, there was little incentive for product improvement. In Europe the situation was almost the reverse. There was so much demand for the existing product that there was little incentive for most producers to improve it. This was somewhat less true in Germany than in the other European markets. Here Vitello and Solo acquired a large share of the market, but in the United Kingdom and the Netherlands these and other superior brands made less progress.

Product improvement: the 1920s

During the 1920s margarine was considerably improved in quality. Hardened vegetable oils were used to a greater extent as raw materials, although usually in combination with animal fat. Improved production technology, combined with the use of the newer raw materials, made for a better flavour and especially for improved texture. Not only did margarine become superior to butter in spreadability, but some manufacturers even varied the hardness and softness of the product from winter to summer.

The introduction of Nucoa in the U.S.A. in 1917 and of Blue Band in the Netherlands in 1923 were important advances in product quality in the two countries. Nucoa, introduced by a company later merged into Best Foods, used hardened coconut oil as its basic raw material. The resulting product quickly became the top-selling margarine in the country, and maintained this position for at least the next two decades. Blue Band, a Van den Bergh product, required more time to win widespread consumer acceptance in the Netherlands. But product quality was strictly maintained by the manufacturer, and by the mid 1930s it was the leading brand, a position that it still holds today.

M.—17

The significance of the 1920s for product quality is not to be measured by the development of a few quality brands, but rather by an improvement in the general level of products available in the market. Before this time, quality control was attempted only by a few manufacturers, and by them only on a relatively small part of total output. There were a great many manufacturers and few of them attempted, or even desired, national distribution. Their objective generally was to produce an inexpensive margarine which could be sold at a low price to local middlemen. Also, there was little product identification that would link a specific manufacturer to a particular batch of margarine, at least by the time the product reached the consumer. Thus there was little incentive for the manufacturer to improve the product. The result was that the retailer took the principal responsibility for the product he sold, and in most countries he was not too scrupulous. In the U.S.A., he coloured the margarine—even after it became illegal to do so without the payment of high taxes—and often sold it as butter. The same sort of thing happened in the Netherlands. The situation was much better in Germany, partly because most food retailers did not sell butter in the early days and were anxious to develop the margarine industry on its own merits. These problems of distribution will be discussed later. For the moment, it is sufficient to note that the large number of manufacturers and the lack of product identification to the consumer resulted in a product of variable quality in most countries during the first half-century of the margarine industry.

By 1920 the structure of the industry had changed considerably. In the Netherlands the number of margarine manufacturers had declined from 70 in 1880 to fewer than 20. In Germany there was considerable consolidation after 1910. In the U.S.A., there were perhaps as many manufacturers in the early 1920s as there had been in 1886, the year in which adverse federal legislation was passed. But the turnover of the firms had been substantial, some 50 per cent having left the industry between 1886 and 1892 to be replaced later by new entrants (8). Presumably these new firms had some purpose in entering the industry other than quick profits, and were attempting to build a permanent business.

Thus in all countries the margarine industry was attaining a certain degree of stability during the 1920s. There was still surplus capacity in Europe; this led to periodic price wars and a series of mergers near the end of the decade. But there was an increasing emphasis by most firms during the decade on the long-term development of the industry. This led to improved products and processes and to product identification. On the whole margarine was a good product during the 1920s although still regarded by most consumers as inferior to butter.

Product development: 1930–50

Depression in the 1930s and war in the 1940s hardly constituted the proper environment for new product development. In the U.S.A. in 1930, all margarine consisted predominantly of vegetable oils, and two-thirds of the total production contained no animal fat at all (9). Two new brands achieved a high degree of market acceptance during the period. Parkay was introduced by Kraft Foods in 1937. In 1943 Standard Brands took over a local margarine, Blue Bonnet, in a merger and successfully placed it in national distribution. But the industry was still subject to severe government regulation and high taxes, and the development of new products and new brands was discouraged accordingly.

The advent of war, however, did increase the consumption of margarine a great deal as a result of the shortage of butter. Because of the taxes on coloured margarine, the product was produced and marketed largely in an uncoloured state with a colouring capsule included in each package for the use of the housewife. The war also changed the available raw materials. Domestically produced cottonseed and soya bean oils replaced imported coconut and palm-kernel oils, a change that had already begun in the 1930s. By the end of the war, animal fat (oleo oil) had almost completely disappeared as a raw material for even the cheapest margarines (10). By 1950, therefore, the industry in the U.S.A. had virtually completed the change-over from an animal-fat product to one composed largely of vegetable oils. With the relaxing of government restrictions in 1950, the industry was ready for an era of new product development based on the utilization of various vegetable oils as raw materials.

In Europe there was little product change during the 1930s and 1940s so far as new materials and new technology were concerned. The mergers of the late 1920s resulted in the establishment of Unilever as the dominant firm in the margarine industry in most countries. With literally hundreds of products and brands available to it, Unilever entered into a period of product consolidation rather than one of product development. Depression and war, moreover, led to great government control. Quota limitations placed on the production of margarine in Germany after 1932 resulted in the closing of a number of plants. Compulsory mixing of butter with margarine in the Netherlands between 1931 and 1937 left little incentive to improve margarine. And to the extent that margarine was produced at all after the start of the Second World War it tended to become—as in the United Kingdom—a uniform product distributed under government allocation orders.

Nevertheless, there was one significant product development during this period, the addition of vitamins. First introduced by Lever Brothers in the United Kingdom in 1927 (11), the practice became more general after 1935 in both Europe and the U.S.A. Because of poor wartime nutrition, the addition of vitamins was required by law in the United Kingdom in 1940, a requirement which was adopted by some other countries in the early 1950s. The addition of vitamins thus corrected the only nutritional deficiency of margarine in comparison with butter and provided the base from which further product improvement could take place in the 1950s.

Trading-up the product: 1950–67

Since 1950 the developed countries of the world have had constantly rising incomes and generally increasing prices, but the net result has been a substantial rise in the level of living For a product such as margarine, which had long carried an image of inferior status, these rising incomes could have meant the loss to butter of a significant portion of the market. One way to combat this possibility was to offer the consumer a better-quality margarine at, if necessary, a higher price. Through this trading-up process, the consumer's desire for better-quality products could be satisfied without his changing to butter. Even those consumers who no longer cared for butter might well be interested in a better-quality margarine. The margarine industry has therefore done a great deal since 1950 to improve the product and to offer the consumer a wider choice. In general, consumers have been willing to trade-up their margarine purchases to the higher-priced and higher-quality products, but there have been significant differences among the various countries.

Of the countries studied here, efforts at trading-up have been perhaps least successful in the Netherlands. Margarine made entirely of vegetable oils still constituted only 10 per cent of the total market in 1965, although this may be a matter of consumer taste. But the total market share of the premium-priced brands which were introduced or reintroduced into the market after 1950 was only 15 per cent. On the other hand, the Dutch consumer has traded-up at least to the extent that he is no longer a buyer of the lowest grades of margarine—which in 1965 had only a market share of 10–12 per cent.

What the Dutch consumer has shown so far is an overwhelming preference for the medium-priced products. This group includes Blue Band, the dominant Unilever brand, which is advertised and promoted as a quality product, and a number of other brands which are sold with premiums or savings schemes. Thus the failure of the Dutch consumer to trade-up may well be due to the unusually successful promotional efforts that have been made on behalf of the middle brands. In any case, the Dutch consumer appears to be satisfied with existing products. He has not increased his consumption of butter during the postwar period, and has not shown much disposition to trade-up his margarine purchases to the more expensive brands.

The German consumer has been much more willing to trade-up his margarine purchases than has the Dutch consumer. Butter consumption has made some recovery in Germany during the postwar period, despite its very high price in relation to margarine, and probably would have made even greater inroads on margarine had not the latter product been improved regularly. In the early 1950s the better grades of margarine had a market share of 35–40 per cent, the medium grades from 40 to 45 per cent, and the lowest grades about 20 per cent. The introduction of Rama in 1954 (12) as a margarine superior in quality to anything then existing was so successful that within three years it had over half of the consumer market. In the 1960s, additional brands were introduced at prices even higher than Rama.

What has happened in Germany in a period of about fifteen years is that all margarine has been upgraded about one level. The lowest grade of the early 1950s has virtually disappeared. The lowest grade of the mid 1960s, with a market share of less than 30 per cent, is at least equivalent in quality to the medium grade of the early 1950s. Rama and other brands of similar quality are now medium priced, and have about 65 per cent of the market. The highest-priced brands, introduced largely in 1965 and 1966, immediately captured some 7 per cent of the market. All of the medium- and high-priced brands now use entirely vegetable oils for the raw material, although there is still some animal fat in the lowest grades.

The trading-up experience of the United Kingdom resembles that of the Netherlands more than it does that of Germany. The British consumer, like the German, has shown a disposition in the postwar period to revert to the consumption of butter. In the United Kingdom, however, the price of butter is much lower relative to that of margarine than it is in Germany. Occasionally, it is even cheaper in price than a premium margarine. Thus it has probably been more difficult to trade-up margarine in the United Kingdom than in Germany. The introduction in 1955 of the brand Summer County, with a 10 per cent butter content, and in 1957 of Blue Band, the first and until recently the only all-vegetable-oil margarine, represent attempts to improve quality and trade-up the product. And yet the market share of these and other premium brands in 1964 was only 34 per cent, compared with a market share of 28 per cent in 1955 for the best grades. Medium grades had 51–2 per cent of the market in both years, while the lowest grades declined from 21 to 14 per cent.

As the data indicate, the British consumer buys more premium-priced margarine than does the Dutch consumer. There has been some increase during the postwar period, but the rate of increase has not been as great as it has been in Germany. Again, in the United Kingdom as in the Netherlands, there is a dominant brand—Stork—in the medium-priced field that has been long promoted as a quality product. Both Stork in the United Kingdom and Blue Band in the Netherlands were well-known and popular brands before the Second World War. Germany did not have such a dominant brand in the 1930s, and in fact had no significant product improvement in the 1930s. Perhaps trading-up merely came earlier to the United Kingdom and the Netherlands than to Germany, since both Stork and Blue Band attained their dominant positions in the mid 1930s. A more likely explanation for these differences in degree of product development and acceptance is that the German consumer of the 1950s and 1960s was simply more interested in new and better products than were the British and Dutch consumers.

Business firms operating internationally believe that consumers in some countries are more willing to try new products and to change brands than are those in other countries. They say that the American consumer is the most flexible and has the least brand loyalty of any. So far as margarine is concerned, the rate of new product development in the U.S.A. since 1956 has been almost chaotic.

The period after 1950 was one of rapid growth for the American margarine industry. Most margarine was then being made from vegetable oils, and there were basically two qualities of product: the standard nationally distributed brands such as Good Luck, Nucoa, Parkay, and Blue Bonnet, and the cheaper local and distributor (or private) brands. By 1956 the consumption of margarine had almost reached that of butter, incomes were rising rapidly, and the market was ready for new and more expensive products.

Imperial, a product containing some butter, was introduced by Lever Brothers in 1956 as the first margarine of premium quality with a premium price. It was followed by Standard Brands' Fleischmann's in 1959 and Best Foods' Mazola in 1960. Both of these latter products used corn oil as the basic raw material and the health claim of high polyunsaturated fat content as the promotion. The success of these products led to imitation and further product innovation. More and more margarines adopted corn oil as an ingredient. Safflower seed oil was used by at least one brand, as having even more polyunsaturated fat than corn oil. Liquid margarine and whipped margarine were developed and improved. Soft margarine was developed in 1964 under the name Chiffon by Anderson, Clayton & Co., a firm which had previously manufactured and sold margarine only under private brands. It rapidly became one of the better-selling brands, and has been widely imitated. The most recent product development appears to be low-calorie margarines with only half the fat content of the regular product.

Not all of these new products are sold at premium prices, but most of them are in the premium price category, which in 1967 had a market share of perhaps 28–30 per cent compared with 20 per cent in 1965 and less than 5 per cent in 1956. The lowest-priced brands have not changed appreciably in market share during this period, holding steady at 47–8 per cent. The medium-priced brands, however, have declined from almost half the market in 1955 to about one-fourth in 1967. This product-category includes several brands which were best sellers before 1950.

Thus the American trading-up experience is quite different from that of Europe, where there has been trading-up all along the line, from low to medium and from medium to high. The net result has been stability in market-share at the medium level with high quality gaining and low quality losing. Even the German experience follows a pattern of this type if one makes allowance for changes in quality at each level. In the U.S.A., however, the trading-up process has resulted mainly in a diversion of consumption from the medium-grade products to the higher grades. Only the lower grades of margarine, which are definitely sold on a price basis, seem to have attained some degree of stability in terms of market share. This is not necessarily an unusual phenomenon in American marketing experience, but in the case of margarine its increased use for cooking purposes in recent years may have contributed to this stability of the low-priced market.

Product development in the U.S.A. since 1956 has been a very dynamic part of the marketing mix for margarine. It has probably been more dynamic than it would have been otherwise because of the long period of relative product stagnation, but we cannot be certain of this. Great changes took place in the American economy after the Second World War which led to the development of a tremendous number of new and improved products. Margarine participated fully in this revolution. It is in product development especially that American marketing tends to surpass marketing in other countries, and margarine in the postwar period appears to illustrate this fact. Much was done in product development and improvement in the European countries, but more was done in the U.S.A.

Product identification: the use of brands

Obviously, there is little reason for product development and improvement if the consumer cannot identify the improved product in the shop. Thus the use of brand names is an important and necessary aspect of product policy in the modern world. The mere use of a brand name does not mean, however, that the product can be easily identified by the consumer. Brand names were used for margarine in the 1880s, as indicated by price lists circulated at that time to the wholesale trade. But the product was distributed in bulk packages, and there was little product-identification by the consumer.

As mentioned previously, brand merchandising of margarine began in the late nineteenth century with the introduction of Vitello and Solo in Europe, and Good Luck and the meat-packer brands—notably Swift's All Sweet—in the U.S.A. These brands were advertised to the consumer and obtained a considerable degree of consumer acceptance, especially in Germany and the U.S.A. Nevertheless, up to the time of the First World War, margarine was still generally

41. Dutch, German, and French margarine packs in use at the beginning of the century.

42. This poster appeared in 1935 when it was compulsory for butter to be added to margarine.

Giudicate Imparzialmente!

La Giustizia, con gli occhi bendati assaggia per poter dare il suo giudizio e sentenziare quale sia burro e quale sia " ERA ", MA NON RIESCE DISTINGUERE !

Avete voi già giudicato? Vi sarete certamente convinti che è cosa impossibile trovare una qualsiasi differenza tra il burro e l'ERA

COMPRATE OGGI

Era SOSTITUISCE IL BURRO

BURRO

Era

In vendita presso tutti gli spacci dell'Alleanza Cooperativa Torinese e nei migliori Negozi Alimentari,

Società *Anonima VAN DEN BERGH*
Villastellone (Piemonte)

43. In 1927 this Italian newspaper advertisement emphasized the similarity between butter and margarine. The slogan 'You can't tell the difference' is still widely used.

44. In 1930, at an exhibition in Milan, visitors were able to sample pastry made with margarine.

being sold in bulk without adequate means of consumer identification. During the 1920s considerable progress was made in brand merchandising, although it was not until after the Second World War that margarine in Europe became almost universally a branded and packaged product. In the early 1950s, even in Germany, branded identifiable items constituted only about 60 per cent of the retail turnover of margarine compared with virtually 100 per cent today.

The multiplicity of brands. Today in Germany perhaps 200–50 brands of margarine are sold. In the U.S.A. there are 700–800, or even more. These figures include all brands of local manufacturers and all distributor brands, as well as the manufacturers' brands which are distributed and advertised nationally. The latter are relatively few in number but obtain a large share of the sales volume.

What is interesting about these brands is not the absolute number in existence now but the changes that have taken place over a period of time. Because of the low volume of margarine sold in the U.S.A. before the Second World War, the number of brands in existence was relatively small. After the removal of restrictions in 1950, new manufacturers entered the industry and existing manufacturers added new brands to their line of products. The result is a large number of brands of varying quality and price.

In Europe, however, the peak of brand proliferation in margarine came during the 1920s. A single manufacturer in Germany may have had as many as 300 brands. Estimates of the total number of margarine brands in the late 1920s range as high as 1,600 in the Netherlands and 2,000 in the United Kingdom. This does not mean, of course, that all of these names carried through to the consumer or were even used on consumer packages. Many were used in wholesale trade and for commercial products. But in the Netherlands in 1929, five margarine manufacturers actually had in stock at one time consumer wrappers using a total of 172 different brand names.

The merger of several margarine manufacturers into Unilever in 1929 left the new organization with hundreds of brand names in each country. The problem was to sort these out and decide which ones to keep and to promote. In the United Kingdom, Stork was retained as the standard quality brand and Echo as the lower-priced competitive brand. Between 1933 and 1938, Stork increased its share of Unilever consumer volume from 5 per cent to more than 40. Echo increased from 8 to 18 per cent.

From time to time since the 1930s, Unilever has added new brands of margarine. More often perhaps, as with Rama in Germany in 1954, it has developed a new product and assigned it a previously existing name which had not been in use for a time. But Unilever brand names in a single country, including special dietary products and commercial products, probably do not ordinarily exceed a dozen, and may be fewer in number. The remaining brands belong to smaller manufacturers and to distributors.

Private brands versus national brands. Distributor brands—those owned and distributed by wholesalers or retailers—are usually referred to as private brands. Manufacturers' brands are usually designated as national brands, indicating that they are nationally advertised and distributed. The terms are not very precise, since many private brands are nationally distributed through retailing chains who may even own and operate their own manufacturing facilities, and many manufacturers' brands only attain local or regional distribution. Nevertheless, the terms are generally understood and will be used here.

Wholesalers may establish private brands for their local trade, but are most likely to do so when there is the possibility of a wider distribution. Thus the development of wholesaler-sponsored voluntary chains in various countries has greatly aided the development of wholesaler brands. The larger retail chains have created and used their own private brands on an even larger scale. The extent to which private brands take trade away from manufacturers' brands depends largely on the relative strength of distributors and manufacturers, and in particular upon the development of large-scale retailing institutions.

Wholesaler brands of margarine came into existence around 1900, and retailer brands about 1910. Few manufacturers' brands were distributed nationally at this time, and few brands in any case had consumer recognition. Thus the consumer co-operatives, which were especially strong in the United Kingdom, and the retail chains, which were starting to develop in a number of countries, found it relatively easy to establish their own brands. A few distributors even established their own manufacturing facilities, although most obtained the product from existing manufacturers, both local and national.

As a result of the aggressiveness of the distributors and the growth of large-scale retailing, it is probable that at least half of the margarine distributed during the 1920s and 1930s in the Netherlands and the United Kingdom consisted of private brands. In Germany, however, the retail chains did not develop until after the Second World War, and private brands were relatively unimportant in the total sales of margarine. The situation in the U.S.A. is not clear, and it probably varied greatly from city to city and from state to state. The variety of state regulations, not to mention the restrictions imposed by the federal government, made it difficult for a national retailer to establish a uniform product and package. Private brands apparently were most used by local chains, especially when there was a nearby local manufacturer to supply the product.

The strength of private brands since the Second World War again shows little uniformity among the various countries. In Germany the chains have developed rapidly since 1950, but have not concentrated on private brands. They account for some 5 per cent of turnover of margarine. In both the Netherlands and the United Kingdom private brands have declined in market share, to perhaps 20 per cent in the former and rather less in the latter. There appear to be several reasons for this. In the first place, there has been a significant improvement in the quality of the national brands and greater promotional effort. Moreover, price differentials between national and private brands do not seem to be great, especially for a period of rising incomes. Many private brands in the Netherlands actually sell at the same price as Blue Band, and in the United Kingdom Echo is sold at a price competitive with the private brands. In the U.S.A., on the other hand, private brands sell at one-fourth to one-half the price of premium brands, and one-half to two-thirds of the price of regular brands. With no competition from national manufacturers in their price bracket, private brands are generally believed to account for 50–60 per cent of total sales volume at the present time. And this has been accomplished during a period of rising incomes, when there was a great deal of product improvement in margarine.

Thus the 'battle of the brands' is being resolved in different ways in different countries. There are probably several reasons for this, but the different marketing strategies used by the participants may well be the most important. In the U.S.A. the distributors have sold private brands at significantly lower prices than those charged by the national manufacturers, and the latter have permitted the private brands to take over the low-priced margarine market. In Europe there is less difference in the prices of private and national brands.

Many private brands are sold at standard prices, and the national manufacturers have also elected to compete in the low-priced field (13). Exactly how this has affected the entire trading-up process is difficult to say, but it is interesting to note that trading-up has been most successful in Germany where private brands have the least market penetration, and in the U.S.A. where direct competition with them has not been attempted. Other market factors, however, such as the relative prices of butter and margarine, are probably of greater importance in determining the success of trading-up efforts.

Packaging

There is a close relationship between the development of packaging and the sale of margarine by brand name. There is often a relationship also between improvement in product and improvement in packaging. In other words, an attempt to trade-up the product is likely to call for a more convenient and more attractive package, as the latter gives the consumer her first impression of the product.

Margarine has been packaged in a wide variety of materials and in many types of containers of various sizes (14). Moreover, most countries have government regulations that inhibit in one way or another the complete freedom of the manufacturer with respect to the packaging of margarine. Nevertheless, there are certain aspects of packaging that are more or less common to all countries. We shall be concerned here with these main points and not with the multitude of details, which are too numerous to mention anyway. We shall also be concerned primarily with the marketing aspects of packaging rather than with the technical aspects. The basic purpose of packaging is to give protection to the product, but this can be achieved in many ways. More and more in our economy, packaging helps to make the sale.

Originally, margarine, like other food products, was sold in bulk. It was packed by the manufacturers in barrels or wooden tubs containing 10 lb or more, and the retailer filled the consumer's order from these containers. The product was not easily identified and there were instances in most countries of margarine being sold as butter.

The introduction of small consumer-sized packages took place in the late 1890s, concurrently with the use and promotion of brand names. The use of these packages, however, developed more rapidly in some countries than in others. In the U.S.A. 90 per cent of the margarine was being sold in 1-lb packages by 1920 (15), but in the

Netherlands at this time bulk margarine probably still constituted well over half of the turnover. Packaged margarine developed more rapidly in Germany than in the Netherlands, but a certain amount was still being sold there in bulk as recently as the early 1950s.

The first packaging for margarine was a vegetable parchment wrapper. In the U.S.A., Jelke first started using such wrappers in the 1890s. The practice had been adopted generally by other manufacturers by 1905. Jelke added the folding carton in 1907 or 1908, a practice which was again widely imitated within a few years (16). The margarine was first wrapped in parchment and then encased in addition in a paperboard carton. By 1926 this practice was almost universal in the U.S.A. (17), bulk margarine having virtually disappeared.

In Europe the parchment wrapper was introduced at about the same time as in the U.S.A., but the paperboard container was generally considered too expensive to use. It is believed that Solo during the 1920s did introduce a paperboard carton in the Netherlands. It was discontinued after a time and apparently did not stimulate sales, since Vitello, the principal competing brand, stayed with parchment wrappers. Even today, the standard paperboard container is little used in Europe. Blue Band, the most expensive premium brand in the United Kingdom, uses a foil wrapper and a foil-laminated board carton; the new soft Blue Band is packed in tubs.

There has been a good deal of trading-up of the package since 1950, however, both in Europe and the U.S.A. In all countries, an aluminium foil wrapper has replaced parchment in the premium brands. In the United Kingdom and the Netherlands foil is used only for these brands. In the U.S.A. it is likely to be used also for the standard, or medium-priced brands, but not for the low-priced brands. In Germany it is used for the low-priced brands also.

Another development which has occurred in several countries, is the use of the consumer-sized paperboard or plastic tub. Introduced into Germany about 1955, the practice soon became common there. By 1965 some 35 per cent of the margarine sold to the ultimate consumer was packaged in tubs. One reason for this rapid development was the added convenience to the consumer in serving the product. In the U.S.A. tubs began to be used in 1963 with the development of soft margarine, a product with a creamy texture unlike any previous margarine, and are still used primarily for this product.

Packaging improvement has thus to some extent followed product improvement. Those countries which have been most successful in trading-up margarine as a product have also made the greatest advances in packaging. On the whole, however, except perhaps in postwar Germany, packaging does not seem to have been as dynamic a part of the marketing process as product development has been. We shall now turn our attention to the selection of distribution channels, a phase of marketing in which the European countries have been especially aggressive.

CHANNELS OF DISTRIBUTION

In traditional marketing terminology margarine would tend to be classified as a convenience good, one which normally would be purchased at the most convenient retail outlet. The manufacturer of a convenience good usually attempts to obtain as widespread distribution as possible through all retail outlets that normally handle that type of product. The regular channel of distribution, therefore, is from manufacturer to wholesaler—sometimes with the assistance of an agent middleman or broker who does not take title to the product —to retailer to consumer. Such a channel usually gives the widest distribution of the product at the lowest cost. Bypassing the wholesaler to sell directly to every retailer normally increases the cost of distribution, since the manufacturer cannot achieve the economies obtained by the wholesaler who sells the products of many manufacturers. The manufacturer of a wide line of products, all of which are distributed to the same retailers, may, however, be able to sell directly at a cost comparable to that of the regular wholesaler.

The principal disadvantage to the manufacturer in using wholesalers is that he does not receive aggressive selling support from the wholesaler, who handles the products of many manufacturers. To overcome this, the manufacturer may well spend rather large sums of money in consumer-advertising and other promotional efforts in order to 'pull' his product through the distribution channels. There is another disadvantage if the product is perishable. The wholesaler-retailer channel tends to be a long one, and the manufacturer can exercise little if any control over the handling of the product once it leaves his possession. If the product has suffered a significant deterioration in quality by the time it reaches the consumer, and if it is sold under the manufacturer's brand name, the result may well be a substantial decline in the consumer's acceptance of the product and in the manufacturer's reputation for producing quality products.

These various conflicting considerations have played an important part in the selection of distribution channels for margarine throughout the 100 years that the product has been in existence. On the one hand, the regular wholesaler–retailer channel has been widely used because of its low cost and general availability. Until the late 1920s, except perhaps in the U.S.A., margarine manufacturers were largely single-product firms. Therefore the relatively low cost of the regular wholesaler–retailer channel had considerable attraction, especially for the smaller manufacturers with limited financial resources. They could hardly afford to sell directly to retailers anyway over any very widespread marketing area. On the other hand, margarine was a product which required aggressive selling. Moreover, it was perishable, highly perishable until about 1950. These two considerations led at various times to a significant amount of direct distribution to retailers, especially by the larger manufacturers. In addition, institutional influences have affected distribution policy over the years.

The basic channel: direct distribution versus wholesalers, 1900–50
When the Dutch firm of Jurgens first began to sell margarine in the United Kingdom in the early 1870s, it utilized existing market facilities. Wilson speaks of the traditional Dutch market at Brewers' Quay in Water Lane (18). Presumably retailers, and perhaps wholesalers, came to this market to buy goods imported from the Netherlands. This market was soon replaced in the distribution of margarine, as it was an ineffective device in obtaining distribution to shops located in the provinces outside London. By the late 1870s the Dutch firms were using wholesalers, and in the 1890s Jurgens began some direct selling to retailers. Early marketing in Germany by Jurgens and Van den Bergh followed a similar course, first the use of wholesalers and then some direct selling in the 1890s. When the two firms entered the Dutch market in 1884, they started immediately with a policy of direct distribution to retailers.

This early emphasis on direct marketing might be assumed to result from difficulties in getting wholesalers to handle the new product, but this does not seem to have been the case. In fact, many of the wholesalers (and retailers) who handled margarine had little opportunity to sell butter, since locally produced butter was often sold, especially in Germany, directly by the farmer to the consumer. Those wholesalers who did handle butter often were not averse to mixing it with margarine and then selling the resulting product as butter at butter prices.

In the Netherlands, Van den Bergh and Jurgens did adopt direct marketing in order to achieve distribution, but for a different reason. As late entrants into the Dutch market, they found it difficult to locate wholesalers who were not tied up with competitive margarine producers. In the United Kingdom and Germany, however, an important reason for direct marketing was the manufacturers' lack of confidence in the prices quoted by wholesalers. By selling directly, they exercised a degree of control over the prices at which the product was sold and discouraged price-cutting by wholesalers.

Direct marketing received an additional impetus about 1900 when the larger manufacturers began to use brand names for their better-quality margarine. Some wholesalers, especially those in the United Kingdom, refused to handle branded merchandise, thus giving the manufacturer an additional reason for selling direct to retailers. A policy was thus inaugurated, and continued for a long time, whereby some of the larger manufacturers sold their top brand directly while using wholesalers to distribute lesser brands and unbranded margarine. When Blue Band was introduced in the Netherlands in 1923, it was sold only directly to retailers for some time.

It is difficult to know how much margarine was sold directly between 1900 and 1950, and the proportion undoubtedly varied from time to time and from country to country. Organization and regulation of the margarine trade in the United Kingdom during the First World War is said to have been relatively easy, because there were no organized wholesale markets and very few wholesalers. The normal channel was 'direct from importer or manufacturer to retailer' (19). At about the same time in Germany, margarine was probably distributed about 50 per cent through wholesalers and 50 per cent directly to retailers, proportions that probably continued through the 1920s. The larger manufacturers, however, with an elaborate organization of regional sales offices and hundreds of salesmen, must have sold directly more than 50 per cent of their output, especially by the 1920s.

In the Netherlands, despite the early beginning of direct marketing, the predominant channel of distribution between 1900 and 1920 involved the use of wholesalers. It is estimated that in 1920 80 per cent of margarine sales were made through wholesalers. A significant change took place, however, during the 1920s, and by 1932 perhaps as much as 80 per cent of sales were being made directly to the

45. From about 1910, Jurgens assisted retailers to set out attractive shop-window displays, a method of advertising which played a major part in market strategy for several decades.

VERSCHIJNT ELKE 14 DAGEN EN IS GRATIS VERKRIJGBAAR VOOR DE VERBRUIKERS VAN SOLO-MARGARINE.	REDACTIE: „DE SOLIST" OSS MET MEDEWERKING VAN BEKENDE SCHRIJVERS EN TEEKENAARS.	UITGAVE: N. V. ANT. JURGENS' MARGARINEFABRIEKEN, OSS

EEN ERNSTIG WOORDJE VOORAF.

Ja, hoe zal ik daar nu mee beginnen ?

Ik heb de pen, ik weet niet hoe vaak al, in de inkt gedoopt, ik zit met mijn linkerhand mijn kroeskop te bewerken, maar hoe vlot het nu gaat als ik jullie d'een of andere grap of iets leuks te vertellen heb, zoo moeielijk is het nu voor me om wat op 't papier te krijgen.

Ik zal je zeggen, hoe dat komt.

Zooals ik je al verteld heb, valt ons tijdschriftje verbazend in den smaak onzer Solo-verbruikers. Het beste bewijs daarvan is het groot aantal brieven, dat we telkens mogen ontvangen en de menigte raadseloplossingen, die ons worden gezonden.

Telkens weer lees ik vol blijdschap en laat dan die brieven met stralende kijkers aan den chef onzer afdeeling zien, dat »de Solist" zoo'n gezellig boekje is, dat de verhaaltjes zoo aardig zijn en de bus zoo prettig is en dat de verschillende andere stukjes, die tot afwisseling er in geschreven worden, zoo leuk of zoo leerzaam of zoo geschikt zijn.

Maar er is iets anders

Onder de vele brieven, die ik te beantwoorden krijg, zijn er ook verscheidene van groote menschen ! Niet, dat ik niet heel vereerd ben met zulke brieven, vooral als ze vol aanmoediging zijn voor Keesje's werk, maar die brieven bevatten heel dikwijls raadseloplossingen door groote menschen voor of namens kinderen in zonden.

En, (nu ben ik er eindelijk), daar kan ik niet best over uit.

Want, beste jongens en meisjes, het tijdschiftje we door onze firma ten geschenke gegeven aan de kir ren en de kinderen moeten dus aan de wedstrij meedoen en de raadsels oplossen. Nu, iedereen begri dat met die kinderen alleen bedoeld worden, zij, lezen en schrijven kunnen en dus in staat zijn raadsels te ontcijferen en wedstrijdwerkjes uit te vo

De directie, die graag *allen* genoegen wil doen, h den termijn van deelname gesteld tot 17 jaar (er n toch een grens zijn), maar de ouderen kunnen meedoen, omdat het niet eerlijk zou wezen jegens jongeren, en de zeer kleinen niet, omdat ze 't een dig niet kunnen.

't Is natuurlijk niets prettig mooie, wijze brieve krijgen met raadseloplossingen van een kind van 4 jaar ; dan weet je en zie je aan 't schrift dat het gr menschen werk is, en groote menschen werk kan meedingen aan 't kinderwerk.

De firma Jurgens geeft »de Solist" uit om reclam maken voor haar fabrikaat, dat zoovelen tegemoet ko omdat natuurboter zoo duur is en Solo en Vero l volkomen vervangen kunnen, omdat ze uitstekend kwaliteit en welsmakend en bovendien in 't bereik

Lees vooral bladz 140 : **Onze Teekenwedstrijd".**

46. With every packet of 'Solo' margarine Jurgens Margarine Factory at Oss was giving away a fortnightly magazine for young people as early as 1910.

retailer. The introduction of new brands of relatively high quality, and the intense competition for sales among the larger manufacturers, were the factors primarily responsible for the change.

In the U.S.A., distribution developed in a somewhat different way, partly because of low sales volume until about 1950 and partly because margarine was a minor product for a number of multi-product firms. The large national meat-packers were the first important manufacturers of margarine in the U.S.A. In 1900 they and Jelke constituted the major portion of the industry. The meat-packers already had their own distribution facilities for meat, selling and delivering it directly to general grocery stores and meat retailers. It was a simple matter, therefore, to add margarine to the product line and distribute it in the same way. Some of the later entrants into the margarine business in the 1930s, such as Kraft and Standard Brands, distributed in the same way for the same reason. They were already distributing directly to grocery retailers a wide line of food products, some of them relatively perishable. For Jelke, a single-product manufacturer, it was uneconomic to set up a distribution system. Moreover, the regular grocery wholesalers of the time were not a suitable channel for perishable goods, nor were they interested in such a small-volume product. Jelke, therefore, utilized wagon-jobbers to sell to retailers. This method of distribution was also utilized for Nucoa when it was introduced in 1917, and by a number of local and regional manufacturers of margarine, although some of the latter were able to make satisfactory arrangements with regular wholesalers.

The wagon-jobber was a particularly suitable means of distribution for a low-volume perishable product. He stocked his delivery wagon or truck with a limited number of perishable and semi-perishable items, operated over a regular route, and took orders from retailers and made delivery at the same time (20). Because of the small number of items handled, the wagon-jobber could give each one a certain amount of speciality selling effort. Because of the limited space in the delivery vehicle, however, he could not distribute products having a large volume of sales. Thus the greatly increased sales volume for margarine during and after the Second World War led to the eventual demise of the wagon-jobber.

The change to wholesalers after 1950

After the Second World War, a change began to take place in many countries in the channel of distribution for margarine. This change

M.—18

involved a shift from direct selling to retailers to distribution through wholesalers by the large firms with national distribution. In Germany by the mid 1960s, Unilever was selling less than 5 per cent of its retail volume directly to retailers, compared with 70 per cent in the early 1950s. A similar change took place in the Netherlands (21). In the United Kingdom, however, Unilever was still selling about half of its retail volume directly in 1965, a situation that also prevailed in France. In Sweden, Denmark, and Belgium, the direct method of distribution, developed in the 1920s or even earlier, remained relatively unchanged in the 1960s. In Finland, however, wholesalers began to be used in place of direct distribution in 1967.

The change from direct to indirect distribution, in those countries where it has occurred, was influenced by two considerations: changes in retail organization and the relative costs of the two methods. As previously stated, the use of wholesalers is ordinarily a less expensive method of distribution than is direct marketing to retailers. In some countries, however, the gross margins obtained by wholesalers are relatively high, and there is little cost-advantage to the use of wholesalers. Even when wholesalers' marsins are low there is still the problem of product perishability, and the manufacturer may prefer to sell directly to retailers in order to exercise greater control over the marketing of his product. Savings in cost, therefore, do not appear to be the main reason for the greater use of wholesalers, although it probably will be a more and more important consideration in the future in the manufacturers' determination of distribution policy.

The change that has taken place in retail organization in recent years is the principal reason for the increased use of wholesalers. The independent retailers began to organize themselves into voluntary chains and buying associations in the 1930s. By the 1950s, these organizations had become sufficiently strong in Germany and the Netherlands to induce manufacturers to distribute through the sponsoring wholesaler of the voluntary group rather than directly to the member retailers. Perhaps the manufacturers were not too reluctant to effect this change in distribution, in view of the economies to be achieved in distributing through wholesalers who were affiliated with a strong and well-organized voluntary chain. In countries such as Belgium, in which direct distribution still prevails, one is likely to find a limited development of the voluntary chain. In the United Kingdom, where the direct distribution of margarine is still significant, the voluntary chains are not so strong as they are in Germany and the

Netherlands, and some such chains still permit direct sale to member retailers.

In the U.S.A. a similar trend toward wholesaler distribution took place during the 1950s and early 1960s. Again, the rise of the voluntary chains and the demise of the small independent grocer was an important factor in the change for those margarine manufacturers with direct distribution. In the U.S.A., however, much of the change involved substituting the regular wholesaler for the wagon-jobber. This substitution was brought about largely by the improved refrigeration facilities made available by the regular wholesaler. In addition, as the sales volume of margarine increased in the 1940s and 1950s, the regular wholesaler became more eager to distribute the product.

The use of agent middlemen

It is not uncommon in the food industry, especially in large countries, to use agent middlemen to assist in distribution. Such middlemen, usually called manufacturers' representatives or brokers, do not take title to the product and seldom take possession. They are particularly useful in introducing new products, in assisting manufacturers who are either unable or unwilling to establish their own marketing operation, and in selling in the more remote and less-populated areas of a country. Although there is some record of the use of agents in the Netherlands and Belgium in the 1880s and 1890s by the major manufacturers, agents appear to have played a minor role in margarine marketing except perhaps in Germany.

In the latter country, both Jurgens and Van den Bergh employed many independent representatives to make sales contacts with wholesalers and retailers. These representatives even contracted with sub-agents to further promote and sell the product. It is believed that by 1914 these agents were responsible for two-thirds of the margarine sales of the two companies. They played an even more important role in the distribution systems of the smaller manufacturers.

These representatives were gradually replaced, especially in the larger cities and the more densely populated areas, by full-time sales employees in the larger companies. In many cases, the representatives were employed as regular salesmen by the manufacturers. In the late 1920s, however, representatives still were selling about one-third of the German margarine volume, and in the 1960s there were still some representatives engaged in selling margarine, especially in the more remote parts of the country.

In the U.S.A. food brokers have been used from time to time in the distribution of margarine, especially by the smaller manufacturers who did not wish to establish their own marketing operations. As mentioned previously, margarine sales before the Second World War were too small to interest the orthodox channels of distribution, of which the food broker may be regarded as a part. Thus the food broker has probably had greater use since 1950 than before. On the whole, it is the small manufacturer with regional distribution who has been most likely to rely on brokers. Anderson, Clayton & Co., however, have used food brokers to achieve national distribution for its new soft margarine, Chiffon. Since this manufacturer does not produce many other products for sale in retail food stores, the use of brokers to achieve distribution for its margarine appears to be much more economical than any alternative method that might be devised.

Retailing institutions and methods

One of the important problems confronting the early manufacturers of margarine was the selection of suitable retailers. In many countries butter was sold largely house-to-house, either by the farmers who produced it or by independent dairy firms and milkmen. The characteristic of perishability was undoubtedly an important reason for this system of direct distribution, and margarine was also a perishable product. Thus, a logical conclusion was to attempt to use the existing butter retailers to distribute margarine. But they were not necessarily willing to do so, depending upon how they viewed their vested interests. The contrasting solutions obtained in Germany and in the Netherlands illustrate the diverse institutional interests involved.

In Germany margarine was regarded as a threat to butter by those engaged in the distribution of butter, especially by the farmers who sold much of their output directly to the consumer anyway. Thus the manufacturer of margarine turned to the retail food-store as a logical outlet for margarine, since the latter had little if any vested interest in the sale of butter. The sale of margarine through the regular retail shops appears to have progressed as rapidly in Germany as anywhere, except perhaps for the United Kingdom where there is little evidence that margarine was retailed in any other way.

There was also some house-to-house sale and delivery of margarine in Germany, starting before 1914, both by specialized retail organizations and by some margarine manufacturers. The situation in Germany differed greatly from that which developed in the

Netherlands, where milkmen sold margarine house-to-house with their regular deliveries of milk. In Germany the house-to-house retailers were organized specifically for the purpose of selling margarine on a wide scale. Between 1924 and 1933, at the peak of their development, there were three large organizations of this type with national distribution and several smaller firms with regional distribution. One of the national firms even had its own manufacturing facilities, but most of the house-to-house sellers purchased margarine in bulk and repacked it into consumer-sized packages.

Another development in the retailing of margarine which was unique to Germany was the mail-order selling of margarine, which was of some importance during the same time as house-to-house selling. Mail-order marketing permitted the housewife to conceal from her friends and neighbours the fact that she was buying margarine. House-to-house and mail-order distribution together, however, probably accounted for only some 10 per cent of retail sales in Germany in the 1920s, and attempts to revive these methods of distribution in the early 1950s were unsuccessful. Thus in Germany, the bulk of the margarine output was distributed from the beginning through regular grocery and food stores.

In the Netherlands, before 1900, butter was generally sold house-to-house by independent butter-vendors, and the new margarine industry utilized these agencies in the distribution of margarine. Although distribution through regular retail shops was started about 1900, these 'butter-pot' vendors, as they came to be called, remained important in the distribution of margarine for some time. Operating largely on a local basis, they mixed margarine with butter and usually sold the resulting product as butter. As the laws regarding adulteration became more definite and better enforced, the 'butter-pot' vendors were replaced by mixers who sold legally a blend of margarine and butter by house-to-house methods. It is believed that by 1929 the sale of margarine by mixers, milkmen, and other house-to-house retailers may have amounted to as much as 40 per cent of total retail sales.

As mentioned previously, the sale of margarine through retail shops started in the Netherlands about 1900. Presumably these first efforts at retail-store distribution were made through the regular grocery and food stores. By 1910, however, special shops geared to the selling of margarine, including dairy stores, had largely taken over the task of distribution. It is not clear exactly why this happened.

Perhaps the regular grocery stores did not promote the sale of margarine enough to satisfy the manufacturers, or perhaps they were not equipped to handle a perishable product. In any event, it was after the First World War before the regular grocery store began to attain the importance in margarine distribution in the Netherlands that it had attained at an earlier date in most other countries.

Mixers and repackers

Although reprocessors are known to have existed in Belgium and northern France in the 1880s, the Dutch mixer and repacker is really a unique institution in the marketing of margarine. By 1914 the 'butter-pot' vendors had become, or were being replaced by, mixers or blenders who were mixing margarine with butter and selling the resulting product honestly as a mixture on a house-to-house basis. Since the butter was purchased from local farmers and the blended product was distributed only locally, the result was a product of good quality which was always fresh. Although there were some exceptions, most of these mixers were not large businesses, and they operated mainly in the western part of the Netherlands. By the late 1920s the largest firms tended to concentrate on mixing, selling their output to roundsmen who in turn sold to consumers house-to-house.

In 1931, in an effort to assist farmers during the depression, a law was passed requiring the addition of butter to margarine. Since the mixers were experienced in doing this, they became the nucleus of a rapidly expanded repacking industry. During the remainder of the 1930s, the repackers constituted an important factor in the margarine industry. In 1937 the law regarding compulsory mixture was repealed, and in 1940 the addition of butter to margarine was prohibited. Many repackers attempted to remain in business by buying margarine in bulk and wrapping and packing it for retail sale. A number managed to stay in business into the 1950s, but very few are left today.

Vertical integration by the manufacturers

One of the more interesting aspects of distribution policy in Europe was the acquisition of financial interests in retail shops by the larger margarine manufacturers. These interests were acquired, especially in the United Kingdom and the Netherlands, primarily and deliberately to promote the distribution of margarine. Although the Van den Bergh family had acquired stock in one shop company in England as early as 1896, it was in 1905 and 1906 that Van den Bergh began to purchase stock extensively and to make financial investments on a large scale in the English multiple shop companies. A part of the consideration for these investments was that Van den Bergh would acquire the right to supply all margarine requirements of the retailer for a specified period of time (22). At about the same time, Van den Bergh also began to acquire minor interests in a number of Dutch retail grocery firms (23). Jurgens and other large margarine manufacturers soon followed the Van den Bergh example.

By 1920 this policy of acquiring financial interests in retail shops, and especially in the multiples, in order to secure the retail distribution of margarine was well established in both the United Kingdom and the Netherlands. These ownership interests were maintained, and even expanded, for some time, probably reaching their peak in 1927 with an investment in Thomas Lipton in England by Van den Bergh. Even as this was taking place, however, the multiples were losing their dominant position in the retail distribution of margarine in the United Kingdom (24). This fact, together with the merger later the same year of Van den Bergh and Jurgens and the creation of Unilever in 1929, made the ownership of retail distribution facilities both less feasible and less necessary. Accordingly, between 1935 and 1950, Unilever gradually withdrew its investments in the retail shops, and ceased to regard these as ways of achieving margarine distribution.

The use of vertical integration as an instrument of margarine marketing policy was largely confined to the United Kingdom and the Netherlands. In Belgium similar integrative attempts were unsuccessful, and in Germany the relatively small amount of integration that existed was not generally an important consideration in the marketing of margarine. The reason for this divergence lay in the differing structures of the retail markets. In Germany and Belgium, the retail grocery business was dominated between 1910 and 1930 by the small independent store. To achieve vertical integration, it would have been necessary for the margarine manufacturers to become financially involved in a large number of small businesses. Even if the manufacturers had been willing to do this, it would have created a substantial amount of ill-will among competitive retailers, who usually resent having a supplier enter into direct competition at the retail level. In the United Kingdom and in the Netherlands the multiples developed earlier as an important form of retail organization, and it was easier for the margarine manufacturers to achieve a degree of vertical integration. Even in these countries, there was some resentment by competitive retailers of the margarine manufacturers' investments (25), but on balance the volume to be derived by integration presumably outweighed that which was lost because of it.

Channels serving the industrial market

Manufacturers often sell directly to the business buyers that make up the industrial market, especially if purchases are made in large quantities. In many industrial markets, however, specialized wholesalers exist who often are able to give superior service at a relatively low cost, especially to small buyers.

Whether wholesalers are used to distribute margarine to bakeries, hotels, restaurants, and other business buyers appears to depend mainly upon the importance of these markets. In the United Kingdom and the Netherlands, where sales to business buyers are large both absolutely and relatively to the total market for margarine, most sales to business buyers (75–80 per cent) are now made directly without the use of wholesale middlemen. In France, where the industrial market is a relatively large part of a small total market, sales are also made directly. In Germany the industrial market is a relatively small part of a large total market, and sales are made largely through wholesalers. A similar situation exists in the U.S.A.

There is not a great deal of historical information about the channels used to reach business buyers, but some changes are known to have taken place since 1950. In the Netherlands, for example, direct marketing has largely replaced the use of wholesalers since that date. The reason appears to be the growth of the industrial market and the effort to serve that market better with specialized products and improved distribution service. In Germany the opposite has happened, apparently partly for the same reason that wholesalers are now being used to serve the consumer market. Organized buying associations have made their appearance in Germany, especially in the bakery trade; and the members insist on buying through the sponsoring wholesalers rather than directly, as they did before. Cash-and-carry wholesalers have also made their appearance in recent years in Germany, the Netherlands, and the United Kingdom, and have attained considerable importance in the industrial market.

In the U.S.A. there were attempts to sell directly in the industrial market, especially to the bakery trade, before 1950, but it was too expensive for most manufacturers. Unless other products were also being sold by the manufacturer to the same business buyers, it was much less expensive to use wholesalers. Since 1950 the institutional market for margarine in the U.S.A. has expanded considerably, but it is mostly served by brokers and specialized wholesalers such as restaurant supply houses, hotel supply houses, ship's chandlers, and the institutional departments of regular grocery wholesalers. It may be noted that the potential industrial market for margarine is still restricted in many states by laws which prohibit the serving of the product in restaurants.

Concluding observations on marketing channels

It is evident that the channels used in marketing margarine have been varied and diverse. Cost and effectiveness are the two basic considerations that have led to the selection of one channel in preference to another at any particular time. Perishability of the product has always been a problem and the desire to maintain quality and avoid product-deterioration has been an important consideration in evaluating channel effectiveness. The institutional arrangements existing in a country or a market have also been of considerable importance at various times.

An important factor in the major margarine markets, perhaps the most important over the years in evaluating channel effectiveness, has been whether a given channel would obtain sales volume for the manufacturer. In markets with a limited volume of sales and without much prospect of growth, cost has been the dominant factor in selecting channels of distribution. In the larger markets, however, there has been a great deal of direct marketing, much of it for the purpose of obtaining a competitive advantage in the sale of the product. Margarine has at times been distributed in ways that are more typical of a specialty food than of a convenience food. This in turn has affected the promotional methods used to stimulate demand for the product. These methods constitute the subject of the next section.

STIMULATION OF DEMAND

Demand for a product may be stimulated by personal selling, by advertising, and through the use of a wide variety of sales-promotional devices such as premiums, contests, trading stamps, and the like. All of these methods have been widely used in the promotion and sale of margarine. For convenience goods of low unit value, advertising is more likely to be used than personal selling in stimulating demand. This is particularly true for large companies with widespread distribution. The reason for this is that advertising is the more economical method of selling such a product to a mass market. As a convenience good, margarine has had extensive advertising support, but personal selling has also been an important factor in its promotional mix, possibly because of the low-status image of the product and the consequent need for aggressive marketing. Information is not available as to the proportionate amounts spent at various times for personal selling, advertising, and sales-promotional activities involving margarine, but the following discussion will attempt to develop some perspective with respect to the promotional mix.

Personal selling

The establishment of branch sales offices and the employment of salesmen to work from these offices were related to the direct channels of distribution used by the major manufacturers of margarine. Since direct marketing was undertaken during the late 1890s in both Germany and the United Kingdom, sales offices were opened and salesmen employed at the same time (26). Beginning in 1897, Jurgens opened a number of sales offices in the United Kingdom to serve independent grocers. Van den Bergh followed the Jurgens example, but only to a limited extent as Van den Bergh had established better relations with wholesalers and the large shop companies than had Jurgens. In Germany, however, when Jurgens began to follow the same policy at about the same time, Van den Bergh moved very rapidly. By 1906 it had 53 sales offices and 750 salesmen there.

It is not clear that all of these salesmen were regular employees of the companies that they represented. In the early days, many were probably independent representatives working on a commission basis. The distinction may not be of great importance as they appear to have represented mainly, if not entirely, the one company, and to have sold primarily the one product, margarine.

In any event, the utilization of such large sales forces primarily for one product, and that one a product of low unit value, was undoubtedly an expensive method of stimulating demand. But the intensive competition for sales volume led to an even greater use of personal selling effort for some time. The peak period for the employment of salesmen probably came between 1923 and 1925. In 1927 Van den Bergh had reduced its sales offices in Germany to nine in a successful effort to reduce selling costs, and Jurgens had followed this example (27). In the Netherlands and in Sweden, as well as in Germany, reductions in sales forces took place before 1927, the year in which Van den Bergh and Jurgens merged to create Margarine Unie. Nevertheless, the great emphasis on the use of personal selling in the margarine industry prior to 1927 is perhaps best illustrated by the fact that Margarine Unie after its creation found itself with 5,600 margarine salesmen in Germany alone (28).

The mergers of 1927 and 1929, culminating in the creation of Unilever, resulted in substantial reductions in the sales forces of the merged companies. For example, the 5,600 margarine salesmen in Germany were soon cut by half. The depression of the 1930s no doubt resulted in further reductions, and the trend towards the use of wholesalers after 1950 further curtailed the number of salesmen used in the marketing of margarine.

Of even greater importance perhaps, in reducing the cost of demand stimulation for margarine, is the fact that the merger of 1929 permitted the addition of other products for the salesmen's line. The development of additional products since then, both through the creation of new products and through further mergers, has resulted in much greater product variety. The Unilever salesmen of the 1960s, numbering fewer than 800 in West Germany for example, provide selling service for several food products as well as margarine.

Another very important factor in reducing the number of salesmen is the development of the supermarket and other large food stores. There are now fewer stores to serve, and thus fewer salesmen needed. This is particularly important to the small margarine manufacturer who must rely more on personal selling than on advertising because of his limited market area. With fewer but larger potential customers, the cost of sales solicitation can be reduced as a percentage of sales volume.

The margarine salesman of the 1960s is likely to have a very different type of job from that of his predecessor of many years ago. The latter took orders, and in many instances even made delivery and collected payment for the sale. With the trend toward the use of wholesalers since 1950, the modern salesman may not even solicit orders from retailers, and certainly will not make deliveries and collections. His job with retailers is rather to check stocks for freshness, to arrange displays and promotions and in general to see that his product is properly merchandised by the retailer. When orders are obtained, they may merely be turned over to a wholesaler. Thus the emphasis of modern marketing is on co-operation among the various elements of the channel of distribution to serve better the ultimate consumer.

There is also a considerable emphasis on the more efficient allocation of personal selling effort. Salesmen's calls may be restricted to retailers handling a certain minimum weekly volume, and the smaller accounts are called upon less frequently than the larger ones. Sales offices are being consolidated into larger and more efficient units as better communication and transport facilities reduce the time required to get products to the market. Thus the modern emphasis, regardless of the number of salesmen employed, is on the more efficient utilization of the personnel involved in the personal selling effort. The greater use of wholesalers in place of direct marketing by manufacturers, the great acceptance of the product by consumers with a resulting stabilization of the level of consumption, and the constantly increasing level of salesmen's salaries are factors that tend to result in many countries in less use of personal selling in relation to advertising and other elements of the promotional mix of margarine.

Advertising

Advertising is most likely to be used as a means of demand-stimulation when it is cheaper than personal selling and more effective than the various forms of sales promotion. For advertising to be economical, widespread distribution of the advertised product and a mass market are required. For it to be effective, the consumer must be able to identify the product in the market place. To the extent that advertising is conducted through the use of printed media, as much of it is even today, the existence of a literate population is essential. Moreover, the use of a common language over a relatively large market area is of considerable importance in reducing the cost and increasing the effectiveness of advertising. The history of margarine advertising reflects and illustrates the importance of these and other considerations.

Although little reliable information is available, it may be assumed that there was little margarine advertising prior to 1900. The market was not sufficiently well-developed to warrant large expenditures, and the manufacturers were not distributing margarine over a sufficiently widespread market area. Of even greater importance was the lack of product identification; as previously mentioned, brand names were not generally used until about 1900, and most margarine was sold in bulk until about 1920. The literacy rate and the lack of a common language in some countries were probably at most minor handicaps in the principal margarine markets of the time.

With the introduction of the Vitello brand in Germany by Van den Bergh in 1898, the advertising situation changed rapidly. Jurgens countered with Solo the following year, and by 1905 its advertising 'reached staggering proportions' (29). Both Van den Bergh and Jurgens, according to Wilson, increased advertising expenditure by 300–400 per cent per year over previously existing levels in the 1904–6 period when competition between the two firms reached a peak.

Most margarine manufacturers did not develop a consistent advertising policy for margarine for some time. When new and improved products were developed, they were likely to be introduced with considerable advertising support. In times of extreme competition, advertising expenditures tended to be much greater than they were during periods of agreement and market-sharing. War and depression played their part in interrupting distribution and restricting advertising. So far as the U.S.A. is concerned, there is the additional factor that the market for margarine was artificially restricted before the Second World War. Thus only since 1950 has advertising become an integrated part of the marketing mix, with a planned and consistent programme from year to year. This development can be illustrated by showing some of the changes that have taken place over the years in the appeals used and the media selected for advertising.

Themes and appeals. The early advertising of margarine tended to state or imply a comparison with butter. Few countries had laws regulating advertising, and there was little restriction of the statements that could be made in support of margarine. In some countries, Germany and France especially, care was exercised by margarine advertisers not to offend the farmer. But this was probably not a major consideration in most countries, as the dairy farmer was already violently opposed to the manufacture and sale of margarine and his attitude could hardly be changed by margarine advertising.

Early advertising, therefore, emphasized quality and similarity to butter at a lower price. In the U.S.A. slogans used before 1915 included: 'churned especially for lovers of good butter', 'made in the milky way', 'creamy richness' (30). In the Netherlands, Blue Band was advertised in the 1920s as 'just like the best butter'. Subsequent legislation in both countries resulted in the prohibition of such advertising, although the United Kingdom still permits the slogan used for one brand, 'most people can't tell the difference'.

By the 1930s, margarine was being advertised largely on its own merits. Snodgrass analysed advertisements in the U.S.A. in 1929 and found only a few that openly suggested a comparison with butter (31). These appear to be still fewer in number today, although advertising of one margarine brand does refer to 'the more expensive spread'.

The particular themes and appeals used in advertising margarine on its own merits have also changed over the years, but perhaps not so much as has the general philosophy. There has always been a good deal of emphasis on taste and flavour and freshness, and these appeals are still used. Ease of spreading is an appeal still used in Europe, but largely discarded in the U.S.A. as margarine has become easier and easier to spread. Nutritional value has been an important appeal over the years. At first it was used somewhat defensively to indicate that margarine was not nutritionally inferior to butter. But as vitamins were added and new raw materials utilized, the approach became a more positive one of promoting the superiority of margarine.

Now this appeal has been expanded to include certain health claims for particular ingredients. There has always been some margarine advertising that included reference to the nature of the ingredients, especially as vegetable fats and oils replaced animal fats, but the present advertising, especially in the U.S.A., relates the ingredients to health very positively and definitely. 'Highest in polyunsaturated fats', 'lowest in saturated fat', 'made from 100 % golden corn oil', and similar claims are frequently used. Margarine advertising in Europe has not yet placed so much stress on health claims.

Media. The media used in advertising margarine vary from country to country, depending upon custom and legality. For example, television advertising is not permitted in some countries and is significantly restricted in others, and the situation is similar for radio advertising. In any event, these media are relatively recent in origin and use. Before the advent of radio in the 1920s, visual media were used by necessity, but advertising was by no means confined to newspapers and magazines. The latter had low circulations by modern standards and in any case did not reach the people who constituted the market for margarine.

The first advertising for margarine utilized wall-posters, usually hand-painted, and posters and cards located in or immediately outside the shops which sold the product. The advertising of Vitello in Germany in the early 1900s has been described as follows: 'Vitello was painted everywhere, on the walls, in the best and most prominent spots, and beautifully enamelled plates hung outside the shops . . .' (32). Advertising in the Netherlands and in Belgium was similar: painted wall-posters, shop posters, and cards. In Rotterdam special showcases were set up along Coolsingel, the main street, for advertising posters.

Modern margarine advertising still has some of these characteristics in those African and Asian countries where literacy rates are low and several languages exist within one country. Considerable reliance tends to be placed on posters which emphasize pictorial representation of the product as a substitute for words. In addition, advertising reaches the consumer through audio means, such as demonstrations using loud-speakers mounted on moving vans.

In the developed countries where there is no restriction on television and radio advertising, television has now replaced radio as the main advertising medium for margarine. In the U.S.A., most heavily advertised brands of margarine spend from two-thirds to three-fourths of their appropriations on television. Magazines and radio receive most of the rest. There is at least one brand, however, which reverses the percentages, spending about two-thirds on radio and a small amount on television. Newspapers, once an important advertising medium for margarine in the U.S.A., have declined significantly in relation to television.

In the United Kingdom also, television has become the dominant advertising medium for margarine, followed by newspapers and magazines. In Germany television advertising is restricted and claims only about one-fourth of the margarine advertising budget. Magazines constitute the dominant medium there, newspapers being less important than television. In the Netherlands, where television advertising was not permitted until early 1967, newspapers and magazines have been the principal media. It seems clear that television takes over as the principal advertising medium for margarine wherever it is permitted to do so.

Co-operative advertising. Co-operative advertising is advertising in which the manufacturer gives allowances to the retailer to promote the manufacturer's product. Although Wilson mentions the existence in the United Kingdom in 1912 of co-operative advertising involving the multiples and the margarine manufacturers (33), advertising allowances generally have been used to a greater extent in the food field in the U.S.A. than in Europe, for a rather obvious reason. The small size of the typical food retailer in Europe has not made it worthwhile for the manufacturer to participate in such an arrangement. As European retailers have become larger, special co-operative promotions have occasionally taken place, but little has been done on a regular and sustained basis.

In the U.S.A. co-operative advertising allowances have sometimes been used a great deal. It is often difficult to determine whether the retailer actually uses the allowance to pay fully for advertising of the manufacturer's brand and in many cases, such allowances may have merely served as price discounts granted to large buyers. At the present time, allowances are more likely to be given for display than for advertising. In a modern self-service store, display space is often more valuable than advertising space. Moreover, the manufacturer finds it easier with display allowances to check on the retailer to see if he is keeping his agreement.

Sales promotion

Successful advertising usually requires a large potential market or a premium product or both. Thus a large manufacturer with a national market and a high degree of market penetration is more likely to spend heavily on advertising than is a small regional manufacturer with limited market penetration. In addition, the higher-quality and higher-priced brands are usually more effectively advertised than other brands. The cheapest brands may be sold on the basis of price alone with a minimum of advertising. Middle-priced brands are in a particularly difficult situation, and may well look for some basis of promotion other than advertising or price.

The promotional mix for margarine again illustrates a number of these ideas. The large manufacturer has emphasized advertising, causing the small manufacturer to seek out various forms of sales promotion. Advertising has also been concentrated on the main brands of each manufacturer. In Europe these are brands of high quality, although the dominant brand of a manufacturer has not always been

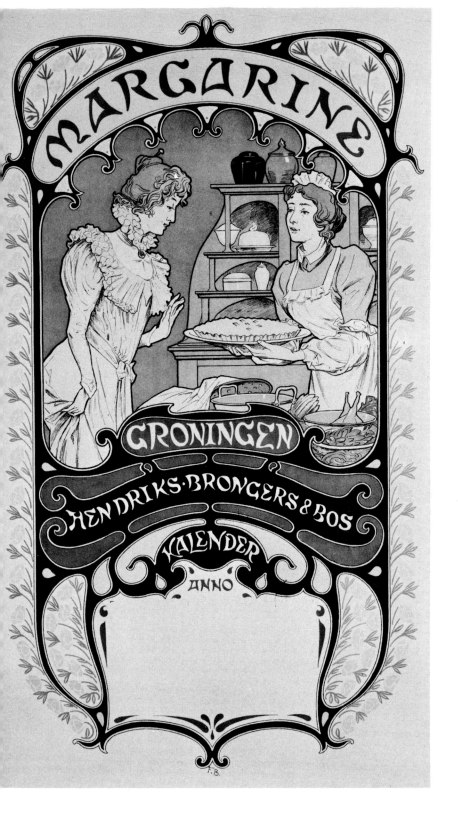

47. A calendar as an advertising medium. *Art nouveau* of high quality
published in the Netherlands in 1910.

48. A German advertisement published in 1930 in which the similarity between butter and margarine is emphasized.

his highest-priced brand. In the U.S.A. advertising is more likely to be concentrated on the highest-priced brand, leaving other forms of sales promotion to the middle brands. In any event, the sales-promotional devices used, either in conjunction with one's own advertising or to combat the advertising of one's competitors, have been many and varied.

The devices used to appeal to the consumer have included the giving of free samples (especially when new brands were introduced or existing brands improved), money-off coupons, pricing specials (buy 1 lb and get ½ lb free), and especially the use of premiums and savings stamps. Premium merchandising in particular has had a long and interesting history. In the United Kingdom and the U.S.A., it has been used somewhat sparingly; but in countries such as Germany, the Netherlands, and Belgium, premium merchandising—or the 'free gift' system as it is called there—has been very important in the promotion of margarine.

Like so many other elements of the marketing mix for margarine, the gift system was introduced in Europe shortly after 1900 when the competition between Jurgens and Van den Bergh was particularly severe. It was utilized especially by large wholesalers and retailers for their private brands, and by small manufacturers. The success of this type of promotion forced the larger manufacturers to use it for one or more secondary brands. The gift system was seldom, if ever, used by the large manufacturers for their top-quality brands. Media advertising was the primary means of promotion for the latter.

The premiums selected for the gift schemes varied from children's magazines, picture cards, and toys, to all types of household products. The emphasis was often on premiums for children. In Germany, for example, children's magazines were the most important type of premium until 1914. Along with picture cards, they were also important between 1924 and 1933; but many household products were added after 1925. For example, for coupons from 45 lb of margarine the housewife could choose from more than 30 items offered by one manufacturer, including 6 dinner plates, 12 breakfast plates, a coffee grinder, a kitchen clock, or a fountain pen. The complete premium list exceeded 60 items, requiring coupons from as few as 3 lb to as many as 900 lb of margarine.

Although gift schemes were eliminated by government order in Germany for a time after 1933, they were revived in 1950. Competitive excesses resulting in more and more costly gifts led to agreement in 1954 to eliminate the gift system. Free gifts continue to exist in the Netherlands, however, where they are still an important means of sales promotion for some firms. At various times, both in Germany and the Netherlands, gifts have been offered to retailers and to the commercial buyers of margarine, as well as to ultimate consumers. The gift system has generally been an effective competitive weapon for those who have used it.

PRICES AND PRICE POLICIES

Price is the fourth element of the marketing mix. It has been an important one in the development of the margarine industry. The early demand for margarine was created primarily by the low price of the product, and price has continued to be an important consideration in the minds of consumers. Other chapters of this book contain discussions of the price and income elasticities of demand and of the role of the government in regulating margarine prices, and these discussions will not be repeated here. Some attention will be paid, however, to the effect upon margarine sales of the comparative prices of butter and margarine. The history of price competition among margarine producers will then be reviewed, along with certain efforts to stabilize prices. The present stability of margarine prices in Europe presents a sharp contrast to the price competition and instability that existed there in the earlier days of the industry, and that now exist in the U.S.A. Over the years, price has become a more dynamic element of the marketing mix in the U.S.A. and a less dynamic one in Europe.

Relationship of margarine and butter prices

An essential element of the marketing mix for margarine over the years has been its low price, and in particular its low price in relation to butter. Most studies of demand elasticity have concluded that changes in the price of butter have a much greater effect upon the consumption of margarine than do changes in the price of margarine itself. It also seems that the difference, or relationship, between margarine prices and butter prices have long-term effects on the consumption of margarine, as well as the short-term effects that are measurable by computing price elasticities. Since many factors affect the relative consumption of margarine and butter, it would not be logical for these price differences to explain completely the trends in margarine consumption, but there should be some relationship.

There does not appear to be an extensive analysis of this relationship, and none is attempted here. One of the difficulties is the accuracy and comparability of price data, especially during the early years of the margarine industry. Even today, price statistics are subject to varying degrees of error, depending upon the country and the commodity. It must be assumed that data from the early years of this century would lack a great deal in precision and validity. Nevertheless there are data available from which some tentative conclusions can be drawn (34).

Between 1900 and 1913, margarine generally sold at some 50–65 per cent of butter prices. These figures are presumably averages for a year although such information is not always stated definitely. Since butter prices tended to vary seasonally, the ratio of margarine prices to butter prices probably varied seasonally also. In addition the annual ratios vary considerably. In general, however, they appear to have been higher in the Netherlands and in the U.S.A. than in the United Kingdom and Germany by some 5–10 per cent. By 1913 the *per capita* consumption of margarine in the two latter countries was almost twice that of the Netherlands, and several times that of the U.S.A. The differences in the price ratios may have been partly responsible, although government regulation in the U.S.A. was obviously the principal reason for the low consumption in that country. The Scandinavian countries had much higher rates of consumption in 1913 than did Germany and the United Kingdom, but no information is available to the present author on price ratios in these countries.

During the 1920s, the ratio of margarine prices to butter prices declined in most countries. The decline was greatest in Germany and the United Kingdom, where margarine prices tended to average 33–5 per cent of butter prices in the former, and 38–9 per cent in the latter. In the Netherlands there was an increasingly favourable price relationship for margarine compared with butter (35), but the ratio remained some 10–15 per cent above those for the United Kingdom and Germany. *Per capita* consumption continued to lag behind that of the other two countries. In the U.S.A. there was a good percentage increase in the *per capita* consumption of margarine as the margarine-to-butter price ratio gradually declined to less than 50 in 1927 (36). Total consumption, however, was still small.

Depression and war during the 1930s and 1940s resulted in a great deal of government regulation, which disrupted market–price relationships. In the United Kingdom during the 1930s the margarine-to-butter price ratio remained at about 40, and in the U.S.A. it varied from 43 to 55 with an average of about 50. In both Germany and the Netherlands ratios increased significantly during the 1930s, reaching a level of 60 and higher by the latter part of the decade. Despite these unfavourable price ratios, *per capita* consumption in both Germany and the Netherlands in 1938 was considerably higher than in the United Kingdom. Denmark and Norway still had much higher rates of consumption, however; Denmark in particular had a relatively low price ratio (37).

Better and more complete data are available for the period since the Second World War. Norway, Denmark, and the Netherlands consumed the largest amounts of margarine *per capita*, more than 40 lb in 1960. In Norway the annual margarine-to-butter ratios ranged from 24 to 32 between 1952 and 1964. During the same period, comparable ratios for the Netherlands varied from 30 to 39. The typical ratios were about 30 for Norway and 33–4 for the Netherlands. The ratios for Denmark were somewhat higher, and quite variable because of variable butter prices. Typically they ranged from 37 to 46, but there were several years in which they were higher, and one in which the percentage was lower.

Sweden, with a relatively high *per capita* consumption of 35 lb in 1960, had high margarine-to-butter price ratios between 1952 and 1964. Ranging from 45 to 58, the ratios were above 50 in most years. In Germany, however, margarine prices averaged about one-third of butter prices during this period, the percentage ranging from 31 to 38. Percentages were slightly higher in the U.S.A., ranging from 35 to 41 with an average of 37–8.

In the United Kingdom, price ratios of margarine-to-butter have risen since the Second World War. Between 1952 and 1956 they ranged from 42 to 47, except for 1956 when the ratio was much lower. In a majority of years since 1957 the ratio has been at least 55, and in the other years it has been at least 50. It is interesting to note that the consumption of butter has exceeded that of margarine since 1956.

Although other factors obviously influence the consumption of margarine and butter, the relative prices of the two commodities do appear to play a part over the long run. A ratio of margarine prices to butter prices of less than 50 per cent appears to be favourable to margarine. Of the countries mentioned here, only Sweden and the

United Kingdom have generally had ratios above 50 during the post-war period. In the United Kingdom margarine obtained only some 45 per cent of the total market for margarine and butter combined in the early 1960s. Sweden is an exception, however, in that margarine obtained about 60 per cent of the market during the same time.

In two of the three countries with the lowest price ratios, Norway and the Netherlands, margarine has captured over 80 per cent of the combined market. In the third country, Germany, the low price ratio has not been so effective in stimulating the demand for margarine. In fact, consumption had declined by the early 1960s to less than 60 per cent of the total market from somewhat higher levels in the middle 1950s.

In the U.S.A. and Denmark, margarine's market share during the early 1960s was similar to that in Sweden and Germany. In the U.S.A. it was approaching 60 per cent, and gradually increasing. In Denmark margarine had about 65 per cent of the market. In the U.S.A. the price ratio was seldom above 40 per cent during the 1960s; in Denmark it was variable but on the whole a few points higher.

The analysis raises the question of the extent to which margarine should be traded-up in price. The answer undoubtedly is different in different countries, but it does seem that a low price relative to butter is still an important element of the marketing mix for margarine.

Price competition in margarine

In Europe the margarine industry, almost from its beginning, became involved periodically in price wars. These were usually followed by agreements to fix prices and market shares, agreements which met with varying degrees of success in stabilizing prices. The price wars occurred most often because of excess capacity in the margarine industry, occasionally because of a surplus of butter production. They usually started in the cheaper grades of margarine, and it was in these grades that the greatest amount of price instability occurred. The quality brands, however, were also affected in most cases. It is often alleged that the price wars were started by the smaller margarine producers who sold only the less expensive grades. However, the early pooling agreements seem to have involved only Van den Bergh and Jurgens, and it seems likely that the intense competition between these two firms played an important part in the early price wars.

The first Van den Bergh–Jurgens agreement to have any success was made in 1908 as a result of severe weakness in margarine prices in Germany (38). The agreement applied also to the United Kingdom, although it was instituted because of the price situation in Germany and was most effective there. The agreement provided for a pooling of profits, and certain other forms of co-operation such as the exchange of secret product formulas.

This agreement began to run into difficulties in 1911 (39). Jurgens's profits had increased and, rather than share them with Van den Bergh, it increased its advertising expenditure. A new agreement was made in 1913, for one year, to limit advertising as well as to share profits. At the advent of war government regulations over-ruled industrial agreements, and after the war Van den Bergh and Jurgens decided not to renew the agreement. After 1925 the cheaper grades of margarine sold at very low prices for some time.

The 1920s were a period of severe price competition in margarine in other countries. There was excess capacity in the United Kingdom, partly perhaps as a result of Lever's attempt to enter the industry, but principally because of the construction of plants to serve Great Britain's wartime needs. Prices fell rapidly in 1920 and 1921. Several unsuccessful attempts were made by Jurgens and Van den Bergh to establish quotas and fix prices between 1921 and 1923 (40). Finally, in 1925, a pooling agreement was worked out between several Dutch and English companies, but early in 1927 the agreement broke down and severe price-cutting followed (41).

There was also severe price-cutting in the Netherlands during the 1920s. From time to time, quota agreements were made in an attempt to stabilize prices, but these were at best only temporarily successful. By 1927 prices were so low that margarine was even being used as a raw material in the manufacture of soap (42).

The failure of the various pooling and quota agreements to result in the stabilization of margarine prices led to the merger of Van den Bergh and Jurgens in 1927. The two companies had briefly considered the possibility of merger shortly before their pooling agreement of 1908, but had decided that it was not feasible for a number of reasons. By 1927, however, it was evident that price stabilization would not be achieved otherwise. Moreover, the two firms were having difficulty in agreeing upon the amounts due under the pooling agreements (43). A complete merger was therefore accomplished, the new firm being called Margarine Unie. Between 1927 and 1929 several smaller competitors were acquired, and in 1929 Margarine Unie merged with Lever in England to create Unilever. The new company was ready to become the dominant firm in the European margarine industry with market shares, including sales obtained through later acquisitions, of 50–75 per cent or more in many countries.

The merger did not, however, result in complete price stability. The depression of the 1930s reduced butter prices, and this led in turn to some price-cutting in margarine. To overcome this in the United Kingdom, the various margarine manufacturers organized in 1936 into the Margarine Group which assigned tonnage quotas to each manufacturer from early 1936 to the beginning of the Second World War. At that time a trade association took over, under government sponsorship, the responsibility of allocating scarce supplies during the war. There was a considerable feeling, especially among the smaller manufacturers, that a similar market allocation plan should continue after the war, but this was not done.

In the Netherlands the government largely controlled margarine prices during the 1930s and 1940s. In addition, some fifteen producers formed the Margarine Convention in 1932 to fix quotas for each manufacturer. Price uniformity thus resulted, at either minimum or maximum levels. The Convention continued in existence until the beginning of the Second World War, and was re-established in 1947. There was a breakdown in the Convention in the early 1950s, with resulting low prices for the cheaper grades of margarine. In 1954 the Convention was reconstituted, and has remained in existence since that time (see Chapter Seven).

In the Scandinavian countries a somewhat different approach, possibly a less complete one, has been taken to achieve price stability. Starting in Sweden in 1926, the device utilized is the organization of a marketing or selling agency. Several manufacturers agree to supply the selling agency, now known as the Marketing Board, with margarine in proportions established by the agreement. The Marketing Board then performs all of the marketing and selling functions, remitting net proceeds to the producer-members. Marketing Boards exist in Denmark, Norway, and Sweden with producer-members ranging in number from two to fourteen or so in each country. They distribute usually from 45 to 65 per cent of total margarine volume in the countries involved. The purpose of the Marketing Boards, at least originally, was probably not so much to reduce price competition as to compete more effectively with consumer co-operatives which were and are very strong in the Scandinavian countries. The Marketing

Boards really constitute a form of producer co-operation. Like any producer co-operative, they are in a position to influence price in relation to their domination of the market. In addition, for a product such as margarine, they may be able to exercise price leadership. In general, the market shares of the Boards are probably not sufficiently high to permit them to control prices through the manipulation of supplies. Price leadership appears to be exercised in Denmark, and probably also in Sweden.

There is no record in the U.S.A. of price-cutting in the early days of the margarine industry such as took place in Europe between 1900 and 1927. In all probability, the sales volume during that period was insufficient to attract aggressive competitors to the industry. The margarine trade was confined to relatively few producers, and it was not difficult to establish a system of price leadership that would give a large degree of price stability. The anti-trust laws of the U.S.A. have long forbidden the forms of industry agreement and co-operation sometimes used by European margarine producers. Therefore, when competitors are few in number, there tends to emerge a price leader whose actions are followed by the remainder of the industry. This probably was the situation in the margarine industry in the U.S.A. before 1950.

The growth of the industry after 1950 undoubtedly increased the amount of competition. In 1935 the four largest margarine manufacturers accounted for 79 per cent of the total value of shipments of the industry, and in 1947 the ratio was still a high 64 per cent (44). By 1954 the comparable ratio had declined to 39 per cent; after that it increased gradually to a level of 50 per cent in 1963 (45). These figures include, of course, each manufacturer's production of private brands of margarine as well as his own nationally advertised brands. In most cases, a manufacturer can exercise little control over the prices of private brands; thus the concentration ratios may imply more market power than actually exists. It is believed that no single brand of margarine has a market share of more than 10 per cent in the U.S.A. at the present time. This is an average, however, and particular brands do have much larger shares of particular local or regional markets. Thus the degree of market penetration of any brand, and its presumed effect on prices, varies a great deal from place to place. A given brand may sell at different prices in different markets.

Premium-priced brands usually sell within a range of prices in the U.S.A., not at a single uniform price. These products are highly advertised, and more or less differentiated in the minds of consumers. A small difference in price, or sometimes even a rather large one, may not affect sales volume appreciably. The medium-priced brands, under a system of price leadership, are more likely to sell at uniform prices. Price differences between brands in a given market are likely to be small and temporary. A price change by one manufacturer will either be followed by competitors or rescinded by the leader. Most of the low-priced brands are private brands, and at this level prices lack uniformity and stability. Special-price promotions are frequent, and originate with the retailer. The amount and frequency of price-cutting varies greatly by market, however. Some areas tend to have rather stable prices; others do not. The degree of competition that exists among the food retailers in the market is the determining factor, not the degree of competition that exists among manufacturers.

Since the Second World War, pricing has tended to become a more dynamic factor in the marketing mix for margarine in the U.S.A. and a less dynamic factor in Europe. One reason for this is the greater use of resale price maintenance and manufacturers' suggested resale prices in Europe than in the U.S.A.

Resale price maintenance

Agreements between a manufacturer and the retailers of his product to sell the product, a branded item, at a price stipulated by the manufacturer constitute the essence of resale price maintenance. One purpose of designating a resale price is to preserve the manufacturer's reputation for quality, since the consumer often associates low prices with low quality. In addition, retailer co-operation in the distribution of the price-maintained product is more likely to be achieved, as prices cannot be reduced by competitors and profit margins are maintained. Resale price maintenance thus tends to substitute service competition for price competition among retailers. Manufacturers, of course, are still free to compete with respect to price.

The federal government of the U.S.A. has generally taken the position that resale price maintenance constitutes an illegal restriction of competition. The practice has, however, been allowed since the 1930s if authorized by state law. Between 1933 and the end of the Second World War, most states permitted resale price maintenance. Since 1950 an increasing number have withdrawn their permissive laws, although they have not necessarily made an effort to proceed legally against manufacturers who suggest resale prices or retailers who abide by them.

Regardless of this legal status, resale price maintenance agreements have been little used in the U.S.A. in the grocery field. Food retailing has been so competitive that any manufacturer who maintained prices might well find himself losing a significant portion of his sales volume to competitive products selling at lower prices. One or two attempts were made some years ago to maintain the retail prices of margarine, but they were not successful and resulted only in reduced sales. Thus the retailer has always been free in the U.S.A. to set his own price for margarine according to demand and competition. This has probably resulted in a lower level of prices and a higher volume of sales than would have existed under resale price maintenance.

In Europe the retailers are smaller and more inclined to seek a certain uniformity in their selling prices. Moreover, most governments have not interfered with resale price maintenance agreements until recently. There has therefore been much greater use of this device in food retailing in Europe than in the U.S.A. Margarine manufacturers in most European countries were suggesting retail prices for branded items by 1910 and generally entering into resale price agreements by the early or mid 1920s. Because much margarine was still sold unbranded in the 1920s, there remained a great deal of price competition at the retail level. Since the early 1930s, however, these unbranded products have been largely replaced by branded products with relatively uniform prices.

Although many European governments have opposed resale price maintenance in recent years, most retailers still follow the manufacturers' suggested price or the prices of their major competitors. Thus the variety of prices at which margarine is sold in most European countries is likely to be quite limited, with rather definite quality distinctions being made between price lines. In comparison, the variety of prices at which margarine is sold in the U.S.A., and at which it was once sold in Europe, is such as to be almost chaotic. But such a variety of prices may very well stimulate demand.

SUMMARY AND CONCLUSIONS

In traditional marketing terminology, margarine would be classified as a convenience good, and not as a shopping or specialty good.

Such a product is one of low unit value. It is distributed widely through all available retail outlets, so that it can be purchased conveniently by the consumer. To achieve this widespread distribution economically requires the use of wholesalers. Since wholesalers do very little to stimulate demand for any particular product or brand, a convenience good is likely to be heavily advertised to the consumer by the manufacturer.

Thus the marketing mix for the typical convenience good consists of low unit price, mass advertising, and an indirect or 'long' channel of distribution. To these characteristics we might add the following: little product variety, a slow rate of product improvement, and the exercise by the manufacturer of little control over the retail price of the product. In recent years, the product variety of many convenience goods has been increased greatly as a result of the application of the principle of market segmentation, and control over retail prices through resale price maintenance agreements has frequently been attempted to prevent retail price-cutting.

The history of the marketing of margarine shows, of course, many characteristics of the convenience good. Every effort has been made to obtain widespread distribution. Broadcast methods of promotion, for example consumer advertising, have been used on a large scale to stimulate demand, and the product is one of low unit value. But the history of margarine marketing also shows many features not ordinarily associated with the marketing of a convenience good. Product variety and product improvement have always been important elements in the marketing mix for margarine, and the product has participated fully in the modern trend in the U.S.A. toward greater product variety. Obviously, however, margarine has not approached the typical shopping good in these respects.

As for distribution, the margarine manufacturer has attempted to place his product in every possible retail outlet, but his method of achieving this has not until recently been typical of the methods used for convenience goods. In Europe particularly there has been a great deal of direct marketing to the retailer without the use of wholesalers. Marketing theory would hardly visualize the possibility of purchasing financial interests in multiples merely to obtain distribution of a product of low unit value.

Departures from the theory have also taken place in the promotional mix. Margarine has been heavily advertised, and the use of premiums and gifts is consistent with the concept of mass marketing.

But the use of salesmen on a large scale in Europe before 1930 is not really typical.

Despite these costly variations in the basic marketing activities, margarine has consistently sold at a low price. Periodic price-cutting is not necessarily inconsistent with the theory, but in Europe the manufacturers, rather than the retailers, were the price-cutters. This is more unusual and resulted eventually in various attempts by the manufacturers to stabilize prices.

The theory that has been developed for the marketing of convenience goods is unduly simplified for a modern society, assuming as it does a homogeneous product and a homogeneous market. Margarine in particular does not fit these specifications. One reason why margarine has been marketed so aggressively appears to be the image of inferiority that became attached to the product very early, and that still exists in some degree. Combatting this image has been the most important marketing problem of the industry.

Aggressiveness in the marketing of margarine has been especially noticeable in Europe before 1930, and in the U.S.A. since 1950. Changes in the competitive structure of the industry have taken place in Europe since 1930, and these undoubtedly have played a part in the present relative stability of the various elements in the marketing mix. Of even more importance, perhaps, is the fact that European markets for margarine have been cultivated for a long time and are now mature markets. There is less opportunity for growth now than there was at an earlier date. Nevertheless, in some countries margarine does not appear to have reached its potential, and more aggressive marketing might be helpful. The image of product inferiority still exists among some consumers.

Before 1950 the U.S.A. was essentially an undeveloped country so far as the margarine industry was concerned. In that year the federal government repealed most of the restrictive regulations that had previously hampered the industry's development. The result has been a substantial growth in the market for margarine.

There are two aspects of marketing in which the American margarine industry since 1950 has tended to outdo its European counterpart. The first is in the dynamics of new product development and the rapidity with which new and improved products are made available to the market. The second is the great variety of products available, and in particular the wide range of prices at which they are sold. Product improvement and product and price variety can be accomplished, no doubt, in a large market much more easily than in a small one; and probably the American consumer really is more adaptable to change than is the European consumer. One reason for this, however, is that American marketing methods have caused him to expect change. In any event margarine has come a long way in both Europe and America, as well as in many other parts of the world, during the past 100 years.

NOTES AND REFERENCES

1. WILSON, C. *The history of Unilever. A study in economic growth and social change* (London, 1954), vol. 2, chap. 3.

2. See WILSON, op. cit., vol. 2, appendix 5 for data on the export trade of the Netherlands from 1893 to 1930.

3. Ibid., p. 174.

4. For details and exact figures from 1887 to 1929 see SNODGRASS, K. *Margarine as a butter substitute* (Stanford, California, 1930), pp. 312–18.

5. SCHWITZER, M. K. *Margarine and other food fats* (New York, 1956), p. 62.

6. WILSON, op. cit., pp. 48, 73.

7. HOWARD, M. C. 'The margarine industry in the United States: Its development under legislative control' (unpublished doctoral dissertation, Columbia University, 1951), p. 204.

8. RIEPMA, S. F. 'Margarine in the United States, 1873–1967' (unpublished).

9. SNODGRASS, op. cit., pp. 2, 133.

10. Data on the utilization of raw materials from 1930 to 1950 are given in HOWARD, op. cit., p. 336.

11. WILSON, op. cit., vol. 1, pp. 306–7.

12. Rama was first introduced by Jurgens in 1924, and was successful. The 1954 Rama was a new product using the established name.

13. Unilever in Germany also has a low-priced brand, Sanella.

14. See ANDERSEN, A. J. C., and WILLIAMS, P. N. *Margarine* (London and Oxford, 1965), 282–304 and SCHWITZER, op. cit., pp. 310–18.

15. SNODGRASS, op. cit., p. 75.

16. —— Ibid.

17. HOWARD, op. cit., p. 131.

18. WILSON, op. cit., vol. 2, p. 39.

19. LLOYD,E.M.H. *Experiments in state control at the War Office and the Ministry of Food* (Oxford, 1924), p. 236.

20. Because of the way in which the federal margarine regulations were administered, the wagon-jobber was not legally permitted to take orders at the time of the call. The order had to have been recorded previously at the central place of business.

21. Sales to chain retailers, or multiples, are classified as indirect sales in compiling these data. In the Netherlands especially practice varies widely as to whether delivery is made by the manufacturer to wholesale chain headquarters or directly to the retail units. Competitors of Unilever were probably selling more of their output directly to retailers in the mid 1960s than Unilever was; and Unilever itself, especially in Germany, was still delivering directly to retailers perhaps as much as one-fourth of the orders received through wholesalers.

22. WILSON, op. cit., vol. 2, pp. 67–8.

23. —— Ibid., p. 76.

24. —— Ibid., pp. 260–1.

25. —— Ibid., p. 126.

26. The details that follow are recorded in WILSON, op. cit., vol. 2, chap. 3.

27. —— Ibid., p. 246.

28. —— Ibid., p. 295.

29. —— Ibid., p. 75.

30. SNODGRASS, op. cit., pp. 101–2.

31. —— Ibid.

32. A description by Sam Van den Bergh, quoted in WILSON, op. cit., p. 74.

33. —— Ibid., p. 130.

34. The relationship of average margarine prices to average butter prices for a number of countries for 1938 and for 1952–64 is given in SCHÜTTAUF,W., *Die Margarine in Deutschland und der Welt (Margarine in Germany and the world)* (Hamburg, 1966), table 16. Data for Germany for earlier years are given in table 31. Data for the Netherlands for 1900–39 are given in WILSON, op. cit., vol. 2, appendix 7. Statistics for the United Kingdom for 1900–38 are to be found in *The measurement of consumer expenditures and behaviour in the United Kingdom, 1900–19* (PRIEST,A.R.) and ibid., *1920–38*, vol. 1 (STONE,R.). Data for the United States from 1901 are to be found in HOWARD, op. cit., pp. 226–8. Prices used are consumer prices paid to retailers, except that only wholesale prices are available for the U.S.A. in most years before 1920.

35. WILSON, op. cit., vol. 2, p. 248.

36. SNODGRASS, op. cit., pp. 247–8.

37. For 1938, Denmark's margarine-to-butter price ratio was 38, almost the same as the United Kingdom's 39. The ratio for Norway was 47, for the U.S.A. 49, and for Germany and the Netherlands more than 60. See SCHÜTTAUF, op. cit., table 16.

38. WILSON, op. cit., vol. 2, pp. 97–100. An earlier agreement in 1901 had been relatively short-lived.

39. —— Ibid., vol. 2, pp. 139–47.

40. —— Ibid., vol. 1, p. 282.

41. —— Ibid., p. 307.

42. —— Ibid., vol. 2, p. 248.

43. —— Ibid., p. 269.

44. *Report of the Federal Trade Commission on changes in concentration ratios in manufacturing, 1935–47 and 1950.* (U.S. Government Printing Office, Washington D.C., 1954), pp. 94–5.

45. *Concentration ratios in manufacturing industry, 1963* (U.S. Government Printing Office, Washington D.C., 1966), p. 147.

CHAPTER SEVEN

Aspects of Government Intervention

J.H.VAN STUYVENBERG

The background

ALMOST as soon as the consumption of margarine reached significant proportions, the governments of various countries began to intervene in the infant industry. They were especially active in the introduction of margarine legislation during the years after 1885. Initially, such legislation had two objectives. The first is understandable; protection of the consumer by safeguarding the purity of margarine as well as butter. Measures were also taken to help him distinguish between the two products, and thus to clarify the difference between their respective markets. Customers should be able to tell what they were buying. There was no intention to influence the customers' preference for one of the two products or to limit their freedom to choose between them.

On the other hand, an intention to exert influence did exist in the measures taken—and now we come to the second objective—to protect the butter producers by obstructing the expansion of the margarine industry. The sole purpose of these measures was to direct the consumers' choice towards butter and to restrict their freedom of choice so that the flow of purchasing power for edible oils and fats would be channelled as much as possible from margarine to butter. Complete prohibition of margarine production, accompanied by embargoes on margarine imports, is an instance of the most extreme and at the same time the most effective forms which these measures took. They completely removed the consumers' freedom of choice.

Guaranteeing the purity of these products has been maintained as the basis of margarine legislation. On the other hand, obstruction of expansion in the margarine industry has lost much of its importance as a motive for legislation over the years, particularly since the Second

World War. Especially in the U.S.A., Canada, and various countries of Western Europe, legislation on margarine has grown more lenient.

Some decades after the advent of this legislation, when margarine, despite all the opposition of the authorities, had nevertheless succeeded in becoming a food of the masses, a third motive for legislation emerged. This arose from the desire to guarantee a minimum quality for the product, and considerations of public health played a decisive part in the matter. The compulsory addition of certain vitamins is one example. Other more incidental and transitory considerations also led to government intervention; these have included attempts to safeguard the population's food supplies in times of war and economic depression. These measures sometimes led to extensive rationing and price control, which therefore meant that margarine had won recognition as an indispensable food. Some government intervention in the determination of margarine prices, sometimes merely the maintenance of a close watch on them, can still be found in various countries. These various motives and the consequent regulations often formed a tangled mass, difficult to sort out in practice. Thus the veto on colouring agents in margarine helps to make the product more recognizable; but at the same time it slows down production. Similarly a compulsory maximum water content increases the purity of the product; yet it also benefits the health of the public. However, this does not excuse a failure to differentiate between the motives of the legislators.

Margarine legislation, which has been constantly subject to change, came into being at a time when government intervention in economic affairs in general was no longer frowned upon. Margarine was invented in 1869. In the same year came the first signs of a breakdown in the short-lived system of international free trade, which dated only from the 1860 Cobden treaty between England and France. In 1869, the world was on the threshold of renewed government intervention in the economic field. Economic individualism, which had been characterized by the application of the policy of *laissez-faire*, came to an end before long. The theories upon which this policy was based— namely a proper understanding of the markets, and the smooth mobility of production factors—appeared to find no confirmation in practice.

On the one hand, industry itself attempted to meet this situation by joining forces: cartels, trusts, and trade unions were formed in order to control the market, and even the economic situation. On the other hand, the state again concerned itself with economic and social matters: social laws were introduced, protectionism—which also brought in the farmers—was revived, and intervention in communications and transport was extended and intensified. After mercantilism, which had been abolished almost completely in the first half of the nineteenth century, the wheel of government policy on economic and social matters had now come full circle.

Here, then, is the economic and political background against which margarine legislation was initiated. In this climate hardly anyone raised any general objections to government intervention in economic affairs. Such objections as were raised soon disappeared: government intervention as such had won acceptance.

This chapter will deal with the history of margarine legislation. Particular attention will be paid to government regulations guaranteeing the purity of margarine as well as to those obstructing the expansion of the margarine industry. Margarine policy in the war years and during times of depression will also be discussed. The regulations regarding a minimum quality in the interests of public health are not considered here; they are discussed in Chapter Five. Nor will the policies in all countries to be reviewed, for they are often analogous in many respects. I shall therefore only deal with the policies in the foremost margarine-producing and consuming countries: the U.S.A., Germany, Holland, Britain, and Russia. I shall then briefly discuss other countries wherever their policies contain any features worthy of note. France will also be discussed because of her great importance within the E.E.C.

THE UNITED STATES

The crusade begins

The production of margarine was first undertaken in the U.S.A. in 1874, and quickly got well under way. As early as 1880 it was being stated that, 'oleo-margarine is a fact in the commercial world and must be treated as such'. A favourable verdict on the new product as a foodstuff had already been given in the following words: 'superior to poor butter as regards taste, odour and healthfulness. There can be no valid objections if no deception is practised upon the buyers.'

Dr. S. F. Riepma, President of the National Association of Margarine Manufacturers, Washington, has put me greatly in his debt by writing, to help me in the preparation of this chapter, a review of the history of margarine in the U.S.A., entitled: 'Margarine in the United States 1873–1967'. I have made grateful use of it. I am greatly indebted to him and thank him sincerely for his collaboration and interest.

When the meat-processing industry, under the leadership of Armour & Company, entered the newly introduced industry in 1883, the margarine industry was placed on a firmer economic footing (1). Its rapid and vigorous expansion seemed to be within the realms of possibility, but there were shoals ahead.

By 1877, New York State had already taken the initative in proposing an act 'for protection of dairymen and to prevent the deception in sales of butter'. Other states followed with similar acts which had little effect. This caused the federal legislators to enter this field in 1886, and in that year Congress passed a law 'defining butter, also imposing a tax upon and regulating the manufacture, sale, importation and exportation of oleomargarine' (2).

Margarine policy in the U.S.A. was characterized by a marked enmity towards the new foodstuff (3). Measures went much further than just enabling consumers to distinguish between the two products. They were aimed more at protecting the dairy farmers by suppressing the new industry. A crusade against margarine started up, which came to an end only in 1950. What are the reasons for the remarkable severity of this policy?

There are numerous clues to throw light on the factors that influenced this situation. For instance, butter-making in the U.S.A. at that time took place almost exclusively on the farms. Thousands of small, independent manufacturers were engaged in butter-making, and they felt their livelihood was threatened by the rise of margarine. For this was not only an industrial product; the main part of it soon began to come from the large slaughter-houses, from 'big business', which was accused of unacceptable monopolistic practices in those unsettled times. The first anti-trust law dates from 1890. Moreover, agriculture had to fight against over-production in this period. Partly as the result of the economic depression which followed the crisis of 1873, the general level of prices fell; prices for agricultural produce were the first to tumble.

Agriculture, which still employed a large proportion of the population at that time, was put into an awkward position. This caused feelings of uneasiness and insecurity in the agricultural section of the population. Lastly, butter exports showed a downward trend which lasted from about 1880 until the First World War. This was put down to corrupt practices affecting the quality of the butter. Margarine and blends of butter and margarine were exported as pure butter (4). There was also cheating in this way on the home market.

The disturbed feelings of the farmers which this situation caused found their outlet in two ways. First, in the political field in the Populists' movement, which had a strong agricultural bias. It exercised a distinct political influence in opposition to 'big business' (5). Secondly, violent agitation began among agricultural organizations in defence of farming interests. This, of course, also had its political aspects. The battle against margarine occupied a central position in this. 'In a process not very clear, dairy leadership located a fighting issue in oleo-margarine, choosing to see it not as a new outlet for beef fat but as a dangerous competitor' (6).

In speeches and publications, the organizations waged a violent campaign over the heads of the consumers for measures to be taken against the margarine threat; and the authorities were willing to listen. By 1886 there were already twenty-two state laws in force against margarine. At first they were of a restrictive nature laying down strict conditions for the manufacture and sale of margarine. One of the best known is the regulation that margarine should be coloured pink, which was enforced by New Jersey and other states (7). These laws had little effect. They were, therefore, replaced by prohibitive laws, especially in the dairy states, where production and sale of margarine was simply banned.

An attempt to have these laws declared unconstitutional failed. The Supreme Court ruled that they did not affect the principle of the 'equal protection of the laws'.

The federal law of 1886

The abuses which the state laws were meant to combat continued, as no special organizations were deputed to check that the laws were being observed. The campaign against margarine was intensified. Pressure on the federal government to place the dairy industry on 'an equal footing with its dangerous competitors' became stronger. After violent controversy, a federal law of a regulative nature came into force in 1886. It was stated that margarine was only allowed to be called 'oleomargarine'. A high tax in the form of licences was imposed on manufacturers, wholesalers, and retailers, amounting to $600, $480, and $48 per year respectively. On top of this, there was a manufacturing tax of 2 cents per lb. Packaging and book-keeping regulations were proclaimed. The law contained no regulations on margarine colouring, despite the fact that this very thing had been the main reason for the ineffectiveness of the state laws. Yet the purpose of the act was clear: the protection of dairy farming at the expense of the margarine industry (8).

An analysis of the motives of those who were for and against the act was made at the time by Bannard. Some of the advocates thought that margarine was 'foul in its nature and deleterious to the public health or perhaps a positive poison', and that it was manufactured under unhygienic conditions using poor raw materials. This prejudice seemed ineradicable at the time, notwithstanding evidence to the contrary by leading chemists. The representatives of dairy interests welcomed the act, though they would have preferred the complete prohibition of the margarine industry, or its annihilation through a tax-levy. Some advocates of the law were, however, merely attempting to put an end to fraudulent practices in the sale of margarine.

The main opponents of the act were, of course, the margarine manufacturers, but the suppliers of raw materials to the margarine industry also opposed it. These included the cattle-farmers from the West and the cotton-growers in the South, who were interested in their sales of pork and beef fat on the one hand, and cottonseed oil on the other. Therefore, there was no single, united, and tightly knit agricultural front against margarine; within agriculture there were conflicting interests with regard to the margarine industry. There were also opponents who considered the act to be unconstitutional, or who denied that Congress was authorized to impose taxes on one branch of industry in order to favour another.

One thing is striking: 'The interests of the consumer have not been seriously considered at any time in this entire struggle' (9).

The 1886 Act had a profound influence on state legislation. The federal government had at any rate recognized margarine as a legally permitted article of trade; according to the Supreme Court, therefore, the bans on production in the state laws had no legal basis. Thereafter, the prohibitive restrictions disappeared from state legislation. Many states—no fewer than thirty-two in 1902—also banned the colouring of the product. The natural colouring of margarine at that time was nearly white; not very attractive to the consumer.

The whole system of government regulation turned out to be ineffective, for there was no machinery to maintain it. Only small quantities of uncoloured margarine reached the consumer; the retailers were busy colouring the product yellow. Fraudulent practices continued to exist. Margarine-tax evasion also occurred; not much by the manufacturers, to some extent by the wholesalers, and a great deal by the retailers. Not much had changed; the margarine industry suffered no lasting hindrance in its development. In 1893, the Commissioner of Internal Revenue reported that margarine production had become an established industry. Margarine had developed into a recognized foodstuff.

Everywhere there was a rising demand for it 'under its proper name and by persons fully informed as to the nature of its substance' (10). This caused great annoyance to the opponents of margarine, and they began to think about tightening up the legislation.

More far-reaching discriminations: 1902 and 1931

The idea had arisen within the National Dairy Union that a tax of 10 cents per lb should be levied on margarine which was artificially coloured in such a way that it resembled butter. In the face of violent opposition, an amendment embodying this idea was added to the 1886 Act in 1902. This would do away with the price difference which existed at that time between butter and coloured margarine, and would get rid of the inducement to commit fraud. The tax on uncoloured margarine was reduced to the nominal sum of $\frac{1}{4}$ cent per lb. The annual licence fee for retailers selling uncoloured margarine was also substantially reduced. The Act struck a heavy blow. Margarine production dropped sharply; not until 1910 did it finally achieve its 1901 level again. But this did not suppress fraudulent practices. 'The high tax fired up the very illegal selling that it was supposed to prevent' (11). The retailers were able to make a nice profit if they sold margarine they coloured themselves as butter, or as the heavily taxed, legally coloured, margarine.

It was almost impossible to trace this type of fraud, and it was hardly ever punished. The Commissioner estimated the amount of tax evaded throughout the year 1914 at $15 million (12).

The first reaction of the margarine industry to the 1902 amendment was to provide its small packs with tubes or little bags containing yellow colouring material, in order to enable the consumers to colour the margarine themselves. Secondly, the manufacturers made increased use of groundnut and soya bean oil as raw materials, especially in the 1920s. These imparted a natural yellow colour to the finished product, and were legally permitted ingredients. Margarine manufactured in this way was not artificially coloured, and was therefore taxed only at $\frac{1}{4}$ per cent per lb. The high tax had been sidestepped. This reaction of the margarine manufacturers thus robbed the 1902 amendment of part of its effectiveness (13). In the following decades, federal legislation underwent no further fundamental changes. Apparently a balance of power had been reached; but this was to prove short-lived.

During the First World War, there was a shortage in the home supply of animal raw materials. The hardening of oils, introduced from Europe in 1915, offered a solution to this. It opened up the possibility of processing imported vegetable oils. The use of coconut oil in particular expanded considerably, even after the war was over. In 1932, this type of oil accounted for as much as 75 per cent of the raw materials used.

The production of 'nut-margarine' with the help of the 'coconut-cow' had an effect which had not been adequately foreseen, for cattle- and pig-farmers and cotton-growers lost interest in the margarine industry. It had become an un-American industry, and so they withdrew all further political support. They went even further, and formed a united agricultural front against the margarine industry by joining up with the dairy farmers. The industry defended itself by appealing to the consumers, 'Don't tax the spread on the people's bread' (14). The response to this was just as weak as the political results it achieved.

A new wave of state laws against margarine rolled up in the 1920s, and grew in size during the 1930s as a result of the agricultural depression. In 1939 margarine was taxed in over half the states, and the colouring of the product was prohibited in more than thirty states. The federal government once more increased the severity of its measures against margarine: the equilibrium in the field of power had been destroyed. In 1931, margarine coloured by natural means was also made subject to a tax of 10 cents per lb. The loophole in the laws had finally been sealed after almost thirty years. Coloured oils even had to be bleached. In addition, heavy taxes were put on imported oils in 1934 (15).

The margarine industry, almost completely isolated politically, was having a hard time of it. How did it react to this situation?

Out into the open sea

For its raw materials the industry reorientated itself from the foreign to the home supply. The discovery of chemical processes for making cottonseed oil tasteless and for giving it the required plasticity facilitated this transition. The development of soya bean cultivation into one of the large cultivations in the U.S.A. likewise helped in the changeover. By 1940, the share of coconut oil in the total raw materials consumption had already dropped as low as 8·5 per cent. Three years later, during the Second World War, cottonseed oil formed 50 per cent, soya bean oil 40 per cent, and animal fats 7 per cent of the raw materials. In 1966 no less than 74 per cent of margarine production was based on soya bean oil. The margarine industry came to form a recognized market for one of America's largest staple agricultural products. Margarine regained political support from the agricultural side, from the cotton-growers in the South and the soya bean-growers in the Midwest. The united agricultural front against margarine collapsed.

This support was augmented by that of the consumers. Because of the fat shortage, margarine had been rationed during the Second World War. As a result of constant research, the product's quality had improved considerably over the years. It had become a palatable, wholesome product, notable for its excellent quality, and distributed throughout wide strata of the population. A process began which led towards a positive approval of margarine by the consumers. They no longer regarded the serving of margarine as socially unacceptable. They wondered why this product had to be coloured in the home, and could not understand why it was the only foodstuff subject to taxation. They became increasingly opposed to all this. This upsurge of positive recognition for margarine by numerous large sections of the nation was greatly encouraged by the National Association of Margarine Manufacturers, reorganized in 1942. It forcefully pursued 'a program of consumer and farmer education'. But of course it met with pockets of resistance. 'The ensuing struggle lasted more than two crowded years. Agricultural, consumer, and scientific testimony deployed as never before on behalf of margarine, receiving nation wide press coverage . . . Prominent in the action . . . were cottonseed, soya-bean and consumer organizations' (16). The workers' organizations, too, supported this campaign, which was fully consistent with the changes that had gradually come about in social policy.

Under this strong pressure, the House of Representatives rescinded the vexatious tax on coloured margarine in 1949, although only by the small majority of 152 to 140 votes. The Senate followed suit in 1950. Another factor influencing the emergence of a more favourable climate for margarine was a decline in the importance of butter production as an element in dairy farming. Different destinies for milk had come into the foreground. An important milestone had been reached in sweeping away the discriminative treatment of margarine.

The positive appreciation of margarine also led to radical changes in the state laws. A typical example of this is the ban on the colouring of margarine. The abolition of this restriction had already begun before 1947; at that time it still existed in twenty-two states. Later the ban was swept away in almost all states, the last one being Wisconsin in 1967.

In 1966 the United States government stated that margarine was to be consumed by the armed forces. It seemed to have realized that the product's quality was irreproachable. One could scarcely imagine a clearer demonstration of the change in government policy.

GERMANY

Introduction

As far as the amount and the motives of government intervention are concerned, German margarine policy lies midway between the policies in the U.S.A. and Holland. The battle against the margarine industry was in the forefront of American legislation, and was also important, though to a lesser degree, in German legislation. Yet measures directed against the margarine industry were also taken in Germany. In Holland the primary policy objective was to protect consumers at home and abroad by guaranteeing the purity both of butter and of margarine. This was likewise an important aspect of German policy, but the steps taken there to achieve it went much further than they did in Holland. In the end they affected the consumer's freedom of choice, for butter sales were promoted at the expense of margarine sales.

The first acts of parliament

The Frankfurter Margarine Gesellschaft began making margarine in Germany in 1872 (17). The new industry thrived. It was faced with an almost insatiable demand, particularly from the working population in German industry which was expanding rapidly at that time. Its growth was stimulated by Germany's change-over to a protectionist

In writing this section I have greatly benefited from Dr. W. Schüttauf's work, Die Margarine in Deutschland und der Welt, *Hamburg, 1966.*

policy in 1879, which meant that the new industry was protected against foreign competition (18).

The dairy organizations pointed to the cases of butter adulteration as their reason for trying to check the expansion of the margarine industry by legal regulations. They provoked increasingly fierce arguments which, about 1886, when butter prices were low, developed into a violent anti-margarine campaign (19). Under the pressure of this agitation the first Margarine Act was passed in 1887. Its provisions were few but far-reaching. Places where margarine was sold had to be clearly indicated; blending butter into margarine was prohibited; the tubs and packages containing the product had to bear the word 'margarine'; and lastly, margarine had to be retailed in the form of a cube. If the intention was merely to combat malpractices, then these provisions were certainly harsher than necessary. But owing to very inadequate enforcement, the Act had almost no effect at all. Numerous petitions were sent to the government from the dairy industry to make the legal measures more stringent. When no notice was taken of these, the butter producers soon made it their business to take action against adulteration (20). In Berlin, for instance, samples of butter bought in shops were tested for purity, and the findings were published. Despite the fact that the sampling was far from being objective, the reports succeeded in causing public disquiet (21). The agitation reached a peak in 1894, when butter prices dropped to a new low. The situation was similar to that before the 1887 Act.

Various ideas and proposals were put forward, not just to restrict malpractice, but even to curb the expansion of the margarine industry. With such an object in mind, Count von Kanitz-Podangen proposed in the Reichstag that a tax on margarine should be levied to help cover increased defence expenditure. A Reichstag Commission wanted margarine to have the brown colour of 'der eichenen Vertäfelung des Reichstagsgebäudes' ('the oak wainscoting in the Reichstag building'), and some people even favoured a blue colouring for the product.

A new margarine bill was presented in 1895. The Reichstag finally adopted this, but it was not accepted by the Bundesrat, which thought that the veto on the colouring of margarine created an insurmountable obstacle. A number of political groupings then initiated new proposals, which resulted in a new Margarine Act in 1897. The latent colouring of margarine with sesame oil which the

Act stipulated was the price which had to be paid in order to avoid the imposition, under pressure from agricultural interests, of some peculiar colour (22). Retail packets had to bear a red band of a specified width, as the cube shape alone was apparently considered insufficient for identification. A system of registration and supervision was introduced for margarine manufacturers. It was forbidden to manufacture, store, pack, or sell butter and margarine at the same premises. Towns with less than 5,000 inhabitants were excluded from these last two restrictions.

In towns of more than 5,000 inhabitants, most of the retailers who could not or would not partition off their shop opted to sell margarine, especially in industrial areas where margarine consumption was fairly high. The regulation did not seem to apply to co-operative retail societies whose operations, the courts ruled, were not *gewerbsmässig* ('for commercial gain') but were aimed at effecting a saving for their members (23).

The Bund der Landwirte (corresponding to the National Farmers' Union) did not get everything its own way. Its demand for a ban on the use of milk in margarine manufacture, which would have been harmful to the product's taste and quality, was not met. One member pointed out that the government might just as well ban the production of margarine altogether. Nor were there any orders against the use of wooden containers or margarine colouring, for such proposals found no majority in the Reichstag. Nevertheless, the new regulations were a great nuisance to the margarine industry and the trade, mainly because of the uncertainty about their precise implications.

Uncertainties arising from legislation

When was the separate sale of butter and margarine mentioned? Very early on the Centralverband deutscher Kaufleute (Central Association of German Traders) had asked the government for an assurance on this point. The replies they received were based on a fairly literal interpretation of the Act by the government officials, since only the courts were considered competent to give a definition.

The object of the regulation, they argued, was to prevent margarine from being passed off, inconspicuously and unnoticed, as butter. Premises where these products were sold had to have reasonably robust partitions of wood, glass, or plasterboard; fireproof material was not necessary. A common entrance was allowed, and also one or more *Durchgangsöffnungen* through the partitions, which usually had to be closed only with doors. The courts later ruled that a cupboard for margarine on premises selling butter did not constitute an adequate partition.

The question of separate sale was not definitely solved until 1926, when a ministerial circular, based on established practice, amended the interpretation of the paragraph in question. The requisite partition was said to exist if, in places where butter was sold, margarine was kept in such a way *'dass eine Verwechslung ausgeschlossen ist'* ('that confusion of the two is precluded') (24). A keystone of margarine legislation had been removed.

Secondly, there were also differing opinions as to whether the Act allowed butter and margarine to be sold together. Apparently, owing to an error in formulation, the Act merely stipulated that these products should not be offered for sale together. It was decided in the supreme court that it should be permissible to sell them together, but the lower courts remained hesitant. No uniform interpretation of this clause had been achieved by the time the First World War broke out. A third source of uncertainty related to the types of fat that were definable as margarine. Legally, a product (*Zubereitung*) was treated as margarine if, for instance, it resembled butter. But did it need to have the colour, taste, smell, and consistency of butter, or would just one of these characteristics suffice? Should the criterion be the purpose for which it was intended and, if so, did the consumer decide this? Could it 'resemble' butter in one way and be different from it in another? The courts were also unable to agree on these important, hotly discussed questions in 1914. Uncertainty remained on many other points as well, some of them amusing (25).

Teichmann believes that the Act had little practical significance. It may even have stimulated margarine sales as it guaranteed consumers hygienic production and good quality. On the other hand, many customers may have felt embarrassed about buying the cube-shaped, red-banded products in a partitioned-off space. Strangely enough, these acts are still in force.

The blockade during the First World War caused a severe shortage of fats in Germany, and this was scarcely alleviated even by the increased cultivation of rape-seed. Consequently fat consumption declined and, by 1917, had fallen to a third of the pre-war level.

These perilous conditions made it necessary to ration fats, including margarine, and fix maximum prices for them. Raw materials were allocated to margarine manufacturers and production was concentrated. In 1918 only 26 margarine factories were in operation, compared with 101 in 1916.

The fat shortage had come to an end by 1921, and the wartime regulations were abolished (26).

Legislation during the depression

The depression that followed the 1929 economic crises had almost halved butter prices in Germany by early 1933, despite the fact that duties on imported butter had been trebled. Butter production had increased because sales of liquid milk had declined with the drop in purchasing power. At first margarine consumption rose as well, since the margarine industry had succeeded in greatly reducing its prices by using different raw materials. There was still widespread aversion to margarine in agricultural quarters because of the conviction that it was a dangerous rival to butter. The farmers had never entirely ceased their complaints, and these now increased in volume. There were strong demands for anti-margarine regulations, which seemed to fulfil some psychological need (27).

The National Socialist regime, which drew much of its support from rural areas and disapproved of margarine, listened sympathetically. It did so with a conviction made all the firmer by the fact that such regulations would naturally fit in with the autarchic striving for import restrictions which was prompted by the lack of foreign exchange. As from 1 May 1933, a margarine tax was introduced, the *Ausgleichsabgabe für Margarine, Oel und Fette* (equalization levy for margarine, oil and fats), since it was expected that the consequent price increase would lead to a reduction in consumption of margarine. In addition, margarine production was curtailed by 50 per cent. The measures were expected to increase sales of butter, but in fact they proved too harsh. The tax, combined with the cutting down of production, sent margarine prices up, and the increase was intensified by an import levy imposed to bridge the gap between home and foreign raw material prices. Fats were becoming too dear for the poorest members of the population, and production quotas had to be eased. By the end of 1934 they had been completely abolished.

Some shortage of edible fats was deliberately created, however, especially of those made from imported raw materials, in order to release scarce supplies of foreign exchange for other purposes. The measures relating to margarine were reminiscent of the wartime economics of austerity. Margarine prices were fixed for the benefit of the poorer population. Of the only three kinds of margarine production allowed, one-half had to consist of household margarine, which was at first untaxed. People in the lower-income groups received *Fettverbilligungsscheine* (fat price-reduction certificates) entitling them to a general reduction in the price of fats. A further reduction was obtainable on household margarine in exchange for *Bezugsscheine* (ration cards).

Fat consumption was felt to be too high compared with 1913, so household margarine was rationed in 1936, and all purchases of it were made subject to *Bezugsscheine*. In order to reduce consumption, open competition between various types of fat by advertising was prohibited in 1937. Restrictions were also placed on stocks of raw materials kept in the margarine and fat factories (28) whereas consumption of jams, fish, cream cheese, and low-fat cheese was encouraged for nutritional and economic reasons.

Thus the margarine industry was clearly involved in the efforts to save foreign exchange. It was used in other ways to promote the interests of agriculture. In order to raise pig prices, the use of lard in margarine remained compulsory until mid 1934. Thereafter beef fat was added on a voluntary basis to a quantity of 8,000 tons a year. There was an element of compulsion, however, in that the margarine industry had drawn up the contract in question with the renderers so as to avoid a legal ruling on this point (29).

During and after the Second World War
During the Second World War, the fat shortage in Germany became even more acute, and rationing was introduced as early as September 1939. Moreover, the anti-margarine National Socialist government took advantage of the situation which had arisen, to further its previous policy; it made compulsory the production of one uniform, unbranded quality of *Tafelmargarine*.

The manufacture of margarine was again concentrated into a small number of factories. Out of 148 margarine factories only 7 were still operating in 1948. Consumption, which had declined from 8 kg to 6 kg *per capita* from 1932 to 1938, reached its lowest level of a little under 1 kg *per capita* in 1946. And even though butter production showed an increase up to 1943, this occurred at the expense of a decrease in the consumption of full-cream milk. Butter consumption fell from 9 kg *per capita* in 1938 to 4 kg in 1946–7. The gradual improvement in fat supplies after the war permitted the easing of government restrictions. A contributory factor here was that the new Democratic government—in contrast to the National Socialists—was not hostile, but took an objective attitude towards margarine. The relaxing of the regulation fitted in with this new government's economic and political ideals, which were inspired by the concept of *Soziale Marktwirtschaft* (a free market economy in the interests of the community).

The restrictions on over-all margarine production were removed in 1949, and brands were restored. Rationing of fat ended in January 1950. The fixed margarine prices introduced in 1936 had been abolished by 1948 and replaced by a compulsory costing system for pricing purposes.

There has been no official price control since 1951. The Bundes-kartellamt (Federal Cartel Office), however, functions as a price-controller for price-maintained products, including margarine. Government supervision in the pricing sphere therefore still exists.

After the Second World War, the German oil industry was compelled to supply cattle cake at very low prices. It sought compensation for the loss of income by putting up prices of oil for the margarine industry, which retaliated by stepping up imports of cheaper oil from abroad. The oil industry, feeling the adverse effects of this, pressed for the ending of price controls on cattle cake, and they were abolished in 1950. The margarine industry no longer had to help in promoting sales of cheap butter by producing dear margarine and cheap cattle cake (30).

What the industry did have to do, however, was to collaborate in providing a market for home-produced rape-seed oil. Since 1935, in order to supplement fat supplies, rape-seed cultivation had been stimulated by means of high prices and subsidies. The subsidies were abolished in 1950. When prices fell after the boom at the time of the Korean war, German rape-seed growers were demanding 20 per cent more than the world market price. The Federal government ultimately responded in 1953 by making it compulsory for the margarine industry to cover 5 per cent—later 10 per cent—of its raw material supplies with German seed, and 1 per cent with German beef fat. It must be borne in mind that the industry, though compelled to buy the rape-seed oil, was not really bound to use it. In cases where German industry considered rape-seed oil unsuitable for margarine manu-facture, it was exported at a loss. The obligation to use home-produced rape-seed was withdrawn as from 1 January 1967.

Despite the fact that various regulations, which certainly did nothing to promote the growth of the margarine industry, are still in existence, we need not end on a pessimistic note. The 1933 tax on fats was abolished in 1940. Its reintroduction was being seriously considered in 1950, mainly in order to raise the price of margarine in relation to that of butter. But at that time the situation was different. In 1933 the agricultural organizations had had their way. In 1950, on the other hand, the proposals were defeated by opposition and fierce criticism from the trade unions, the consumers' organizations, and the pensioners' representatives. For the first time in Germany's margarine policy, measures directed against the market position of this product were abandoned because of pressure and protests from consumers (31).

Margarine had acquired an indispensable role in the nation's eating habits, and the German government recognized this fact. When prices of raw materials used in margarine began to rise because of the Korea boom, margarine was temporarily subsidized to keep its price down and to safeguard fat supplies.

The legislation and its motives

The Dutch margarine laws have always shown moderation. Generally speaking, their sole purpose has been to enable the consumers to distinguish margarine from butter more easily, and to provide them with safeguards for the purity of the respective products. Unlike the Americans, the Dutch legislators only made a brief attempt, during the depression in the 1930s, to obstruct the expansion of the margarine industry with the aim of encouraging the sales of butter.

Dutch legislation on margarine began in 1889 when there was a slump in exports of butter. Dutch butter—largely produced in the province of Friesland—had been faced with difficulties over export to Britain.

New producers were emerging: Normandy, Denmark, and later Australia and New Zealand, were gaining ground on Dutch butter producers in the British market. Their up-to-date, scientific manufacturing methods made it possible for them to supply vast quantities of butter of a uniform quality to the English manufacturing towns where there was a great demand for it. Holland could not meet this demand, for butter production there was still based on empiricism

M.—21

and tradition (32). Moreover, Dutch butter producers, lulled by the high prices in the third quarter of last century, had neglected quality. The tendency towards a slump in prices for this butter was aggravated by the agricultural crisis which began about 1875; at Leeuwarden butter prices dropped from f 1·60 per kg in 1876 to f 1·01 in 1895 (33).

Butter adulteration, which took place on a large scale, was another contributory factor in this slump. Adulteration can be divided into two phases. At first, water—as much as 30 per cent—was added, or potato flour, lard, gum syrup, and similar substances; or else inferior, non-Friesland butter. Such practices became so widespread that in 1871 Friesland apparently exported 60 per cent more 'butter' than was marketed there in that year (34).

The advent of margarine heralded the second phase of adulteration. Anton Jurgens the margarine manufacturer commented in 1884, 'But as always happens in such cases, the avarice of the sellers has been so kindled by the similarity in appearance to pure butter that they have tried to increase their profits by selling butterine for butter at butter prices, even though they themselves buy it from the manufacturers for what it is and at a low price' (35). Not only was margarine passed off as butter, but the mixing of butter and margarine flourished, growing almost into an industry.

The corrupt practices of the earlier period died out (36), but the consequences were inevitable. Friesland butter, the highest priced on the London market in 1860, was the cheapest of all twenty-five years later. Holland was facing a butter slump (37).

The first acts of parliament

Originally, in the view of the farming community, government action against these abuses was 'useless and unnecessary'; they thought the problem would be solved automatically by the 'natural relationship between buyer and seller'. Around 1860, thinking in Holland was dominated to such an extent by economic individualism that even voluntary supervision to ensure the production of genuine butter was rejected (38).

However, views changed; in 1885 a Vereeniging tot Bestrijding van de Knoeierjen in de Boterhandel (Association for Combating Corrupt Practices in the Butter Trade) was founded. Even though a State Commission on Agriculture set up in 1886 called for action to prevent products from being passed off as butter when in fact they were nothing but fat, it nevertheless emphasized 'that good margarine deserves to be classed as an excellent item in the nation's diet' (39). Nevertheless, the Dutch margarine manufacturers' association, the Vereeniging van Margarineboterfabrikanten in Nederland, formed in the meantime, perhaps for safety's sake strongly resisted the proposed measures. To obstruct the mixing of butter and margarine might cause a reversion to the worst practices, 'which now belong to the past'. And the Association claimed that the State Commission conveniently ignored that form of fraud which amounted to the 'substitution of butter for butter'. After all, the Dutch dairy industry, the Association argued, was behind that of other countries, and 'only improved methods and consistency in quality' could halt its decline (40).

The government readily recognized 'that good artificial butter . . . was of great value to the national diet' (41) but remained unconvinced. A bill 'for the prevention of deception in the butter trade' became law in 1889, despite the opposition's claim that it would place too much restriction on free enterprise, and that it was unnecessary because it would have little effect.

The Act treated margarine as a butter substitute. It was not to be supplied or stocked in shops or other places of public sale without the word 'margarine' in distinct characters on the pack, or 'if not there, on the product itself'. This was the main provision, obviously intended to make margarine distinguishable, though with the least possible recourse to regulation.

It soon became apparent that the Act had brought no improvement. It was not enforced properly: the 1890 budget merely allotted the ridiculously low sum of ƒ 200 for this purpose. What is more, the legislators had overlooked one important aspect: legal delivery is effected by handing goods over, and the inspectors were naturally not given the opportunity of seeing this take place with adulterated butter. Nor was there any obligation upon retailers to display the words 'margarine' or 'substitute' in such a way that 'customers are bound to see them' (42).

Adulteration of butter was also encouraged in the following way. A Reichert–Meissl–Wollny number of 25, indicating the volatile fatty acid content, was regarded by experts as the absolute minimum for pure butter. But in the south of the country a butter came on the market which in autumn had a very high fatty acid content, and margarine could thus be safely mixed with it. An added complication was that a value below 25 also proved to be possible for pure butter.

Holland had now gained the unenviable notoriety abroad as a country where butter adulteration was rife (43). Stricter regulations to combat this problem were deemed necessary, yet the principle of 'protecting the reputable butter trade without harming the margarine industry', as it had been formulated in the 1900 amendment, was not to be interfered with (44). That did not happen, but the laws certainly went further than they had gone in 1889. Henceforth, the word 'margarine' had to be clearly displayed on all occasions, even during transportation. Shops and other places of sale had to display the word 'margarine', while the two products had to be distinctly separated by a partition. Lastly, a government butter inspectorate was established. The obvious aim was to avoid harming the margarine industry (45).

Even if these regulations had been observed, however, the margarine industry would not have been very adversely affected. But they were evaded, and did not seem adequate to suppress fraud.

Voluntary butter inspection: the indicator conflict (46)

The dairy industry now took action itself by introducing voluntary inspection of butter production on an individual basis, supervised by the dairying organizations. There was now a supply of guaranteed pure butter, but there was such deep-rooted distrust of Dutch butter abroad that more convincing evidence of a change of heart was demanded. Where, it was asked, was official government recognition of the inspection system?

Where was the compulsory latent colouring of margarine, for instance with sesame oil, so that adulteration would be very easy to detect? Other countries thought this very important.

The butter inspection system was, in fact, officially recognized in 1904; inspection stations were set up under government control, and a government butter mark was introduced as an official guarantee of purity. The government and industry saw eye to eye on this point. Belgium recognized this Dutch government butter mark in the same year.

Though addition of sesame oil had been made compulsory in Germany, Belgium, Austria, France, Denmark, and Sweden, this was never so in Holland, but the question did receive much attention at the time. The margarine manufacturer, S. Van den Bergh Jr., wrote a pamphlet opposing it (47). The Dutch delegations at the International Dairy Congresses in 1903, 1905, and 1907 were also against it. Their main objections were that sesame oil spoilt the taste of margarine and made it dearer—naturally this objection was not raised by the dairy industry. The compulsory latent colouring, it was further objected, was considered much too expensive in relation to the trifling effect to be expected. What was more, it merely hampered inspection; the fact that a sample contained no indicator did not necessarily mean it was butter. Strictly speaking, therefore, the inspectors were checking up whether the obligation to add sesame oil was being complied with. Lastly, butter was liable to be adulterated with other substances besides margarine; with other fats, for instance, or with water (48). At the beginning of this century the trick of adding water was so common that special equipment was on sale for the purpose (49). There seemed to have been some justification for the fear expressed by the Vereeniging van Margarineboterfabrikanten in 1887 that the old malpractices would be revived immediately there was any interference with the margarine trade.

By about 1914, the value of the voluntary butter inspection system in Holland had been recognized abroad. Dutch butter regained its reputation without the compulsory addition of an indicator to margarine. A contributory factor was the movement of production from the farm to the factory, with the result that large quantities of butter of uniform quality became available for export. With the object of restoring the good reputation of Dutch butter abroad, margarine regulations were intensified once more. Instructions now covered the production of butter, margarine, and blends.

The 1908 amendment prescribed a minimum fat content for butter to combat adulteration with water. Producers had to be licensed and the manufacture of butter and margarine had to be kept separate. Blends were permitted, but the maximum amount of margarine which could be mixed with the butter was determined. There was special supervision of factories manufacturing blends, as well as of butter factories and stores owned by margarine manufacturers, and of butter imports. This was more than the Vereeniging tot bestrijding van de Knoeierijen in de Boterhandel had wanted in 1905, for it had considered supervision of margarine manufacture and restriction of blending unnecessary. The Association's committee 'did not want to obstruct fair trading by the margarine industry' in Holland, as it was an industry 'whose existence had to be accepted' (50).

Supervised butter production quickly expanded to such an extent that the entire export market could be supplied; it is thus difficult to say what effect the Act really had on exports. The same applies to the home market, which had not been a major factor during the consideration of possible courses of action.

The wars and the depression

The First World War presented problems of a different kind. For fear Dutch margarine would be re-exported to Germany, whether after reworking or not, the Allies kept a close watch on supplies of raw materials to the Dutch margarine industry. In reaction to the embargo on margarine exports declared in Holland, the British government stopped exports of raw materials to Holland completely in 1918. These conditions meant an increasing shortage of edible oils and fats for the population, and forms of price control and rationing were gradually introduced. From 1914 onwards permits were required for the export of butter. Margarine sales were controlled from 1915, and stricter measures followed in 1916. Wholesalers and retailers received no allocations beyond their customary quantities of margarine. The government made contracts for the manufacture of a subsidized 'standard margarine' in order to keep its prices down. There were no restrictions on the remaining margarine either for price or for quantity, at least in so far as raw materials were available. Rationing of standard margarine began a year later. Margarine exports were prohibited in March 1918, and rigorous, full-scale rationing of all edible oils and fats followed on 1 June. Step by step the government had taken more drastic action as fat supplies became increasingly difficult to come by. After the Armistice, conditions returned to normal; the restrictions were abolished, and 1919 saw the end of margarine and butter rationing (51).

From then on, the relationship between butter and margarine remained stable as far as government policy was concerned, and there was a pause in legislation.

The difficult export markets of the 1930s caused heavy losses for Dutch agriculture, including dairy farming, and the government took measures, both comprehensive and complex, to counteract the agricultural depression (52). The dairy policy behind these measures also involved the margarine industry. A levy on margarine and other edible fats helped to raise money to support butter prices. It was made compulsory to add butter to margarine; the amount of butter added varied according to the size of the surplus, and an indirect market for butter was thereby created. But the blend sold so well that there was a net decline in butter consumption—something which had been neither provided for nor intended. In 1933, therefore, the government cut the total margarine production by almost 20 per cent, down to a level of 1,050 tons per week.

The government, desirous of an instrument of policy for margarine, now took steps to establish a convention between margarine manufacturers. Because of its dairy policy, the government could allow neither an unlimited expansion of margarine production nor an unlimited decline in margarine prices. The convention operated as a cartel on production quotas. Each manufacturer was allotted a quota based on his former market share, for any excess of which he paid a penalty for the benefit of those who had failed to reach their quotas. There was now no longer any sense in offering lower-priced products; in fact, an official minimum price was prescribed for margarine (53). As economic recovery gradually advanced the butter surplus disappeared; compulsory blending was abolished in 1937, and at the same time margarine production quotas were eased.

During the Second World War the situation was reversed. Again, as in the First World War, there was a severe shortage of fats. Mixing of butter and margarine was prohibited in 1942 (54). Minimum prices for margarine were superseded by maximum prices in order to keep the cost of living down. For this same reason, the still existing margarine levy made way for a raw materials subsidy, which lasted until after the war.

Moreover, the rationing of margarine made essential by the shortage of fats lasted until 1949, and raw materials were allocated *pro rata* to the manufacturers' convention quotas.

The convention remained in existence after the war, to the satisfaction of both government and manufacturers. But the quota system was made more flexible through being given scope for quality competition. In 1951 the manufacturers were again granted freedom to determine the extent of their production themselves. At the present time prices are negotiated between the government and the industry, as official supervision is considered essential for such an important product as margarine.

The position consolidated

Government butter inspection had put an end to adulteration. Nevertheless, potato flour was prescribed as an indicator for margarine in 1935, in order to remove any doubts that might still exist abroad about Dutch butter (55). Such regulations were already in existence in other countries. Pressure from the dairy industry, which had apparently forgotten the fight against the addition of sesame oil, was the main reason for this new regulation. This pressure was applied again in 1953, when any reference to farming or dairying or any related subject was forbidden in margarine advertising or on margarine packaging; there had to be no suggestion to the consumer that the product he was buying was butter or its equivalent.

The consumer's interests were the main consideration, but whether he really needed this protection is a moot point, because margarine, after eighty years' existence, had become an established food in its own right.

This is clear from the official motives behind the abolition, in the same year, of the regulations in regard to labelling and partitions in shops. They were no longer being enforced anyway; in fact it was officially stated that they had no further significance in protecting butter against adulteration 'in the present situation in which it must be recognised that margarine has acquired next after butter an individual, independent place in the market' (56).

This development was reflected in legislation, for in 1960 the Butter Act was repealed. The regulations on margarine included in it were then largely superseded by provisions in a special ordinance of the 'Produktschap' of margarine, fats, and oils. Margarine had captured an independent position on the market, and with it the road to independence for legislation on margarine.

THE UNITED KINGDOM

Introduction

The British government's attitude of moderation and leniency in its legislation on the margarine industry is accounted for by the country's international position and economic structure.

After the industrial revolution around 1800, the emphasis of Britain's economy was on industry, transport, and banking. With the repeal of the Corn Laws in 1846, the country's agricultural basis was abandoned, and it became the 'workshop of the world'. During the agricultural depression in the last quarter of the nineteenth century this trend continued.

Unlike Germany, Britain took no steps to shield agriculture from foreign competition, and became more and more dependent on imports to feed and even provide semi-luxuries for the expanding population of the manufacturing towns. Margarine was imported mainly from the Netherlands until 1889, when Otto Mønsted, a Dane, built Britain's first margarine factory. In such circumstances the dairy organizations obviously had some influence on government policy, but this was not decisive. The primary purpose of the regulations was to protect consumers against fraud, by making butter and margarine readily distinguishable and safeguarding the purity of these commodities.

Legislation up to 1914
Some initiative was taken by the British Dairy Farmers' Association, in calling for inspection of margarine factories to prevent their products from being passed off as butter, and in asking that all butter substitutes should bear a government stamp. All these requirements were reasonable.

As a result of two bills presented by Members of the House of Lords and the House of Commons, a Parliamentary Select Committee was appointed to 'inquire into the problems of sales (of margarine) and the possibility of fraud' (57). It heard the detailed evidence of many witnesses, and had regard not only to the interests of butter producers, but also to those of 'large classes of the community in our great towns'.

The Committee became convinced that large-scale fraud existed, and called for measures against this. An Act, in 1887, provided that margarine must be sold only under the name 'margarine'. The popular name 'butterine', suggestive of butter, was prohibited. Packings had to bear the word margarine in distinct characters, and manufacturers had to be registered; Food and Drugs Act inspectors were to ensure that the Act was complied with (58).

As in other countries, this first piece of legislation proved ineffective. A second Committee found that more drastic action was needed, including a veto on colouring margarine, limitation of blending, and compulsory analysis of imported butter and margarine.

Little came of these proposals in practice. When the Margarine Act was amended in 1899, registration of margarine sellers too was introduced. Moreover, the Food and Drugs Act provided that margarine should not contain more than 10 per cent butter. The Margarine Act of 1908 did not add much that was new, except the limitation of water content to 16 per cent, thereby resolving a problem on which experts had differed for many years.

The First World War and after

At the outbreak of the First World War, Britain's supremacy at sea seemed likely to guarantee the regular food supplies. The need to save on shipping space, combined with the effort to cut the cost of the convoy system which was soon introduced, prompted the British government to encourage home production of a number of goods, including margarine. A couple of years later the British margarine industry was able to supply nearly all the home demand (59). The unlimited submarine warfare resorted to by Germany in 1917 changed this, and the British nation faced a severe food shortage. 'The public rushed from shop to shop, and realizing that supplies were limited, began to wait outside the shops even before they opened. The food queue made its first appearance' (60). The makeshift food regulations were tightened up and made more comprehensive. They had lacked uniformity in allocation of supplies and pricing; prices in the case of margarine were fixed from stage to stage. Consumers now had to register with retailers, and some products even had to be rationed, including butter and margarine from 22 December 1917. The restrictions were abolished after the war, and the ending of margarine rationing in February 1919 began a new era which lasted until the outbreak of the Second World War.

Between the wars the margarine regulations changed. The 1908 Act disappeared, and in 1938 the margarine provisions were embodied in the Food and Drugs Act which—following some minor modifications in 1954—is still '. . . the basic law governing the manufacture, distribution and sale of margarine in England and Wales' (61). Besides defining margarine and regulating imports, it stipulates in regard to packaging the size of the characters in which the word 'margarine' must appear and the weight of 'cartons and boxes in which margarine packets are distributed' (62).

The packet must clearly state the butter content, if any. The Act gives government officials access to margarine factories. The product is not required to have a particular colour, and the regulations as a whole indicate the reasonable attitude always adopted by the British government towards the margarine industry.

During and after the Second World War (63)

The worsening international situation with the growing danger of war in the late 1930s prompted the British government to take timely action for safeguarding food supplies. By 1937 a Sub-committee on Food Supplies had prepared a complex of four plans for stockpiling a number of important materials. When hostilities broke out in 1939, margarine was not rationed at first because it was possible to provide a weekly ration of 4 oz of butter. But the German occupation of Denmark and Holland, both major butter-producing countries, deprived Britain of two important sources of supply, so that margarine and cooking fats had to be rationed from 22 July 1940. The system was based on combining allocations with freedom of choice for the consumer, who was not restricted to any significant extent. The fat ration totalled 8 oz a week, of which 2 oz had to be in the form of margarine. The rest was available either as butter or margarine. A mere two months later, the strong demand for butter possible under this system made a modification necessary, and the butter ration was reduced to 2 oz. Because adequate supplies of margarine and cooking fats were available, it proved possible to maintain the total fat ration at 8 oz.

The government also wished to curb the rising cost of living. The policy was that consumer goods should be within the consumers' reach, and maximum prices were fixed for many essential foods. The margarine industry standardized its products voluntarily and stated the prices on the packs, thereby adopting the policy of indirect price-fixing.

The fact that the margarine industry was highly concentrated facilitated this collaboration with the government. The entire production, distribution, and sale of margarine was assembled by the margarine industry in one central organization—Marcom Ltd.—which co-operated closely with the Ministry of Food and acted as its selling agents. Only two kinds of margarine were made: high-priced Special and low-priced Standard. The profits on one were intended to subsidize the other. In fact, Special was in big demand, though there was much less difference in quality than the prices suggested.

The shortage of oils and fats persisted long after the war, compelling maintenance of the restrictions already in force, and it was 1954 before conditions returned to normal.

The mildness of the English margarine legislation is striking (64). Its main concern has been to prevent butter adulteration and guarantee purity. 'The law's primary aim has been to protect the consumer against fraud and misrepresentation and to help to ensure a proper standard of hygiene and quality . . . No restrictions have been made as to colour or flavouring and as to shape of packages and no discriminating taxes have been imposed. This may be the reason why the law relating to this food is simple, is not hedged about by legal obscurities and is easily understood by the ordinary man' (65). The British government has realized the importance of margarine. This, together with the fact that there has been little or no pressure by the dairy industry, has accounted for the attitude in the government's relevant legislation that made widespread consumption of this fat product possible.

RUSSIA

In contrast to the Tsarist administration, which attempted to oppose the rise of the margarine industry, the Communist regime gave a powerful stimulus to this industry's development and had every reason for doing so.

Up to now the U.S.S.R. has been involved in a process of industrialization, which, considering the fairly minor significance of the country's agricultural imports, necessitated the development of agriculture in order to supply food to the industrial population concentrated in the cities. Agricultural development has been relatively backward in Russia, including the dairy sector, and still poses a constant problem for the Russian government. It is clear from this situation that the margarine industry has been stimulated during the Communist regime, as it supplies valuable fats for human consumption. There have also been no important problems as to raw materials, for climatic and natural conditions favoured the cultivation of sufficient sunflower seeds and cottonseeds within Russia itself; the cultivation of soya beans is nowadays gradually increasing in importance.

Margarine was first manufactured in Russia at a fairly early date— in 1874. Production remained small and amounted only to 1,000 tons in the year 1910. Because of the regulation that the manufacture of margarine was only permitted in towns which had public slaughterhouses, the industry was concentrated in Moscow, Odessa, and Leningrad. Only sound raw tallow could be used as raw material, and a close watch was kept on the standards of production hygiene. These were the methods used to ensure a good-quality product.

Margarine legislation in Russia dates from 1891, and was later tightened up with the addition of police regulations. It was fairly far-reaching and included a ban on mixing margarine with butter, a ban on colouring margarine, a prohibition on imports, and compulsory notification of margarine factories. The product could be sold only in special shops, and packaging regulations intended to prevent deception of consumers were also enforced. Animosity towards margarine went so far that articles describing margarine factories were censored up to 1914. Curiously enough, the ban on mixing was apparently not maintained, with the result that pure margarine was not consumed even among the poorest people in Russia (66).

The Communist Revolution introduced the change described above, and margarine production was soon being encouraged; in 1930, at the beginning of the first five-year plan, it amounted to 6,000 tons. This subsequently rose to no less than 107,000 tons in 1939, 200,000 tons in 1950, and 662,000 tons in 1965, which meant a 1965 *per capita* consumption of 3 kg. Butter production, 445,000 tons in 1930, amounted to 1·1 million tons in 1965, or 5 kg *per capita*, and was therefore higher than *per capita* margarine production. It turns out, however, that the total margarine production since 1930 has not only increased in actual terms, but also shown an increase in comparison with butter production. The production of raw materials, which, in contrast to the pre-1914 period, consisted largely of vegetable fats and oils, has similarly shown a strong increase (67).

This was achieved through the purposeful policy of the centrally controlled Russian economic system. Originally the margarine industry was concentrated to a great extent within the big cities, but now attempts are being made to spread the industry further afield in order to supply margarine to the remoter industrial regions.

A factor contributing to this movement is the attempt to bring the production centres closer to the districts where the raw materials are produced.

In order to encourage margarine consumption a price policy is operated, whereby the price ratio between margarine and butter is fixed at 1:2.

Margarine is coloured yellow. The addition of colouring agents was prohibited before 1914. There are two qualities of margarine— kitchen and table margarine. The pack of top-quality margarine bears a picture of a cow to indicate the product's uses, and the necessary attention is also being paid to the flavouring of margarine. This was prohibited before 1914.

Attempts are being made to produce a margarine with a quality 'not inferior to butter in its organoleptic characteristics and nutritive value' (68). Despite these measures, which strikingly demonstrate the change in climate and which clearly show the attempts being made to encourage margarine consumption, the product is still used mainly for baking purposes. It seems that the Russian housewife is not as yet very margarine-minded. In fact this is generally true of customers in the countries behind the Iron Curtain. Margarine is not rationed in Russia; the product is sold freely and the shops have plentiful stocks of it.

THE EUROPEAN ECONOMIC COMMUNITY

In 1957 six European states—Belgium, West Germany, France, Italy, Luxembourg, and Holland—by the Treaty of Rome entered into an economic union, the European Economic Community (E.E.C.).

As a natural consequence of the striving after economic unity, in principle the economic policy of the individual countries, both in aims and in ways and means, is subordinated to the fulfilment of the purposes declared in common. The creation of a great free trade area, of its very nature, takes time; for the complete disappearance of internal tariffs should not be possible ideally before the price and cost structures of the various countries are mutually adjusted. Even so the abolition of internal tariffs was completed by July 1968. Running parallel with the abolition of internal dues, a common external tariff was introduced in full on 1 July 1968.

For the margarine industry, quite understandably, this development is not a matter of indifference. The first cause of concern is its supply of raw materials; and the industry is also involved in so far as regulations affecting its end-product are under consideration. These being still at the preparatory stage, can be dismissed briefly; any pronouncement on them would be premature. With regard to the raw materials, however, regulations have also been drawn up. These ought to be considered against the background of the position occupied by agriculture within the E.E.C. as a whole, and with reference to the common agricultural policy resulting from that.

World market prices for agricultural products are lower on the whole than prices in the E.E.C. countries. A free flow of agricultural commodities to the E.E.C. would therefore cause hardship for farming in the economic community, a state of affairs which is regarded as unacceptable, especially from the aspect of social welfare. Protection of agriculture within the E.E.C. by means of an external tariff and variable levies on the import of farm products offer possibilities of a solution. In the case of commodities the consumption of which is entirely or largely covered by production within the E.E.C., the levies on import are varied in accordance with the fluctuations of the difference between the world market prices and the prices within the E.E.C.

If, on the contrary, production of specified foodstuffs—or their raw materials—forms only a small part of the consumption in the E.E.C. area, then a subsidy should be given to the producers to bridge the gap between prices in the world market and the home prices to the grower. For the benefit of the consumers, prices can then be held on this relatively low world market level. This system of protection for farming is known as the system of deficiency payments, additional payment of the difference in price.

This system has great significance for the margarine industry in the E.E.C.—an industry which for its supply of raw materials is largely dependent on vegetable oils and fats, only 20 per cent of the production of which is covered within the E.E.C. The system of deficiency payments is applied here. Margarine manufacturers are thus enabled to buy their raw materials without restriction in the world market, even when a common external tariff is enforced. Apart from this tariff the prices of processed raw materials are in principle on the world market level, and thus are lower than they would have been if the system of variable levies had been applied.

The markets in vegetable oils and fats, including marine oils, on the one hand, and those in animal fats on the other hand are regarded as different markets, unless—for this possibility is kept open—the sale ratios alter significantly as a result of Common Market regulations. Essentially therefore the regulations for the two groups of products are kept separate.

Against this background, measures for unification of the E.E.C. market in olives and fats were planned and put into effect. Late in 1964 the European Commission made three proposals, the first of which related to the market organization concerning these products in the Common Market. This came into force, though not unaltered, by 1 July 1967. In this market ordinance all the tariffs and quantitative trade restrictions within the E.E.C. are abolished. The import of olive oil is subject to a system of variable levies, while imports of all other vegetable oils and fats from non-member states come under a common external tariff. Imports from the Associated African States, however, are entirely exempt from import duties. Producers of some types of oil-seed within the E.E.C. are given direct financial support by means of deficiency payments, and for these seeds common minimum prices are fixed, which—if necessary—can be maintained by market intervention, through purchases made by official bodies.

The position of olive oil is exceptional, for it is subject to a combination of deficiency payments to the producers and variable levies at the frontier. This arrangement results in a market price which is lower than the producers' price but higher than the price on the world market. The latter is chosen in such a way that the ratio of competition with other vegetable oils and fats is approximately the same as that formerly current in Italy, the only E.E.C. country where an extreme form of protection prevailed in this sector before the Common Market materialized.

The second proposal of the European Commission concerned the relation to the African countries that have a treaty of association with the E.E.C.: for the oleaginous products from these countries a special adjustment was effected, which has also been in force since 1 July 1967. It stipulated that oil imports from the Associated African States to the E.E.C. countries should be duty-free. Oils imported from other countries are subject to the common external tariff of the E.E.C., although oil-seeds, irrespective of the country of origin, are duty-free —while if necessary, for instance, if the import of these seeds from the Associated African States were to fall sharply, special measures to meet the case could be taken.

In addition to this protection of the market position of African oils and oil-seeds, action was taken on a wider scale, since the Associated African States sell their products within the E.E.C. at world market prices. If these prices drop below the so-called 'reference prices', the deficiency is made up by the E.E.C. In this way a minimum level of output is maintained for oil-seed products in the Associated African States.

The third proposal put forward by the European Commission in 1964 dealt with an E.E.C. duty on all vegetable oils and fats used for human consumption, up to a maximum of $87·5 million yearly. This was intended as a contribution to the E.E.C. agricultural fund in connection with the financial support measures for both the E.E.C. producers and the Associated African States. Although the above-mentioned measures came into force on 1 July 1967, no decision has yet been taken with respect to this special tax.

The measures adopted cannot be called unpropitious for the margarine industry in the E.E.C. area, for it can continue to purchase raw materials at world market prices as before, through having retained almost free access to this market.

We will now consider several other countries whose margarine policy differs in one way or another from that of those already dealt with.

New Zealand

In New Zealand there is complete prohibition of both the production and the import of margarine for household use. This extreme measure is explained by the great importance of the dairy industry in the nation's economy.

South Africa

The margarine policy of South Africa (69) has been marked by two special characteristics: regulations have shown increasing severity, and there is an annual production quota for margarine. This line of policy is determined by the dairy-farming interests.

Sales of margarine containing milk fat, milk, or a colouring agent, were banned in 1918. The margarine industry reacted against these severe regulations by using certain raw materials which gave its product a natural yellow colouring. But this was of no avail, for in 1930 regulations came into effect prohibiting the sale of products manufactured from vegetable or animal oils which were 'indistinguishable from butter in appearance'. This meant that 'an attractive and palatable table margarine could not be produced'. Towards the end of the Second World War, however, the shortage of fats made it necessary for the production of coloured margarine to be allowed again, though not without some strings attached. When this production became substantial after 1947, dairy interests protested and received a favourable hearing. The severe shortage of fats had meanwhile disappeared, and the production and sale of yellow-coloured margarine was prohibited again in 1950. This was not all, for the manufacture of uncoloured margarine was made dependent on a special permit from the Department of Agriculture. Every factory was also limited to a certain annual quota, but the production maximum has gradually been increased since then.

Obviously the growth of the South African margarine industry has been seriously hampered by vexatious government regulations.

M.—22

Italy

The chequered history of Italian margarine legislation has been characterized by alternating periods of leniency and severity. For a time the production of margarine was completely prohibited. At other times it was permitted, though not officially recognized by law. The industry has also had to fight against a heavy burden of taxation.

Once the production of margarine—mainly as a product for bakeries—had developed somewhat during the 1920s, the agricultural and bakers' organizations banded together to start up a campaign against the product. They scored their first success in 1934 with a ban on the manufacture of margarine for household use, and this was followed by a complete ban on production in 1937. The striving for self-sufficiency played no mean part in this. After the liberation of Rome, there were no supplies of the cheapest fat—margarine—available to help the Americans combat the serious food shortage with which they were confronted. They promptly began to import it for the benefit of the food-kitchens. Some of this margarine filtered through the walls of the official rationing pipelines, which were apparently somewhat leaky here and there. This meant that margarine came on to the open market, which caused the former margarine manufacturers to press for permission to restart production. Tentative consent was given by means of a ministerial circular, despite the fact that the legal ban on margarine production was still in force. It was indeed a very dubious legal situation.

After pressure from margarine producers, however, a legal regulation on margarine manufacture came into effect in 1951. In this move, the margarine makers were trying to knock the wind out of the sails of the agricultural organizations which had again been campaigning against margarine. Nevertheless, the regulation showed anything but goodwill towards margarine. It was forbidden to mix fats derived from milk with margarine. Bakery margarine could not be coloured. The addition of sesame oil was made compulsory. Every packet of margarine had to be closed with lead seals; the maximum weight per package was put at only 200 g in 1960.

During the Korean war the Italian government had taken the precaution of stocking up with large quantities of edible oils and fats, including sesame oil, but the prices of these raw materials dropped after the end of the war. To get rid of its stocks the government therefore introduced a system of compulsory purchase. Anyone wishing to obtain an import licence for oil or oil-seeds was compelled to buy a certain amount of oil from the national stocks at high prices. When these had all been sold, the obligation to pay a fixed sum—called the *abbinamento*—for import licences was retained. Compulsory purchase had led to nothing less than an import levy—founded on a ministerial circular. This was abolished in 1967 under E.E.C. regulations. Since edible fats such as coconut fat, palm fat, and palm kernel fat, did not come under the *abbinamento*, the margarine industry began to use these fats as raw materials.

A second factor also lay behind this move; in 1952, the Italian government had imposed a tax which increased prices for seed oils in order to protect olive oil production. This tax did not affect edible fats either.

Despite these difficult circumstances, the margarine industry developed somewhat in the 1950s, although the share of margarine in the total consumption of edible oils and fats still remained below 5 per cent. Nevertheless this increase in consumption annoyed the producers of edible seed oils, and in 1959 they induced the government to put a special tax of 120 lire per kg on the competing margarine as well. Some of the proceeds from this tax went towards increases in the salaries of civil servants. The various taxes naturally produced a price ratio between butter and margarine which was very prejudicial to margarine. However, in 1966 the margarine tax, which did not apply to bakery margarine, was lowered considerably by the Italian parliament.

Italian margarine policy has definitely hampered the expansion of margarine production. Originally the butter producers were being protected, but, especially after 1950, the protection of olive oil producers has come to the fore as the purpose of legislation.

Denmark

Denmark (70) is worth closer study for three reasons: it was the first country to impose national regulations on the margarine industry (in 1885); its policy has been much more severe than has generally been claimed in the literature; and a unique, ingeniously contrived, colour chart is used in this country to define the admissible shades of yellow for margarine colouring.

In the relevant literature one may come across the opinion that the margarine industry in such countries as Denmark, Holland, and the Baltic states has been able to develop in comparative freedom. Yet these were butter-exporting countries where the cost price of butter was comparatively high, both compared with its price in Australia and New Zealand and compared with margarine. They therefore began exporting their expensive butter, and cheap margarine took its place in the home market. The national economy in these cases profited from the benefits of this exchange, so that the expansion of the margarine industry was not impeded. In Denmark—a country which offers a striking example of this—even the farmers went over in great numbers to the consumption of margarine, whilst their own butter was exported. This reasoning certainly contains a grain of truth, but still needs some qualification.

The Danish margarine industry did not develop in a mild climate. The fear of losing the reputation of Danish butter, especially on the English market, led to the first legal measures in 1885. Needless to say, they did not appear to be far-reaching enough. Fairly forceful measures, including a ban on the mixing of butter with margarine and a ban on the colouring of the product, were then put forward by a special advisory committee in order to quell persistent deception. When these recommendations were accepted by the government, they unleashed a violent clash of opinions between the government and parliament, for the latter did not want to see anything put in the way of fair competition between butter and margarine. This episode, which went down in history as the 'butter war', even led to the dissolution of parliament.

The attempt to prevent the introduction of harsher regulations did not succeed, especially as regards trade, packaging, and supervision. There was no ban on mixing, nor, strictly speaking, on the yellow colouring of margarine. In the 1888 act, however, the degree of yellow colouring was governed by the fourteen shades of yellow on the official colour chart. These had been so selected that, even if the darkest shade of yellow was used, the margarine would still not equal the yellow of butter. These colour regulations caused much trouble, because temperature and sunlight both affect the colour of margarine (71). In 1905, the addition of sesame oil was made obligatory.

Later, a milder attitude towards the margarine industry gradually developed and the farmers lost much of their suspicion about the product. After much preparation and discussion, the colour regulations were eventually abolished in 1925; yet this move was accompanied by a ban on mixing.

Thereafter, the Danish legislators made no more fundamental alterations, but there was no question of a mild governmental climate for the Danish margarine industry, at any rate up to 1945.

Norway

The Norwegian government has positively encouraged the production and consumption of margarine since the end of the Second World War. This is not just a coincidence; the policy can be explained by the fact that the margarine industry offered a good market for valuable home-produced raw materials, such as marine oils, which were supplied by the Norwegian fishing industry.

The policy of Norwegian governments, almost always Socialist, has likewise been a contributory factor, for they aimed to provide the population with sufficient fat products at low prices; and margarine benefited most from this because of the types of raw materials available. The extent to which sales of marine oils have become dependent on the margarine industry is clearly demonstrated by the fact that at present almost half the production of these raw materials finds its way into this industry. The proportion of marine oils used in margarine rose from about 25 per cent in 1928 to more than 70 per cent in 1966.

Margarine is subsidized to encourage consumption. At first, after the Second World War, raw materials were made available to the margarine industry at constant, low prices. This was followed in 1957 by direct subsidies on the finished product. The level of this subsidy, which was not the same for all types of margarine up to 1958, tended to fluctuate; and between 1958 and 1960, when a Conservative government was in power, margarine was not subsidized at all.

Government policy meant that, in 1966, the price ratio of butter—also subsidized—to margarine was 1:3·4 in favour of margarine. In the last couple of years this ratio has shown a downward trend.

It is little wonder that, in such circumstances, *per capita* margarine consumption in Norway is the highest in the world. In 1966 it amounted to no less than 21·5 kg per head, as compared to 4·1 kg for butter.

The history of margarine policy in these countries just mentioned seems to offer us bans on production, permanent production quotas, exceptionally high taxes, and colour charts for inclusion in the already extremely varied legislative armoury. Consumption of margarine has been encouraged in Norway, and the country occupies an exceptional position in this respect.

France

The important position occupied by France in the E.E.C. leads us finally to a consideration of the legislative measures on margarine in that country. As in other countries, both production and sale of margarine were brought under regulation. In 1872, at the suggestion of the Conseil d'Hygiène et de Salubrité de la Seine, an embargo was laid on the selling of this product under the name of 'butter'. The year 1887 saw the passing of the first laws in this connection, mainly for the protection of the consumer in the first instance through the checking of fraudulent practices.

The success was very slight. In 1891 it had to be stated that 'the sale of margarine under its true name remains null and void among the retailers, while cases of the most shameless misrepresentation have become daily more frequent . . .'.

It was judged necessary to take more effectual measures, and these were embodied in the Act of 1897, which still forms the basis of current legislation on margarine in France.

The guiding principle of this law was the decision to mark out a clear boundary between butter and margarine, with absolute separation of the two industries and the two trades. With this in view definitions were provided for both products. The colouring of margarine was banned. Later the Cour de Cassation made a definite statement that this ban did not apply to the margarines whose yellow colouring has been obtained by the use of oil with natural colour. Furthermore, producers of butter and dealers in it were forbidden to make or to store margarine in the premises they used for the production of butter or for dealing in it. The regulation in relation to the retail trade was later modified. Lastly, margarine was not to contain more than 10 per cent of butter, and had to be put on sale in cube-shaped packets.

Observance of these provisions was subject to strict supervision, and they have since been tightened up. All margarine stores had to be shown as such by display of a signboard. In 1931 the law directed manufacturers to add an indicator to margarine. These orders were far-reaching; this was admitted in 1935 by the Minister of Agriculture, who stated in a circular that the various laws 'contain a set of very strict provisions offering every possible guarantee to the protection of public health'. In this context it will be well to point out that the Act of 29 June 1934 relating to protection of milk products (the title of this law is significant) prohibited the use of the words 'butter', 'cream', 'milk' in all advertising of margarine. 'This law', said the Minister of Agriculture, 'directly ensures the protection of butter. . . .'

'The new law also has the purpose, in particular, of safeguarding the interests of butter producers against the possible extension of margarine.'

A new objective had thus been officially introduced into the legislation on margarine: the protection of dairy-farming interests. To this end the Act of 1935 gave the government powers to fix quotas, under certain conditions, for the import into France of raw materials used especially for the manufacture of margarine, and to prescribe the inclusion in margarine of a certain percentage of beef fat.

Moreover, the law banned the addition of any kind of perfume to margarine. During the Second World War, just as during the First, there was a shortage of fats, and the severity of certain measures was relaxed: in wartime the position in legislation is always propitious for margarine. After the war the orders for relaxation were largely cancelled. No legislative action of any importance has been taken since that time.

Finally, we must draw attention to the fact that butter, in comparison with margarine, has profited by advantageous fiscal measures.

French legislation on margarine is in fact *très rigoureuse*. It is worth recording that there have often been attempts in ministerial circulars —which have no legal validity—to interpret or to shade legislation, in that they 'have permitted adaptation of this legislation to the realities of the situation'.

Nevertheless, margarine consumption rose from 0·8 kg a head in 1938 to 2·6 kg in 1965. Improvement in the quality of the product was an important contributory factor in this development.

CONCLUSION

If we review the evolution of margarine legislation in the countries discussed—which may be considered representative of the countries where margarine production and consumption have reached significant proportions—we can find evidence of some broad trends. The first legislative measures relating to margarine appear to have been adopted about 1885. Agriculture was then in a state of depression, and had to contend with low butter prices. An important factor influencing the margarine policy of all countries was their protection of butter producers against competition from margarine, and their resistance of the dishonest practices provoked by the existence of margarine. At the same time there were endeavours to protect the consumers by means of ensuring purity and good quality in their margarine. In the first phase of this margarine policy there was no question, generally speaking, of extreme measures. One element was common to all the relevant legislation: invariably it proved fruitless, causing little if any change in the situation it attempted to contest. This state of affairs must be attributed mainly to the absence of an efficient system for keeping a check on observance of the laws. About the year 1900 there was a second wave of legislation, and more stringent measures were taken in the effort to gain the proposed objects—in the U.S.A. particularly, and to a lesser extent in Germany—regulations were published which aimed at arresting the expansion of the margarine industry. In this case also, one of the motives was protection of the consumer; but the measures were excessive. Artificial colouring of margarine was prohibited or taxed—whereas the customary artificial colouring of butter was allowed; a red band round the cube-shaped pack was compulsory, and only a certain range of shades in the yellow colouring permitted. The margarine legislation in England and Holland offers convincing proof that such extreme measures were not necessary for guaranteeing that margarine could be identified. Then too, under a show of consumer protection, an anti-margarine policy was initiated that ignored the consumers and their organizations and had not been requested by them, nor could they influence it to any appreciable extent; in fact, legislators in several countries treated the consumers as 'infants under the law'. Reaping no advantage from the above-mentioned measures, consumers found on the contrary that the purchase of margarine stamped them as social inferiors.

After this second phase there came a period of balance of power and of consolidation, which lasted for a few decades. It was in Denmark, where the regulations were relaxed in 1925, that the first move to end this took place. Yet in other countries we see a revival of the anti-margarine legislation, in which quite different measures from those prevailing so far were put into operation. Bans and restrictions on production, until then all but unknown, and duties and taxes, so far applied only in the U.S.A., were proclaimed in several countries, with the object of securing an unfavourable price ratio for margarine by comparison with butter. In Italy, for example, a ban was imposed on the production of margarine; in the U.S.A. all coloured margarine was taxed; in Holland there was a duty on margarine and production was restricted; in Germany the imported raw materials were taxed, as well as the end-product, and consumption of margarine was partially rationed. These measures, as much as any, were taken because butter producers—as in the 1880s—had to contend with low prices as a result of the depression then prevailing. These producers were given extra protection, over and above the existing standard. The reasons for this were of a temporary nature, and the measures, too, were supposed to be temporary. That proved to be so during the Second World War, when over-production of fats turned into a fat shortage. In Germany and Holland there was a switch to price control and a subsidy on margarine to keep down the cost of living and guarantee the food supply. Not until after the Second World War could any evidence be found of a more lenient attitude in general towards margarine, it was then shown in legislation particularly in the U.S.A. By then margarine, being also under the influence of the distribution rules during the Second World War, had reached the status of a widely valued food. A contributory factor here was that influence on social policy was exerted by the working population; and consumers had on the whole become much more powerful. Through their organizations they managed, for the first time in the history of margarine politics, to bring a clearly perceptible influence to bear on margarine legislation in a number of cases. Very stringent regulations do undoubtedly still operate against margarine in certain countries, among them New Zealand, South Africa, Italy, Finland, and Switzerland. In contrast, however, legislation on margarine has shown greater leniency in other countries.

In the U.S.A. the federal tax on yellow-coloured margarine was abolished; prohibition orders with regard to the colouring of margarine no longer exist in any state, although some state taxes still remain in effect. In Canada also the colouring of margarine was permitted, and in Holland some superfluous regulations disappeared. Germany's consumer organizations succeeded in preventing the proposed reintroduction of the margarine tax; Norway deliberately promoted the consumption of margarine, while in Italy the taxation on it was appreciably reduced. In Germany, under the influence of the E.E.C., the compulsory purchase of home-grown rape-seed by the margarine industry was suspended; on the same grounds the tax on rape-seed oils was cancelled in Italy.

These are all symptoms which reveal that margarine has now gained an established and recognized place in the pattern of consumption. The beneficial effect on health attributed to its use has been a contributory factor, in the U.S.A. especially, but also in Germany and, to a rather lesser extent, in England. The great importance at present attached to margarine for its usefulness as a popular food is apparent from the fact that in a number of countries the price-regulation of this product is influenced to a greater or lesser extent by the government.

Evidently the sharp edges of the butter–margarine confrontation are going through a process of attrition.

What factors have brought about this relaxation of the legislative measures against margarine? First of all, it can be shown that in many countries a large section of the population now depends to a great extent on margarine for its supply of fats. In the higher-income groups, too, this product, which has much improved in quality over the years, is of undoubtedly nutritional value, digestible, and wholesome, has secured its own market. No other edible fat can possibly take its place at equally low prices and in such ample supply. In these circumstances the maintenance of restrictions on margarine production meets with ever-increasing opposition.

Secondly, it must be borne in mind that more and more of the milk produced is being processed, under the influence of rising prosperity, into products such as cheese, condensed milk, and milk powder, which are more profitable financially than butter production. Naturally this is not equally true for all countries; but that does not alter the fact that in large areas of the world butter looks like becoming something in the nature of a by-product in the dairy-farming industry.

A parallel development is the increasing economic importance attached to cattle as producers of meat rather than of milk. Besides, economic growth has been responsible for a relatively substantial reduction in the number of agricultural workers in the total employed population. The outcome of this development has been a fall in the proportion of the population dependent for its income on the financial results of butter production.

A third factor enters here. After the margarine industry had turned to the processing of vegetable oils and fats it began to use soya bean oil; this was especially in evidence in the U.S.A., which had embarked on its own widespread cultivation of soya beans. As a result the soya bean growers—just like the cultivators of cottonseed and sunflower seeds—became involved in the expansion of the margarine industry. They were in the forefront when the question arose of doing away with the restrictions placed on this industry. The important categories of agricultural producers mentioned above lent their support. In the matter of cattle-breeding also, relations had altered. Owing to expansion in the margarine industry, the oil industry that supplies raw materials for margarine production now has a role as a producer of raw materials for animal feeding-stuffs. Through research in laboratories and on experimental farms this industry has made a positive contribution to the rationalization of cattle feeding. It is a development which has occurred everywhere; more especially in countries such as England, because there co-operative farming, which elsewhere has taken a prominent part in promoting the rationalization of animal feeding, has not expanded to any great extent. The effect has been that cattle-breeding has had an interest in the existence of the margarine industry for the sake of its supply of fodder.

A fourth factor appears in the provision of employment which the margarine industry affords; obstruction of this industry might lead to unemployment. But at the same time we must not lose sight of the fact that the margarine industry is not a high-powered activity: the number of people depending on the industry for their livelihood is relatively small.

There are some factors that provide an explanation of the change which is beginning to show in legislation, consequent on the changing relation between butter and margarine production and consumption.

A prominent representative of the farming industry in Holland remarked recently that the freedom claimed by the consumer—that is a freedom which no right-minded person will in normal circumstances relinquish—makes the process of supplying food something dynamic. Its most successful operation is to be found in an evenly balanced interaction between interest groups that respect one another's position.

Let us express the hope that everyone will in future take this dictum as a standard in business dealings, so that more and more it may be realized in practice.

NOTES AND REFERENCES

1. RIEPMA, S. 'Margarine in the United States 1873–1967' (unpublished), p. 3.

2. WIEST, E. *The butter industry in the United States* (New York, 1916), pp. 234, 239.

3. HEFTER, G. *Technologie der Fette und Öle* (*Technology of fats and oils*) (Berlin, 1910), vol. 3, p. 256.

4. SNODGRASS, K. *Margarine as a butter substitute* (Stanford, California, 1930), p. 16.

5. BEARD, C. A., and BEARD, M. R. *A basic history of the United States* (New York, 1944), p. 333.

6. RIEPMA, op. cit., p. 4.

7. WIEST, op. cit., p. 242.

8. MEISSNER, F. 'Consumer protection or butter politics?', *Cartel* (October 1952), p. 50.

9. SNODGRASS, op. cit., p. 36.

10. MEISSNER, op. cit., p. 51.

11. RIEPMA, op. cit., p. 6.

12. SNODGRASS, op. cit., p. 71.

13. WIEST, op. cit., p. 259.

14. MEISSNER, op. cit., p. 53.

15. RIEPMA, op. cit., p. 8.

16. —— Ibid., p. 9. To the organizations mentioned here belong, among others, the National Association of Consumers, the Consumers' Union, the National League of Women Shoppers, the National Council of Jewish Women, the New York City Branch of the American Association of University Women, the Consumers' Conference of Greater Cincinnati, and the League of Women Voters of the United States. The American Veterans of World War I and the American Home Economics Association might also be mentioned here. But cf. *Oleomargarine tax repeal, Hearings before the Committee on Agriculture, House of Representatives, Eighteenth Congress* (Washington, 1948).

17. FRÄNKEL, H. *Der Kampf gegen die Margarine* (*The fight against margarine*) (Weimar, 1894), p. 7.

18. WILSON, C. *The history of Unilever. A study in economic growth and social change* (London, 1954), vol. 2, pp. 55 and 102.

19. TEICHMANN, U. *Die Politik der Agrarpreisstützung* (*The policy of agricultural price support*) (Köln-Deutz, 1955), p. 463.

20. LAVALLE, A. *Die Margarine-Gesetzgebung und ihre Entwicklung in den einzelnen Kulturstaaten* (*Margarine legislation and its evolution in certain developed countries*) (Bremen, 1896), p. 217.

21. SOXHLET, F. *Über Margarine* (*On margarine*) (Munich, 1895), p. 78.

22. HEFTER, op. cit., p. 215.

23. —— Ibid., p. 231.

24. TEICHMANN, op. cit., p. 481.

25. HEFTER, op. cit., p. 222.

26. SCHÜTTAUF, W. *Die Margarine in Deutschland und in der Welt* (*Margarine in Germany and the world*) (Hamburg, 1966), p. 16.

27. TEICHMANN, op. cit., p. 509.

28. SCHÜTTAUF, op. cit., p. 21.

29. TEICHMANN, op. cit., p. 496.

30. SCHÜTTAUF, op. cit., p. 25.

31. —— Ibid.

32. CROESEN, V. R. Y. *De Geschiedenis van de ontwikkeling van de Nederlandsche zuivelbereiding in het laatst van de negentiende en het begin van de twintigste eeuw.* (*History of the development of the Dutch dairy industry towards the end of the nineteenth and early in the twentieth century*) (The Hague, 1931), pp. 46 and 79.

33. RINKES BORGER, J. *De Boterkwestie* (*The butter question*) (1886), p. 19.
VAN DER ZEE, T. *De Friesche boerencoöperaties in haar maatschappelijk verband.* (*The Friesian farm co-operatives in their association*) (Sneek, 1933), p. 14.

34. CROESEN, op. cit., p. 40.
RINKES BORGER, op. cit., p. 25.
VAN DER ZEE, op. cit., p. 20.
HOLLENBERG, P. *Gerlachus van den Elsen* ('s-Hertogenbosch, 1956), p. 328.

35. JURGENS, A. 'Butterine of margarineboter' ('Butterine or margarine butter'), lecture to the Society of Arts, 12 December 1884.

36. CROESEN, op. cit., p. 40.
RINKES BORGER, op. cit., p. 26.

37. VAN DER ZEE, op. cit., p. 11.

38. CROESEN, op. cit., p. 44.

39. *Collection of recommendations by the Agricultural Commission* (The Hague, 1891), p. 3.

40. HIJLKEMA, H. B. *Gedenkboek van de Vereeniging tot bestrijding van knoeirerijen in den boter-en kaashandel* (*Records of the association for combating corrupt practices in the butter and cheese trade*) (1885–1914), p. 206.

41. *Memorie van Toelichting, Handelingen Staten-Generaal* (*Explanatory memorandum from the proceedings of the Dutch parliament*) (1888–9), appendices 63.3.

42. KNAPP, W. H. C. *Botercontrole in Nederland* (*Butter inspection in the Netherlands*) (Schiedam, 1927), p. 76.

43. CROESEN, op. cit., p. 58.
KNAPP, op. cit., pp. 91 and 112.

44. *Memorie van Toelichting, Handelingen Staten-Generaal* (1888–9), appendices 129.3.

45. *Memorie van Antwoord, Handelingen Staten-Generaal* (*Memorandum in reply from the proceedings of the Dutch parliament*) (1888–9), appendices 129.5.

46. An indicator is a substance that must, by law, be included in the product; in this case a fixed small percentage of sesame oil had to be processed with the margarine. This gives the product latent colour. By means of a simple chemical test which stains sesame oil red, it is then simple to determine if the substance tested is margarine.

47. VAN DEN BERGH, S., JR. *De verplichte toevoeging van sesamolie bij de margarine* (*The obligatory addition of sesame oil to margarine*) (Rotterdam, 1904).

48. *Memorie van Toelichting, Handelingen Staten-Generaal* (1906–7), appendices 127.3.

49. HIJLKEMA, op. cit., pp. 105 and 262.

50. —— Ibid., p. 287.

51. For the war years, see:
VAN MANEN, C. A. *De Nederlandsche Overzee Trustmaatschappij* (*The Dutch Overseas Trust Company*) (The Hague, 1935), vol. 3, p. 486; vol. 5, pp. 18, 25, and 27; vol. 6, p. 101.
De levensmiddelenvoorziening en het gemeentebestuur van Amsterdam (*The supply of foodstuffs and the Amsterdam City Council*), vol. 6, p. 198; vol. 5, pp. 85, 120, 193, and 204.
POSTHUMA, F. E. 'Food supply and agriculture', in *The Netherlands and the world war* (New Haven, 1928), vol. 2, p. 279.
ZAALBERG, C. J. P. 'The manufacturing industry', ibid., p. 103.
TREUB, M. W. F. *Oorlogstijd* (*Wartime*) (Haarlem and Amsterdam, 1916), p. 53.
Verslagen en mededelingen van de Directie van den landbouw (*Reports and comments from the Agricultural Commission*), no. 3 (1915), p. 81.

52. *De landbouw-crisiswetgeving* (*The legislation of the agricultural crisis*) (The Hague, 1937–40).
STEENBERGHE, M. P. L. *Landbouwcrisispolitiek* (*The politics of the agricultural crisis*) (The Hague, 1939).
VAN STUYVENBERG, J. H. 'De landbouw op de stroom van de tijd' ('Agriculture in the tide of time'), in *Ondernemend Nederland* (Haarlem, 1959).

53. HERWEIJER, P. *De Margarineconventie* (1943).

54. *La Margarine, sa réglementation dans le monde* (World regulation of margarine) (Rome, 1956), p. 125.

55. *Memorie van Toelichting, Handelingen Staten-Generaal* (1934–5), appendices 270.1–3. Royal Decree, 1 June 1935.

56. *Memorie van Toelichting, Handelingen Staten-Generaal* (1952–3), appendices 2920.

57. WILSON, op. cit., vol. 2, p. 87.

58. LAVALLE, op. cit., p. 142.

59. SAUNDERS, H. 'Margarine: the development and status of oleomargarine legislation in the United Kingdom', *Food, drug, and cosmetic law journal* (July 1952).

60. BEVERIDGE, W. H. *British food control* (London, 1928), p. 195.

61. SCHWITZER, M. K. *Margarine and other food fats* (New York, 1956), p. 371.

62. Ibid., p. 372.

63. This section is based mainly on data from records of Unilever Limited in Great Britain, on SAUNDERS, op. cit., and on HAMMOND, R. J., 'Food', in *History of the Second World War*, vols. 1–3 (London, 1951–62).

64. SNODGRASS, op. cit., p. 177.

65. SAUNDERS, op. cit., p. 427.

66. HEFTER, G. op. cit., p. 249.

67. SLASTCHEV-GREGOROVITCH, N. N. 'The development trends of the margarine industry in the U.S.S.R.' (unpublished).

68. NAUMENKO, P. V. *On the main problems of scientific and technological improvements in the oil and fat industry of the U.S.S.R.* (1966).

69. MARAIS, G. *Butter and margarine* (Pretoria, 1966).

70. COHN, E. *De margarine-industrie in Denemarken, 1833–1933* (*The margarine industry in Denmark, 1833–1933*) (Copenhagen, 1953).

71. This mass of regulations drove Otto Mønsted, a leading manufacturer and exporter of margarine, to open a factory in England in 1889. There colouring was not necessary.

Index of Names

This index contains the names of individuals mentioned in the text, notes, and references. Organizations and firms will be found in the subject index. Numbers in italic indicate a bibliographical reference

Subject Index